CLIMATE CHANGE ADAPTATION AND DEVELOPMENT

Climate change poses multiple challenges to development. It affects lives and livelihoods, infrastructure and institutions, as well as beliefs, cultures and identities. There is a growing recognition that the social dimensions of vulnerability and adaptation now need to move to the forefront of development policies and practices.

This book presents case studies showing that climate change is as much a problem *of* development as *for* development, with many of the risks closely linked to past, present and future development pathways. Development policies and practices can play a key role in addressing climate change, but it is critical to question to what extent such actions and interventions reproduce, rather than address, the social and political structures and development pathways driving vulnerability. The chapters emphasise that adaptation is about much more than a set of projects or interventions to reduce specific impacts of climate change; it is about living with change while also transforming the processes that contribute to vulnerability in the first place.

This book will help students in the field of climate change and development to make sense of adaptation as a social process, and it will provide practitioners, policymakers and researchers working at the interface between climate change and development with useful insights for approaching adaptation as part of a larger transformation to sustainability.

Tor Håkon Inderberg is Senior Research Fellow and Director of the European Programme at the Fridtjof Nansen Institute, Norway.

Siri Eriksen is Associate Professor at the Department of International Environment and Development Studies, Norwegian University of Life Sciences, Norway.

Karen O'Brien is a Professor of Human Geography at the Department of Sociology and Human Geography, University of Oslo, Norway.

Linda Sygna is Co-Founder of cCHANGE – Transformation in a Changing Climate, cchange.no.

CLIMATE CHANGE ADAPTATION AND DEVELOPMENT

Transforming paradigms and practices

Edited by Tor Håkon Inderberg, Siri Eriksen, Karen O'Brien and Linda Sygna

Routledge
Taylor & Francis Group

LONDON AND NEW YORK

First published 2015
by Routledge
2 Park Square, Milton Park, Abingdon, Oxon OX14 4RN

and by Routledge
711 Third Avenue, New York, NY 10017

Routledge is an imprint of the Taylor & Francis Group, an informa business

British Library Cataloguing-in-Publication Data
A catalogue record for this book is available from the British Library

Library of Congress Cataloging-in-Publication Data
Climate change adaptation and development : transforming paradigms
and practices / edited by Tor Håkon Inderberg, Siri Eriksen, Karen
O'Brien and Linda Sygna.
     pages cm
   1. Sustainable development – Case studies. 2. Economic development –
Environmental aspects – Case studies. 3. Climatic changes – Social
aspects – Case studies. I. Inderberg, Tor Håkon, editor of compilation.
II. Eriksen, Siri H., editor of compilation. III. O'Brien, Karen L., editor
of compilation. IV. Sygna, Linda, editor of compilation.
HC79.E5C594 2014
338.9′27–dc23   2014021427

ISBN: 978-1-138-02596-7 (hbk)
ISBN: 978-1-138-02598-1 (pbk)
ISBN: 978-1-315-77465-7 (ebk)

Typeset in Bembo
by HWA Text and Data Management, Lo

Printed and bound by CPI Group (UK) Ltd, Croydon, CR0 4YY

CONTENTS

FIGURES

TABLES

CONTRIBUTORS

Emily Boyd is a professor at the School of Archaeology, Geography and Environmental Science (SAGES), University of Reading. She is recognised for scholarship in the field of resilience and climate change, making theoretical contributions to advance social science research at the intersection between social and natural sciences. Her current research focuses on the way that contemporary societies understand, adapt and manage social change under multiple economic and environmental risks. In particular she researches how societies will continue to prosper under uncertain futures through processes of building resilience.

Ebba Brink is a doctoral candidate at the Lund University Centre for Sustainability Studies (LUCSUS). Her research interests centre around cities' adaptation to climate-related risk, in particular how people deal with and engage in the governance of urban risk in Sweden, as well as in Brazil.

Vanesa Castán Broto is a lecturer at the Bartlett Development Planning Unit. Her research is concerned with cities, development and climate change. She has undertaken research on the role of knowledge in environmental conflicts; the role of experiments in reconfiguring governance; the possibilities and implications of participatory planning for climate change; and, most recently, the role of energy transitions in cities in the global south. She currently holds an ESRC Future Research Leaders Fellowship to study energy landscapes.

Lars Christiansen has a master's degree in environmental geography and is a task manager at the UNEP Risø Centre where he supervises a number of United Nations Environmental Programme (UNEP) adaptation projects in Africa and Asia. From 2007 to 2011 he worked as a programme manager for climate adaptation at the Global Environment Facility Secretariat.

Jonathan Ensor is a senior researcher at the Stockholm Environment Institute at York. His work as an academic and development practitioner has focused on understanding the relationship between climate change and development, with a particular interest in community-based adaptation. His recent research explores resilience in practice, in particular through attention to how scholarship on participation, social learning and human rights can help bring considerations of equity and justice into adaptation planning.

Siri Eriksen is an assistant professor at the Norwegian University of Life Sciences. Her research interests focus on social vulnerability, in particular how people manage climatic variability and change in eastern and southern Africa as well as in Norway, and the politics involved in adaptation processes.

Sara Gabrielsson has a PhD in sustainability science from Lund University, Sweden. Her research focuses on integral community-based approaches to achieve social change in rural areas of the global south. She is currently doing research on the scalability and sustainability of community-based water and sanitation systems in rural Tanzania.

Jennifer Hays, PhD, is based at the Institute for Archaeology and Social Anthropology at the University of Tromsø, Norway. She is also a member of the Paris-based research project Scales of Governance: the UN and Indigenous Peoples (SOGIP). Her main focus is on the intersection of indigenous rights, education, and land.

Siri Bjerkreim Hellevik, PhD, is a senior advisor in Sund Energy, a consulting company providing strategic and commercial advice to energy companies, clean tech industries, investors and authorities globally. Hellevik was previously Senior Researcher at the Norwegian Institute of Urban and Regional Research (NIBR). She has experience from research and consultancies in several African and some Asian countries.

Mattias Hjerpe is an associate professor at the Centre for Climate Science and Policy Research and at Water and Environmental Studies, Linköping University, Sweden. His principal research areas are adaptation to global climate and economic change, political leadership and nonstate actors' roles in climate change. Recent work has been published in *Climatic Change*, *Global Environmental Politics*, *Local Environment and Mitigation* and *Adaptation Strategies for Global Change*.

Tor Håkon Inderberg is a senior research fellow and Director of the European Programme at the Fridtjof Nansen Institute, Norway. He is a political scientist whose research investigates climate change adaptive capacity in public organizations as well as energy and climate-related politics. His work focuses on a number of countries within and outside Europe.

Francis X. Johnson is a senior research fellow with Stockholm Environment Institute. His research and policy analyses focus on the socio-economic and environmental implications of shifts in energy and biomass use from local to global scales, focusing especially on policies and institutions related to developing countries.

Sirkku Juhola, PhD, is an assistant professor in urban environmental policy at the Department of Environmental Sciences at University of Helsinki and a visiting scholar at the Department of Real Estate, Planning and Geoinformatics at Aalto University. She specialises in adaptation policy in developed and developing countries.

Wilbard Kombe is Professor of Urban Planning and Management at Ardhi University, Tanzania, and specialises in urban land management. His major areas of research include urban land management, urban governance and climate change, basic services and livelihoods of the urban poor, institutional dynamics, and urbanisation in poverty in the South.

Jakob Kronik, PhD, runs F7 Consult from Copenhagen and has published widely on rural and indigenous peoples' knowledge, institutions and adaptation strategies to socio-economic and environmental change in Latin America, North Africa and the Middle East. He is currently the Vice President of the non-governmental organisation (NGO) Forests of the World.

Kassim Kulindwa, PhD, is a trained economist and associate professor and researcher at the Department of International Environment and Development Studies, Norwegian University of Life Sciences at Ås, Norway. For 32 years his academic and research interest included issues on natural resource and environmental management, energy, climate change mitigation and adaptation in the context of sustainable development.

Andrei Marin is a researcher at the Department of International Environment and Development Studies, Norwegian University of Life Sciences. His work focuses on political, social, and economic aspects of climate change adaptation and vulnerability, resource rights and access, and political ecology, in Mongolia, Kenya and Norway.

Clara Kweka Msale is an assistant lecturer at Ardhi University, Dar es Salaam, and a PhD candidate in the same university. Her PhD focuses on land use planning, governance and institutional setting on climate change flooding settlements.

Clara has more than seven years' experience on research and consultancy in Tanzania.

Baruani Mshale is concurrently finalising his doctoral studies in the School of Natural Resources and Environment (SNRE), University of Michigan (Ann Arbor), and working as a postdoctoral research fellow at the Centre for International Forestry Research (CIFOR), Nairobi office. His research interests include human–environment interactions, sustainable development, natural resource conservation, climate change mitigation and adaptation.

Sigrid Nagoda is a research fellow at the Department of International Environment and Development Studies, Noragric at the Norwegian University of Life Sciences. She is interested in how local-level social dynamics lead to different levels of vulnerability between people and over time, and how these dynamics relate to societal processes of change. Her PhD focuses on the effects of humanitarian aid on food security and multi-stress vulnerability in northwestern Nepal.

Andrea J. Nightingale is an associate professor in the School of Global Studies, University of Gothenburg, Sweden. Her research in Nepal and Scotland explores collective action, environmental governance, conflict and social justice through the lens of community forestry, fisheries and state transition. She uses this work to problematize linear explanations of nature–society interactions.

Karen O'Brien is a professor in the Department of Sociology and Human Geography at the University of Oslo, and co-founder of cCHANGE – Transformation in a Changing Climate. She is interested in how transdisciplinary and integral approaches to global change research can contribute to a better understanding of how societies respond to change, and in particular how deliberate, ethical, equitable and sustainable transformations can be catalysed in response to climate change.

Caroline A. Ochieng, PhD, is a research fellow at the Stockholm Environment Institute. Her research interests lie in understanding the impact of lack of energy access at local and regional scales. Her research has focused on indoor air pollution from biomass fuel use, health impacts and interventions for reducing the health risk. She has particular interest in health promoting technologies such as clean cookstoves, barriers for technology adoption and use, and household energy interventions.

Birgitta Rydhagen is an associate professor in technoscience studies at Blekinge Institute of Technology, Sweden. Her profile is feminist and gender research within technoscience, environmental and postcolonial studies. She works in the fields of water and sanitation, water and climate change and inclusive innovation.

Linda Sygna is a co-founder of cCHANGE –Transformation in a Changing Climate and has worked with transdisciplinary research projects and events, science-policy dialogues and communication on social science perspectives on climate change at the University of Oslo. She is an economist by training and her research has focused on the social and human dimensions of climate change, and in particular on social impacts, adaptation and vulnerability in both developed and developing country contexts.

Sara Trærup is an agricultural economist and a researcher, and has been with UNEP Risø Centre since 2005. Throughout the years, Sara has been working on socio-economic aspects related to climate change adaptation in a development context. Most of her work is currently focused on issues related to deployment and diffusion of climate change adaptation technologies in developing countries.

Trond Vedeld, PhD, is a senior researcher in the international department of the Norwegian Institute of Urban and Regional Research (NIBR). His research focus is on climate change, urban governance, decentralisation, and the institutional dimension of development. He has more than 30 years of experience with applied research in Africa and India.

Christine Wamsler is an associate professor at Lund University Centre for Sustainability Studies (LUCSUS), honorary fellow at the University of Manchester, visiting professor at the Technical University of Munich (TUM) and an international consultant. She specialises in sustainable city development with a focus on climate change adaptation, disaster risk reduction, urban resilience and transformation planning.

Jennifer West is a research fellow at CICERO, the Center for International Climate and Environmental Research – Oslo and a PhD student at the Norwegian University of Life Sciences, Department of International Environment and Development Studies. Her doctoral research explores the interface between agricultural investment, climate adaptation and agricultural development policy and practice, with a special focus on Tanzania.

Julie Wilk is the Director of the Centre for Climate Science and Policy Research and an associate professor at Water and Environmental Studies, Linköping University, Sweden. Her main research area is holistic water resource management in low- and middle-income countries. More recent research has focused on vulnerability assessments of climate variability and change and using drought early warning systems for increasing community resilience.

FOREWORD

This publication focuses on the consequences of climate change particularly for the poorest countries, and within them the poorest people. They are often among the most affected and most vulnerable to the impacts of climate change.

There is a growing body of evidence of ways in which rigorous social analysis has been highly successful in guiding development efforts. The general objective of this book is to stimulate awareness of the role that social analysis can play in supporting efforts to adapt to climate change.

The book argues that technical solutions alone to address adaptation to climate change are insufficient. Failure to adequately address social, structural and political aspects is necessary in order to properly recognize and deal with the various (and sometimes conflicting or vested) interests and agendas involved.

The book brings closer to one another the traditional development and climate change adaptation paradigms and recommends changes to the way that climate change adaptation is addressed in development cooperation. Focusing on the social, structural and political factors, which cause vulnerability and influence adaptation processes, will be key factors for successful outcomes at the activity/project level. The analyses contained in the book can also be seen as reinforcing, complementing, and providing more in-depth understanding of many of the arguments made in the recent reports of the Intergovernmental Panel on Climate Change (IPCC).

★ ★ ★

As the joint development finance institution of the Nordic countries, the Nordic Development Fund (NDF) is in a special position to have taken the initiative to support this research and publication. With a strong background since 1989 in focusing on economic and social development in low-income countries in

Africa, Asia and Latin America, and with a new focus in 2009 on climate change, NDF has been among the forerunners internationally to integrate climate change related objectives to 'traditional' development activities and projects.

NDF traditionally focuses on supporting project type activities, and not so much on research or general policy level work. Through supporting in-depth academic research, we have taken an exceptional (to NDF) measure, and hope that this can lead to better and more effective operations by development practitioners and communities.

Through advances in theory and policy, one is able to also improve the quality of action in integrating development, climate change adaptation and social analysis at the field and operational level.

Pasi Hellman
Managing Director
Nordic Development Fund

1

INTRODUCTION

Development as usual is not enough

*Siri Eriksen, Tor Håkon Inderberg, Karen O'Brien
and Linda Sygna*

In many parts of the world, climate change has become more than an abstract problem to be discussed at international conferences or debated in the media: it is an everyday reality with implications for people's livelihoods and lives. It is a process that is experienced both through slow long-term changes in ecological conditions and through extreme climate events. While long-term changes can influence agriculture, water, health and other sectors, it is often the shifting frequencies and magnitudes of storms, floods, droughts and other extremes that bring home the significance of climate change for vulnerable populations (SREX 2012; IPCC 2014a). Both types of changes underscore the importance of adaptation *and* mitigation responses, particularly in the context of sustainable development.

The IPCC Fifth Assessment Report (IPCC 2014a, 2014b) clearly indicates that the future is a choice. According to the IPCC, continuation along current trajectories of greenhouse gas (GHG) emissions is very likely to lead to global temperature increases of 4°C or more in this century, contributing to changes in social, economic, political, technological and ecological systems and functioning at a rate and on a scale unparalleled in human history (IPCC 2014a). These fundamental, systemic changes introduce potential thresholds and tipping points, such as disruption of the Indian and West African monsoons (Lenton et al. 2008). However, we can still achieve low-emission pathways that minimize temperature increases, sea-level rise, loss of sea ice, ocean acidification, and other impacts. But these will require transformations of a different sort – not only in energy, food, water and urban systems, but also in social systems and structures, and in development pathways. Even such low-emission pathways will lead to dramatic impacts and potential tipping points for some groups, so there is a need to adapt to imminent climate changes, in addition to transforming developmental pathways.

The rate and magnitude of climate change and its social impacts are linked to the dominant developmental pathways currently driving accelerated warming and heightened vulnerability (Olsson et al. 2014). These pathways, based on fossil-fuel-driven economic growth, are the product of systems, policies, practices and actions at many levels. Development and aid interventions form part of such practices and actions. Here a key question is: to what extent are they contributing to, or countering, current development pathways that are based on fossil-fuel-driven economic growth?

In response to increased adaptation finance through, for example, developed country commitments to the climate change convention (United Nations Framework Convention on Climate Change (UNFCCC)), governments, development agencies and non-governmental organizations (NGOs) are funding and implementing an increasing number of adaptation projects in developing countries. For example, the Adaptation Fund has spent more than USD 225 million over three years to finance adaptation projects and programmes in 34 developing countries (Adaptation Fund 2014). The Green Climate Fund (GCF), an output of COP15 in Copenhagen, is intended to become the main multilateral climate financing mechanism to support climate action in developing countries. It is expected to channel over USD 100 billion a year in climate financing to developing countries from 2020, to support them in limiting or reducing their GHG emissions and adapting to the impacts of climate change. Here the larger objective is to promote a 'paradigm shift towards low-emission and climate-resilient development pathways' (Green Climate Fund 2014).

However, we know less about how such interventions actually fare in terms of addressing the underlying reasons why people and areas are vulnerable to climate change. There is a large literature showing that vulnerability is closely linked to development processes and pathways, including issues of power, access, livelihoods, rights and voice, and – not least – poverty (Liverman 1990; Watts and Bohle 1993; Adger and Kelly 1999; Luers 2005; Eakin 2006). Nonetheless, the IPCC recently concluded that poverty dynamics are insufficiently accounted for in climate change research; further, an evaluation of the limited experience to date with mitigation and adaptation policies indicates that they have had at best a negligible effect on poverty – in some cases they may have even undermined the livelihoods of marginalized groups (Olsson et al. 2014). A critical question is whether adaptation measures are merely incremental adjustments to 'development as usual', or whether they can indeed influence current development pathways in ways that bring about fundamental transformations and paradigm shifts. This question emerges from a growing body of research showing that many local and global responses to climate change, such as forestry programmes and sea walls, contribute to business-as-usual development and land grabbing that may in fact exacerbate vulnerability to climate change, rather than reduce it (Beymer-Farris and Bassett 2011; Marino and Ribot 2012).

This book is a collection of case studies that contribute to critical understandings of the relationship between climate change adaptation and development. In exploring the implications of 'development-as-usual' approaches, these case studies recognize adaptation as a social process that unfolds differently in different contexts. While many studies and analyses of adaptation in developing countries focus on important practical and technical challenges of planning, funding and implementing projects (Gagnon-Lebrun and Agrawala 2006; Gigli and Agrawala 2007; Mapfumo, Mtambanengwe and Chikowo 2010; Biagini et al. 2014), the chapters in this book draw attention to the systemic and structural factors that define adaptation as a *social* processes. They describe the types of interventions and actions that impede or support adaptation in different local contexts. More broadly, they investigate the extent to which adaptation interventions by governments, NGOs and aid agencies either reproduce or challenge dominant development paradigms. Such knowledge is essential if adaptation actions are to engage with and support more equitable and sustainable pathways.

In this introductory chapter, we describe why climate change adaptation and development need to be taken more seriously, what is meant by 'development as usual', and how adaptation is framed, financed and practised within this paradigm. We then describe the contributions to this book, and show that there is significant empirical research to support arguments for new approaches to adaptation and development which can serve as an entry point for creating sustainable and resilient development pathways.

Taking adaptation and development seriously

Communities, sectors, states and institutions have to adapt not only to the changes that are currently observed, but also to the impacts that are likely to occur over the next decades. Adaptation has been defined by the IPCC (2014a: 5) as '[t]he process of adjustment to actual or expected climate and its effects. In human systems, adaptation seeks to moderate or avoid harm or exploit beneficial opportunities.' Looking towards the second half of the 21st century and beyond, the types of adaptation required will be closely linked to the success or failure of near-term and sustained climate change mitigation: the challenges of adapting to a world that is more than 4°C warmer are exponentially higher than adapting to a world of less than 2°C warming, and there are recognized limits to adaptation (Dow et al. 2013). Adaptation and mitigation cannot be seen as discrete, independent policies. Although mitigation and adaptation are often discussed as two separate policy arenas, they are closely related in practice, as mitigation of GHG emissions will influence both how much and what kind of adaptation will be necessary in the future (Pelling 2011). Indeed, some practices, such as the provision of renewable energy to poor households, can create synergies and co-benefits between mitigation and adaptation (IPCC 2014a).

The process of adaptation presents significant challenges to development – not only because of the financial costs of adaptation, but also because failure to adapt will incur significant losses and damages (Warner and van der Geest 2013).

Yet vulnerability to climate change and other social stressors is not created by the impact of climate change alone: social factors such as inequity, marginalization, lack of access and rights to resources, and poverty are also involved (O'Brien et al. 2007). Development interventions themselves may add to vulnerability or reduce adaptive capacity (Barnett and O'Neill 2010). For example, in the Pacific island of Niue, development aid undermined existing government structures and legitimacy, providing the financing for adaptation while eroding the capacity to adapt (Barnett 2008). Lessons from community-based adaptation also show that adaptation is first and foremost a process whereby communities become increasingly enabled and empowered to make choices about their own lives and livelihoods (Ensor and Berger 2010; Schipper et al. 2014). Since social adaptation to climate change is not a politically neutral process, addressing the underlying drivers of vulnerability will also necessitate challenging some of the key dependencies, inequities and power structures.

Climate change is thus as much a problem *of* development as *for* development, because the risks are closely linked to past, present and future development pathways. As Pelling (2011: 25) argues, 'the vastness of climate change and the multitude of pathways through which it can affect life and wellbeing for any individual or organization make it almost impossible for "climate change" in a holistic sense to be the target of adaptation'. Seeing climate change not as an external threat to development, but instead both a driver and product of development, he contends that we should not be talking about adapting *to* climate change, but about adapting *with* climate change.

What do these insights mean for the growing field of 'adaptation and development'? First, more than a simple integration of adaptation into 'development-as-usual' paradigms is required in order to avoid perpetuating many of the factors that contributed to vulnerability in the first place. Merely adapting to the impacts without transforming development paradigms and practices is likely to contribute to increasingly negative outcomes, especially for those who are currently most vulnerable to shocks and stressors of all sorts. Second, fossil-fuel-based global development pathways driven by goals of rapid economic growth are likely to fuel the dynamics of vulnerability over time: as the rate and magnitude of climate change increases, the costs of adaptation rise dramatically, while the possibilities become more and more limited (IPCC 2014a). For these reasons, climate change is not just another issue to absorb or mainstream into current development paradigms and practices. It calls for a different type of development – one that can take adaptation seriously.

Development as usual

Climate change has strong links to development, whether in relation to the causes and consequences of climate change or to responses related to adaptation and mitigation (Leary et al. 2008). As noted in the IPCC 'Summary for Policymakers' in *Mitigation of Climate Change* (2014b: 4), 'a comprehensive assessment of climate policies involves going beyond a focus on mitigation and adaptation policies alone to examine development pathways more broadly, along with their determinants'. This is consistent with Pelling's (2011: 167) view that '[c]limate change presents the early twenty-first century with a grand opportunity to reconfigure the meaning and trajectory of development'.

However, as discussed by Tanner and Horn-Phathanothai (2014), development may have several different meanings. It can refer to a *process*, such as industrial development or modernization, or a *project*, such as deliberate efforts to improve human wellbeing through policies, plans and development initiatives. Development can also refer to a *discourse*, such as that of social progress (Tanner and Horn-Phathanothai 2014). Dominant processes, projects and discourses of development have together resulted in a development paradigm that has influenced how 'adaptation' is translated into policies and practices.

Development as a discourse emerged in the post-World War II period and was closely associated with ideas of growth, progress, modernization and globalization; in short, modern technologies, management systems and values were expected to lead to growing consumption and prosperity in developing countries (Brooks, Grist and Brown 2009). Although the political context changed with the end of the Cold War, the underlying paradigm was kept intact. Some of the consequences of this approach could be seen by the introduction of structural policy reforms, which included deregulation, privatization of markets, and imposition of fees for schools and health services (Kingsbury 2007).

The direct links between the environment and development were emphasized through the Brundtland Commission Report *Our Common Future* (WCED 1987), and global environmental issues and politics increasingly came on the agenda after the 1992 United Nations Conference on Environment and Development. Nonetheless, both poverty and environmental issues have generally been framed as externalities of development, and have often been seen as implicit obstacles to further growth (Brooks, Grist and Brown 2009). Recent years have seen a growing focus on private–public partnerships and an expanding role for the business sector, including 'green' investments. The explicit or implicit goal of development within this paradigm is arguably still economic growth through a capitalist market system, with socially based indicators often seen solely as a means towards economic ends (Hamann 2012).

Development as a modernization process has been criticized for its overarching goals and also for its lack of reflexivity on political and ideological dimensions (Sachs 1992; Escobar 1995). Many alternative approaches have been pursued, including those emphasizing Women in Development, Gender and Development, and Participatory Learning and Action (Ireland and McKinnon 2013). Tanner and Horn-Phathanothai (2014) describe these as people-centred paradigms, new economic paradigms, and new environmental approaches. These approaches have influenced the way development interventions are carried out; nevertheless, development funding and projects are often criticized for being primarily oriented towards economic growth (Peet and Hartwick

2009). Modernization-led economic growth remains the dominant development discourse, constituting 'development as usual'.

Climate change as a new development issue

The shortcomings of the dominant development paradigm have become even more evident and critical in the context of climate change because existing inequities are a key social cause of climate change vulnerability and because energy and resource-intensive growth drive GHG emissions and hence the climate change problem (Pelling 2011; Marino and Ribot 2012; Olsson et al. 2014). Newell (2009: 189) notes the contradictions between development as usual and climate change:

> Perhaps most alarming of all is the fact that the governments and leading international institutions charged with serving the public interest on climate change continue to promote a model of economic development that is clearly unsustainable, one that is energy intensive, export-oriented, and produces widespread social and environmental externalities. Rather than being part of the solution, through their own activities many of these actors are exacerbating the problem.

Nonetheless, climate change has entered into the world of development planning and practice unaccompanied by much rethinking of 'what is new to development thinking' (Boyd and Juhola 2009). Traditional adaptation interventions within development have tended to focus directly on climate impacts, without addressing the underlying causes of vulnerability that are linked to social structures, economic relations, the distribution of power and access to resources (Vincent et al. 2013). In practice, the focus has often been narrow and sectoral, aimed largely at mainstreaming climate change considerations into current activities rather than questioning how current activities and structures contribute to the social and political drivers of vulnerability. As Tanner and Horn-Phathanothai (2014: 6) point out, '[c]limate change issues are often relegated to specialized environmental or disaster-response authorities that view them in narrow technical terms. These specialized authorities are ill-equipped to respond to the full spectrum of development challenges that climate change raises.'

The integration of adaptation activities into development activities has taken many forms and labels, such as Climate Friendly Development, Climate Compatible Development, Conservation Agriculture, Climate Smart Agriculture, or simply 'mainstreaming' adaptation into existing policies and projects, whether related to poverty reduction, agriculture, energy, health or disaster-risk reduction (Kok and de Coninck 2007). Leary et al. (2008: 16) describe how the adaptation process 'needs to be integrated into policy formulation, planning, programme management, project design and project implementation of the agencies that are responsible for human and economic development, finance, agriculture, forestry, land use, and conservation, biodiversity conservation, water, energy, public health, transportation, housing, disaster management, and other sectors and activities'. This approach to adaptation and development is consistent with ecological modernization theory, which promotes change within current systems and structures, in contrast to 'a critical ecopolitics of change that involves some subversion of existing modern configurations of states, markets and social institutions' (Warner 2010: 539). Adaptation is in this form seen as part of the 'technical fix' paradigm that is at the heart of modernity. Within this paradigm, technological advances and innovations are prioritized as the solution to most of the world's problems (Hoogma et al. 2002).

Adaptation under 'development as usual' has nonetheless been criticized by many scholars. Bassett and Fogelman (2013: 48) reflect that 'adaptation always seems to take place in relation to a list of proximate factors that can be more or less addressed without upsetting the social-political order'. Brooks et al. (2009) similarly express concern that efforts such as 'climate proofing' implicitly protect existing developmental policies, plans, programmes and practices against the impacts of climate change, with the ultimate objective of maintaining the status quo. Pelling (2011) considers this a form of resilience that does not threaten core aspects of the dominant system. As a result, Ireland and McKinnon (2013: 158) draw attention to the 'urgent need to question the underlying assumptions of adaptation and to investigate the ideologies and agendas that are shaping adaptation discourses'.

Funding adaptation through development

As a response to increases in climate funding, there is a growing diversity of actors involved in formal adaptation initiatives, including bilateral and multilateral development agencies, humanitarian organizations, local and international NGOs, businesses and community-based organizations (though arguably, many of the most important adaptation strategies are carried out 'informally' by individuals, households and communities themselves, see Olsson et al. 2014). The donor landscape today includes bilateral donors, multilateral donors, and various funds for adaptation projects and programmes, while there are also initiatives run by local or regional organizations jointly sponsored by several donors. Specific adaptation projects, for example, have been funded either bilaterally or multilaterally through organizations such as the World Bank and regional development banks. Despite the diversity of actors involved in adaptation, an institutional structure of partnerships and financing originally created for development (e.g., through institutional infrastructures in place for Official Development Assistance (ODA)) have in effect supported adaptation through 'development as usual' (Brooks, Grist and Brown 2009).

In addition to traditional development finance structures, specific climate financing structures and institutions have been put in place. There are several climate change funds, and specific adaptation funds, such as the

Global Environment Facility (GEF), the official financing mechanism for the UNFCCC. Initially the GEF focused mainly on climate change mitigation and biodiversity activities, with some limited financing of vulnerability and adaptation assessments and studies, and with less focus on capacity building and almost no emphasis on implementation of adaptation actions (Young 2002). In order to increase adaptation financing, GEF launched a Strategic Priority on Adaptation (SPA) in 2004. The GEF also hosts the Least Developed Countries Fund (LDCF) and the Special Climate Change Fund (SCCF). The Adaptation Fund (AF) is a financial instrument under the UNFCCC and its Kyoto Protocol (KP), financed through a share of proceeds from the Clean Development Mechanism (CDM) and voluntary donor contributions.

The 'absorption' of climate change and adaptation into a development-as-usual paradigm is further indicated in the tools used by the various financing funds, such as the LDCF/SCCF Adaptation Monitoring and Assessment Tool, where the explicit goal is to integrate adaptation measures in development policies, plans, programmes, projects and actions (GEF 2010). As pointed out by Klein (2010), mainstreaming has been a challenge, especially with respect to evaluation, monitoring and financing. It is sometimes difficult to single out the climate component, and the question of 'additionality' in funding has been raised by developing countries who are worried that adaptation funding is merely a reallocation of existing development funding (Michaelowa and Michaelowa 2010). This has especially been the case since the financial crisis, which resulted in significant cuts in development funding (Kirigia et al. 2011).[1]

Against this backdrop, the total amount of funding currently available for adaptation is considered insufficient and difficult to access. This has led to calls, such as at the 8th international conference on Community Based Adaptation to Climate Change, for not only greater commitment of funds, but also greater inclusivity and transparency (Kathmandu Declaration 2014).

Donors have a strong influence on adaptation discourses and what types of formal adaptation efforts are carried out in practice. However, common to most of the adaptation projects funded bilaterally or through the GEF, including the 'softer measures', is that they tend to focus on reducing the direct impact(s) of climate change, often through skills transfer or provision of specific information such as land-management techniques. Adaptation interventions have mainly taken the form of supporting activities that deal with current climate variability, such as disaster-risk reduction (flood control, drought mitigation and relief), social safety nets, water management, ecosystems management (forests, mangrove plantations), agricultural practices, improved meteorological services and forecasting, microfinance, and insurance such as index-based insurance. Some infrastructural measures (dimensioning of roads, pipes, flood and coastal defences) and agricultural adjustments (promoting drought-resistant crops, climate-smart agriculture, irrigation) as well as institutional changes (land-tenure change, land-use planning and building regulations, support of local institutions) have also been promoted as adaptation to climate change (Mapfumo, Mtambanengwe and Chikowo 2010; Nkem, Munang and Jallow 2011; Bahinipati and Sahu 2012; IEG 2012). An analysis of the adaptation projects funded by the GEF identified ten categories of projects: capacity building, management and planning, practice and behaviour, policy, information, physical infrastructure, warning and observing systems, green infrastructure, financing, and technology (Biagini et al. 2014).

In many cases adaptation projects are seen as development projects aimed at reducing specific impacts of climate change (Lamhauge, Lanzi and Agrawala 2012). Importantly, they seldom appear to address the social structures that cause vulnerability in the first place. And although the development of 'green' infrastructure may be included in the programme, such efforts tend to focus on actions like reforestation or afforestation, with somewhat less emphasis on projects for developing energy infrastructure and low-carbon solutions. This approach to adaptation has been criticized for representing little new in response to climate change, and for repeating earlier strategies, policies and practices – now justified by climate change (Ireland 2012; Bassett and Fogelman 2013).

In summary, climate change is typically seen as a threat to development that has to be addressed by changing crops, management practices, institutions, or behaviours in order to reduce risk and vulnerability. And so, adaptation to climate change gets subsumed within current development policies and practices. Piecemeal adaptation efforts that reduce impacts often fail to deal with the underlying causes of vulnerability. With the growing recognition of the importance of climate change in the development context, effective development assistance activities need to fit with larger social and environmental goals. For this, how adaptation is understood and approached within the development sector will be crucial.

Adaptation as a social process

Moving beyond development as usual means viewing adaptation through a much broader lens, recognizing that it is not merely about minimizing discrete 'climate impacts', but about addressing the systemic risks that are embedded in current development pathways. What does this mean for how adaptation is approached in policy and practice? An underlying theme that runs throughout the chapters in this book is an emphasis on adaptation as more than one single intervention that can be implemented based on scenarios of future climate change impacts. Instead, adaptation is a social process that requires attention to the systems and structures that influence vulnerability and the practical, on-the-ground actions to address the observed or future impacts of climate change. It also calls for greater attention to the values, beliefs, worldviews and assumptions that influence processes of change. In short, adaptation involves addressing the social and human dimensions of climate change – including how social and economic structures as well as gender and power relations influence vulnerability and the capacity to adapt.

This does not mean that technical adaptations are irrelevant or unnecessary, but rather that they are insufficient and unlikely to improve the wellbeing of current and future generations unless also social relations and structural issues, including power and political processes, are dealt with. The chapters in this book show what recognizing adaptation as a process of development and change means in practice, hence providing entry points for approaching it in practical terms. Several features of adaptation (as a social process) emerge: first, local capacity is a critical part of the adaptation process and is closely linked to empowerment; second, the framework for adaptation is set by decisions on several levels and within multiple spheres of policy; and third, because adaptation is about change and processes where decisions, interests and implications are negotiated, it is a highly political process. The rich empirical material presented in this book exemplifies how adaptation can address social relations and processes with the aim of reducing vulnerability and transforming development towards more sustainable pathways.

The importance of vulnerability context and local capacity

The local level is where the impacts of climate change will be felt, and adaptation is often targeted at this level. What is striking, however, is that existing local strategies and vulnerability contexts are seldom at the heart of interventions. In Chapter 2, Jon Ensor, Emily Boyd, Sirrku Juhola and Vanesa Castán Broto argue that development actors have focused more on reducing the impacts than building capacities to adapt and transform. Capacity building is not only a matter of strengthening strategies at the community level; it is also vitally important for influencing and creating change at higher levels, the very levels where marginalization and inequality originate. Ensor and colleagues find that a community's access to power sharing, knowledge and experimentation is an important premise for building strong adaptive capacity and thus a way for communities to participate effectively, gaining recognition for local understandings, needs and values in the higher bureaucracies. Such access is also critical for influencing the structural causes of vulnerability to climate change, instead of being reduced to passive recipients of a given governance arrangement or set of actions.

Affirming and empowering local livelihood strategies through adaptation processes is further elaborated in Chapter 3. Using the case of charcoal production, Caroline Ochieng, Sirkku Juhola and Francis X. Johnson argue that local strategies that have often been seen as merely short-term survival strategies detrimental to the local environment are, in fact, an important part of longer-term adaptation. Therefore, policy efforts should shift away from focusing on technical adjustments and interventions that are delinked from, or even undermine, local strategies – and instead take these as a starting point in supporting a wider adaptation process. Crucially, such a change of perspective means that the social and economic relations of production through which local strategies are carried out need to be improved, in effect challenging current processes of marginalization. For example, the legal frameworks and trade structures that leave rural producers of charcoal with very little revenue, while quite literally fuelling a large part of the national economy through the provision of cheap energy, need to be reformed. Supporting local capacity also involves enhancing the position of small-scale producers of charcoal (as well as other local strategies) in trade relations and within legal frameworks, so that they can have a fair income and influence over their own circumstances. Recognizing local strategies as far more than short-term survival strategies turn what might be considered 'good adaptation' on its head.

The observation that rural people's own strategies are important for adaptation, yet remain ignored in formal policies, is mirrored in urban contexts in San Salvador and Rio de Janeiro. In Chapter 4, Christine Wamsler and Ebba Brink argue that urban dwellers' strategies for coping with disasters and climate change should not automatically be seen as maladaptive. Instead, understanding of such strategies and their strengths and weaknesses should form the basis for formulating development policies and projects. Wamsler and Brink show that disaster resilience depends on the level of flexibility and inclusiveness of the combined set of strategies employed, rather than the effectiveness of a single strategy. Supporting adaptive capacity in this context is not about targeting one particular local response, but empowering urban dwellers more generally in securing such flexibility and inclusiveness in their coping systems. Such socially based adaptation can lead to transformation of the power relations and development pathways that influence the opportunity space for managing risks.

Importantly, adaptive capacity is not uniform within a community. In Chapter 5, Sara Gabrielsson analyses adaptation in communities around the Lake Victoria Basin. The study shows how social relations create differentiated access to adaptation strategies and how these relations are an important aspect of the vulnerability context and local adaptive capacity. Gender-differentiated rights and responsibilities, for example, often limit the opportunities for women. At the same time, the local 'economy of affection' is becoming increasingly unreliable as an adaptation strategy. Hence, it is not sufficient to empower local adaptation strategies within formal economic and legal frameworks without considering the issue of gender-differentiated rights and responsibilities. Gabrielsson's observations show that it is critical for development organizations to understand how social relations drive vulnerability patterns; they also indicate that local adaptation processes can be a driver of change towards more sustainable and equitable development pathways.

Nonetheless, technologies, and not social measures, often take precedence in national adaptation planning. In Chapter 6, Sara Trærup and Lars Christiansen show how technologically focused adaptation can also provide an entry point for targeting the social drivers of vulnerability and generating social development. They point out that adaptation technologies often emphasize the soft aspects of technology, like orgware and software, which have benefits for livelihoods, institutions and local capacity building. How adaptation technologies are implemented does matter; in particular, smaller-scale technologies suited to community-level interventions and participation can contribute to equitable and pro-poor development.

Adaptation beyond the local level

Focusing on adaptation solely on the local level may not be enough to reduce vulnerability. Several chapters show how adaptation must take place simultaneously across levels. In Chapter 7, Trond Vedeld, Wilbard Kombe, Clara Kweka Msale and Siri Bjerkreim Hellevik draw attention to the importance of multilevel governance and the coordination between different levels and actors. In the case of Dar es Salaam, they find that integrating adaptation into urban governance and building adaptive capacity at the local level can be severely constrained by deep-seated institutional deficiencies: policies and mandates are unclear, and a lack of finances, resources and technologies characterizes all levels. The authors show how informal settlements in Dar es Salaam that are at risk from flooding remain largely outside the realm of spatial planning. This has led to large informal settlements in flood-prone areas, with a significantly unequal distribution of vulnerability between different groups. Adding climate change adaptation to an already highly pressured governance system that is failing to meet the basic needs of the population may seem challenging. However, the authors point to the potential for bringing coherence to planning processes, recognizing that broader development plans play an important role in determining who is at risk, and why.

Diverse actions and policies beyond official or explicit adaptation measures can ultimately provide a much wider and more effective solution space for addressing risks. In Chapter 8, Jennifer West describes how in Tanzania, climate policies have identified the agricultural sector as particularly vulnerable and a top priority for adaptation. However, West describes how vulnerability among small-scale farmers has been driven by structural changes in agriculture, such as efforts to modernize and commercialize smallholder production in breadbasket regions of the country. In order for policy efforts to support the adaptation process, the effect of such structural changes on the adaptive capacity of rural smallholders must be understood. West describes how some types of agricultural investments can support local capacity – but she also notes that it matters *how* agricultural investments are made, not just for farmer sensitivity to climate factors but also for market risk, access to land and water, equity outcomes and empowerment.

Unintended community adaptation opportunities sometimes arise from technological and socio-economic changes. In Chapter 9, Julie Wilk, Mattias Hjerpe and Birgitta Rydhagen investigate how such unplanned side effects or *spinoffs* often materialize outside the aims of development programmes or government interventions. Examining the cases of information and communication technology (ICT) in South Africa, changing lifestyles in China, and empowerment in India, they show that such spinoffs often can be utilized to strengthen adaptive capacity. Adaptation approaches would benefit from paying specific attention to such spinoffs from development.

Adaptation as a political process

Adaptation involves changes, whether in technologies, infrastructure, social structures or policies, and these changes involve decisions and choices that may have widespread consequences. Adaptation is a political process where different interests and agendas (not always transparent) are involved and affected. The needs, values and interests of some actors are often prioritized, while those of others are ignored. Adaptation is not a neutral process that benefits all, therefore; it is a matter of politics that involves addressing the social and power relations through which resources, costs and benefits are distributed in society.

In Chapter 10, Siri Eriksen and Andrei Marin argue that supporting adaptation as a social process that contributes towards sustainable development pathways entails transforming negotiation processes between the diverse actors through which decisions are reached and actions formed. Such transformation includes empowering people not only in the adaptation process, but in the development process more widely, since development discourses and goals often drive adaptation choices. The case of Afar, Ethiopia, illustrates how a modernization-influenced development model, pressuring people to shift from pastoralism to settled cultivation, has played a central role in driving both the vulnerability context and adaptation pathways. Reduced ability to face droughts and climatic changes is an unintended consequence of development interventions. Supporting the adaptation process towards more sustainable pathways will mean making more explicit the development goals and values of diverse actors, and how they affect different adaptation interests.

Clearly, some interests are heard and prioritized while others are ignored in the various decisions that underpin the adaptation process. In Chapter 11, Sigrid Nagoda and Siri Eriksen show how vulnerability reduction framed by 'development as usual' ignore differing values, interests and power structures, thereby serving to reinforce inequities and inequalities in rural Humla, Nepal. When faced with stressors like climate change, the dependency and inequality between households with access to power and those excluded is often deepened, exacerbating vulnerability patterns. Adaptation is highly political: it is critical to understand, and if necessary challenge, local power relations, if humanitarian and development communities are to succeed in reducing the vulnerability of the poor and contribute to an adaptation process towards greater equity and social sustainability. Such interventions that support adaptation as a social process can empower the vulnerable and counteract power imbalances and processes of marginalization.

In Chapter 12, Andrea Nightingale suggests that formal adaptation programmes specifically need to address the political context through which adaptation takes place. Examining the case of Nepal, she argues that adaptation is a socionatural political process: it both constitutes and is derived from current social–political changes and relations. Social and political power relations determine who can harness changes in resources and services to their own benefit, and influence adaptation outcomes. Climate change programmes become embroiled in already-politicized relationships and networks, without challenging the relations that create inequities and vulnerability. However, programmes tend to emphasize institution building and positive trajectories for adaptation, largely delinked from the political context and institutional fragilities. Such 'development-as-usual' approaches prove inadequate for tackling vulnerability. Rather than treating politics as a negative externality that threatens 'positive' adaptation, politics should be understood as constituting adaptation. Nightingale argues that the current emphasis on *how* to adapt needs to be replaced with a focus on adaptation *for whom.*

In order to go beyond 'development-as-usual' adaptation, the research process itself may have to change. In Chapter 13, Kassim Kulindwa and Baruani Mshale investigate which actors are involved in generating and applying knowledge for climate change adaptation, as well as which narratives are employed in advancing different interests. Focusing on Tanzania, they find that applying a participatory action research approach can help narrow the gap between research and policy, providing an arena for testing and negotiating the various interests and positions of different actors, and highlighting shared and competing narratives. Importantly, involving relevant actors at all levels in the research process, including policy-makers, civil servants, private sector and civil society, combined with a policy-process analysis of actors' roles and power relations, helped make explicit the different interests. In turn, this contributed to making project outcomes more relevant to the actors involved, and to identifying practical and workable adaptation activities.

Empowerment emerges as a critical part of adaptation. In Chapter 14, Jakob Kronik and Jennifer Hays investigate the vulnerability of indigenous peoples, drawing on five case studies in Latin America, North Africa and the Middle East. They argue that indigenous groups are particularly vulnerable to climate change since their livelihoods are often dependent on climate-sensitive resources. At the same time, environmental, social, economic and political processes, in addition to many development initiatives, limit the room for manoeuvre for these groups, undermining their ability to respond effectively to climate change. Furthermore, the role of indigenous knowledge is often overlooked in development initiatives aimed at reducing climate risk. The chapter also shows the importance of empowerment for the adaptation process. Not only is the socio-economic, legal and political room for manoeuvre available to any given group in itself critical for the success of their adaptation strategies, even more important for adaptive capacity is indigenous groups' ability to exercise their rights and challenge this space, influencing their own space for manoeuvre.

The chapters in this book show that adaptation must be understood in different contexts, and how such adaptation challenges development as usual. In

Chapter 15, we draw out some key conclusions, focusing on what a rethinking of adaptation and development can actually mean, and the implications for practical actions. We describe the three spheres of transformation as a way of identifying how adaptation can contribute to climate resilient pathways, arguing that adaptation so far has focused primarily on the practical sphere, while ignoring the political and personal sphere of change. Operationalizing adaptation approaches requires a diverse set of tools and changes in the mode of operation. The insights derived from the case studies presented here contribute to six recommendations for approaching adaptation through multiple entry points. These draw attention to the significance of the political and personal spheres as a means for making changes in the practical sphere more effective.

Conclusions

This book shows how climate change poses challenges to institutions, infrastructure, economic sectors, livelihoods and lives, but also to beliefs, cultures and identities – not just at the local level where impacts are often most evident, but at regional, national and international levels where the policies and politics of development and aid are discussed and debated. Adaption to climate change is thus not a matter of a single decision, a measure or a quick-fix to deal with specific impacts, but a process driven by actions and decisions at all levels, nested within social and political structures. Supporting adaptation will require addressing these social and political structures specifically, in order to reduce vulnerability and create more equitable and sustainable development pathways. Even though many actions take place at the local level among vulnerable communities, adaptation is a key concern for development in the sense of challenging global development processes.

Adaptation as framed by current development paradigms is not enough. Climate change adaptation must drive fundamental changes in how we approach 'development'. Climate change also gives rise to a critical question: Is it possible to truly adapt to changes within the same development paradigms that have generated vulnerability in the first place? The IPCC notes that in order to move towards sustainability 'a fundamental rethinking of poverty and development will need to emphasize equity among poor and non-poor people to collectively address greenhouse gas emissions and vulnerabilities while striving toward a joint, just, and desirable future' (Olsson et al. 2014: 24). Realizing this future is the real challenge of adaptation and development.

Note

1 Aid budgets fell in real terms after the financial crisis of 2008 (OECD 2013), and what was promised as additional funding for climate change instead was often included under traditional ODA. At the same time, there has been a shift in ODA funding away from the poorest countries and towards middle-income countries (OECD 2013). Since 2008, DAC commitments to social infrastructure and services

(sectors like health, education, population programmes, water, sanitation and other social infrastructure) have stagnated (stats.oecd.org). The media have recently raised concerns that an increasing proportion of aid is going towards refugee-related activities *in the host countries*, in effect diluting the poverty reduction component of development aid.

References

Adaptation Fund. 2014. Homepage, www.adaptation-fund.org [accessed 28 April 2014].
Adger, W.N. and Kelly, M. 1999. 'Social vulnerability to climate change and the architecture of entitlements'. *Mitigation and Adaptation Strategies for Global Change* 4 (3-4), 253–266.
Bahinipati, C.S. and Sahu, N.C. 2012. 'Mangrove conservation as sustainable adaptation to cyclonic risk in Kendrapada District of Odisha, India'. *Asian Journal of Environment and Disaster Management* 4 (2), 183–202.
Barnett, J. 2008. 'The effect of aid on capacity to adapt to climate change: Insights from Niue'. *Political Science* 60 (1), 31–45.
Barnett, J. and O'Neill, S. 2010. 'Maladaptation'. *Global Environmental Change* 20 (2), 211–213.
Bassett, T.J. and Fogelman, C. 2013. 'Déjà vu or something new? The adaptation concept in the climate change literature'. *Geoforum* 48 (1), 42–53.
Beymer-Farris, B.A. and Bassett, T.J. 2011. 'The REDD menace: Resurgent protectionism in Tanzania's mangrove forests'. *Global Environmental Change* 22 (2), 332–341.
Biagini, B., Bierbaum, R., Stults, M., Dobardzic, S. and McNeely, S.M. 2014. 'A typology of adaptation actions: A global look at climate adaptation actions financed through the Global Environment Facility'. *Global Environmental Change* 25 (1), 97–108.
Boyd, E. and Juhola, S. 2009. 'Stepping up to the climate change: Opportunities in re-conceptualising development furtures'. *Journal of International Development* 21 (6), 792–804.
Brooks, N., Grist, N. and Brown, K. 2009. 'Development futures in the context of climate change: Challenging the present and learning from the past'. *Development Policy Review* 27 (6), 741–765.
Dow, K., Berkhout, F., Preston, B.L., Klein, R.J.T., Midgley, G. and Shaw, M.R. 2013. 'Limits to adaptation'. *Nature Climate Change* 3 (4), 305–307.
Eakin, H. 2006. *Weathering Risk in Rural Mexico: Climatic, Institutional, and Economic Change.* Tucson, AZ: University of Arizona Press.
Ensor, J. and Berger, R. 2010. *Understanding Climate Change Adaptation: Lessons from Community-based Approaches.* Rugby: Practical Action.
Escobar, A. 1995. *Encountering Development: The Making and Unmaking of the Third World.* Princeton, NJ: Princeton University Press.
Gagnon-Lebrun, F. and Agrawala, S. 2006. *Progress on Adaptation to Climate Change in Developed Countries: An Analysis of Broad Trends.* Paris: OECD.
GEF. 2010. *Updated Results-based Management Framework for the Least Developed Countries Fund (LDCF) and the Special Climate Change Fund (SCCF) and Adaptation Monitoring and Assessment Tool.* Washington, DC: Global Environment Facility.
Gigli, S. and Agrawala, S. 2007. *Stocktaking of Progress on Integrating Adaptation to Climate Change into Development Co-operation Activities.* Paris: OECD.
Green Climate Fund. 2014. *Mandate and governance* http://www.gcfund.org/about-the-fund/mandate-and-governance.html [accessed 02 May 2014].
Hamann, R. 2012. The business of development: Revisiting strategies for a sustainable future. *Environment: Linking Science and Policy for Sustainable Development* 54 (2), 18–29.

Available at: http://www.environmentmagazine.org/Archives/Back%20Issues/2012/March-April%202012/sustainable_full.html

Hoogma, R., Kemp, R., Schot, J. and Truffer, B. 2002. *Experimenting for Sustainable Transport*. London: Spon Press.

IEG. 2012. *Adapting to Climate Change: Assessing the World Bank Group Experience Phase III*. Independent Evaluation Group of the World Bank. Washington, DC: World Bank.

IPCC. 2014a. 'Summary for Policymakers'. In: *Climate Change 2014: Impacts, Adaptation, and Vulnerability. Contribution of Working Group III to the Fifth Assessment Report of the Intergovernmental Panel on Climate Change*. Cambridge: Cambridge University Press.

IPCC. 2014b. 'Summary for Policymakers'. In: *Climate Change 2014, Mitigation of Climate Change. Contribution of Working Group III to the Fifth Assessment Report of the Intergovernmental Panel on Climate Change*. Cambridge: Cambridge University Press.

Ireland, P. 2012. 'Nepalganj, the centre of the world: Local perceptions of environmental change and the roles of climate-change adaptation actors'. *Local Environment* 17 (2), 187–201.

Ireland, P. and McKinnon, K. 2013. 'Strategic localism for an uncertain world: A postdevelopment approach to climate change adaptation'. *Geoforum* 47 (4), 158–166.

Kathmandu Declaration. 2014. 'Kathmandu Declaration on Financing Local Adaptation to Climate Change'. Paper read at 8th International Conference on Community Based Adaptation to Climate Change, 26–30 April 2014, Kathmandu.

Kingsbury, D. 2007. *Political Development*. London: Routledge.

Kirigia, J.M., Nganda, B.M., Mwikisa, C.N. and Cardoso, B. 2011. 'Effects of global financial crisis on funding for health development in nineteen countries of the WHO African Region'. *BMC International Health and Human Rights* 11 (4), doi: 10.1186/1472-698X-11-4.

Klein, R. 2010. 'Mainstreaming climate adaptation into development: A policy dilemma'. In: A. Ansohn and B. Pleskovic (eds), *Climate Governance and Development*. Berlin workshop series 2010. Washington, DC: World Bank.

Kok, M.T.J. and de Coninck, H.C. 2007. 'Widening the scope of policies to address climate change: Directions for mainstreaming'. *Environmental Science & Policy* 10 (7-8), 587–599.

Lamhauge, N., Lanzi, E. and Agrawala, S. 2012. *Monitoring and Evaluation for Adaptation: Lessons from Development Co-operation Agencies*. Paris: OECD.

Leary, N., Adejuwon, J., Barros, V., Batima, P., Biagini, B., Burton, I., Chinvanno, S. et al. 2008. 'A stitch in time: General lessons from specific cases'. In: N. Leary, J. Adejuwon, V. Barros, I. Burton, J. Kulkarni and R. Lasco (eds), *Climate Change and Adaptation, Vol.1*. London: Earthscan.

Lenton, T.M., Held, H., Kriegler, E., Hall, J.W., Lucht, W., Rahmstorf, S. and Schellnhuber, H.J. 2008. Inaugural Article: 'Tipping elements in the Earth's climate system'. *Proceedings of the National Academy of Sciences* 105 (6), 1786-1793.

Liverman, D.M. 1990. 'Drought impacts in Mexico: Climate, agriculture, technology, and land tenure in Sonora and Puebla'. *Annals of the American Association of Geographers* 80 (1), 49–72.

Luers, A.L. 2005. 'The surface of vulnerability: An analytical framework for examining environmental change'. *Global Environmental Change* 15 (3), 214–223.

Mapfumo, P., Mtambanengwe, F. and Chikowo, R. 2010. 'Mobilizing local safety nets for enhanced adaptive capacity to climate change and variability in Zimbabwe', *Adaptation Insights* November 2010. Ottawa: IDRC.

Marino, E. and Ribot, J. 2012. 'Adding insult to injury: Climate change and the inequities of climate intervention'. *Global Environmental Change* 22 (2), 323–328.

Michaelowa, A. and Michaelowa, K. 2010. *Coding Error or Statistical Embellishment? The Political Economy of Reporting Climate Aid.* Zürich: Zürich University.

Newell, P. 2009. 'Fit for purpose: Towards a development architecture that can deliver'. In: E. Palosuo (ed.), *Rethinking Development in a Carbon-Constrained World.* Helsinki: Ministry of Foreign Affairs.

Nkem, J., Munang, R. and Jallow, B.P. 2011. *Lessons for Adaptation in Sub-Saharan Africa.* Climate change adaptation & development programme (CC Dare). Nairobi: UNEP/ UNDP.

O'Brien, K., Eriksen, S., Nygaard, L. and Schjolden, A. 2007. 'Why different interpretations of vulnerabilty matter in climate change discourses'. *Climate Policy* 7 (1), 73–88.

OECD. 2008. The Paris Declaration on Aid Effectiveness and the Accra Agenda for Action. Paris: OECD.

OECD. 2013. Development Co-operation Report 2013: Ending Poverty. Paris: OECD.

Olsson, L., Opondo, M., Tschakert, P., Agrawal, A., Eriksen, S., Ma, S., Perch, L. and Zakeildeen, S. 2014. Capter 13 'Livelihoods and poverty'. In: C.B. Field, V.R. Barros, D.J. Dokken, K.J. Mach, M.D. Mastrandrea, T.E. Bilir, M. Chatterjee, K.L. Ebi, Y.O. Estrada, R.C. Genova, B. Girma, E.S. Kissel, A.N. Levy, S. MacCracken, P.R. Mastrandrea, and L.L. White (eds), *Climate Change 2014: Impacts, Adaptation, and Vulnerability. Contribution of Working Group II to the Fifth Assessment Report of the Intergovernmental Panel on Climate Change.* Cambridge: Cambridge University Press.

Peet, R. and Hartwick, E. 2009. *Theories of Development: Contentions, Arguments, Alternatives,* 2nd edn. New York: Guilford Press.

Pelling, M. 2011. *Adaptation to Climate Change. From Resilience to Transformation.* London: Routledge.

Sachs, W. 1992. *The Development Dictionary. A Guide to Knowledge as Power.* New York: Zed Books.

Schipper, E.L.F., Ayers, J., Reid, H., Huq, S. and Rahman, A.E. 2014. *Community-based Adaptation to Climate Change.* London: Routledge.

SREX. 2012. *Managing the Risks of Extreme Events and Disasters to Advance Climate Change Adaptation.* IPCC. Cambridge: Cambridge University Press.

Tanner, T. and Horn-Phathanothai, L. 2014. *Climate Change and Development.* London: Routledge.

Warner, K. and van der Geest, K. 2013. 'Loss and damage from climate change: Local-level evidence from nine vulnerable countries'. *International Journal of Global Warming* 5 (4), 1–20.

Warner, R. 2010. 'Ecologial modernisation theory: Towards a critical ecopolitics of change?' *Environmental Politics* 19 (4), 538–556.

Watts, M. and Bohle, H.G. 1993. 'The space of vulnerability. The causal structure of hunger and famine'. *Progress in Human Geography* 17 (1), 43–67.

WCED. 1987. *Our Common Future.* United Nations Report of the World Commission on Environment and Development. Available at: http://www.un-documents.net/wced-ocf.htm

Young, Z. 2002. *A New Green Order? The World Bank and the Politics of the Global Environment Facility.* London: Pluto Press.

2

BUILDING ADAPTIVE CAPACITY IN THE INFORMAL SETTLEMENTS OF MAPUTO

Lessons for development from a resilience perspective

Jonathan Ensor, Emily Boyd, Sirkku Juhola and Vanesa Castán Broto

Introduction

Increasing numbers of development practitioners are turning their attention to community-based adaptation as a response to the emerging reality and threat of climate change (Reid et al. 2009; Ensor et al. 2014). At the heart of adaptation is the need to address future uncertainty and, as a consequence, the role that adaptive capacity plays in enabling communities to make changes to their lives and livelihoods. But this understanding presents twin challenges: first, to develop a clear picture of adaptive capacity, so that the demands placed on development can be articulated; and second, to find development models and modes of practice that meet those demands.

The premise of this chapter is that adaptive capacity, while now part of the development lexicon, has still to be fully explored as to its meaning for development practice. Here, as elsewhere, the term is assumed to capture the ability to carry out adaptation measures. These measures may be aimed at reducing vulnerability to specific weather-related threats or at building the ability to cope with and recover from unexpected events. The vulnerability of communities[1] to future climate change therefore depends in part on their adaptive capacity, through which timely adaptation measures can be adopted. Development actions on adaptation commonly include some or all of the following: vulnerability-reducing measures, support for coping or absorbing capacity, and efforts to build adaptive capacity. At the local level, they are often directed to place-specific climate impacts and their perceived consequences. In this chapter, we adopt an explicit contextual understanding of vulnerability, one which emphasizes a multi-dimensional view on climate–society interactions and thus characterizes vulnerability in relation to both social-ecological relations and institutional responses to climate change impacts (O'Brien et al. 2007).

While the emphasis that is placed on each of these components will vary according to local needs, a lack of clarity around understanding 'adaptive capacity' means that it can easily be overlooked or underplayed. The aim of this chapter is to show how studies of resilience can help to shed light on the nature of the challenges that adaptive capacity must overcome. All communities live in complex environments, where cross-scale relationships and self-organizing dynamics make understanding the impacts of and responses to change difficult to predict, thereby revealing uncertainty as a central feature not only of climate change but of all aspects of life. From this perspective, the function of adaptive capacity is not only to enable change, but to do so in ways that can reduce the likelihood that communities in a particular social-ecological system will experience the worst consequences of future climate change, or will find their wellbeing undermined by current adaptation actions.

We explore this resilience framing further in 'Resilience, adaptive capacity and development' below. In 'Adaptive capacity: power, knowledge and experimentation' we look to understand adaptive capacity from this perspective, identifying crucial social dimensions often overlooked by development actors. We suggest that a focus on power sharing, knowledge and information, and experimentation and testing in adaptation planning is necessary if climate change responses are to be able to engage with complexity and build opportunities to meet future change. In so doing, we seek to move towards a concrete understanding of how resilience revises our understanding of development, and the contribution that development can make to supporting resilience in practice. In particular, we identify how a focus on these three components within adaptation planning can contribute to the emergence of a flexible, adaptive governance system that fosters local adaptive capacity. 'Adaptation planning in Maputo, Mozambique' draws on fieldwork in Maputo, Mozambique, presenting a case study analysed using this framework. Finally, in 'Lessons from a resilience perspective' we present conclusions that can help to explain the role of adaptive capacity in development under climate change, highlighting the challenges to overcoming existing structures of power and knowledge.

Resilience, adaptive capacity and development

Resilience thinking recognizes that people co-exist with and have co-evolved within their natural (ecological) environments. One consequence is that we live with complexity and uncertainty (Berkes and Folke 1998). In resilience discourse, complexity arises because people and their environments, linked together in 'social-ecological systems', are constantly changing in response to external influences and as internal relationships are reworked (Holling and Gunderson 2002; Walker and Salt 2006). Linear, cause-and-effect responses are not the norm: people and environments adapt in response to external changes, making the consequences difficult to predict (Scheffer et al. 2012). From a development and adaptation perspective, complexity means that we need to recognize the unpredictable nature of change. It requires a mind-set shift away from the assumption that understanding the current ecological and social context is sufficient, and towards a focus on the capacity to adapt to changes not yet known and yet to be experienced. Complexity in climate change introduces the prospect of nonlinear change and uncertainty in climate projections, making it hard to predict specific effects such as how the intensity of cyclones, or the frequency of droughts and floods, may change in a warmer world. Uncertainty is significant to adaptation not just as a result of our limited understanding of climate science, but also because it is inherent in social-ecological contexts – in the life of communities – due to the potential for surprises inherent in complex systems.

In the context of climate change, resilience is significant as it refers to the amount of disturbance or change that a system can withstand before it changes function – with the attendant loss of wellbeing if the desirable characteristics of human systems are lost. It does so by drawing attention to the different connections and timescales that operate within systems. First, the resilience perspective draws attention to *cross-scale relationships*: how the local, national and international levels are connected by people, institutions and organizations in ways that create links and dependencies between actors and changes to the environment at these different levels. Second, it demands both *shorter- and longer-term thinking*, drawing attention to the different speeds at which parts of the system change or react (often more quickly in terms of individuals and more slowly in terms of policy-making, for example) and the consequences of actions today and in the future. Third, the resilience perspective alerts us to how these relationships shift *thresholds* through the conscious or unconscious changing of the socio-ecological system, in ways that can bring the system closer to the tipping points (or thresholds) after which irreversible processes of change occur. For example, national fertilizer subsidies may be linked (across scales) to the loss of local fisheries through the gradual accumulation (over long timescales) of nutrients in waterways, ultimately leading to the threshold beyond which oxygenation declines rapidly, and the sudden and unexpected loss of productive aquatic ecosystems occurs. The emergence of thresholds can be relatively easy to spot in simple systems, but remains poorly understood in complex systems – and in social systems in particular (Scheffer et al. 2012). For communities in general, low resilience and the breaching of thresholds can mean unexpected and fundamental changes to lives and livelihoods.

Climate change and its impacts have emerged as key variables that shift thresholds and render communities vulnerable to what might otherwise be minor shocks or stresses. Adaptive capacity is significant, as it represents the ability of social actors to make deliberate changes and thus influences the resilience of their social-ecological systems. However, case-study evidence indicates that adaptation interventions by development actors are frequently focused more on meeting immediate-term challenges – such as through the provision of technologies to enhance food or water security in the face of existing climate variability – than the reality of on-going climate change (Ensor and Berger 2009). While the academic literature has discussed adaptive capacity for some time now (Smit and Wandel 2006; Engle and Lemos 2010; Eakin et al. 2011; Engle 2011; Gupta et al. 2011; Juhola & Kruse 2013), it is only recently that publications from major development organizations have recognized addressing adaptive capacity as a component of their adaptation actions. As a result, there remains a shortage of development experiences that explore the meaning of adaptive capacity (Mitchell and Tanner 2006; Nelson et al. 2007), and definitions vary considerably (CARE 2010; CCCD 2010; Pettengell 2010; Ludi et al. 2012). Meanwhile, for many development actors, adaptation remains based on notions of 'good' development – which reinforce existing development paradigms and fail to engage with what is new and different about climate change (Ireland 2012).

Adaptive capacity can be supported by the opportunities that emerge from small-scale experiments with livelihood practices that, if adopted at the local scale, can increase resilience, shifting communities away from thresholds. Yet adaptive capacity is also shaped by the social and political context. The formal and informal institutions that intersect with local communities play a key role in mediating interests across scales, shaping the opportunities and constraints for local-level changes (Agrawal 2010; Eakin and Lemos 2010; Gupta et al. 2010). In poor or marginalized communities where the continuity (and resilience) of inequitable or unsustainable resource access and distribution arrangements is undesirable, the capacity to influence and create change at the higher scale can be critical. Creating the conditions for effective participation that disaggregates communities, providing opportunities for the range of local understandings, needs and values to gain traction in the bureaucracies at higher scales, is thus a key challenge for local adaptive capacity.

Conversely, it has been shown that informing people that the risks of climate-change impacts are increasing is not enough to engage the local population to act (Patt and Schröter 2008): climate-change risks and adaptations need to be made meaningful in context. As such, the dissemination and bridging of both scientific and local knowledge through multi-scalar institutions is a key process in building adaptive capacity for climate change. As noted by Pelling (2010:3), adaptation can also be 'an opportunity for social reform, for questioning the values that drive inequalities in development and our unsustainable relationship with the environment'. For adaptive capacity, such reform needs to include opportunities for communities to engage with others in learning cycles, so that they can test and revise alternative ways of living in the face of emerging environmental change (Collins and Ison 2009; Tschakert and Dietrich 2010). Adaptive governance is one model for adaptation planning in which multiple actors come together to identify the interests, values and uncertainties at different scales, and to learn from activities that are collectively defined and reflected upon (Folke et al. 2005). In this way, the manner in which adaptation planning proceeds and is governed can be central to supporting local adaptive capacity.

From this discussion we may conclude that the focus of development actions on adaptive capacity must be structural rather than narrowly needs-based, technical or economic. In the following, therefore, we attend to the structures and processes that shape adaptation planning, thereby mediating the distribution of information, knowledge and resources.

Adaptive capacity: power, knowledge and experimentation

The task of adaptation, then, is to identify thresholds, and do one of two things: either increase the resilience of the existing system, reducing the risk of crossing thresholds whereby the system may lose its ability to serve its desirable function; or stimulate a deliberate transformation (O'Brien 2012) to a re-organized system of new livelihoods and associated environmental management. 'Deliberate transformation' here is understood, in line with O'Brien (2012), as changes carried out with a particular purpose or goal in mind, often by a group of committed individuals, in order to bring about fundamental shifts in the way that societies are organized. This is distinct from adaptation actions that reinforce the status quo and support the existing system. Within these processes, adaptive capacity is employed by actors to make livelihood changes that increase resilience or transform the system altogether. Table 2.1 summarizes practical lessons derived from the resilience thinking described in the section above, along with the implications for adaptive capacity.

TABLE 2.1 Implications of resilience thinking for adaptive capacity

	Insights from resilience thinking	Implications for adaptive capacity
1.	Opportunities for local livelihood changes are limited, constrained or regulated by processes that act at larger scales	Securing local adaptation actions may require influence over policies, processes and regulations at the district, national or even international scales
2.	The perspective of actors at different scales are needed to build an understanding of complex systems and to respond to thresholds and changes occurring at those scales	Adaptation decision-making needs to integrate the knowledge of multiple stakeholders, including but extending beyond local actors
3.	Links to cycles of experimenting and testing provide the learning necessary to respond to uncertainty and to prevent systems passing dangerous thresholds	The availability of appropriate local adaptation options will depend on access to information and knowledge gained from experimentation and testing

These insights indicate that support for adaptive capacity at the community scale should focus on three interconnected areas (Ensor 2011):

- the *power-sharing* arrangements that are in place to expand communities' networks, voice and influence (rows 1 and 2 in Table 2.1);
- the sources and processes that give rise to the *knowledge and information* that inform adaptation decisions (rows 2 and 3); and,
- the availability of *experimentation and testing* of adaptation options that are relevant at the local level (row 3).

These three dimensions provide a framework for supporting adaptive capacity, focusing attention onto important aspects of social systems that are frequently overlooked in development actions. Attention is directed explicitly to the processes that can be supported and sustained that in context expand a community's power sharing, knowledge and information, and experimentation and testing opportunities. This makes it possible for communities to expand their capabilities in ways that enable them to engage with the challenges of climate change in a complex world – rather than achieving a specific governance arrangement or set of actions. As Figure 2.1 illustrates, the dimensions are linked and interdependent: the sources and processes that give rise to knowledge and information feed into power-sharing relationships and emerge as collaborative actions – experiments and tests – that apply new understandings and produce learning in the form of new knowledge and information.

Power sharing

Power is significant because of its central role in defining the opportunities and resources that communities can access, and is thus an essential step in addressing adaptive capacity. Competing claims and differing understandings of value are subject to unequal power and representation in social processes, undermining and excluding the poor while cementing their vulnerability – including vulnerability to climate impacts (Ribot 2009). Poor and marginalized communities are most threatened by climate change because of relations of power, politics and economics. And here, women are often particularly vulnerable, as in Maputo (Figueiredo & Perkins 2012), the case study in this chapter. Unequal gendered power relations can mean that adaptation strategies are pursued because 'they reflect and reinforce gender inequalities, rather than because they represent the best adaptation choices' (Terry 2009).

The significance for those working to support adaptive capacity lies in recognizing that 'business as usual' is likely to repeat and reinforce this pattern. Consideration of the *voice and influence* (see Figure 2.1) of adaptation actors is critical. As Nelson et al. observe, 'most adaptation does not necessarily reduce the vulnerability of those most at risk' (2007:411). Adaptations are not politically neutral: winners and losers are created when benefits are redistributed in a changed social-ecological environment. Political alliances and power relationships are therefore inevitable in adaptation decision-making, played out not only in what gets decided, but who gets to decide (O'Brien et al. 2009a). In this way, power directs us to question equity, both in process and in outcome: 'who decides what should be made resilient to what, for whom resilience is managed, for what purpose?' (Nelson et al. 2007:410).

Yet while inequalities in power are unavoidable, power *sharing* requires moving beyond the identification of power as struggle, or the site of conflict between competing claims. With a focus on power, the risk is that it is perceived as immutable and owned by different actors, rather than as determined through relationships that can be reshaped through collective processes (Collins and Ison 2009). In fact, when capabilities are expanded through collective action rather than wresting of power, complex systems can be tackled and benefit secured for and by poor communities. There are several different approaches that, if embedded into development practice, can support the process of analysing and building relationships between actors and institutions in ways that open spaces for power sharing (Borrini-Feyerabend et al. 2004; Ensor 2011).

Knowledge and information

Communities will need to expand their knowledge and access to information, while those with decision-making power in governance regimes will need to recognize the knowledge of vulnerable local actors. *Informing adaptation decisions* (Figure 2.1) by bringing together different actors with a view to

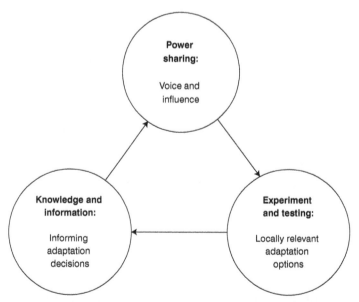

FIGURE 2.1   A framework linking areas for action on adaptive capacity

bridging their understandings of the world is therefore at the heart of adaptive capacity (McCarthy et al. 2011). The networks, institutions and decision-making spaces available to communities play multiple roles in adaptive capacity, helping to build a more complete understanding of the problem in question, of the solutions available, and of the potential consequences and trade-offs. Water catchments, for example, are increasingly recognized as sites of interdependent and interconnected actors and ecologies, which are socially constructed yet understood and valued differently by stakeholders (Ison et al. 2007). As a consequence, catchment management is increasingly concerned with processes for knowledge co-production and sharing (e.g. Lebel et al. 2010; Ducrot 2012). Similarly, previous research in Mozambique has shown that, in order for adaptation to be successful, local populations need to be included in understanding how climate change may place them at greater risk (Patt and Schröter 2008). Unless climate scientists, bureaucrats and community members can come together, recognizing that each interprets and prioritizes the impacts of climate change differently, and then collectively defining what successful adaptations may look like, adaptation will remain partial and maladaptation likely. Lack of this kind of capacity hinders mainstreaming of adaptation, reducing it to a donor-led exercise rather than one that is co-developed across government and civil society (Sietz et al. 2011).

Knowledge implies learning and the ability to use information. In this sense, knowledge makes information useful. But what is often overlooked is that this also means that we construct our knowledge on the basis of our (limited) experiences and (specific, often shared) values. One person's knowledge of a given issue will not necessarily be the same as another's, with understandings shifting across individuals and communities. Power-sharing approaches can overcome this limitation by facilitating knowledge sharing and joint learning experiences (see, for example, Sanginga et al. 2010). Through working together to gain a better understanding of the situation, new and shared ways of knowing are generated (Schusler et al. 2003; Ison et al. 2007; Pahl-Wostl 2009). In this way, power-sharing processes provide participants with a window onto complexity, as each actor recognizes that his or her knowledge is incomplete and is enabled to form and revise this knowledge in light of the multiple perspectives and shared experiences that result from collaborative actions. In most cases, imperfect power sharing means that power remains pertinent. The production of knowledge is political and part of the wider power dynamics that define the relationships between stakeholders, affecting who participates, who speaks and who benefits.

Experimentation and testing

The testing of new technologies and methodologies in the local context links experimentation directly to the processes of knowledge generation described above. Stimulated by an awareness of climate change, new information is turned into new knowledge through its local application, with the emergent learning providing the basis for a subsequent cycle of experimentation, testing and review. This process is at the heart of adaptive capacity, leading to changes that are effective in context and providing *locally relevant adaptation options* (Figure 2.1). Patt (2008) suggests that the most adaptive societies are those with actors who have the capacity to experiment, and institutions in place to support them. Here, we emphasize the need for experimentation with technologies and policies, institutions and processes.

Both opportunities for and constraints on experimentation and testing are significant. At the local level, technology choice encompasses the ability to make informed decisions on alternative adaptation technologies. It results from the amount and quality of information that is available, and the emergent knowledge gained through shared learning and earlier choices. Addressing choice thus places an emphasis on extending information sources through the breadth of stakeholders and the facilitation of visits, exchanges or trials. Technical capacity – or the skills and knowledge to engage in experimentation – brings into focus the inequalities in educational background, prior experience, support or assets that may exist between stakeholders – and that will need to be mediated – if local capacities are to be expanded (Murwira et al. 2000). At larger scales, climate-change experiments are now being conducted in many urban locations, designed to increase understanding of climate impacts and responses; in the process, they are opening new spaces for political engagement and joint actions (Bulkeley and Castán Broto 2012; Castán Broto and Bulkeley 2012).

From 'development as usual' to adaptive capacity

These three dimensions provide a framework for understanding development support for adaptive capacity. That framework offers a model in which multiple participants from different scales are brought together (in power-sharing relationships) to blend their different perspectives (sharing knowledge and information) and to undertake actions that can generate shared learning (testing ideas in context, generating new knowledge and information). The result can be a flexible, collaborative and adaptive governance system. While many examples of adaptive governance approaches are to be found in the literature (Folke et al. 2005), there has been less implementation experience, particularly in contexts of the Global South. This presents an important challenge for development actors seeking to support adaptive capacity through their work. The particular manifestation of and – crucially – how to move towards adaptive governance arrangements is highly context-specific, hinging on a range of factors including existing institutions, the mix and capacities of stakeholders, and the political context at local and higher levels. Table 2.2 illustrates the shift required from conventional to adaptive governance, highlighting the gulf between resilient, adaptive systems, and the conventional, well-established development regime. Table 2.2 thus illustrates the challenges entailed in engendering support for adaptive capacity through development practices.

TABLE 2.2 Characteristics of conventional and adaptive governance (adapted from Brunner and Lynch 2010, in particular re-interpreted from a participation perspective)

Established regime	*Adaptive governance*
Centralized power in decision-making	*Power sharing in decision-making*
Top–down: The important decisions are made by central authorities at the top of international and national hierarchies.	Bottom–up: Facilitated processes support diverse actors (including the voices of the weakest) to share perspectives; enables authorities to allocate resources to support what works on the ground.
Bureaucracies: Policies are implemented uniformly and with little reference to local contexts by subordinates accountable to the central authorities.	Networks: Case studies of local policies and actions that worked can be diffused by networks for voluntary adaptation by other communities.
Expertise: Disinterested experts develop technologies and integrated scientific assessments for the central authorities.	Experience: Local communities working in parallel can adapt and field test policies and actions in their own contexts; diversity is an asset.
Technical knowledge systems	*Procedural knowledge systems*
Formal planning: Policy process is discrete, relying on formal methods and metrics to evaluate planned alternatives and avoid failure.	Appraisal: Learning is at the centre of policies and actions; appraisals allow building on success and moving on from failure.
Targets: Comprehensive policy depends on science-based technologies to realize a given target efficiently and above politics.	Interest: knowledge sharing integrates or balances interests in a community to advance its common interests; politics and power are necessary.
Linear: Unfettered basic research to reduce scientific uncertainty is a prerequisite for rational and cost-effective decisions.	Cooperative: Scientists, policymakers and communities work together toward overlapping practical aims, sharing differently informed insights.
Generalized experimentation and testing	*Contextualized experimentation and testing*
Generalized: Research generalizes across human or natural systems for results of broad national or international scope.	Contextualized: Inquiry follows action research modalities, focusing on understanding single cases and relies on community participation.
Predictive: Stable and standard parts are integrated into numerical predictions to reduce uncertainty.	Integrative: Each factor is contingent on a working 'model' of the whole case; gaps and inconsistencies in it prompt revisions.
Reductive: Research selects from diverse systems separate parts relevant to a stable relationship or standard measure or method.	Systems perspective: situated inquiry strives to cover all the major interacting factors, human and natural, shaping outcomes in the single case.

Adaptation planning in Maputo, Mozambique

In Maputo, communities consisting of households living in informal settlements are poorly connected to municipal governance, including the myriad flows of policy initiatives, knowledge and financial support related to climate change. Yet these people are living in a context where risks are growing and adaptation options are limited by the imperatives of retaining social capital and city-based livelihoods. This section examines the potential for adaptation planning to contribute to the emergence of a flexible, adaptive governance system that can foster local adaptive capacity in Maputo, from the perspective of the dimensions outlined in 'Adaptive capacity: power, knowledge and experimentation' above. This analysis is derived from our engagement with adaptation planning in the Maputo *bairro* (neighbourhood) of Chamanculo C during an 18-month project, funded by the Climate and Development Knowledge Network (CDKN). In this analysis, we draw on two resources: existing scientific and policy documents, with reports sourced through networks and key informants; and two site visits and qualitative key informant interviews ($n=15$) with policy stakeholders representing national governments, non-governmental organization (NGOs), civil society organizations, and private-sector and intergovernmental, bi-lateral and multilateral donors in Maputo, 26 May–3 June 2012 and 5–9 November 2012.

Power sharing

In Maputo, each district is divided into *bairros* (or 'wards'), headed by a *bairros* secretary (*Secretário do Bairro*), below which are *quarteirões* (quarters, or 'neighbourhoods') of 50 to 100 households administered by *chefes de quarteirões* and, finally, a head of ten houses (*Chefe de dez Casas*). It is at the *bairros* level and below that local politics is played out, determining the success of municipal policy strategies and the destination of resources (Paulo et al. 2007). However, the apparent decentralization down to 'ten houses' is in reality characterized by tight Frelimo party control. The *bairros* secretaries, for example, are Frelimo members and de facto appointees of the party, while the ostensibly elected *chefes de quarteirões* are usually appointed by the *bairros* secretary.[2] At the same time, traditional leaders, or *régulos*, occupy inherited positions. Today, in part at least, they derive their power from their ability to represent and maintain the respect of the people.[3] These *régulos* form a 'consultation body' at the *bairro* level, representing the population with a voice that has to be listened to in decision-making – variously described as holding balancing, executive or veto power in decision-making.[4] The traditional families wield considerable influence, and the formal parties need to establish a positive relationship with them if they are to gain and maintain power. The consequence of these dynamics is that parallel systems of governance persist within Maputo. While the accountability that the *régulos* system brings could easily be overstated, it is clear that it exists in tension with the formal system, and that ideas of governance and power in Maputo would be oversimplified through exclusive reference to the formal processes.

There are also inter- and non-governmental groups represented in Maputo. UN Habitat, working through the Cities and Climate Change Initiative (CCCI), has been supporting the development of an adaptation plan for the city. Priority has gone to adaptation planning, identifying the available legal tools, commissioning a pilot project, and locating vulnerable sectors and areas. Events within the city have sought to draw in the perspective of local leaders, but these reflect the structures outlined above.[5] Similarly, the National Disaster Management Institute (Instituto Nacional de Gestão de Calamidades, INGC) has worked to establish Community Emergency Response Committees, but these are constituted of local leaders who include the *Secretário do Bairro* and *chefes de quarteirões*. Finally, the Italian NGO Avsi is working on behalf of the municipal council to produce a plan for the upgrading of drains, roads, water and lighting in Chamanculo C. While not currently integrating climate-change issues, their approach gathers data at the household level.[6] This is the initial phase of their 'integrated requalification' approach that seeks to bring together the physical and socio-economic challenges facing the communities in the *bairro*, prior to the development of plans.

The consequences of these arrangements for adaptive capacity are mixed. Overall, from a resilience perspective, the development challenge lies in identifying or opening spaces in which cross-scale relationships can be developed and power shared between this multiplicity of urban actors, many of whom reside in the informal settlements with little voice or influence in the established patterns of governance. The top-down control exercised by Frelimo, in particular the control exerted by the *chefes de quarteirões,* is likely to act as a brake on community voices entering into decision-making, and the *régulos* system is at best an imperfect mechanism through which sections of the community are able to assert their views. However, a shift to a governance arrangement which could incorporate a greater diversity of voices and opportunities to learn from experiments outside the *bairro* is likely to be challenging, as perhaps reflected in Avsi's cautious approach to integrating communities into the planning process. A final challenge lies in the need for the government to recognize the validity of local interests: as one local academic stated during an interview, 'rainfall inundation and lack of formal drains are the problem in the informal settlements, and the government must shift from thinking about their population as illegal'.[7] The outlook for these communities in the face of climate change will remain poor as long as those in authority continue to overlook their responsibility for essential services, citing the 'illegality' of the settlements.

Knowledge and information

Much of the knowledge on the impacts of climate change for Mozambique is generated outside the country with the help of international organizations. The most comprehensive translation of this into and assessment of impacts and vulnerability in Mozambique has been carried out by the INGC, although smaller-scale case study examples also exist (Hahn et al. 2009). In discussing the potential climate change impacts and the resulting vulnerability, their approach mirrors that taken by the established management approach to adaptation (Table 2.2). The knowledge technologies adopted so far have focused on identifying impacts through scenarios, risk analysis and planning, and to a limited extent on wider concepts of vulnerability (Keskitalo et al. 2012). Vulnerability to climate change has been framed through scenarios, with socio-economic vulnerability seen mainly in terms of economic assessments and the total number of people affected.[8] What this implies is not only an outlook that focuses on the economic – rather than the social and environmental – wellbeing of the city, but also that knowledge is narrowly constructed in terms of the perspectives that are assumed to be significant in its creation. Overall, this approach reflects first-generation adaptation approaches that rely on predicted impacts to stimulate technical and infrastructural changes. This contrasts with more contextualized assessments of social and ecological vulnerability that recognize future uncertainty and the potential for maladaptation (Burton et al. 2002; Eriksen et al. 2007; Eriksen and Brown 2011). Furthermore, this approach fails to recognize the strong awareness that the people of Mozambique have as regards flooding events and other potential impacts of climate change, as well as their clear understanding of the consequences for their livelihoods (see also O'Brien et al. 2009b).

More recently, greater localized knowledge and information is being generated and collated by the municipal council. Under the CCCI initiative, an Environmental Information Management System has been constructed to create a database mapping vulnerability to impacts across Maputo, with the intention of linking into the city cadastre system to integrate environmental risks into planning. The CCCI project is also working with the municipality to explore local perceptions of risk. This development entails small group studies, and has come in response to the experience of flooding in January 2012 and recognition of the need to understand where and how decisions are made in responding to risks.[9] Avsi's work for the municipality does not include climate change, so there are no climate-change specialists on the Avsi team. However, they have a focus on environmental education, and their baseline data survey gathered household perceptions of environmental risk, allowing detailed mapping of flood-prone areas within the *bairro*.[10] From the perspective of adaptive capacity, what appears to be lacking with this and other sources of knowledge within the city is a plan for how and with whom such capacities are to be shared so as to be effective in informing decision-making on adaptation.

Experimentation and testing

Experts at the helm of preparing climate resilience and adaptation plans in Maputo are led by INGC and the Physics Department of Universidade Eduardo Mondlane, supported by the Architecture Department. This expertise is combined with the interests of international organization (e.g. UN Habitat) and the local government (municipality) and will set the stage for the development of an urban adaptation plan. Current efforts to draft an adaptation plan involve going into urban settlements as an experiment with greater participation and integration of local risk and response perspectives. However, preliminary findings from our work indicate that, as regards disaster risk reduction, the state supports implementation and forms of consultation, but no new institutions – limiting the extent to which these experiments can inform new planning or governance arrangements for adaptation.[11]

Other environmental experiments with clear local development benefits have been identified in Maputo. These include a waste collection and recycling initiative managed by AMOR (Associação Moçambicana de Reciclagem), which supports ad hoc partnerships between small private waste-collectors, supported by municipal collection services from local 'recycling points'. NGOs and informal waste collectors substitute for the operations of the government here. In the case of small-scale water providers, the state has financed infrastructure and has helped to establish new water providers. Regarding waste collection, the role of government has been more limited, with local *catadores* (usually women) emerging from within the local population who are flexible enough to respond rapidly to existing waste collection needs.[12]

Small-scale projects such as these are examples of how development actors, in various forms of partnership with the state, can engage in experiments necessary for adaptive capacity. That said, the existence of alternatives alone is not enough to stimulate learning. Avsi, for example, has plans for a simple approach to solving major drainage and flooding issues, by building properties on stilts to allow height for improved drainage. While experimenting with this approach could prove critical to informing adaption options for the communities in the informal settlements, this alternative is undesirable to those who seek to use relocation in order to access valuable land. The lack of real engagement between state and local urban settlers in selecting locally relevant experiments may be attributed to the absence of 'a culture of participation', but there also seems to be a significant gap between this level of experimentation and the power issues discussed in 'Knowledge and information'.

Lessons from a resilience perspective

In Chamanculo C, flooding is a significant challenge whenever it rains. This is one of Maputo's oldest *bairros*, and the lack of drainage leads to chronic problems that are likely to worsen if rainfall events become more intense, as predicted under climate change. That means there is an urgent need to build adaptive capacity through processes that can integrate communities into adaptation planning, enabling local voices to be heard when risks and responses are defined for today's challenges, and contributing towards enhanced capacity to adapt to future changes.

Securing opportunities and incentives for power sharing in Maputo is a particular challenge. Engagement with climate change is limited among those affected and those with the responsibility to act, while relationships of power and influence are mediated through formal and informal governance arrangements that make decision-making opaque and outcomes difficult to predict – as also concluded in other studies of adaptation in Mozambique (see Artur and Hillhorst 2012). The challenge of sustaining spaces to meet uncertainty through participatory planning and learning among a mass of interests and conflicting perceptions of risk and capacity is a formidable one. Development actors will need to identify and work through overlapping regimes of power, facilitating interactions that can engage key players and build trust through concrete actions. Avsi's approach, which locates them as an interlocutor, accepted and trusted by both the communities and the authorities, may prove prudent. It also demonstrates the utility of the existing formal and informal structures as channels of communication already existing within the city, even if they may result in imperfect representation of needs. Such imperfection may mean that more needs to be done if adaptive capacity is to be supported. Many voices are not heard – including those of women (who trade within the *quarteirões* and have many ideas for improvement but lack the means to test them) and youth (who dominate the population but lack a voice within the household or at other scales). The interests of effectiveness, fairness and resilience in the face of complexity all suggest that there is an urgent need to disaggregate the 'community', to enable a better understanding of the range of perspectives and experiences, so that these can be built into a shared process of adaptation planning.

In direct contradiction to a resilience perspective on adaptive capacity, knowledge of climate-change risks in Mozambique is dominated by an understanding of environmental change as predictable and controllable, and (possibly because) it is skewed towards identifying threats to current economic assets. This situation is by no means unique to Mozambique. Against this backdrop, the approach taken by the municipality, which aims to inform planning with localized perceptions of risk, is a positive step that appears to build cross-scale linkages between residents and policy-makers. However, the significance of these developments is potentially undermined by the lack of connections to power sharing (through which actors with different perspectives and from different scales could be drawn into shared decision-making), as well as the failure to recognize that different forms of knowledge are pertinent in defining solutions as well as problems. Today it is a challenge to see whether and how these initiatives can overcome the politics inherent in adaptation decision-making and the power relations that define whose knowledge ultimately counts.

Moreover, it remains for external, cross-scale, actors to supply information on climate change. Building knowledge will require relating this information to the lives of those at risk, as well as identifying local thresholds and securing the opportunity to observe or participate in adaptation experiments or tests of alternative livelihood or infrastructure approaches. If adaptations are to be viable in context, local knowledge and localized information will need to feed into power-sharing relationships, emerging as collaborative actions (experiments and tests) that apply new understandings and produce learning that is relevant to those living and governing in Maputo. Experimentation and testing exists in different forms, such as disaster-risk reduction experiments in informal settlements and the establishment of water providers or waste management systems; however, while it appears that local communities are often consulted and informed, there is less evidence of serious engagement between state and local urban settlers. This may be attributed to the absence of 'a culture of participation', lack of familiarity with participatory action research methodologies, and, more broadly, a gap between this level of experimentation, building knowledge and power sharing.

In conclusion, we remain optimistic about adaptation planning in Maputo. Our work has identified opportunities to link experiments with community approaches to adaptation planning into legislation currently being discussed within the municipality. We hold that adaptation planning processes can and must build adaptive capacity from a *resilience perspective*. In this way, current and future challenges can be met in ways that shift communities away from thresholds and build the potential for deliberate transformation. This we see as a real possibility. However, for this possibility to be realized, the resilience perspective needs to be unpacked and, in particular, linked to accumulated experience of power, knowledge and experiments within the development and social science community, thereby drawing in the human dimensions of change.

The analysis in this chapter has indicated that local politics must be taken seriously when considering adaptation. It is important not only to find ways to work through and with existing channels of power and influence, but also to forge new ways of sharing power, generating knowledge and experimenting with alternatives in order to create large-scale shifts in communities. Moreover, supporting adaptive capacity in communities presents new challenges to development actors. Attention must shift to the processes linking knowledge and experiments, so that the social, political and economic landscape can be navigated towards new, shared ways of understanding the complex challenges of climate change.

Acknowledgements

This work was funded by the Climate Development Knowledge Network, CDKN, a project funded by the UK Department for International Development and the Netherlands Directorate-General for International Cooperation (DGIS), led and administered by PricewaterhouseCoopers LLP. Management of the delivery of CDKN is undertaken by PricewaterhouseCoopers LLP and an alliance of organizations that includes Fundación Futuro Latinoamericano, INTRAC, LEAD International, the Overseas Development Institute, and SouthSouthNorth. The authors are also grateful to the two anonymous reviewers, and the editors, whose constructive comments were valuable in the drafting of this chapter.

Notes

1 The term 'community' is used, following Smit and Wandel (2006), to refer to an aggregation of households, interconnected in some way, and with a limited spatial extent.
2 Anonymous 1, Maputo, 2012.
3 Anonymous 1, Maputo, 2012.
4 Anonymous 1, Maputo, 2012.
5 Anonymous 2, Maputo, 2012
6 Avsi interview, Maputo, 2012.
7 Anonymous 3, Maputo, 2012.
8 INGC interview, Maputo, 2012; see also INGC 2009b.
9 Anonymous 2, Maputo, 2012
10 Avsi interview, Maputo, 2012.
11 Interviews with INGC, UN Habitat, Avsi and Anonymous 2, Maputo, 2012.
12 AMOR interview, Maputo, 2012.

References

Agrawal, A. (2010). 'Local Institutions and Adaptation to Climate Change', in Mearns, R., and Norton, A. (eds), *Social Dimensions of Climate Change: Equity and Vulnerability in a Warming World*. Washington, DC: World Bank.

Artur, L., and Hillhorst, D. (2012). 'Everyday Realities of Climate Change Adaptation in Mozambique'. *Global Environmental Change* 22: 529–536.

Berkes, F., and Folke, C. eds. (1998). *Linking Sociological and Ecological Systems: Management Practices and Social Mechanisms for Building Resilience*. New York: Cambridge University Press.

Borrini-Feyerabend, G., Pimbert, M., Farvar, M., Kothari, A., and Renard, Y. (2004). *Sharing Power. Learning by Doing in Co-Management of Natural Resources Throughout the World*. Cenesta, Tehran: IIED and IUCN/CEESP/CMWG.

Bulkeley, H., and Castán Broto, V. (2012). 'Government by Experiment? Global Cities and the Governing of Climate Change'. *Transactions of the Institute of British Geographers* 38(3): 361–75.

Burton, I., Huq, S., Lim, B., Pilifosova, O., and Schipper, E. (2002). 'From Impacts Assessment to Adaptation Priorities: the Shaping of Adaptation Policy'. *Climate Policy* 2(2): 145–59.

CARE (2010). 'Community-based adaptation in action' http://www.care.org/getinvolved/advocacy/climatechange/ourwork_adaptation_initiatives.asp (accessed 15/09/2010).

Castán Broto, V., and Bulkeley, H. (2012). 'A Survey of Urban Climate Change Experiments in 100 Cities'. *Global Environmental Change* 23(1): 92–102.

Collins, K., and Ison, R. (2009). 'Jumping Off Arnstein's Ladder: Social Learning as a New Policy Paradigm for Climate Change Adaptation'. *Environmental Policy and Governance* 19(6): 358–73.

Ducrot, R. (2012). 'Gaming Across Scale in Peri-Urban Water Management: Contribution From Two Experiences in Bolivia and Brazil'. *Third World Quarterly* 16(4): 240–52.

Eakin, H., Bojórquez-Tapia, L., Monterde Diaz, R., Castellanos, E., and Haggar, J. (2011). 'Adaptive Capacity and Social-Environmental Change: Theoretical and Operational Modeling of Smallholder Coffee Systems Response in Mesoamerican Pacific Rim'. *Environmental Management* 47(3): 352–67.

Engle, N. (2011). 'Adaptive Capacity and its Assessment'. *Global Environmental Change* 21(2): 647–56

Engle, N., and Lemos, M. (2010). 'Unpacking Governance: Building Adaptive Capacity to Climate Change of River Basins in Brazil'. *Global Environmental Change* 20(1): 4–13.

Ensor, J. (2011). *Uncertain Futures*. Rugby: Practical Action Publishing.

Ensor, J., and Berger, R. (2009). *Understanding Climate Change Adaptation*. Rugby: Practical Action Publishing.

Ensor, J., Berger, R., and Huq, S. eds. (2014). *Community-Based Adaptation to Climate Change: Emerging Lessons*. Rugby: Practical Action Publishing.

Eriksen, S., and Brown, K. (2011). 'Sustainable Adaptation to Climate Change'. *Climate and Development* 3(1): 3–6.

Eriksen, S., Klein, R., Ulsrud, K., Næss, L., and O'Brien, K. (2007). 'Climate Change Adaptation and Poverty Reduction: Key Interactions and Critical Measures'. Oslo: University of Oslo (GECHS Report 1).

Figueiredo, P., and Perkins, P. (2012). 'Women and Water Management in Times of Climate Change: Participatory and Inclusive Process'. *Journal of Cleaner Production*, 60(December): 1–7.

Folke, C., Hahn, T., Olsson, P., and Norberg, J. (2005). 'Adaptive Governance of Social-Ecological Systems'. *Annual Review of Environment and Resources* 30(1): 441–73.

Gupta, J., Termeer, C., Klostermann, J., Meijerink, S., van den Brink, M., Jong, P., Nooteboom, S., and Bergsma, E. (2010). 'The Adaptive Capacity Wheel: a Method to Assess the Inherent Characteristics of Institutions to Enable the Adaptive Capacity of Society'. *Environmental Science & Policy* 13(6): 459–71.

Hahn, M., Riederer, A., and Foster, S. (2009). 'The Livelihood Vulnerability Index: a Pragmatic Approach to Assessing Risks from Climate Variability and Change: a Case Study in Mozambique'. *Global Environmental Change* 19: 74–88.

Holling, C., and Gunderson, L. (2002). 'Resilience and Adaptive Cycles', in Gunderson, L., and Holling, C. (eds), *Panarchy: Understanding Transformations in Human and Natural Systems*. Washington, DC: Island Press.

Ireland, P. (2012). 'Climate Change Adaptation: Business-as-Usual Aid and Development or an Emerging Discourse for Change?'. *International Journal of Development Issues* 11(2): 92–110.

Ison, R., Roling, N., and Watson, D. (2007). 'Challenges to Science and Society in the Sustainable Management and Use of Water: Investigating the Role of Social Learning'. *Environmental Science and Policy* 10(6): 499–511.

Juhola, S., and Kruse, S. (2013). 'A Framework for Analysing Regional Adaptive Capacity Assessments: Challenges for Methodology and Policy Making'. *Mitigation and Adaptation Strategies for Global Change* doi:10.1007/s11027-013-9481-z 1:22

Keskitalo, E., Carina, H., Juhola, S., and Westerhoff, L. (2012). 'Climate Change as Governmentality: Technologies of Government for Adaptation in Three European Countries'. *Journal of Environmental Planning and Management* 55(4): 435–52.

Lebel, L., Grothmann, T., and Siebenhüner, B. (2010). 'The Role of Social Learning in Adaptiveness: Insights From Water Management'. *International Environmental Agreements: Politics, Law and Economics* 10(4): 333–53.

Ludi, E., Jones, L., and Levine, S. (2012). *Changing Focus? How to Start Taking Adaptive Capacity Seriously*. London: Overseas Development Institute.

McCarthy, D., Crandall, D., Whitelaw, G., General, Z., and Tsuji, L. (2011). 'A Critical Systems Approach to Social Learning: Building Adaptive Capacity in Social, Ecological, Epistemological (SEE) Systems'. *Ecology and Society* 16(3): 18.

Mitchell, T., and Tanner, T. (2006). *Adapting to Climate Change*. Brighton: Institute of Development Studies and Tearfund.

Murwira, K., Wedgewood, K., Watson, H., Win, W., and Tawney, C. (2000). *Beating Hunger: the Chivi Experience*. Rugby: Intermediate Technology Publications.

Nelson, D., Adger, W., and Brown, K. (2007). 'Adaptation to Environmental Change: Contributions of a Resilience Framework'. *Annual Review of Environment and Resources* 32(1): 395–419.

O'Brien, K. (2012). 'Global Environmental Change II: From Adaptation to Deliberate Transformation.' *Progress in Human Geography* 36(5): 667–76.

O'Brien, K., Eriksen, S., Nygaard, L., and Schjolden, A. (2007). 'Why Different Interpretations of Vulnerability Matter in Climate Change Discourses'. *Climate Policy* 7(1): 73–88.

O'Brien, K., Hayward, B., and Berkes, F. (2009a). 'Rethinking Social Contracts: Building Resilience in a Changing Climate'. *Ecology and Society* 14(2): 12.

O'Brien, K., Quinlan, T., and Ziervogel, G. (2009b). 'Vulnerability Interventions in the Context of Multiple Stressors: Lessons from the Southern Africa Vulnerability Initiative (SAVI)'. *Environmental Science & Policy* 12(1): 23–32.

Pahl-Wostl, C. (2009). 'A Conceptual Framework for Analysing Adaptive Capacity and Multi-Level Learning Processes in Resource Governance Regimes'. *Global Environmental Change* 19(3): 354–65.

Patt, A., and Schröter, D. (2008). 'Perceptions of Climate Risk In Mozambique: Implications for the Success of Adaptation Strategies'. *Global Environmental Change* 18: 458–67.

Paulo, M., Rosário, C., and Tvedten, I. (2007). *'Xiculungo' Social Relations of Urban Poverty in Maputo, Mozambique*. Bergen, Norway: Chr. Michelsen Institute.

Pelling, M. (2010). *Adaptation to Climate Change: From Resilience to Transformation*. London: Routledge.

Pettengell, C. (2010). *Climate Change Adaptation: Enabling People Living in Poverty to Adapt*. Oxford: Oxfam Research Report.

Reid, H., Alam, M., Berger, R., and Cannon, T. (2009). 'Community-Based Adaptation to Climate Change'. *Participatory Learning and Action* 60: 11–29.

Ribot, J. (2009). 'Vulnerability Does Not Fall From the Sky: Toward Multiscale, Pro-Poor Climate Policy', in Mearns, R., and Norton, A. (eds), *Social Dimensions of Climate Change: Equity and Vulnerability in a Warming World*. Washington, DC: World Bank.

Sanginga, P., Kamugisha, R., and Martin, A. (2010). 'Strengthening Social Capital for Adaptive Governance of Natural Resources: a Participatory Learning and Action Research for Bylaws Reforms in Uganda'. *Society & Natural Resources* 23(8): 695–710.

Scheffer, M., Carpenter, S., Lenton, T., Bascompte, J., Brock, W., Dakos, V., van de Koppel, J., van de Leemput, I., Levin, S., van Nes, E., Pascual, M., and Vandermeer, J. (2012). 'Anticipating Critical Transitions'. *Science* 338(6105): 344–48.

Schusler, T., Daniel, J., and Pfeffer, M. (2003). 'Social Learning for Collaborative Natural Resource Management'. *Society & Natural Resources* 16(4): 309–26.

Sietz, D., Boschutz, M., and Klein, R. (2011). 'Mainstreaming Climate Adaptation into Development Assistance: Rationale, Institutional Barriers and Opportunities in Mozambique'. *Environmental Science & Policy* 14: 493–502.

Smit, B., and Wandel, J. (2006). 'Adaptation, Adaptive Capacity and Vulnerability'. *Global Environmental Change – Human and Policy Dimensions* 16(3): 282–92.

Terry, G. (2009). *Climate Change and Gender Justice*. Rugby: Practical Action Publishing.

Tschakert, P., and Dietrich, K. (2010). 'Anticipatory Learning for Climate Change Adaptation and Resilience'. *Ecology and Society* 15(2): 11.

Walker, B., and Salt, S. (2006). *Resilience Thinking*. Washington, DC: Island Press.

3

THE SOCIETAL ROLE OF CHARCOAL PRODUCTION IN CLIMATE-CHANGE ADAPTATION OF THE ARID AND SEMI-ARID LANDS OF KENYA

Caroline A. Ochieng, Sirkku Juhola and Francis X. Johnson

Introduction

The vulnerability of drylands populations is subject to varying interpretations. How 'vulnerability' is perceived is important in influencing how the community or development organizations in the dryland regions respond to climate change (Füssel 2010). In this chapter, we use 'community' as defined by Smit and Wandel (2006) as an aggregation of households, interconnected in some way, and with a limited spatial extent, recognizing that interests and responses may vary between individuals in a community. The ability of the community to cope with adverse recurring events such as droughts as well as the risks posed by climate change forms an important part of adaptive capacity. Communities living in drylands are generally perceived as vulnerable, given the biophysical characteristics of the environment upon which their livelihoods depend (Adger et al. 2004), such as water scarcity. This conceptualization has led to the widely observed application of physical response measures in addressing vulnerability, and in defining coping and adaptation strategies (Turner 1994; Bohle 2001; Eriksen et al. 2005; O'Brien et al. 2007).

While some successes have been registered from these 'hard' measures,[1] there are also instances where the results have been undesirable. This is clearly seen in Kenyan arid and semi-arid lands (ASALs), where attempts to sedentarize nomadic practices of dryland communities have inadvertently contributed to their vulnerability (Eriksen and Lind 2009; Ruto et al. 2009). In our era of climate change, the ASALs have been described as more vulnerable than ever, making adaptation an imperative for local communities (IUCN, IISD, SEI & SDC 2003). Without careful consideration of the factors that underlie the perception and response to vulnerability in these regions, efforts to reduce climate risk might ignore valuable lessons from earlier development efforts.

How then should the vulnerability, including coping and adaptation, of ASAL communities be conceptualized, and how would this conceptualization influence policy and development response to it? Some authors (Kelly and Adger 2000; Wisner 2004) have drawn a distinction between physical and social vulnerability, whereby the former refers to exposure to stress and crises resulting from physical hazards, and the latter refers to the capacity of individuals and communities to respond to physical impacts. Those who adhere to the former concept often see vulnerability as an 'outcome process', which then requires physical adaptation measures (O'Brien et al. 2007). In this chapter, we adopt a definition that conforms to the *Sustainable livelihood approach* framework (IFAD 2013), which places people rather than the resources they depend on in the centre of the analysis. How people create their livelihoods depends on the resources and *livelihood assets* that they have access to and use, which in turn depends on their *vulnerability context*, as well as prevailing social, institutional and political environment. According to this framework, the vulnerability context is made up of trends, shocks (such as drought) and seasonality. Thus, vulnerability to climate variability and change occur in the context of political, institutional, economic and social structures and changes, which interact dynamically. This has been referred to as 'contextual vulnerability' (O'Brien et al. 2007; Eriksen and Silva 2009), as opposed to 'outcome vulnerability' manifested through physical processes. With this conceptualization, marginalization and its resultant poverty in the ASALs are as important as the biophysical environment in contributing to the vulnerability of different communities, and addressing them should be a core part of the adaptation process.

Charcoal production – taken here to encompass the process of (small-scale) fuel wood production and/or harvesting, and conversion of the fuel wood into charcoal through carbonization – has been widely documented as a drought-coping measure in ASALs (Eriksen et al. 2005; Getachew et al. 2008), but has not been considered as a means of adaptation. Quite the contrary, development efforts towards adaptation have discouraged the practice in an effort to promote good environmental management in ASALs. However, we argue that charcoal production could actually be a climate adaption measure, and that banning it may in fact increase the vulnerability of ASAL communities. Taken further, this case illustrates that it is indeed possible for development measures, also those aimed at promoting climate-change mitigation and adaptation, to contribute to vulnerability.

Here we draw on literature that conceptually distinguishes coping from adaptation; and empirical findings from a case study in Kenya that compares community drought responses with those of development agencies.

We use these information sources to address the following questions:

- How do community-initiated drought-coping measures compare to those promoted by development actors in the region?
- How does the conceptual framing of vulnerability and coping influence development practice on the ground?

Perspectives from the literature on charcoal production and its potential role in coping and adaptation in ASALs

A fairly clear distinction is usually drawn between coping and adaptation in the academic literature, with coping viewed as unfavourable in relation to adaptation. According to an IPCC task force report, coping 'focuses on the moment, constraint, and survival; while adapting focuses on the future, where learning and reinvention are key features and short-term survival is less in question' (IPCC 2012: 51). A United Nations Convention to Combat Desertification (UNCCD) report on options for climate-change adaptation in the African drylands further makes the following distinction: that coping strategies emanate from experience of dealing with short-term and known hazards such as seasonal variations; adaptive strategies are more long term, enabling people to respond to evolving conditions not previously experienced (UNCCD, UNDP & UNEP 2009: 12). In support of this view, Taylor et al. (2010: 10–13) cite the following example:

> Selling off productive assets (like livestock) and/or boosting incomes through artisanal charcoaling are two examples of 'traditional coping mechanisms' common across much of semi-arid Africa. But while these strategies may work well enough when drought occurs only once every five or so years, they are a dead-end when it comes to dealing with the contemporary reality of accelerating drought cycles.

Some authors have also warned of the risk of classifying coping measures as adaptive measures, holding that coping measures are likely to undermine opportunities for adaptation in the future through unplanned and un-strategic use of resources (Taylor et al. 2010; IRIN 2013). Here we are interested in understanding the extent to which this division is helpful in understanding the livelihood strategies and ways of responding to the climatic stressors of the ASAL communities in Makueni, Kenya.

In Kenya, charcoal is the primary energy source for 82 per cent of the urban population. With an annual market value of over USD 400 million, the charcoal market is equivalent to 43 per cent of the revenues from the tourism industry, the top income earner in the country (PISCES 2011). Most charcoal production takes place in ASALs, the region with the worst development indicators and poverty incidence in Kenya (Office of the Prime Minister 2011). Rural communities produce the charcoal that is transported to the urban centres. There have been efforts to curb or ban the production of charcoal out of concern for deforestation and unsustainable resource use. However, the portability and high energy content of charcoal – nearly twice the energy density of wood – have made it valuable to consumers and thus demand continues to grow. Lifecycle management approaches could improve the sustainability of charcoal, but that will require enabling institutions and policies (Kituyi 2004; Njenga et al. 2013).

In the whole value-chain of charcoal, those who benefit the least are the producers. This is primarily due to unfavourable policies that have driven the practice underground, leading to corruption and low income for small-scale producers. Until recently, Kenya had conflicting and contradictory charcoal policies, whereby it was legal to consume charcoal but illegal to produce it, leading to an unfavourable policy environment. A similar situation is found in other countries in eastern and southern Africa (Zulu 2010). Enforcement of such laws not only denies government revenues, but also creates social exclusion, as it targets poor people and small-scale operators, without affecting those who are well connected and politically protected. Although energy and forestry policies and acts have recently legalized sustainable charcoal production, players in the industry continue to operate just as they did before the policies and legislation were enacted, partly due to low awareness and complicated licensing procedures. Under a regime of regulated wood supplies and unobtrusive policies, it is estimated that a small-scale charcoal producer can on average earn the equivalent of USD 2700 a year (PISCES 2011).

In ASALs, the negative image of charcoal production by government and development agencies is reinforced by the long prevailing perception that coping strategies that entail utilization of local environmental resources are degrading to the environment and should not be promoted. Charcoal is acknowledged as a drought-coping measure, but 'coping' is implicitly viewed as bad for adaptation, as it diverts attention away from addressing structural problems, leading to a focus on 'surviving' instead of 'thriving' (Speranza et al. 2010). Taken literally, this view can lead to curbing of charcoal production as a means of promoting adaptation, while leaving the community more vulnerable. Such vulnerability can contribute to deforestation which further limits future livelihood strategies, both on-farm and off-farm (Paavola 2008). As an example, the Millennium Ecosystem Assessment report (2005) focuses on unsustainable community practices in the semi-arid zone, and how climate change will exacerbate the situation. The report proposes soil and water management, while acknowledging that poor farmers are reluctant to invest in such measures because they are unable to forego the immediate income generated by conventional land-use practices in favour of long-term benefits. According to Tschakert (2007: 382), such physical environmental measures mirror anti-desertification plans, and the adaptive role that these solutions offer to subsistence farmers, the vulnerable 'target' population, is tangential at best. Further, Anderson et al. (2004) attribute the failure of past policies on drylands to being focused on the presumed limitations of the natural resource base, ignoring the richness of local knowledge, skills and capacity for innovation in overcoming or circumventing environmental constraints.

Development and policy actors tend to pay more attention to the environmental consequences of charcoal production (assumed to be negative) with little attention to its social aspects. What the community is doing is viewed as wrong, so other, more 'sustainable', measures are needed for adaptation. In tandem, there is a general assumption that these environmental protection measures would benefit marginalized communities, and this then is used to justify the immediate negative consequences that are observed (Girard 2002). In this chapter, we do not conduct a thorough investigation of the environmental consequences of various forms of charcoal production. Instead we focus on the societal aspects of charcoal production, acknowledging that the activity may also have negative environmental consequences. That said, it should be noted that various sustainable methods for charcoal production and use also exist (Kituyi 2004; Njenga et al. 2013).

Case study in Makueni District

Background

Makueni District (now Makueni County) is an administrative unit in the Eastern Province of Kenya. The district has a population of 884,527 and an area of about 8000 km². The district is divided into various agro-ecological zones, ranging from semi-arid zones which support mixed farming activities, to very arid zones. Farming is the main economic activity, and is almost entirely rain-fed. The climate is hot and dry for most of the year. There is semi-arid vegetation, with low and erratic rainfall. Makueni is one of the most food-insecure counties in Kenya, with the majority of the population (73 per cent) living below the poverty line.

In 2008, the present authors conducted a study of household vulnerability and adaptive capacity in Makueni to food security threats posed by drought and climate change (Ochieng and Yitambe 2012). The study was carried out soon after a drought in 2006 that had devastating effects on livelihoods. This led to a surge in the number of development agencies (DAs) working in the region, seeking to respond to the disaster but also to boost adaptive capacity to minimize the impact of future disasters.

The study entailed a questionnaire to 342 household heads, and interviews with 12 DAs. The interviews were held with those responsible for the design and implementation of the drought management and climate-change adaptation programmes. Information on the DAs was obtained from the households, who were asked to report on DAs they were involved with, or that they knew were working on issues of drought and food security in the region. Interview findings from DAs were validated through interviews with community groups involved in the DA activities.

The case study revealed that the production of charcoal was one of a range of coping measures used in the community (Ochieng and Yitambe 2012). The initial conclusion of the work was that most community members were coping with climate change rather than adapting to it – a view supported by previous studies of the region (Nelson 2000; Ifejika et al. 2008; Speranza et al. 2010).

For illustrative purpose, here we focus our analysis on one activity, charcoal production, amongst the range of coping measures identified. This is to enable a clear perspective on how different perceptions on vulnerability, coping and adaptation can influence policy action, leading to conditions that might themselves also result in vulnerability. We do not attempt to generalize this study to all other coping measures, but a similar analysis could be applied to other coping strategies in assessing whether they act to undermine adaptation.

Results and discussion

Household-level coping strategies

Figure 3.1 shows the primary household-level strategies for reducing drought impact among the study households in Makueni. The responses were drawn from household heads, most of whom (79 per cent) had lived in the region all their lives. Many were middle-aged, although 14 per cent were above 55 years and could therefore describe how they perceived local climatic conditions to have changed over several decades. Despite the reported unreliable rainfall patterns, the main source of livelihood for most households was small-scale subsistence farming: crops and livestock production (61 per cent). Many farmers had low levels of education and no formal employment.

To cope with drought, the households employed various coping measures either concurrently or in sequence, whereby different sets of options were tried and abandoned whenever they failed.

As can be seen from Figure 3.1, a large proportion of the households changed their food consumption patterns and sold their assets, in addition to borrowing from existing social support systems. In these situations the households also needed to purchase all their food items, which required additional income. Additional income sources were not easily available, however, forcing people to sell important livelihood assets. Such loss of livelihood assets meant that the drought recovery process was prolonged and left them increasingly vulnerable to the impacts of future droughts. Furthermore, the choice of coping strategies varied during the phase of drought. Activities that were weather-dependent were quickly abandoned as the drought period became prolonged, with many switching to non-farm measures. These findings illustrate the important role of income diversification, not just for coping but also adaptation. Successful income diversification can eliminate the need to sell off productive assets. Increased income is therefore critical not only in the short term, but also for drought recovery and longer-term ability to manage droughts. In this sense,

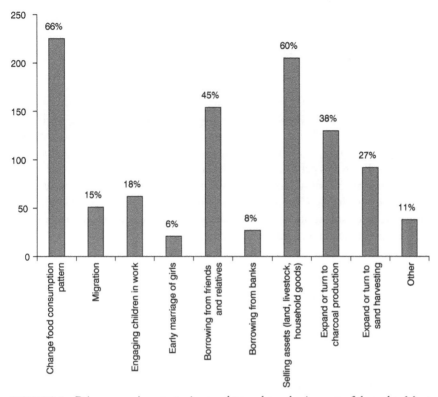

FIGURE 3.1   Primary coping strategies used to reduce the impact of drought. Most of these activities were complemented by others, and their dominance varied with season (N=250 households)

therefore, the role of charcoal production could be considered as adaptive rather than coping.

There was a gender dimension to the coping strategies employed, including charcoal production. While women had more diversified income sources than men, the measures they employed appeared less economically viable than those of most men. Activities in which women engaged when the drought peaked included sale of sisal ropes, baskets, fruits, honey and other small-scale produce that targeted the local market. In contrast, men engaged in charcoal production and sand harvesting, activities that targeted markets outside Makueni likely to be less affected by drought. In addition to the fear of legal reprisals, women reported lack of prior experience with charcoal production as a barrier to engaging in the activity. This is supported by the finding that those who had engaged in charcoal production prior to the drought episode continued with the activity.

Overall, the coping measures we observed can be divided into two categories: principal activities, and complementary ones. This conforms to the categorization of Eriksen et al. (2005) from neighbouring Kitui County. Similar to their observations, we found that the principal measures could substitute for farming as a main source of household food income, and were regular and reliable over extended periods. Complementary measures, by contrast, were less regular and could not be sustained over extended periods.

Many of the observed coping strategies such as sale of livestock or taking children out of school to provide labour were complementary, and engaging in them could contribute to further impoverishment by decreasing livelihood assets or personal wellbeing. Charcoal production seemed to fall in the principal category, by helping to accumulate assets to the household, albeit somewhat marginally. From this perspective, our findings indicate that charcoal production is a coping strategy that supports communities in adaptation, rather than eroding their ability to do so. Charcoal production as a coping measure can support and sometimes substitute for vital livelihood measures and thus enable those engaged in it to generate additional income.

DA-promoted measures

A high presence of DAs was observed in the district, as well as many organized community groups which formed an entry point for development programmes. The agencies had varied goals, many of which were presented as drought preparedness and resilience rather than climate-change adaptation. There were, however, common characteristics to their activities with regard to the theme of this study: 1) none of them explored the role of charcoal production as a possible adaptive measure or an important livelihood measure; 2) there was heavy promotion of environmental conservation measures, such as protection of catchment areas; and 3) most activities could be characterized as technical 'hard' measures, generally targeting agriculture (see Table 3.1).

Most of the projects did not support existing community-level coping strategies explicitly, but rather focused on agricultural development that targeted only a segment of the community in trying to see them through seasonal variation. Thus, there appears to be a disconnect between how DAs address coping measures and adaptation and what communities in fact do themselves to respond to droughts.

Various perspectives emerged from the study findings. Firstly, comparison of the results in Table 3.1 with the findings presented in Figure 3.1 shows a clear difference between the DA approach and that of the communities. DA measures appear to focus more on environmental conservation and development, some of which may enhance adaptive capacity, whereas local strategies are more geared towards diversified livelihoods that can manage drought and climatic variations. Most DA measures did not directly support those livelihood and coping strategies that are most critical for local communities in managing climatic variation and change. To use the terminology of the academic literature, the community's approach would be seen more as coping, leading to a perceived need to provide them with a new set of measures for adapting. By contrast, the same literature

TABLE 3.1 Development agency (DA) measures for improved drought tolerance and climate-change adaptation in Makueni

Measures promoted	Number of individuals covered by the programmes in the study population (%)	Type of DA
Diversification of production	72 (21)	Government
Weather bulletins	294 (86)	Government
Micro-finance	All	Private, Government
Full basket and school feeding programmes	All	NGO
Rainwater harvesting	34 (10)	NGO
Small-scale irrigation	10 (3)	NGO
Early-maturing or drought-tolerant crops	All	Government
Drought-tolerant livestock breeds	14 (4)	Government
Agricultural extension services	All	Government
Fodder preservation	All	NGO and community groups
Farm credit facilities	41 (12)	Private and government
Sustainable sand-harvesting project for schools	7 (2)	Government
Seed replication and seed banking	10 (3)	Government and NGO
Protection of catchment areas	All	Government

would consider the DA approach as adaptive precisely because the measures are geared towards minimizing the use of the coping strategies presented in Figure 3.1. This could help to explain why there is no stronger link between the two approaches even though both aim at reducing the impact of drought on the households.

Secondly, the set of measures in Table 3.1 generally fall in the category of 'hard' measures (Tschakert 2007; Collins and Ison 2009). They not only incorporate technical measures that are heavily biased towards agriculture, but also include environmental conservation measures aimed at curbing natural resource harvesting practices in Figure 3.1. Because they are mostly externally generated, it is not clear how well-adapted they would be for each individual's needs in terms of gender, age and other socio-demographic characteristics.

Finally, we observed very low replication of DA-promoted activities, making their positive impact negligible at community level. This also raises concerns about the social sustainability of these pilot measures. The fact that certain segments of the population are systematically not reached by these measures should also be of concern, not least as regards whether the measures effectively support the adaptive capacity of those who need it the most – the most marginalized and vulnerable groups. Other authors have shown that replication of new technology and development initiatives requires more than mere physical proximity. Citing the example of pineapple farmers in Ghana, Maddison (2007) reports that only 7 per cent of farmers in the same village could provide some information about others' activities. The authors argue that information flows through social networks and does not necessarily spread simply because of geographical proximity.

The low level of local adoption of DA measures could also be because they were generally not linked in any meaningful way to what the community was already doing. While some agencies reported that they would sit with the community and discuss with them project ideas before inception, other DA activities were externally determined. In the next section, we explore possible reasons for the disconnect in the type of coping measures employed by households and those employed by the agencies. We find two possible reasons: differing views on vulnerability, and conceptual framing of coping and adaptation.

Differing views of vulnerability, coping and adaptation

As noted, vulnerability does not refer merely to exposure to stress, but also the context in which stressors are experienced, which in turn creates the conditions for people's ability to cope with and adapt to the changes.

Although our study did not seek to explore local perceptions on vulnerability, some inferences can be drawn from what the households reported as causing climate stress in the region. There is no contention that ASAL regions have unique biophysical characteristics that pose stress to livelihoods of communities living in these regions. People living in drylands are aware of the climatic stress within their borders; hence migration to regions with less physical stress is a coping strategy that has long been employed. However, perceptions differ between and within the local community on the one hand, and scholars as well as development actors on the other hand on the causes of vulnerability beyond actual physical stress. Turner (1994) attributes this to the imbalance in the knowledge of monitoring human causes and responses to adverse events as compared to the ability to observe the physical aspects of environmental changes.

Most participants observed that the causes of drought and its impact at household level was not limited rainfall but the unreliability of it. A large proportion (85 per cent) of the respondents felt that the patterns of rainfall had changed, becoming more and more unreliable, making it difficult to cope. The long rains which used to indicate the beginning of planting seasons were no longer reliable, so that it became necessary to undertake the drastic shift to planting during the short rains. But now also the short rains had become unreliable. Other indicators of climatic changes were inability to spend the entire day working on the farm as in the past, due to the intense heat. Respondents also reported that children were growing up without knowing what a mature maize crop looks like. In terms of physical stressors, climate variability was thus seen as the main concern, rather than the overall climatic pattern of the region. This salient difference in perceptions can have long-term consequences if not acknowledged. One inference that could be drawn from these findings is that before climate change the community was not as vulnerable as had been thought, because the people were accustomed to dry conditions. Yet the dry climatic conditions were the driver for several decades of development efforts in the ASAL region.

In the case of Makueni, we see 'vulnerability' in terms of people not knowing that what they are experiencing is beyond the regular shift in weather patterns that they are accustomed to, but something more long term. The measures needed for coping with this stressor may not be the same as those that enabled them to live through past drought episodes, resulting in a need to explore new options. Asked whether they would change their practices in light of these changed rainfall patterns, half of the participants reported that they would not, and there were expectations that rainfall patterns would become more predictable in future (Ochieng and Yitambe 2012). Only 2.5 per cent of participants who reported the long-term shift in rainfall patterns came close to articulating the science behind climate change.

Although the DAs were aware of climate change and a few had climate-change adaptation programmes in place, only one agency classified its activity as a climate-change adaptation programme, with the rest working on 'drought management'. In addition, there was no clear recognition from the DAs with regard to the role that charcoal might play as a coping strategy, or how it could contribute to sustainable adaptation, by balancing between the community's ability to maintain livelihoods without irreparably eroding the environment. Various other measures had been tested and failed, like planting during the short rains. The fact that charcoal production had been sustained over several years shows its potential as an adaptation measure. Continued disregard of the important role of charcoal as a coping measure could result in situations similar to what Bassett and Zuéli (2000: 68) describe from Côte d'Ivoire: the ongoing ecological and human consequences of ignoring ongoing biophysical changes while planners are busy addressing imagined environmental problems. The ban on charcoal did not stop the practice: it simply drove it underground.

With regard to the distinction in the conceptual framing between coping and adaptation, this case study brings out findings that indicate that such a distinction is not always useful for understanding how ASAL communities diversify their livelihood strategies and how this in turn can build adaptive capacity. Indeed, if the conceptual framing of coping and adaptation is incorrect, then not only is vulnerability of ASAL communities incorrectly perceived, but also how the communities should adapt to it. Views based on an artificial distinction between coping and adaption conceptualizations can serve to reinforce the power structures, through the failure of 'educated' DA officials to value local knowledge sufficiently. The findings of this study underscore the importance of challenging power structures that disempower *local knowledge* as compared to 'scientific' knowledge embodied in DAs. Consequently, instead of supporting activities such as charcoal production to ensure that it is sustainable or adaptive, the practice is simply banned.

Adger et al. (2004) observe that coping measures take place within existing structures (e.g. production systems), whereas adaptation frequently involves changing the framework within which coping takes place. This is similar to what we observed in Makueni. But we argue that factors that shape capacity to cope with present-day vulnerability may complement factors that shape the ability to adapt over longer timescales. The DA approach and the community approach to coping and adaptation can therefore be complementary. Realizing the intrinsic linkage between coping and adaptation is important – otherwise, promoting external adaptation measures in a bid to limit the need for coping may actually leave people with less ability to cope, let alone adapt to new threats.

Conclusions and recommendations

In this chapter we have shown how the conceptualization of vulnerability and differing notions of coping and adaptation can influence practices on climate-change adaptation. Such influence may be negative (as widely documented with historical attempts to sedentarize pastoral communities), or may lead to inaction on the underlying social causes of vulnerability and the means of addressing them. In this study we have seen how having opportunities for income can be a strong measure for coping and adaptation – but development efforts are more focused on environmental and 'hard' measures not available or beneficial to all. Strengthening existing local strategies is critical for reaching the most vulnerable, empowering local knowledge and influence in decision-making processes, and probably in enhancing equity, thereby supporting social sustainability.

We have also shown how the dominant view of coping as counterproductive to or disconnected from adaptation can lead to ignoring important measures such as charcoal production that can diversify incomes and can thus be used to build adaptation. Challenging this prevailing view, we argue that coping and adaptation can be complementary. Future development options for Makueni and other ASAL regions should not be foreclosed by policy measures that inhibit the abilities of the local people to respond to the changing natural and economic circumstances.

With specific reference to charcoal production in ASALs, it is time to reconsider its role in coping with climate change and adapting to its impacts. Thus far the only linkage that has been drawn between charcoal production and climate change is on mitigation, which supports curbing the practice in order to reduce deforestation rates. Exploring the potential of the charcoal sector can provide an opportunity for reducing not only vulnerability to climate change, but also ecosystem vulnerability, as the practice would become regulated with proper controls of production measures. For this to occur, coping measures would need to be viewed as part of adaptation, rather than a separate process. Part of the adaptation process would therefore be to look for ways of making charcoal production both environmentally and socially sustainable and inclusive. However, making charcoal production available to a larger section of the community can at best form one part of a broader, more socially sustainable approach to adaptation – it must be complemented with strengthening other local strategies too. Moreover, the arguments advanced in this chapter should not be interpreted as holding that all the measures that communities utilize in disaster situations should necessarily be built upon, but that they should be taken into account in trying to support diverse livelihoods.

Acknowledgements

The case study fieldwork was funded by ProVention research and Action Grants for disaster risk reduction. We thank several people who made significant contributions to the initial fieldwork: the Makueni households and development agencies who took part in the study, fieldwork assistant Martin Kamwanza, and Kenyatta University supervisors Drs Isaac Mwanzo and Andre Yitambe. Further analysis and reproduction of the earlier work that forms the content of this chapter were funded by Europe Aid through a grant to the Stockholm Environment Institute. The views expressed in this chapter are solely those of the authors and do not represent the views of the funding or supporting institutions.

Note

1 Tschakert (2007) describes these as technical types of adaptive responses that have been proposed in many countries' reports on climate change vulnerability, and the National Adaptation Programmes for Action (NAPAs). She cites examples such as drought-resistant crop varieties, micro-irrigation, construction of dykes, reforestation and seasonal climate forecasts.

References

Adger, W. N., Brooks, N., Bentham, G., Agnew, M. & Eriksen, S. (2004). *New indicators of vulnerability and adaptive capacity*. Technical Report 7. Norwich: Tyndall Centre for Climate Change Research.

Anderson, J., Bryceson, D., Campbell, B., Chitundu, D., Clarke, J., Drinkwater, M., Fakir, S., Frost, P., Gambiza, J. & Grundy, I. (2004). *Chance, change and choice in African drylands: A new perspective on policy priorities*. Report of the Workshop on Development Assistance in the African Drylands, Durban.

Bassett, T. J. & Zuéli, K. B. (2000). 'Environmental discourses and the Ivorian savanna'. *Annals of the Association of American Geographers*, 90, 67–95.

Bohle, H. G. (2001). 'Vulnerability and criticality: perspectives from social geography'. *IHDP update*, 2, 3–5.

Collins, K. & Ison, R. (2009). 'Jumping off Arnstein's ladder: social learning as a new policy paradigm for climate change adaptation'. *Environmental Policy and Governance*, 19, 358–373.

Eriksen, S. & Lind, J. (2009). 'Adaptation as a political process: adjusting to drought and conflict in Kenya's Drylands'. *Environmental Management*, 43, 817–835.

Eriksen, S. & Silva, J. A. (2009). 'The vulnerability context of a savanna area in Mozambique: household drought coping strategies and responses to economic change'. *Environmental Science & Policy*, 12, 33–52.

Eriksen, S. H., Brown, K. & Kelly, P. M. (2005). 'The dynamics of vulnerability: locating coping strategies in Kenya and Tanzania'. *Geographical Journal*, 171, 287–305.

Füssel, H. M. (2010). *Review and quantitative analysis of indices of climate change exposure, adaptive capacity, sensitivity, and impacts*. Background note to the World Development Report 2010, The World Bank. Potsdam: Institute for Climate Impact Research.

Getachew, G., Tolossa, D. & Gebru, G. (2008). 'Risk perception and coping strategies among the Karrayu pastoralists of Upper Awash Valley, Central Ethiopia'. *Nomadic Peoples*, 12(1): 93–107.

Girard, P. (2002). 'Charcoal production and use in Africa: what future?' *Unasylva*, 53, 30–35.

IFAD. (2013). *Sustainable livelihood framework*. Available from: <http://www.ifad.org/sla/>. (18 April 2014).

Ifejika Speranza, C., Kiteme, B. & Wiesmann, U. (2008). 'Droughts and famines: the underlying factors and the causal links among agro-pastoral households in semi-arid Makueni district, Kenya'. *Global Environmental Change*, 18, 220–233.

IPCC. 2012. 'Managing the Risks of Extreme Events and Disasters to Advance Climate Change Adaptation'. A Special Report of Working Groups I and II of the Intergovernmental Panel on Climate Change [Field, C.B., V. Barros, T.F. Stocker, D. Qin, D.J. Dokken, K.L. Ebi, M.D. Mastrandrea, K.J. Mach, G.-K. Plattner, S.K. Allen, M. Tignor, and P.M. Midgley (eds.)]. Cambridge: Cambridge University Press.

IRIN. (2013). *Climate change: coping versus adapting*. IRINnews. Available from <http://www.irinnews.org/Report/95224/CLIMATE-CHANGE-Coping-versus-adapting> (20 November 2013).

IUCN, IISD, SEI & SDC (2003). *Livelihoods and climate change: combining disaster risk reduction, natural resource management and climate change adaptation in a new approach to the reduction of vulnerability and poverty*. A Conceptual Framework Paper Prepared by the IPCC Task Force on Climate Change, Vulnerable Communities and Adaptation. Canada: International Institute for Sustainable Development.

Kelly, P. M. & Adger, W. N. (2000). 'Theory and practice in assessing vulnerability to climate change and facilitating adaptation'. *Climatic Change*, 47, 325–352.

Kituyi, E. (2004). 'Towards sustainable production and use of charcoal in Kenya: exploring the potential in life cycle management approach'. *Journal of Cleaner Production*, 12, 1047–1057.

Maddison, D. (2007). *The perception of and adaptation to climate change in Africa*. Volume 4308, Pretoria: World Bank Publications.

Millennium Ecosystem Assessment. (2005). *Ecosystems and human well-being: synthesis*. Washington, DC: Island Press.

Nelson, J. (2000). 'Makueni district profile: income diversification and farm investment, 1989-1999'. Drylands Research Working Paper 10. Crewkerne: Drylands Research.

Njenga, M., Karanja, N., Munster, C., Iiyama, M., Neufeldt, H., Kithinji, J. & Jamnadass, R. (2013). 'Charcoal production and strategies to enhance its sustainability in Kenya'. *Development in Practice*, 23, 359–371.

O'Brien, K., Eriksen, S., Nygaard, L. P. & Schjolden, A. (2007). 'Why different interpretations of vulnerability matter in climate change discourses'. *Climate Policy*, 7, 73–88.

Ochieng, C. A. & Yitambe, A. (2012). 'Climate change risk and food insecurity in arid and semi-arid lands of Kenya. In: Bloemetrz, L., Doevenspeck, M., Macamo, E. & Müller-Mahn, D. (eds.) *Risk and Africa: multi-disciplinary empirical approaches*. Berlin: LIT Verlag Münster.

Office of the Prime Minister. (2011). *Releasing our full potential – draft sessional paper on national policy for the sustainable development of Northern Kenya and other arid lands: 2009*. Nairobi: Government of Kenya.

Paavola, J. (2008). 'Livelihoods, vulnerability and adaptation to climate change in Morogoro, Tanzania'. *Environmental Science & Policy*, 11, 642–654.

PISCES. (2011). *The Kenya charcoal policy handbook: current regulations for a sustainable charcoal sector*. Policy Innovation Systems for Clean Energy Security (PISCES). Available from http://www.pisces.or.ke/sites/default/files/The%20Kenya%20Charcoal%20Policy%20 Handbook.pdf (30 June 2014).

Ruto, S. J., Ongwenyi, Z. N. & Mugo, J. K. (2009). *Educational marginalisation in Northern Kenya*. Background paper prepared for the Education for All Global Monitoring Report 2010: Reaching the marginalized. Nairobi: UNESCO.

Smit, B. & Wandel, J. (2006). 'Adaptation, adaptive capacity and vulnerability'. *Global Environmental Change*, 16, 282–292.

Speranza, C. I., Kiteme, B., Ambenje, P., Wiesmann, U. & Makali, S. (2010). 'Indigenous knowledge related to climate variability and change: insights from droughts in semi-arid areas of former Makueni District, Kenya'. *Climatic Change*, 100, 295–315.

Taylor, A., Harris, K. & Ehrhart, C. (2010). 'Adaptation: key terms'. *Tiempo*, 78, 10–13.

Tschakert, P. (2007). 'Views from the vulnerable: understanding climatic and other stressors in the Sahel'. *Global Environmental Change*, 17, 381–396.

Turner, B. (1994). 'Local faces, global flows: the role of land use and land cover in global environmental change'. *Land Degradation & Development*, 5, 71–78.

UNCCD, UNDP & UNEP. (2009). *Climate change in the African drylands: options and opportunities for adaptation and mitigation*. New York, Bonn, Nairobi: UNCCD, UNDP, UNEP.

Wisner, B., Pires, B., Cannon, T & Davies, I. eds. (2004). *At risk: natural hazards, people's vulnerability and disasters*. New York: Routledge.

Zulu, L. C. (2010). 'The forbidden fuel: charcoal, urban woodfuel demand and supply dynamics, community forest management and woodfuel policy in Malawi'. *Energy Policy*, 38, 3717–3730.

4

ADAPTIVE CAPACITY

From coping to sustainable transformation

Christine Wamsler and Ebba Brink

Introduction

Climate change and increasing disasters are among the most serious risks to sustainable urban development today.[1] Worldwide, the number of disasters has almost quadrupled during the past 30 years (UNISDR 2012), and there is widespread consensus that urban disasters are increasing exponentially,[2] resulting in escalating human and economic losses (IPCC 2012a).

Throughout history, humans have managed to cope with their environment and adapt to it (Easterling et al. 2004; Shaw et al. 2008). This accumulated local capacity is increasingly recognized as critical for reducing risk and vulnerability (see e.g. Shaw et al. 2008; IPCC 2012a; Soltesova et al. 2012; Dodman and Mitlin 2013; Wamsler 2014).

Urbanization finds expression in characteristic physical, environmental, socio-cultural, economic and institutional features – which inevitably create specific conditions of risk (Wamsler 2014). However, comparatively little focus is placed on the adaptive capacities of city dwellers; and such capacities are rarely considered by city authorities (Satterthwaite et al. 2007; Shaw et al. 2008; Carmin et al. 2012). Moreover, environmental changes are occurring at an unprecedented rate and magnitude (Steffen et al. 2004; O'Brien and Leichenko 2008), placing new demands on human capacity to adapt.

Without adequate support from city authorities and aid organizations, urban dwellers cannot use their adaptive capacity to its fullest extent. Even worse, inadequate assistance may result in city authorities and city dwellers obstructing each other's adaptation efforts (Ahammad 2011; Hamza et al. 2012; Wamsler 2014).

This study probes the consequences of the local adaptation efforts of city dwellers, and why they should be considered when developing policies and projects to promote resilience and transformation. We provide a framework for analysing people's efforts to reduce and adapt to urban risk; identify the strengths and weaknesses of such capacities, especially as regards climate change; and discuss the importance of local adaptive capacities for achieving sustainable urban transformation.

We first analysed urban dwellers' adaptive practices, drawing on data from field studies conducted between 2006 and 2012 in marginal at-risk settlements in San Salvador and Rio de Janeiro. This was complemented by a meta-evaluation of cross-country studies, as well as single-case or single-country studies.[3] After the primary data from the field studies and the secondary data from the meta-evaluation had been synthesized to provide a general overview of people's adaptive behaviour, we assessed coping practices from a larger sustainability perspective. This approach allowed a qualitative and locally focused, yet comprehensive, perspective often missing in climate-related science. It also highlighted the many similarities in the problems faced by urban residents across the developing world and their ways of tackling them. The research presented in this chapter draws partially from two broader research projects regarding risk and adaptation planning in cities (see Wamsler 2014) and the role of formal education in shaping adaptive capacity (see Lutz 2008; Wamsler et al. 2012).[4]

This chapter is divided into five sections. The next section presents key concepts and introduces criteria for assessing people's adaptive action. We then present a systematic overview of city dwellers' coping practices and discuss them in a larger sustainability perspective. Finally, we examine how the findings can contribute to policy development that acknowledges and supports city dwellers' local capacities, instead of following development pathways that have created risk in the first place and therefore only reinforce existing vulnerabilities. We argue that a more distributed urban risk governance system is a necessary step for a sustainable urban transformation to take place.

Coping and adaptive capacity – an analytical framework

The terms 'coping capacity' and 'adaptive capacity' are often used to denote similar issues and generally include both *used* and *unused* capacities. UNISDR (2009:8) defines coping capacity as 'the ability of people, organisations and systems, using available skills and resources, to face and manage adverse conditions, emergencies or disasters', which 'contribute to the reduction of disaster risks'. Adaptive capacity can be defined as 'the ability of a system to adjust to climate change to moderate potential damages, to take advantage of opportunities, or to cope with the consequences' (IPCC 2007:21). Used adaptive capacity is seen in how people reduce and adapt to urban risk.

Some scholars differentiate between coping (local adjustments made to deal with extreme weather events) and adaptive practices (more long-term or fundamental changes aimed at systematically reducing potential harm or taking advantage of opportunities from changing weather patterns) (e.g. Gallopín

2006; Smit and Wandel 2006; Cutter et al. 2008; IPCC 2012a); indeed, some maintain that the two are mutually conflicting (e.g. Barrett and McPeak 2005; Young 2010). Similarly, adaptation policies often overlook local strategies, seeing them as 'coping' and not long-term improvements. However, the differentiation between coping and adaptation seems counterproductive, as it is far from clear-cut and also very context-specific (see e.g. Béné et al. 2012). There is reason to investigate to what extent the local coping efforts of city dwellers form part of a system that represents more long-term adaptive capacity and stimulus for change. The terms coping strategy and coping practice denote here both short- and more long-term risk-reducing activities.

Sustainable urban transformation refers to 'structural transformation processes – multi-dimensional and radical change – that can effectively direct urban development towards ambitious sustainability goals' (McCormick et al. 2012:1). From a disaster risk reduction perspective, it can be understood as the altering of fundamental system attributes (IPCC 2012b) by addressing the root causes[5] of risk and vulnerability in urban societies. This is crucial because solely incremental approaches to adaptation that build on existing structures (instead of altering them) may support the same development pathways that have created risk in the first place, further reproducing risk (Adger et al. 2005; Pelling 2010).

In the disaster literature, disasters (and related risk) are commonly understood as the result of an interaction between hazards (e.g. floods, windstorms, fires and sea-level rise) and vulnerable conditions. Simply put, disaster vulnerability refers to the conditions, characteristics and circumstances that make communities or societies '…susceptible to the damaging effects of a hazard' (UNISDR 2009:30). This can also be termed *contextual* vulnerability, which proves a useful perspective for studying coping strategies, power structures and alternative development pathways related to climate change (O'Brien et al. 2007). In contrast, climate adaptation literature typically presents vulnerability as a function of exposure, sensitivity and adaptive capacity, also called *outcome* vulnerability (O'Brien et al. 2007).

Our framework bridges risk and adaptation literatures and suggests three main dimensions for analysing local strategies for coping and adaptation.[6] First, they can be analysed on the basis of their *objectives*, divided into four types of risk-reducing activities (Wamsler 2014):

1 hazard reduction and avoidance: ability to reduce or avoid existing (and future) hazards
2 vulnerability reduction: ability to reduce existing (and future) susceptibility to hazards and/or drivers of vulnerability
3 preparedness for response (or ad hoc action): having functioning and flexible mechanisms and structures for disaster response in place
4 preparedness for recovery (or ad hoc action): having functioning and flexible mechanisms and structures for disaster recovery in place.

This categorization emphasizes the need for risk reduction and adaptation to address (a) both the natural and societal drivers of risk and (b) all the phases – before, during and after – of a potential disaster. With risk understood as a product of hazard and vulnerability (Wisner et al. 2004; UNISDR 2009), the first activity listed addresses hazards, whereas the following three focus on location-specific vulnerabilities.

A second dimension involves assessing local strategies for coping and adaptation in relation to their *thematic foci* – physical,[7] environmental, socio-cultural, economic or political/institutional (Table 4.3). Third, the strategies can be reviewed on the basis of their underlying *patterns of social behaviour*. This categorization has been established by Cultural Theory (Thompson et al. 1990; Thompson 2011). *Individualistic* behaviour refers to self-help, fixing things without outside assistance. *Communitarian* behaviour is based on the view that everybody sinks or swims together, and is characterized by community efforts. *Hierarchical* patterns relate to belief in, and reliance on, authority structures and strong leadership for assistance, control and organization. *Fatalistic* behaviour is based on the view that taking or not taking action has the same (unfavourable) result: it is a 'non-strategy' for survival.

People do not adapt in a vacuum: practices are constantly shaped and reshaped by governmental and non-governmental policies and actions (Adger et al. 2005; Moser et al. 2010; Pelling 2010; Wamsler 2014). Our framework combines three different dimensions to enable thorough analyses of coping strategies and the conditions in which they are used – a prerequisite for evaluating the effectiveness and sustainability of local practices, as well as the provision of related policies that can assist those most at risk. Effectiveness is described by Adger et al. (2005, p. 81) as 'the capacity of an adaptation action to achieve its expressed objectives'. In practice, effectiveness may signify a strategy's success in preventing deaths and injuries, as well as losses and damages to property, environment and livelihoods related to climate change and variability. Conversely, the sustainability of an adaptation action can be described as being related to its potential impact from a systems perspective, in the sense that it should not compromise the adaptation of others (now or in the future) or further contribute to climate change (see WCED 1987; Adger et al. 2005; Wamsler 2014). Hence, a sustainable coping system is here understood as a system that can assist an individual, household or urban community to reduce their level of risk, whilst maintaining or enhancing local adaptive capacities both now and in the future, and thus not compromising the ability of future generations to meet their own needs.

Our analytical framework considers three factors decisive for effective and sustainable adaptation: *inclusiveness, flexibility* and *equity*. Here, inclusiveness means the inclusion of all four types of risk-reducing activities (described as the first dimension above) in addressing risk before, during and after a potential disaster. Flexibility relates to the diversity of measures (with regard to the second and third dimensions; that is, thematic focus and patterns of social behaviour) used within the four types (Table 4.3). Equity in adaptations can be evaluated based on the distribution of the more and less advantageous outcomes of an adaptation action ('winners' and 'losers'), and with regard to who is involved in decision-making on adaptation (Adger et al. 2005).

Coping practices

This section systematizes coping strategies using the framework described above and based on the authors' case studies in Brazil and El Salvador, and the meta-evaluation of other articles.

Hazard reduction and avoidance

Urban dwellers use various measures to *reduce hazard exposure* (systematized in the first column in Tables 4.1 and 4.2). For example, people build small embankments to improve protection from river or sea flooding, or construct retaining walls to protect their homes from landslides. The materials and techniques used vary considerably, and include bricks, cement, stones, soil, old tyres or combinations of these (Wamsler 2007a; Douglas et al. 2008; Jabeen et al. 2010). Although individualistic physical and environmental measures often prevail, there are also examples of communitarian actions. Residents join together, for instance, to obtain construction materials or build simple flood walls or retaining walls. Community or family members assist in actions taken by individuals. A resident of San Salvador explains:

> 'I got old car tyres from my neighbours' repair shop to build a flood wall next to the river.'
>
> (Wamsler 2014:191)

Other people use biodegradable sandbags filled with soil and seeds, which grow into green retaining walls, for instance in Medellín (Colombia) (Inteligencias Colectivas 2011a) or grow plants to stabilize the soil, counteract soil erosion and create windbreaks (Wamsler 2007a). In San Salvador, covering slopes with plastic sheets to prevent landslides is a common measure.

In addition, people take physical measures that simultaneously *reduce hazards and location-specific vulnerabilities*. Examples from our studies in Brazil and El Salvador include reducing uncontrolled water flows that may cause landslides; improving electrical connections to prevent fires; and measures to reduce the heat island effect, thereby reducing vulnerability in the face of climate-related temperature increase.

Measures to *avoid hazards* are also common among urban dwellers – such as not building in obviously hazard-prone locations; setting up fences to prevent children from getting close to risk zones; or moving to a safer house or location. However, a very different strategy was also noted in San Salvador, where some people moved into risk areas in order to be included in post-disaster resettlement programmes.

TABLE 4.1 Examples of coping and adaptive practices in areas prone to flooding and landslides[a]

	Hazard reduction	Vulnerability reduction	Preparedness for response	Preparedness for recovery
Physical	Building small levees, dams or embankments for flood protection Building retaining walls to stabilize slopes and prevent landslides	Ensuring that water is adequately discharged and drained by: • (illegally) linking drainage to main system; • prolonging length of roof projections and rainwater eaves; • changing direction of roof incline Permanently increasing above-floor height of furniture in dwellings in flood areas (e.g. use of unusually high tables and wardrobes, refrigerator built on high plinth)	Storing sandbags, soil, stones, bricks, etc. to temporarily: • improve flood protection during heavy rains (e.g. in front of entrance door); • increase height of furniture; • block wastewater pipes to avoid flooding, backflow, and related contamination Having an 'extra house' for temporary use in case of emergency	Using materials that recover easily from floods (like wooden plank flooring which is less prone to waterlogging, can be easily cleaned, etc.)
Environmental	Planting (or fighting deforestation) to preserve natural flood protection in surrounding areas, stabilize slopes and prevent landslides	Cleaning waste from slopes, avoiding littering and regularly cleaning gutters to mitigate flooding caused by blocked gutters and landslides triggered by heavy/waterlogged soil, dampness, or methane gas explosions due to accumulated waste	Weather prediction based on observations of nature/natural phenomena for early warning (e.g. noting cloud colour and formation, water-level of rivers, and/or animal behaviour)	Reducing risks of environmental contamination and health hazards during recovery phase (cleaning up debris, keeping surroundings litter-free, repairing public wastewater pipes that pass through the settlement, etc.) (ad hoc measure)

continued …

Table 4.1 continued

	Hazard reduction	Vulnerability reduction	Preparedness for response	Preparedness for recovery
Socio-cultural	Formation of local groups to control and monitor previous slope stabilization works for landslide protection Taking measures to prevent children from getting close to risk areas (awareness raising, establishing 'forbidden areas', etc.)	Sending children to a school outside one's own settlement (where there is less disturbance to their education from natural disasters, poor infrastructure, violence, etc.)	Creating community-based information structures for early warning (e.g. community members going door-to-door with warnings, disaster alarms like sirens or church bells) Collective storage of items to help community members during emergencies (non-perishable food, boats, etc.)	Staying informed about precautions to take during post-disaster rehabilitation and clean-up (with floods: wearing gloves and sturdy shoes; taking care not to step on submerged sharp items or poisonous creatures; not letting children play in floodwater; etc.)
Economic	Saving money in order to be able to move to a lower-risk area	Taking jobs that will not be affected by local disasters (e.g. work outside one's own settlement)	Family members staying at home during disaster impact to secure economic assets (ad hoc measure)	Accessing formal or informal insurance schemes (e.g. formal disaster insurance policy, health insurance through formal employment, or community emergency savings) Getting a formal job, also in order to be eligible for credits from financing institutions
Political/Institutional	Declaring oneself as being at high risk, to become eligible for resettlement programmes that offer at-risk people social housing in areas with less hazard exposure	'Exchanging' political votes for punctual assistance from political parties (food, [money for] housing improvements, etc.) Seeking to obtain legal tenure in order to access formal assistance, legal protection, and other services for vulnerability reduction	Relying on hierarchical structures for emergency assistance Establishing, and engaging in, a local emergency committee	Joining a political party, professional society, religious or spiritual group; or maintaining good contacts with NGOs, the municipality, and national governmental organizations – from which one can seek assistance for post-disaster reconstruction

	Hazard reduction	Vulnerability reduction	Preparedness for response	Preparedness for recovery
Unused capacities	Planting to reduce risks could be upscaled into a community programme, and broadened to include elements of urban agriculture, which also reduce vulnerability by promoting better ecology, heat reduction, social cohesion, and nutrition (e.g. guava and orange are vitamin-rich fruits whose trees help stabilize the soil)	Many informal builders who could be trained in disaster-resistant construction techniques	Many elderly people with knowledge of traditional coping strategies, especially for disaster response; transfer of traditional knowledge, which is so far little used, is important	Existing community-based NGOs that offer free courses (e.g. English and IT) for children and youth; they could serve as a platform for raising awareness about precautions to take during post-disaster rehabilitation and clean-up

a The differentiation between the aspects analysed is not always clear-cut, and there are certainly overlaps

TABLE 4.2 Examples of coping and adaptive practices in areas prone to high winds and storms[a]

	Hazard reduction	Vulnerability reduction	Preparedness for response	Preparedness for recovery
Physical	Improving electrical connections in the house to prevent fire (as a secondary hazard after storms)	Improving roof fixing, and putting objects on the roof to hold it in place during storms	Building an emergency shelter (e.g. hurricane-resistant community centre)	Deliberately not 'improving' the house (e.g. changing from a wooden construction to a brick house) as potential damage can be more easily repaired and/or more cheaply replaced
Environmental	Environmental behaviour that contributes to climate-change mitigation and indirectly to reduction of climatic hazards (buying second-hand, recycling or reusing waste and construction material, using a pressure cooker to reduce cooking time, planting trees, etc.)	Cutting down large branches and trees located close to houses to avoid damage/injury during storms	Storage of water in cisterns, barrels or plastic bottles for use during emergencies Having available filters or chemicals for cleaning up water if necessary (e.g. clay filter)	Drawing on natural resources to help recover and reduce recovery cost (e.g. water from natural springs or rivers, food from urban agriculture, collecting firewood instead of using gas stove) (also ad hoc measure)
Socio-cultural	Use of traditional or indigenous knowledge on storm routes and wind patterns in order to build in lower-risk areas	Interacting with people from the neighbourhood (e.g. buying from local shops, offering labour when needed, employing community members for small jobs) to create social ties for mutual support	Exchange of rooms/apartments between family members so that less mobile members live in the more accessible areas, for easy evacuation	Creating social networks (family, friends, or neighbours) from which to seek assistance for recovery as regards, e.g. money or materials for reconstruction, assistance with clean-up or childcare

	Hazard reduction	Vulnerability reduction	Preparedness for response	Preparedness for recovery
Economic	Use of remittances to allow some family members to move to more secure areas	Economic diversification (taking on several jobs at the same time) so that disasters have less impact on livelihoods	Sharing economic and other assets during hazard impact (ad hoc measure) / Saving in order to have 'extra money' to prepare for emergencies (e.g. to be able to stay somewhere else temporarily)	Acquiring economic assets that can be easily sold, for instance: • use of construction materials for own shelter which can be sold and replaced with other objects; • owning land or property/house (both aspects also part of physical measures) / Changing (or being able to change) jobs, to work where demand rises after disasters (e.g. construction sector) (also ad hoc measure)
Political/Institutional	Linking up with faith-based or other support groups that provide comfort and support to improve one's risk situation/ reduce hazard exposure	Engaging in community matters (e.g. local committees) to influence community-based decision-making / Lobbying political parties, faith-based organizations, NGOs, etc. to obtain assistance for vulnerability reduction	Collaborating with various institutions (NGOs, churches, nurseries, etc.) to prepare for potential evacuations: food distribution points and/or emergency shelters	Improving the possibility of accessing post-disaster help by deliberate increase of risk (e.g. moving in with family members in more affected areas where assistance is available) (ad hoc measure) / Giving preference to employers that can provide post-disaster assistance (e.g. for storage of belongings during recovery phase)
Unused capacities	Good community organizations and interest in training courses for hazard reduction	Possibility for households to access legal tenure if practical issues are supported	Many households have TV or radio, mobile phones, and access to Internet, which can be used for early warning, campaigns, etc.	Community-based savings schemes exist that could be scaled up or expanded (to become emergency funds, micro-insurance)

a The differentiation between the aspects analysed is not always clear-cut, and there are certainly overlaps

Vulnerability reduction

Most deliberate coping strategies are means to *reduce people's physical vulnerability* (systematized in the second column in Tables 4.1 and 4.2). In contrast to hazard reduction and avoidance, these are aimed to withstand potential hazard impacts. Physical or structural protection is often taken into consideration during the construction and maintenance of buildings – for instance, foundation depth, length of roof projections, height of door sills and regular house painting to prevent water infiltration. However, many Rio and San Salvador dwellers describe how they are increasingly being forced to strengthen their housing even further to become better adapted, a point echoed in other studies, for example by a young resident of the Linda compound, Lusaka:

> '[…] people have learned the hard way. If you go around the compound now, people are using burnt bricks or cement blocks because houses built from these are stronger.'
>
> (Simatele 2010:21)

For instance, people replace flimsy doors with more flood-proof ones; improve wall and roof insulation; construct additional drains; build long projecting pipes to discharge rainwater towards the street (a typical measure in Medellín: see Inteligencias Colectivas 2011b); and change the direction or degree of roof incline, to discharge run-off water without causing erosion or damaging roof construction.

Innovative examples of how urban dwellers reduce their physical vulnerability can be found for nearly all hazard types. Examples include floating houses (Tudehope 2011); creating outlets at the rear of the house to allow water levels to sink faster during flooding (Douglas et al. 2008; Jabeen et al. 2010); and construction on poles or other techniques to raise the floor platform to mitigate flooding and improve ventilation (Douglas et al. 2008; Jabeen et al. 2010; Pelling 2011).[8]

People use many other physical measures besides structural improvements to houses to reduce their location-specific vulnerability. Examples are putting wood or bricks on the roof to hold it in place during storms; gluing objects to furniture to prevent them falling during earthquakes; or increasing the height of furniture in flood areas, as illustrated by this statement from a woman in the Alajo community in Accra, Ghana:

> 'Our furniture has been custom-made to help keep our things dry from the water […] our tables are very high and so also are our wardrobes.'
>
> (Douglas et al. 2008:197)

To mitigate heat, people also paint their houses white (Cheikh and Bouchair 2008); and/or use ventilation holes, which they then cover with various materials for mosquito protection (Jabeen et al. 2010).

Physical measures are often combined with environmental ones. To mitigate heat, people in Rio use containers of plants and climbing shrubs to cover walls and roofs, a measure also found in Dhaka, Bangladesh (Jabeen et al. 2010). In both case-study areas, trees and other plants are further used as natural protection against landslides (Wamsler and Umaña 2003; Wamsler et al. 2012). Urban residents also use combined physical-environmental measures to mitigate floods, landslides and water scarcity. For example, they may construct soak pits to allow rainwater or wastewater to filter into the ground (Gensch and Sacher 2012), and draw on their local knowledge to determine where and how to settle (Shaw et al. 2008). To cope with water scarcity, various measures have been developed: freshwater, for instance, can be channelled off roofs for household and communal use (Ayers and Forsyth 2009).

Although physical measures are more visible and better documented, there is increasing evidence that physical and environmental measures often go together with more socially oriented ones. One related example of communitarian behaviour found in Rio and San Salvador is swapping rooms with more vulnerable elderly or disabled people, to give them the less dangerous (less exposed or more accessible) ones.

In addition, city dwellers reduce vulnerability through economic measures aimed at increasing household income and income security: for example, taking low-risk jobs; economic diversification at individual and household levels to reduce dependence on specific sources of income;[9] and taking jobs outside their own district to be less affected by local disasters (Wamsler 2007a; SAARC 2008; Jabeen et al. 2010). Economic diversification is vital, since disasters affect people's livelihoods – even when they do not occur, as pointed out by a resident of hurricane-prone Caye Caulker, Belize:

> 'As long as it is expected to hit anywhere around, the tourists are immediately going to avoid this area for a good two to three weeks, even if the hurricane has passed. And that does a huge amount of damage to your revenue and business total. A hurricane affects whether it hits or it doesn't.'
>
> (Esdahl 2011:14)

More socially oriented measures involve the creation of solidarity and reciprocal relationships with neighbours and other community members. These can serve as a foundation for communitarian action-taking, like establishing local committees for risk reduction, or 'community cleaning days' to reduce the risk of waste, branches and other items clogging up water channels. Other socially oriented measures may relate to education, like sending children to school outside their own district or investing in children's education (Wamsler et al. 2012).

Further communitarian patterns of social behaviour can be seen when people organize to get a more powerful voice in lobbying institutions for better services (including for risk reduction and adaptation). This is the case in the areas studied in Brazil and El Salvador, where local interests are represented by residents' associations or local committees. Another institutional measure is to 'fight' for legal tenure to gain access to formal assistance or credits offered by national or local authorities, banks or aid organizations. Achieving legal tenure means not having to live in constant fear of eviction, and increases people's motivation to improve their risk situation (Wamsler et al. 2012).

People living at risk may also adopt more emotionally oriented strategies, such as accepting or ignoring their high risk; seeking emotional support within their social network (family, relatives, neighbours, religious group, etc.); or fully relying on their faith. Whereas religious faith has sometimes been linked to fatalistic behaviour, it can also be a powerful strategy and lead to effective action (see 'Preparedness for response' below). Other people place their trust in hierarchical structures and rely fully on these for support, another posture that may result in passive behaviour.

Preparedness for response

In *preparing for possible emergencies*, people use a range of measures that allow them to adapt their behaviour temporarily to changed circumstances (systematized in the third column in Tables 4.1 and 4.2). Some preparations may be taken shortly before potential hazard impacts (e.g. after disaster warnings), others the whole year round: typical examples are keeping important documents and money in a safe place, storing food and bottles of water, or having other items on hand, like a portable cooker, air conditioning appliances or a fan. Measures for preparing for floods include storing plastic sheets, sandbags, electric pumps and items to raise furniture or to block wastewater pipes and prevent backflow when water rises (Wamsler 2007a; Douglas et al. 2008; Jabeen et al. 2010).

Physical measures for response preparedness include the construction of temporary or permanent emergency rooms or shelters. The latter can be an example of both communitarian and individualistic behaviour: sometimes whole communities organize or construct their own emergency shelter; those who can afford it, however, may buy or rent an 'extra house' in or outside their own settlement, where they can stay with their families in case of emergency. This was observed in both the Rio and the San Salvador case-study areas.

People also take a range of other non-hazard specific and more communitarian actions to prepare for disaster response, like creating local emergency groups. After Hurricane Mitch in 1998, many low-income settlements in Central America established such groups, often with support from national and international non-governmental organizations (NGOs; Wamsler and Umaña 2003). The creation of social capital can also form the basis for risk-reducing activities. Social cohesion, solidarity and community networks can facilitate mutual aid during disasters and in the immediate aftermath. In the Rio and San

Salvador case-study areas, such aid involves door-to-door advice and evacuation; guarding empty houses; temporary stays with community members living in more secure areas; and sharing food and services (like toilets) with others. Similar measures can be found elsewhere (see Douglas et al. 2008; Jabeen et al. 2010).

An important part of preparedness for response is anticipating and monitoring hazards. Social cohesion and community networks are crucial for local communication structures to ensure rapid diffusion of hazard information for early warning. Sources used for predicting extreme weather events include television, radio, Internet, local religious leaders or places of worship, as well as individuals' observations and traditional monitoring systems (e.g. Wamsler 2007b; SAARC 2008; Singh 2011; Wamsler et al. 2012). In the Rio case-study area, people forecast heavy rains on the basis of clouds, and cockroaches entering houses. In the San Salvador study area, people monitor the flood risk by noting river water-levels, the sound level caused by rain up-hill and the appearance of clouds.

Apart from the numerous preparedness measures in advance of potential emergencies, many responses are ad hoc. To cope with water scarcity, people may have to buy overpriced bottled water, or reduce the amount of water used for drinking, cooking, cleaning and washing to an extent that can create risks to health and hygiene.

Preparedness for recovery

Urban dwellers use various preparedness measures *to recover quickly from disaster impacts* (housing damage, income loss, injury) and bounce back swiftly to their former, or improved, living conditions (systematized in the fourth column in Tables 4.1 and 4.2). Such measures are also called 'self-insurance': the creation of (access to) formal and informal security systems that can provide post-disaster assistance.

Financial assistance for funding post-disaster reconstruction and rehabilitation may come from a range of sources, like formal bank loans; savings accounts; informal credits from employers and relatives; community-based saving schemes, donations; or monetary compensation from insurance schemes (Wamsler 2007a; SAARC 2008; Jabeen et al. 2010). In urban low-income settlements, such as in Rio and San Salvador, people may save money 'under the mattress'; work extra hours; or take on additional jobs to increase their post-disaster income.

In the San Salvador case-study area, people also stockpile assets like construction material, which can be sold quickly as needed (see also Jabeen et al. 2010). For instance, to alleviate financial distress after Hurricane Mitch in 1998, one man sold his corrugated iron roofing sheets and then re-roofed his home with materials from an old car chassis:

> 'I never nail down the iron sheets that I use for roofing my house so that I can sell them if I want; if I need some money, like after Hurricane Mitch.'
>
> (Wamsler 2014:212)

People with limited financial resources sometimes decide not to invest too much in their housing, as losses can then be replaced more cheaply (Moser et al. 2010). Nevertheless, legal home ownership is often seen as city dwellers' most important strategy for 'self-insurance': the house can be sold or sub-let if funds are needed, and ownership provides access to formal assistance for on-site reconstruction and bank credits.

Formal employment is another individualistic strategy that city dwellers use to become less vulnerable and better prepared for recovery. A formal job usually means a more secure income (even when disasters lead to loss of working days); access to insurance (life, health, unemployment, disaster); pension after retirement; direct post-disaster assistance or post-disaster credits from employers; and other workers' benefits. Many people in the Rio and San Salvador case-study areas who have formal employment say that they are less at risk and better prepared to recover after disasters than those who must depend on informal structures and services. In San Salvador, some people have even made deals with entrepreneurs to obtain (illegally) certificates of employment, so they can access health insurance policies and formal credits without being formally employed.

Both legal tenure and a formal job can help to ensure sources of income and ultimately speed up recovery, especially when alternative informal systems are weak or non-existent. However, being fully reliant on hierarchical structures for social protection also has shortcomings, especially in the context of climate change. Insurance – if available to the poorest – is not always reliable as loss payments are often not made as expected (Esdahl 2011).

In addition to measures aimed at securing necessary financial resources, urban residents depend on non-financial assistance to recover quickly after disasters, like a woman from the Mafalala settlement in Maputo, Mozambique:

> 'During the 2000 floods, I lost everything. [...]. Because of my age and being without a husband, I couldn't remove my goods and leave the area. [...] I survive because of family support.'
>
> (Douglas et al. 2008:198)

Non-financial assistance is often based on communitarian patterns of social behaviour. It may include help in looking after or fostering children; labour work to repair damage and reconstruct houses; or clean-up of disaster impacts, as efficient and safe removal of debris, mud and other disaster impacts is crucial for quick recovery. Social cohesion, family and community support networks, as well as good relations with organizations giving assistance (governmental agencies, local committees, and religious, professional and political groups) are crucial for accessing financial and non-financial post-disaster assistance.

Another type of preparedness measure involves the use of construction materials that recover readily (or can be recovered) after hazard impacts. Wooden plank flooring is, for instance, less prone to water-clogging after heavy rainfall (Jabeen et al. 2010).

Strengths and limitations of city dwellers' coping practice

The analysis of coping strategies presented in 'Coping practices' above shows a great richness and diversity in objectives and thematic foci. Further analyses presented here, however, imply huge differences in effectiveness and sustainability, including forward-looking and short-term solutions, and even harmful ('maladaptive') measures.

Coping – in a context of climate change

What can be considered an 'effective' or an 'ineffective' coping practice was found to vary considerably according to context. Some coping strategies that might work well at an individual or household level prove counterproductive in terms of the larger picture. They may increase the vulnerability of others and negatively impact equity issues. For example, during hot summer periods, people from the San Salvador case-study area hoard water taken from private or public taps; and in the Rio case study people drench their rooftops with water to reduce indoor temperature. Both practices inevitably result in growing pressure on water supplies. Also in Rio, the high use of fans and air conditioners during hot periods frequently causes sub-standard electrical connections to short-circuit, resulting in power outages and fires which can spread quickly in the densely built settlements. Air conditioning further increases energy consumption, which exacerbates climate change. Another coping strategy that might work at the individual level but is counterproductive in a larger perspective, are the 'flying toilets' used in informal settlements throughout the world, including the Rio case-study area. If toilets are not available or cannot be flushed due to water scarcity, people often relieve themselves into plastic bags which are simply tossed out of the window – a great environmental and human health risk (UN Water 2007).[10] Other examples from the San Salvador case-study area include flood defence walls, landfills and land expansions out into rivers, which can increase flood risk further downstream.

Coping strategies that might be effective in the short term but not in the long term include borrowing from money-lenders at high interest rates; selling off assets cheaply during the post-disaster period; spending money on temporary arrangements (e.g. short-lived water barriers and channels); felling trees to use as free firewood; or covering slopes with plastic sheets that not only pollute the environment, but may blow into rivers and block them up.

Some coping strategies may be ineffective in both the short and long term, such as passive behaviour (full reliance on hierarchical structures or divine forces, leading to fatalism); and dysfunctional arrangements like using corrugated iron as retaining walls, or roofing houses with loose corrugated iron weighed down by heavy objects that endanger neighbours during windstorms. Other examples might be traditional beliefs or social relations that are manifested in the way hazards and related risk-reducing measures are viewed (SAARC 2008), as shown by these words from an informal settler in Zambia:

> 'The frequent heavy rainfalls that come year after year, and the heat, including the sudden shifts between the two weather conditions are clear signs of a curse. Women must stop wearing trousers, playing football, boxing and going to taverns. They should respect their husbands.'
>
> (Simatele 2010:15)

At the same time, there are numerous examples of coping strategies that, together with other measures, may prove effective in both the short *and* the long term. These include collaborating with neighbours and local committees (e.g. for mutual help or early warning); growing (suitable) plants and fighting deforestation to reduce heat, flood and landslide risk; accumulating assets for use as collateral or to sell in post-disaster times without making a loss; reducing unnecessary expenses; accessing safe and convenient savings arrangements or loans on favourable conditions; implementing physical measures that are incremental and/or flexible (e.g. using detachable roofs as firebreaks, or living in floating houses which rise with the water level); improving waste and wastewater management; greater engagement in decision-making for adaptation planning; and investing in and improving access to formal education.

However, the effectiveness of local coping strategies is threatened by an increase in the rate and magnitude of existing environmental hazards induced by climate change. City dwellers are faced with a new starting point from which they must cope. In the Rio case study, people reported that heavy rains are increasingly occurring outside the normal rainy seasons, making flood and landslide events harder to predict and reducing the time available for preparations and recovery. This means an increased need for coping with more frequent and severe hazards that consume the resources available for subsequent coping or adaptation needs (Adger 1996; Risbey et al. 1999; IPCC 2012a). According to a resident of Caye Caulker, Belize, who is the owner of a hotel where at-risk neighbours increasingly seek refuge during hurricanes:

> 'The people affect us more; because they are not prepared, they can do more damage than the hurricane.'
>
> (Esdahl 2011:15)[11]

This means that with climate change, there will be an increased need for flexible coping mechanisms that do not rely solely on, nor deplete the resources of, other members of the community.

Moreover, climate change could exacerbate the trend towards individualistic measures in urban communities, which can further reduce adaptive capacities at household and community levels. Better-off community members may find themselves challenged and, consequently, opt out of solidarity- and community-based mechanisms. This is because communitarian strategies, which are based on solidarity and reciprocity, work best (a) where there is not too great a disparity in residents' income levels; (b) in settlements where people have family members living close by; (c) where family members or other dependents are not simultaneously affected by disaster impacts; and (d) where disasters happen repeatedly, but not too frequently, and have mostly short-term impacts (Morduch 1999). In urban areas, however, such conditions seldom apply, and are likely to become even less common in a context of climate change (with increased frequency and intensity of disasters, and rising numbers of related migrants).

The effectiveness of citizens' coping strategies can also be adversely affected by the fact that climate change can make traditional or conventional coping strategies obsolete and no longer viable, and increasingly outpace the ability of local coping strategies to adapt to changing conditions through a process of testing and changing (Shaw et al. 2008). A telling example of how such traditional knowledge can become obsolete comes from a Mozambican community which had always been able to predict floods based on ants leaving their underground nests when water is rising. In 2000 unusual cyclone activity resulted in 700 human fatalities (Hamza et al. 2012). The floods came so rapidly that there was no time for ants to react.

From coping strategies to coping systems

Analysing the effectiveness of single coping strategies is important, but the results cannot be taken as an indicator of individual or household adaptive capacity, or the importance of the strategy for enhancing resilience and transformation.

What can be a short-term measure for one person or household can be an effective solution for another, depending on the particular context and conditions, and the set and combination of strategies used. For instance, increased income diversification might mean more working hours and exhaustion for a woman who is already overloaded with other tasks, whereas for another woman, it could translate into more independence, money, pension, insurance and new social networks. Similarly, selling or renting out rooms may help to maintain the status quo; or leave households worse off, if they receive less than they invested or they end up having to move household members to areas with higher risk. However, it may also generate the resources needed for more sustainable changes, like getting a better or safer house, or allowing investment in health,

TABLE 4.3 Framework for analysing coping and adaptive practices: strategies and systems[a]

Thematic focus	Objective	Pattern of social behaviour				Hazard focus		Planned/ ad hoc		Intention (to reduce risk)		Other aspects	Effectiveness	Total No.
		Individual	Communitarian	Hierarchical	Fatalist	Hazard-specific	Multi-hazard	Planned: pre-disaster	Ad hoc: post-disaster	Deliberate	Unintentional			
	*Response preparedness in flood/landslide-prone area**											Related information transfer, financial implication, institutional support and/or unused capacities***	Short-term (ST) and long-term (LT) impact****	
Physical	Storing objects to block wastewater pipes to avoid flooding, backflow and related contamination	x				x		x		x			*Likely to be effective in ST and LT*	
	Having 'extra house' to stay, in case of emergency	x					x	x		x	x	*May prove expensive*	*Likely to be effective in ST and LT*	2
Environmental	Predicting adverse weather based on observations of nature/natural phenomena for early warning (cloud colour and formation, water-level of rivers, animal behaviour)	x	x					x		x		Transfer of traditional knowledge from generation to generation, also through stories and proverbs	*Can be effective in ST and LT if combined with 'modern' knowledge*	
	Cutting down trees to use as firewood to reduce gas expenses in post-disaster period (also recovery phase)	x	x				x		x	x		Successful in reducing costs short term	*Effective in ST, strongly increases risk in LT, should be discouraged*	2

	Coping measure*	Classification (×)	Total no.**	Information*/**	Likely to be effective***	
Socio-cultural	Using community-based information structures for early warning (e.g. community members going door-to-door with information and warnings)	× × ×		Information obtained from TV, radio and church (priest)	Likely to be effective in ST and LT	1
Economic	Family members staying at home during disaster impact/emergencies to secure economic assets	× × ×			Could be effective in preventing ST economic loss, but could also be deadly	1
Political/institutional	Collaborating with organizations/institutions to prepare for possible evacuation	× × ×		Door-to-door information by volunteers trained by local organization	Likely to be effective in ST and LT. But inst. capacity may be limited	1
Total no.	7	5 3 1 0 1 5 5 2 7	1		$\approx$6 S $\approx$5 LT	

a The differentiation between the aspects proposed for systematically analysing coping measures is not always clear-cut and there are certainly overlaps.

* Italic text shows the information to be filled in by the user. For each objective/type of risk-reducing activity (i.e. hazard reduction and avoidance, vulnerability reduction, response preparedness and recovery preparedness) a separate table should be established. The numbers can then be compared to visualize the distribution of measures taken across the four activities (e.g. whether the distribution is relatively even, or there is disproportionate focus on one type of measure, thematic focus, pattern of social behaviour, etc.).

** For examples of unused capacities see Tables 4.1 and 4.2 (under preparedness for response). For an analysis of the possible financial implications of coping strategies see Wamsler 2007a.

*** Effectiveness relates here to single coping strategies and their success in preventing deaths and injuries, as well as losses and damages to property, environment and livelihoods. The effectiveness of the coping system must be assessed on the basis of its flexibility and inclusiveness.

education and business opportunities (e.g. Jabeen et al. 2010; Simatele 2010).[12] Furthermore, while the effectiveness of a single coping strategy might be low, the same strategy might prove vital in complementing other strategies to create a sustainable coping system.

This study has identified two attributes that are crucial in a context of climate change and uncertainty and which determine the sustainability of coping systems: *flexibility* and *inclusiveness*. Flexibility relates to the number of measures that address each risk factor and their diversity with regard to their thematic and hazard-oriented foci and underlying patterns of social behaviour (Table 4.3). Simply put, the more redundant and diverse the back-up measures that a system provides for addressing a specific risk factor, the more flexible that system is. Inclusiveness relates to the use of not just some but all of the four potential risk reduction and adaptation measures to ensure that all types of risk factors are addressed. Flexible and inclusive systems translate into the ability to change in response to altered circumstances and to carry on functioning even when individual parts fail. Take, for example, a coping system in which people individually deploy just one physical measure to address location-specific vulnerabilities. This does not provide any back-up system and is thus more rigid than a system which combines various physical, environmental, socio-cultural, economic and political/institutional measures to address vulnerabilities, through individual and joint efforts. Nor is a system particularly inclusive if only physical vulnerability reduction is used, while hazard reduction and avoidance, preparedness for response and preparedness for recovery are not considered.

The idea of considering coping strategies in interrelated sets, as well as dealing with the potential conflicts between 'strategies for survival' versus 'strategies for success', has been taken up by Ziervogel et al. (2006), albeit in a rural context. They found that coping systems, or 'strategy sets', often include strategies not directly aimed at reducing climate-related risk, an outcome that is supported by this study. Reduced vulnerability to climate variability was shown to be supported by coping systems that reduce the negative impacts of a *range* of stresses, including climate, market variability, social and cultural change. Furthermore, by calling for adaptation policies that are relevant 'firstly to guarantee individuals' and communities' survival and then to help them to succeed' (Ziervogel et al. 2006:302), they pinpoint how the latter cannot take place without the former.

Dismissing people's local adaptation as 'merely coping', in the sense of simply surviving without engendering any long-term improvements, can thus have severe consequences. People's practices are constantly shaped and reshaped by governmental and non-governmental policies and actions – which implies that city authorities can both help and hinder adaptive processes on the ground (see Adger et al. 2005; Moser et al. 2010; Pelling 2010; Wamsler 2014).

Many present-day adaptation interventions reinforce existing inequalities and inequities, and do little to alleviate underlying vulnerabilities (Adger et al. 2003, 2005). Even worse, institutional assistance can, in fact, not only *reinforce* existing inequalities, but also *create* barriers to sustainable coping, given that sustainable coping requires flexible and inclusive systems. Our study found several examples of such barriers: programmes which impose risk reduction and adaptation measures that cannot be locally maintained (e.g. projects where easily maintained local retaining walls were replaced with ones built using complicated modern techniques); programmes that deprive people of their livelihoods without providing alternatives; the construction of physical risk reduction measures that offer a false sense of security; or the provision of social housing that homeowners cannot use as a financial guarantee when applying for credits to improve further disaster resilience (see Wamsler 2007a, 2014). Another example is resettling people from risk areas far away from their schools, income sources and social networks, making them renters rather than homeowners, or exposing them to new and unknown hazards – all factors that can increase social vulnerability and risk (Wamsler 2014).

Our findings suggest that any adaptation approach needs to be based on risk assessment methods that involve consultation with the people actually at risk and are further based on the criteria of equity, flexibility and inclusiveness. They draw attention to the need for measures that are fundamental, addressing societal inequities and developmental shortcomings, rather than isolated, hazard-specific actions. For example, one factor identified as fostering both flexibility and inclusiveness on the part of coping systems is people's level of formal education. Formal education, at all levels, increases people's flexibility as regards finding appropriate and forward-looking solutions to climate-induced problems as they arise, and preparing for anticipated risks (Lutz 2010; Tyler and Moench 2012; Wamsler et al. 2012; Striessnig et al. 2013). This includes improved access to the formal job market (and related workers' benefits) which was identified as critical for urban dwellers' adaptive capacity.[13] Educational level can also be an important determinant of adaptive capacity at the city level. In cities, adaptive capacity is generally influenced by factors like infrastructure, economic resources, technology, institutions and governance structures, equity, information and skills (see Smit et al. 2001). Formal education is related to most of these, as it can positively influence knowledge production and economic growth, and is also a necessary condition for the development and persistence of democratic institutions (Lutz 2010). This comes in addition to education and capacity building focused directly on matters related to climate change adaptation and the mainstreaming of such knowledge in formal education systems.

Conclusions: from coping to sustainable urban transformation

The way that marginal at-risk settlements are viewed influences the types of solutions proposed for them. City authorities and aid organizations may choose to focus on how appalling conditions are, and therefore look for ways of clearing or replacing such 'eyesores'. Alternatively, they can recognize and tap into the wealth of knowledge, experience and capacities that people living in such areas possess and, within that perspective, their need for more disaster-resilient housing, water and sanitation. This second view opens the way to a different path: one that can lead to sustainable transformation, not least by changing the power relations that dictate the management of risk.

This chapter has presented an overview and systematization of the scarce and fragmented knowledge regarding urban residents' coping strategies, together with critical insights into the strengths and weaknesses of these strategies. This analysis shows the richness and diversity of local adaptive capacities, as well as the similarities in problems faced by urban residents across the developing world and their ways of tackling them.

We conclude that city dwellers' ways of coping with climate variability and extremes should not automatically be dismissed as maladaptive. Whether urban communities manage to achieve resilience and move on to sustainable transformation hinges not on the effectiveness of single coping strategies, but on the flexibility and inclusiveness of individual, household and community coping systems – the combined set of strategies used – and in line with this, increased local participation in the governance of urban risk.

To support coping systems for more sustainable adaptation and transformation, the first step is their assessment. For this study, we have elaborated an analytical framework (presented in 'Coping and adaptive capacity – an analytical framework' and Table 4.3) that can be used by city authorities and aid organizations to bring to light the system aspects of coping, inclusiveness, flexibility and equity, which they might otherwise not recognize. If put into practice, that framework can help such bodies take advantage of local capacities, so that they can provide assistance in line with the various perspectives and efforts of urban residents – assistance that ensures that measures are context-specific, and get effectively implemented and maintained. It also ensures that other adaptive capacities not readily apparent in people's coping strategies and associated coping systems are identified, as well as any barriers to using those capacities. The framework can further assist to extract the elements of principles that can be transferred from one location to another, ultimately enabling more flexible and inclusive structures for risk reduction and adaptation.

To act on these findings and transform 'development as usual' into something more sustainable, city authorities and aid organizations need to support urban dwellers in negotiating their needs and rights, so that the coping systems they use become more flexible, more inclusive and more viable in today's society. Specific measures may include improving and accelerating communities' inherent learning mechanisms, shared learning dialogues, raising local educational levels, improving access to the formal job market and providing more end-of-pipe solutions, like encouraging or upscaling existing strategies, and offering new or alternative strategies where needed.[14] The ultimate aim is a better-distributed, flexible and inclusive urban risk-governance system in which people at risk can take an active stake. Greater diffusion or distribution of power to include the local people themselves can trigger more effective learning in a context of rapid change, and provide a better platform for 'experimenting' where conditions are uncertain and situations are in a constant state of flux. This can allow 'home-grown' approaches and methods to evolve, as well as improving the understanding of local causes of harm, which can then be addressed through participatory, community-based efforts formulated within the larger policy context.

Transformation could thus involve a set of incremental improvements that are able, in combination with (more) transformative measures at community and city levels, to alter current coping systems from within. That said, however, the idea of transformation should not become a new pretext for external interference. Ultimately, this is not a debate between inherent local and external institutional systems as such; it is a question of finding the most appropriate approach for each situation.

Notes

1 'Sustainable urban development' is here conceived of as the creation of liveable, inclusive, ecologically healthy, resource-efficient, prosperous and attractive cities (see McCormick et al. 2012).
2 This is despite the lack of global data on urban disasters, because of low emphasis on the urban in development and disaster risk research and policy (Pelling 2007).
3 These studies were identified via databases such as Scopus and Web of Knowledge, in which the following search terms were combined: 'urban', 'cities', 'climate change', 'adaptation', 'disaster risk reduction', 'local', 'community-based', 'community-driven', 'coping', 'grassroots', 'traditional'. Cross-country studies analysed were Douglas et al. 2008; SAARC 2008; Shaw et al. 2008; Pelling 2011; Singh 2011; Béné et al. 2012; Hamza et al. 2012; Soltesova et al. 2012. Single-country studies were Alam and Rabbani 2007; Khan 2008; Shaw et al. 2008b; Ayers and Forsyth 2009; Jabeen et al. 2010; Ahammad 2011; Audefroy 2011; Banks et al. 2011; Carcellar et al. 2011; Esdahl 2011; Johnson 2011; Ramachandraiah 2011; Thompson 2011; Simatele 2012. Cases analysed include studies from Bangladesh, Belize, Dominican Republic, Ghana, Guyana, Haiti, India, Kenya, Mozambique, Nepal, Nigeria, Philippines, Uganda, Vietnam and Zambia.
4 The projects were funded by Resilient Regions (www.resilientregions.org/en/) and the European Research Council, respectively.
5 Root causes can here be defined as an interrelated set of structural factors and processes within a society, which often have arisen in another time or place and are typically so entrenched in today's society that they become 'invisible' and thus hard to detect (Wamsler 2014).
6 Only the three main dimensions of analysis are described here. For further aspects see Table 4.3.
7 The term refers mainly to the shape and the structural or constructed aspects of a cityscape. Physical changes include engineering or constructed measures as well as other changes to the built environment, often referred to as 'hard measures' (as opposed to 'soft measures').
8 An example of the latter from the Dominican Republic can be found at: www.inteligenciascolectivas.org/vivienda-elevada.
9 Economic diversification means that people engage in many different income-earning activities. Renting out rooms, owning a home-based business, and working at different service jobs are common income sources that the urban poor often 'run'

in parallel, not only in the case-study areas (Jabeen et al. 2010). Doing this allows them to recover more quickly after hazard impacts.

10 In the slums of Nairobi, Kenya, 'flying toilets' are also used by girls and women as a strategy to avoid the risk of sexual violence when seeking a public toilet or another place outside their own home (Amnesty International 2010).

11 Explanation: disaster victims often overstay their welcome. For the hotel owner, this means increased workload, stolen goods and a feeling of responsibility that prevents her from evacuating from the island herself.

12 'One householder reported that she took a loan to improve part of her house and was able to accommodate a small shop where her previously unemployed husband started to work. She also got increased rent from the better rooms, and within a year had managed to improve the rest of the house with the extra earnings as well as being able to send the eldest child to college' (Jabeen et al. 2010:428).

13 Many urban dwellers are pushed into informal employment, which can be a structural cause or driving force of vulnerability.

14 Note that discouraging a specific (presumably short-term) solution without considering the entire coping system might result in reduced adaptive capacities.

References

Adger, N. (1996). *Approaches to vulnerability to climate change* (CSERGE Working Paper GEC 96-05). Norwich: Centre for Social and Economic Research on the Global Environment, University of East Anglia; London: University College London.

Adger, N., Arnell, N. and Tompkins, E. (2005). 'Successful adaptation to climate change across scales'. *Global Environmental Change*, 15, 77–86.

Adger, W.N., Huq, S., Brown, K., Conway, D. and Hulme, M. (2003). 'Adaptation to climate change in the developing world'. *Progress in Development Studies*, 3(3), 179–195.

Ahammad, R. (2011). 'Constraints of pro-poor climate change adaptation in Chittagong city'. *Environment and Urbanization*, 23(2), 503–515.

Alam, M. and Rabbani, M. (2007). 'Vulnerabilities and responses to climate change for Dhaka'. *Environment and Urbanization*, 19(1), 81–97.

Amnesty International (2010). *Risking rape to reach a toilet: women's experiences in the slums of Nairobi, Kenya*. At: http://www.amnesty.org/en/library/info/AFR32/006/2010. Accessed 4 November 2012.

Audefroy, J. (2011). 'Haiti: post-earthquake lessons learned from traditional construction'. *Environment and Urbanization*, 23(2), 447–462.

Ayers, J. and Forsyth, T. (2009). 'Community based adaptation to climate change'. *Environment: Science and Policy for Sustainable Development*, 51(4), 22–31.

Barrett, C. and McPeak, J. (2005) 'Poverty traps and safety nets', in A. de Janvry and R. Kanbur (eds), *Poverty, Inequality and Development: Essays in Honor of Erik Thorbecke*. Amsterdam: Kluwer.

Ben Cheikh, H. and Bouchair, A. (2008). 'Experimental studies of a passive cooling roof in hot arid areas'. *Revue des Energies Renouvelables*, 11(4), 515–522.

Béné, C., Godfrey Wood, R., Newsham, A. and Davies, M. (2012). *Resilience: New utopia or new tyranny? Reflection about the potentials and limits of the concept of resilience in relation to vulnerability reduction programmes*. IDS Working Paper Vol. 2012 No. 405, CSP Working Paper No. 006. London: Institute of Development Studies and Centre for Social Protection.

Carcellar, N., Co, J. and Hipolito, Z. (2011). 'Addressing disaster risk reduction through community-rooted interventions in the Philippines: experience of the Homeless People's Federation of the Philippines'. *Environment and Urbanization*, 23(2), 365–381.

Carmin, J., Nadkarni, N. and Rhie, C. (2012). *Progress and challenges in urban climate adaptation planning: Results of a global survey*. Cambridge, MA: MIT.

Cutter, S., Barnes, L., Berry, M., Burton, C., Evans, E., Tate, E. and Webb, J. (2008). 'A place-based model for understanding community resilience to natural disasters'. *Global Environmental Change*, 18(4), 598–606.

Dodman, D. and Mitlin, D. (2013). 'Challenges for community-based adaptation: discovering the potential for transformation'. *Journal of International Development*, 25 (5), 640–659.

Douglas, I., Alam, K., Maghenda, M.A., McDonnell, Y., McLean, L. and Campbell, J. (2008). 'Unjust waters: climate change, flooding and the urban poor in Africa'. *Environment and Urbanization*, 20(1), 187–205.

Easterling, W.E., Hurd, B. and Smith, J.B. (2004). *Coping with global climate change: The role of adaptation in the United States*. Washington, DC: Pew Center on Global Climate Change.

Esdahl, S. (2011). *Supporting societies' adaptive capacities to climate change: Analysis and comparison of local and institutional capacities on Caye Caulker, Belize* [Master's thesis]. Lund University, Sweden.

Gallopín, G. (2006). 'Linkages between vulnerability, resilience, and adaptive capacity'. *Global Environmental Change*, 16, 293–303.

Gensch, R. and Sacher, N. (2012). *Soak pits*. Sustainable Sanitation and Water Management. At: www.sswm.info/category/implementation-tools/wastewater-treatment/hardware/greywater/soak-pit. Accessed 3 November 2012.

Hamza, M., Smith, D. and Vivekananda, J. (2012). *Difficult environments: Bridging concepts and practice for low carbon climate resilient development*. Brighton: IDS Learning Hub.

Inteligencias Colectivas (2011a). *Muros vegetales de contención* [*Green retaining walls*]. Inteligencias Colectivas, 9 March. At: www.inteligenciascolectivas.org/muros-vegetales-de-contencion. Accessed 4 October 2012.

Inteligencias Colectivas (2011b). *Desagues en voladizo/Duchas urbanas* [*Projecting wastepipes/Urban showers*]. Inteligencias Colectivas, 21 January. At: www.inteligenciascolectivas.org/desagues-en-voladizoduchas-urbanas. Accessed 4 October 2012.

IPCC (Intergovernmental Panel on Climate Change) (2007). *Climate change 2007: Synthesis report*. Contribution of Working Groups I, II and III to the Fourth Assessment Report of the Intergovernmental Panel on Climate Change. Geneva: IPCC.

IPCC (Intergovernmental Panel on Climate Change) (2012a). *Managing the risks of extreme events and disasters to advance climate change adaptation (SREX)*. A Special Report of Working Groups I and II of the Intergovernmental Panel on Climate Change [C. Field, V. Barros, T. Stocker, D. Qin, D. Dokken, K. Ebi, M. Mastrandrea et al. (eds)]. Cambridge: Cambridge University Press.

IPCC (Intergovernmental Panel on Climate Change) (2012b). 'Glossary of terms', in *Managing the risks of extreme events and disasters to advance climate change adaptation (SREX)*. A Special Report of Working Groups I and II of the Intergovernmental Panel on Climate Change [ref. *supra*]. Cambridge: Cambridge University Press, 555–564.

Jabeen, H., Johnson, C. and Allen, A. (2010). 'Built-in resilience: learning from grassroots coping strategies for climate variability'. *Environment and Urbanization*, 22, 415–431.

Johnson, C. (2011). 'Kernels of change: civil society challenges to state-led strategies for recovery and risk reduction in Turkey'. *Environment and Urbanization*, 23(2), 415–430.

Khan, A. (2008). 'Earthquake safe traditional house construction practices in Kashmir: state of Jammu & Kashmir, Northern India', in R. Shaw, N. Uy and J. Baumwoll (eds), *Good practices and lessons learned from experiences in the Asia-Pacific Region*. Bangkok: UNISDR.

Lutz, W. (2008). *Forecasting societies' adaptive capacities to climate change (FutureSoc). Annex I – description of work. Funded Research Proposal, European Research Council, Advanced Investigator Grant.* Unpublished document. Laxenburg: International Institute for Applied Systems Analysis (IIASA).

Lutz, W. (2010). 'Improving education as key to enhancing adaptive capacity in developing countries', presented at the International Workshop on 'The Social Dimension of Adaptation to Climate Change', organized by the International Center for Climate Governance (ICCG), 18–19 February, Venice.

McCormick, K., Neij, L., Anderberg, S. and Coenen, L. (2012). 'Advancing sustainable urban transformation', *Cleaner Production*, 50, 1–11.

Morduch, J. (1999). 'Between the state and the market: can informal insurance patch the safety net?' *World Bank Research Observer*, 14(2), 187–207.

Moser, C., Norton, A., Stein, A. and Georgieva, S. (2010). *Pro-poor adaptation to climate change in urban centres: Case studies of vulnerability and resilience in Kenya and Nicaragua.* Social Development Department, Report No. 54947-GLB. Washington DC: The World Bank.

O'Brien, K. and Leichenko, R. (2008). *Environmental change and globalization: Double exposures.* Oxford: Oxford University Press.

O'Brien, K., Eriksen, S., Nygaard, L.P. and Schjolden, A. (2007). 'Why different interpretations of vulnerability matter in climate change discourses'. *Climate Policy*, 7(1), 73–88.

Pelling, M. (2007). 'Urbanization and disaster risk', panel contribution to Population–Environment Research Network Cyberseminar on Population and Natural Hazards (November 2007).

Pelling, M. (2010). *Adaptation to climate change: From resilience to transformation.* London: Routledge.

Pelling, M. (2011). 'Urban governance and disaster risk reduction in the Caribbean: the experiences of Oxfam GB'. *Environment and Urbanization*, 23(2), 383–400.

Ramachandraiah, C. (2011). 'Coping with urban flooding: a study of the 2009 Kurnool floods, India'. *Environment and Urbanization*, 23(2), 431–446.

Risbey, J., Kandlikar, M., Dowlatabadi, H. and Graetz, D. (1999). 'Scale, context, and decision making in agricultural adaptation to climate variability and change'. *Mitigation and Adaptation Strategies for Global Change*, 4(2), 137–165.

SAARC (2008). *Indigenous knowledge for disaster risk reduction in South Asia.* New Delhi: SAARC Disaster Management Centre.

Satterthwaite, D., Huq, S., Pelling, M., Reid, H. and Romero Lankao, P. (2007). *Adapting to climate change in urban areas: The possibilities and constraints in low- and middle-income nations.* Human Settlements Discussion Paper Series: Climate Change and Cities (No. 1). London: IIED.

Shaw, R., Takeuchi, Y., Uy, N. and Sharma, A. (2008). *Policy note: Indigenous knowledge – disaster risk reduction.* Kyoto: EU, UNISDR, Kyoto University, Seeds.

Simatele, D. (2010). *Climate change adaptation in Lusaka, Zambia: A case study of Kalingalinga and Linda Compounds.* Global Urban Research Centre Working Paper #6. Manchester: GURC.

Singh, D. (2011). 'The wave that eats people – the value of indigenous knowledge for disaster risk reduction'. *UNISDR News Archive*, 9 August.

Smit, B. and Wandel, J. (2006). 'Adaptation, adaptive capacity and vulnerability'. *Global Environmental Change*, 16, 282–292.

Smit, B., Pilifosova, O., Burton, I., Challenger, B., Huq, S., Klein, R. and Yohe, G. (2001). 'Adaptation to climate change in the context of sustainable development and equity', in J. McCarthy, O. Canziana, N. Leary, D. Dokken and K. White (eds), *Climate change 2001: Impacts, adaptation, and vulnerability*, 877–912. New York: Cambridge University Press.

Soltesova, K., Brown, A., Dayal, A. and Dodman, D. (2012). 'Community participation in urban adaptation to climate change: potential and limits for CBA approaches', in J. Ayers, S. Huq, H. Reid, A. Rahman and L. Schipper (eds), *Community-based adaptation: Scaling it up*. London: Earthscan.

Steffen, W., Sanderson, A., Tyson, P., Jäger, J., Matson, P., Moore, B., Oldfield, F., et al. (2004). *Global change and the earth system: A planet under pressure*. New York: Springer.

Striessnig, E., Lutz, W. and Patt, A. (2013). 'Effects of educational attainment on climate risk vulnerability'. *Ecology and Society*, 18(1), 16.

Thompson, M. (2011). 'The quest for "clumsy solutions" in Nepal's mountains'. *Options*, Winter 2011/12, 12–13, special issue on 'Human Wellbeing and Sustainable Development'.

Thompson, M., Ellis, R. and Wildavsky, A. (1990). *Cultural theory*. Boulder, CO: Westview Press.

Tudehope, M. (2011). '"Bat people" and "floating houses": hope in the lowliest of Manila's slums'. *The Global Urbanist – Communities*, 29 March.

Twigg, J. (2004). *Disaster risk reduction: Mitigation and preparedness in development and emergency programming*, Good Practice Review no. 9. London, UK: ODI: HPN.

Tyler, S. and Moench, M. (2012). 'A framework for urban climate resilience'. *Climate and Development*, 4(4), 311–326.

UN Water (2007). *World Water Day 2007: Coping with water scarcity – every drop counts* (brochure). Rome: UN Water.

UNISDR (United Nations Office for Disaster Risk Reduction) (2009). *Terminology: Disaster risk reduction*. Geneva: United Nations.

UNISDR (United Nations Office for Disaster Risk Reduction) (2012). *2011 – Disasters in numbers*. UNISDR, USAID, CRED. http://www.preventionweb.net/files/24697_2 46922011disasterstats1.pdf

Wamsler, C. (2007a). 'Bridging the gaps: stakeholder-based strategies for risk reduction and financing for the urban poor'. *Environment and Urbanization*, 19(1), 115–142.

Wamsler, C. (2007b). 'Managing urban disaster risk: analysis and adaptation frameworks for integrated settlement development programming for the urban poor' [Doctoral thesis]. Lund University, Sweden.

Wamsler, C. (2014). *Cities, disaster risk and adaptation* (Routledge Series on Critical Introduction to Urbanism and the City). London: Routledge.

Wamsler, C. and Brink, E. (2014). 'People's adaptive capacity: from coping to sustainable transformation'. *Environment & Urbanization*, special issue on 'Towards resilience and transformation for cities' (forthcoming).

Wamsler, C. and Umaña, C. (2003). *El Salvador: Proyecto de reconstrucción con inclusión de la gestión de riesgo* [*Reconstruction programming with integration of disaster risk management*]. Deutsche Gesellschaft für Technische Zusammenarbeit (GTZ). Eschborn: GTZ.

Wamsler, C., Brink, E. and Rantala, O. (2012). 'Climate change, adaptation, and formal education: the role of schooling for increasing societies' adaptive capacities in El Salvador and Brazil: adaptive capacities'. *Ecology and Society*, 17(2), 2, special issue on 'Education and differential vulnerability to natural disasters'.

WCED (World Commission on Environment and Development) (1987). *Our common future: Report of the world commission on environment and development*. Oxford: Oxford University Press.

Wisner, B., Blaikie, P., Cannon, T. and Davis, I. (2004). *At risk: Natural hazards, people's vulnerability and disasters* (2nd ed.). London: Routledge.

Young, O.R. (2010). *Institutional dynamics: Emergent patterns in international environmental governance*. Cambridge, MA: MIT Press.

Ziervogel, G., Bharwani, S. and Downing, T.E. (2006). 'Adapting to climate variability: pumpkins, people and policy'. *Natural Resources Forum* 30(4), 294–305.

5

GENDER MATTERS

Adaptive capacities to climate variability and change in the Lake Victoria Basin

Sara Gabrielsson

Introduction

The central premise of this book rests on the assumption that both vulnerability and the ability to respond to climate change must be viewed as *processes*, shaped by ongoing multiple stressors that interact on different levels, and with varying impacts across localities and groups of people (see Reid and Vogel 2006; O'Brien and Leichenko 2007). This argument builds on the increasing recognition among scholars, practitioners and policy-makers alike, that adaptation cannot be seen merely as a techno-managerial challenge that involves incremental adjustments to technologies, regulations, policies and practices in order to live with change. Fundamental shifts in societal systems are required, in particular deliberate transformations aimed at influencing future change towards more sustainable pathways. This implies the need to reduce emissions and to deal with the social, political and cultural causes of vulnerability, including injustice and inequity (Pelling 2011; O'Brien 2012). But that in turn requires in-depth understanding of how people in different settings identify risk, make decisions and implement actions, all mediated by their values, norms and traditions (Adger et al. 2012). Few such studies have been conducted, even though socio-cultural understanding is 'no less central to adaptation than financing infrastructural development and reducing carbon emissions' (ibid.: 1).

This chapter attempts to fill some of these gaps by exploring how certain social dimensions inherent in rural farmer livelihoods – specifically, norms linked to gender and the moral economy – may obstruct women from pursuing adaptation strategies that can respond to increased climate risks. Drawing on extensive research among smallholder farmers in the Lake Victoria Basin (LVB), the chapter concludes that failure to understand and incorporate gender dimensions into future adaptation policies and projects may lead to dissatisfactory adaptation results. Such policies and projects are likely to waste precious financial resources and time without reducing climate risks, thus hindering much-needed efforts to bring about deliberate transformations for those most vulnerable to climate change.

Contextualizing vulnerability to climate change in the LVB

The complexity of climate change and its impacts across levels requires adaptation responses that are equally diverse and inclusive. This reality calls for in-depth knowledge and understanding of the specific cultural context and locale (Morton 2007). In the case of the LVB of Kenya and Tanzania examined here, this has been made possible by using an integrative and place-based approach to understand climate vulnerability, drawing on qualitative and quantitative methods as well as data gathered during repeated fieldwork periods between 2007 and 2011 from four communities in Kenya and Tanzania (Onjiko, Thurdibuoro, Kisumwa, Kunsugu) along Lake Victoria. The research included a baseline household survey with 200 households randomly selected from the four communities, covering demography, health, livelihood strategies and climate issues. It also involved engagement with elders through 17 life-history interviews, 12 focus groups centred on coping and adaptation strategies during hardship seasons, in addition to four narrative walks and four participatory mapping and seasonal calendar exercises in the communities. Data also come from interviews with 30 widows and other women from various village-savings and loans groups, focusing on adaptive capacities. What follows is a synopsis of these research findings and a discussion on their implications for the future development of adaptation projects and policy.

Climate risks and their induced stress on livelihoods in the LVB

As rain-fed agriculture is the mainstay of livelihoods in the LVB, grasping the local dynamics of rainfall is vital for understanding how climate variability and change may induce stress on farmers' livelihoods and wellbeing (Odada et al. 2006). According to elderly and currently active farmers in the four communities, rainfall has become increasingly unpredictable in the last 10 to 15 years, deviating from the otherwise dependable bi-modal rainfall patterns. This deviation has been confirmed by regional climate analysis (Thornton et al. 2010; Kizza et al. 2009). Farmers explain that increasingly erratic rainfall makes it difficult for them to know when to plant and harvest optimally. Many of them have witnessed their crops rotting in the fields from too much soil water, or seedlings wilting due to lack of soil moisture, with a decline in agricultural production as the direct result (Gabrielsson et al. 2013). An observable consequence of this is the abandonment of crop-surplus storage as a coping mechanism for food security – a reality shared by other smallholder communities across sub-Saharan Africa (SSA) (Toulmin 2009; Rarieya and Fortun 2010). With less produce to sell, household revenues invariably shrink, while reliance on cash to ensure basic livelihood needs, like staple foods, fodder, water and fuel wood, grows (Gabrielsson et al. 2013).

Life-history interviews with 17 elderly farmers from across the four communities also indicate a rise in the spread of climate-related pests, vectors and pathogens, in turn leading to higher incidence of various crop diseases as well as malaria, cholera, dengue fever and typhoid throughout the year, a trend identified in other areas of East Africa as well (Wandiga 2006; Githeko 2009). According to the seasonal calendar exercises conducted for this study, the costs of these recurring incidences of climate-associated diseases are many: higher expenditures for healthcare; increased work burdens for women; loss of anticipated non-farm incomes; and the added costs of hiring agricultural labour when manpower is reduced or lost. Importantly, it is the *convergence* of these incremental climate-induced stressors *in time and space* that has the most critical effects on farmers' livelihoods. Continued illness, mismanaged crops and ensuing food insecurity bring destructive effects to the human– environment system, creating and maintaining a state of 'chronic livelihood stress' (Gabrielsson et al. 2013: 152).

Farmers' resources and strategies to respond to climate risks

Working the land, for both men and women, entails greater risks and unpredictability today than in the past (Eriksen et al. 2005; Smucker and Wisner 2008; Andersson and Gabrielsson 2012). To optimize yields and market prices through timely planting, harvesting and labour inputs, farmers must utilize their existing, albeit already limited, resources more intensively (Andersson and Gabrielsson 2012). Farmers have several resources available. First, their own able-bodiedness (Cleaver 2005), which enables or disables individuals and households to engage in farming and non-farming. Second, the land they can farm, which enables or disables the production of sufficient amounts of food for home consumption and sales. Third, the cash they may earn, which enables or disables individuals and/or households to secure a buffer to ensure that basic livelihood needs can be met. Finally, access to communities of practices (Wenger 1998), which enables or disables the pooling of time and labour as well as the sharing of resources and tools within and between individuals, households and communities.

In the LVB, and elsewhere across East Africa, these resources may, at least in theory, be manifested through four major livelihood strategies: extensification, intensification, diversification and migration (Ellis 2000). In practice however, migration is no longer as attractive as it used to be, as the competition for unskilled work has increased between rural dwellers and the urban poor (Bryceson 2002a; Cleaver 2005; Ellis and Freeman 2005). Moreover, increased urbanization and price inflation in cities has rendered migratory work less profitable, making remittances an unreliable source of income for rural households (Gabrielsson 2012).

Rapid population increases, from 1 million living in the LVB in 1960 to 30 million in 2001 (UNEP 2006), has led to fragmentation of agricultural land, which in turn has meant that previous strategies to relieve food insecurity, whether through temporary migration to farm or graze animals and/or expansion of agricultural production into new areas, have become less viable (Wandiga 2006). In the four communities studied, agricultural expansion is no longer an option for farmers, who now are forced to sustain an average household of seven on farming plots smaller than three acres (Gabrielsson et al. 2013). Another consequence of the lack of fertile land is that these communities, which previously engaged in heavy livestock rearing, are now seeing livestock numbers being reduced significantly, with increasing dependence on food crops as a result (Gabrielsson 2012). A growing rural population and reduction of land holdings per household have necessitated an intensification of agricultural production throughout the region, with shifting cultivation of diversified crops replaced by predominately sedentary mono-cropping (Odada et al. 2006). This has also contributed to the spread of invasive weeds, soil degradation and a further loss of crop productivity (Smucker and Wisner 2008).

This fairly recent agricultural shift has left farming communities in the LVB with a narrowing range of livelihood strategies available. While intensification is still a viable livelihood strategy, in the short term it requires an increased supply of (healthy) labour power, and in the long term, greater agricultural expertise to make management environmentally and economically sustainable (Pretty et al. 2011). In the four case-study communities, both these resources are currently in short supply, due in part to the risks of exposure to many diseases, including HIV/AIDS, and lack of technology transfer and training (Andersson and Gabrielsson 2012). As a result, diversification is likely to continue to play a key role in livelihoods in the region, especially since the yield-gains of new farming technology display signs of levelling off and farming on its own is unable to provide sufficient means of survival (Ellis 2000; Pretty et al. 2011). Diversification includes the portfolio of activities that farming households engage in *outside* farming, such as small businesses or day labour.

As we will see in the next sections, existing power differentials between men and women may act to limit or support access to the resources necessary for pursuing such diversification and/or intensification strategies – in the longer term impeding or facilitating adaptation to climate change, and the possibilities for smallholder livelihoods to pursue deliberate transformations towards a more sustainable future.

The gender dimensions of farmer livelihoods in the LVB

Besides the biophysical and economic processes affecting adaptation to climate variability and change, social norms play a significant role in rural farmers' ability to respond to climate risks. In the LVB, and across farming communities of SSA at large, there are two social dimensions in particular that delineate people's lives and livelihoods. The first is the presence of a gender regime that assigns gender-differentiated rights and responsibilities (Mies 1986; Agarwal 1997). The second is what Hydén (1980) termed 'an economy of affection' whereby loyalty to one's own kin is expected through imposed social obligations. These social dimensions have considerable bearing on how livelihoods in the LVB are performed and enacted on the individual as well as on the collective level. The synergistic effects of these two dimensions also help to explain the divergence in adaptive capacities between men and women, and the subsequent climate vulnerability felt primarily by women, who generally have less adaptive capacities than their male counterparts.

The gender regime

Farming across SSA is centred on the family. Social norms build on and are determined by the everyday *rights* and *responsibilities* of individuals within a household. In the LVB the functional purpose and rationality of the gender regime is to organize household duties and secure family wellbeing. Women and men are assigned different rights and responsibilities within the rural farming household (Gabrielsson 2012). *Gendered rights* are most evident in how property (i.e. land) is inherited. Customary laws in the LVB prohibit women from owning land; women can only apply their labour to the land owned by their husbands or fathers (Lee-Smith 1997). Marriage is also a signifier of this gendered regime, as husbands and families must exchange bride wealth for the reproductive and productive capabilities of the bride (Rocheleau et al. 1996). Another demonstration of gendered rights within smallholder farming households in the LVB is the practice of 'widow inheritance' – a socially sanctioned re-marriage whereby a male relative of the deceased husband assumes guardianship of the deceased's family, including the wife, to ensure that the property stays in the family (Gunga 2009).

Gendered responsibilities are primarily reflected through the differentiated amounts, types and spheres of labour that women and men engage in. Women are predominately bound to reproductive and productive activities within the domestic sphere, such as childcare, cooking, cleaning, washing, fetching water and fire wood, making charcoal, tending the home garden and food crops as well as small livestock like chickens and goats. Men are seen as responsible for everything else: rearing cattle, tending and selling cash crops, digging and clearing land as well as building and maintaining the homestead (Rocheleau et al. 1996; Francis 2000; Bryceson 2002b). Gender differences are also apparent in how men and women keep and use cash, and their mobility and presence in public domains (Lee-Smith 1997; Gabrielsson and Ramasar 2012).

This agrarian division of labour, whereby male farmers primarily engage in cash crop production and females are responsible for subsistence production, can be traced to the introduction of Christianity in Africa during the colonial and post-colonial era, when the generic ideal of the nuclear family was pioneered

(Mies 1986). This ideal encouraged senior males to become breadwinners and heads of households, while women were idealized as being responsible for taking care of the home and children (ibid.). The division of labour worked because all family members had their assigned duties, which in combination covered the reproductive and consumption needs of the entire family (Tsuruta 2008).

When structural adjustment programs (SAPs) were implemented across SSA in the 1980s and 1990s in an effort to strengthen the continent's failing economies through liberalization, privatization and fiscal stabilization measures, the conditions of this gender division of labour changed (Mohan et al. 2000). Changes began when the SAPs encouraged governments to cut fertilizer subsidies, which led farmers to shift from cash crop development back to crops with quick or regular year-round returns (Bryceson 2002a). With the economic returns from cash cropping declining significantly, many men and children had to seek other income-earning opportunities, to prevent impoverishment (Francis 1998). In the LVB, elderly farmers testify that this shift had devastating impacts on families, as most men were forced to abandon their cotton farms and migrate to urban areas to seek employment. Moreover, SAP conditions prompted bankrupt African governments to remove subsidies on school fees and user fees at health centres, which meant that the cost of welfare services rose radically, to be paid by the patients (Francis 1998; Ellis 2000; Bryceson 2002a). These prices have remained high throughout the LVB, consuming a substantial portion of smallholders' household budgets (Gabrielsson et al. 2013).

Overall, these economic policies have led to significant changes in the organization of labour, and to reliance on cash in rural areas: agricultural work has become increasingly replaced by non-agricultural work, unpaid work has become paid, and activities formerly performed by the household are now usually carried out by an individual (Francis, 2000; Bryceson 2002b). Part of the reason lies in the significant inflation in prices of basic goods like cooking oil, gasoline and sugar, and the price volatility of staple food crops caused by the instability of the global market (Minot 2010). In addition, the widespread impacts of the HIV and AIDS pandemic changes not only the continent's social structures but also its food production systems (Hydén 2013). The devastation of the pandemic is particularly evident in the LVB, where HIV prevalence on the Kenyan side is estimated to be as high as 15 percent of the population and even higher among widowed and divorced women, with many families left traumatized and in financial crisis, in addition to the loss of labour (Gabrielsson and Ramasar 2012).

For rural women in the LVB this stage of socio-economic development is uniquely challenging: they have sole responsibility for feeding their families, but are restricted from accessing and controlling the livelihood assets needed to increase their food production and income diversification possibilities, such as land, money, credits, farming tools and education (Gabrielsson and Ramasar 2012). According to focus groups discussions and individual interviews with married and widowed women, this shift towards more monetary-reliant livelihoods has generally meant that female farmers today are financially dependent on their husbands/fathers/brothers to secure cash to pay for healthcare, basic household needs and school fees. Because of this inequality in financial power, the women interviewed for this study say they have limited opportunities to plan for the future, whether in terms of investment in their children's education, in agricultural production or in business ventures. They also claim that, compared to the past when domestic work could be shared by men and women, the shift towards a more cash-based economy has increased their labour burdens significantly. This leaves them with less time (if any) to rest their bodies, nurture relationships with their children, friends and relatives, test out new agricultural crops and techniques or start up small businesses. Further, they hold, their male counterparts today have not only more time but also the financial means to invest in diversifying activities to increase livelihood incomes as well as intensify agricultural production and output. However, according to many of the interviewed, men and women alike, few male farmers actually engage in such activities. Instead they spend much of their time seeking paid daily work in and around local market places, generally without success, while drinking the local alcoholic beverages frequently and cheaply available there. For many households this new livelihood situation has created instability within the family, with frequent quarrels and domestic violence as a result. A majority of the women interviewed argued that the disparity in financial power between men and women, and the unequal work burdens put on women, are key contributors to this instability, which in the longer term also affects the families' possibilities to adapt to increased climate vulnerabilities.

Many of these families have managed to survive because they have been able to lean on the economy of affection (see below), as a way of coping in times of extreme hardship. However, with the new livelihood context characterized by 'chronic livelihood stress', this strategy is becoming increasingly unreliable, leaving women in particular with few or no alternatives for adapting to the incremental climate-induced stressors affecting their lives.

The economy of affection

When farming households across rural SSA encounter hardships, whether caused by disease, deaths, droughts or flooding, people manage to survive and some even thrive by being able to draw on support from their nearest kin or community. In practice this means that whenever people are in need of assistance, financial or otherwise, 'structurally defined groups connected by blood, kin, community or other affinities, such as religion' (Hydén 1983: 8) will support one another through reciprocal exchange via informal agreements based on mutual accountability and self-enforcement (Tsuruta 2008). These *informal institutions*, legitimated by close emotional ties, enable people to meet both basic survival needs, such as food, cash, clothing or childcare (ibid.) as well as maintain social activities and rituals, such as loans to pay for weddings and funerals (Hydén 1983). These personal networks also play a significant role for local development, through informal loan arrangements to develop small-scale businesses, expand farming practices or construct houses. The system may also involve calling on family members and relatives to support schooling for less fortunate members of an extended family, whether by covering school fees or by providing free accommodation (ibid.: 14).

In a society where the state is generally weak, such an economy of affection largely 'works' because for those in need of assistance the transaction costs are low; moreover, free-riding is not a problem, because patrons take pride in providing assistance even if others do not contribute, as this gives the patron power. Also the hazards are low because it is less risky to seek out others informally for problem solution than relying on formal institutions to do so (Hydén 2007). The robustness of these informal institutions (as opposed to formal ones) is thus legitimized by the local (private) realm and driven by the 'trust and sense of mutual obligation that the face-to-face exchange creates' (Hydén 1983: 11).

In the domestic sphere such reciprocal exchanges can be observed when women share and take turns looking after each other's children, give food for emergencies and work on each other's plots, without any monetary transactions taking place. Similarly, loyalty to one's own kin is a significant element in the sustainability of local business ventures (Njogu et al. 2010). In the LVB this can be seen primarily in the kin-based separation of location and/or timing of market places for vegetables, livestock and consumer goods (Gabrielsson 2012). The economy of affection also plays a significant role in the national and local political arena in both Kenya and Tanzania, paving the way for a 'clientelist' form of politics: some political rulers treat the exercise of power as an extension of their private realm, thereby giving precedence to their own kinship networks, rather than the public realm of formal institutions (Hydén 2013). An indication of this in the LVB may be seen in how politicians, predominately males, have majority rule in those areas where their kinship ties originate.

In this socio-political reality, where informal exchange is significant and direct reciprocities are deemed necessary to get things done, *who* you know is often more important than *what* you know. Nor is it unusual for people to value sharing personal wealth more than investing in economic ventures, or that people trust that giving a helping hand today will generate returns tomorrow (Hydén 2013). In such an economy, accumulation of money is therefore not an end in itself, but rather a means to strengthen social ties – and for politicians to acquire more votes.

But in patriarchal societies, common in SSA, where women are deemed subordinate to men and thereby lack access to financial capital, political voice, social networks and mobility, the economy of affection may be a perilous system to navigate. While the exchanges made within the economy of affection are reciprocal, they are certainly not power-neutral. The power relation is determined by the person who is least dependent on what is being exchanged, thus giving patrons the power to deny others their influence (Hydén 2008). When these patrons are men – and in the LVB they generally are – it tends to makes women unable to negotiate the terms of the exchange. Subsequently, women become reliant on their husbands/sons/brothers/brothers-in-law to negotiate in their place for the assistance they need to uphold the gendered responsibilities that the gender regime has assigned to them. But in a livelihood context where the males are generally reluctant to plan for the future or engage in diversification of incomes or intensification of agricultural production, it may be difficult for women to persuade their men to negotiate on their behalf. Similarly, it may be difficult for women to convince their men of the need to buy new agricultural equipment or a bike to facilitate transport of goods to the market, when the economy of affection can give patrons instant rewards through the strengthening of social ties to those who share their personal wealth rather than investing in long-term economic ventures.

Moreover, as the trend of greater need for cash among rural farming families continues to rise and women's labour burdens become heavier, demands on the economy of affection grow to such an extent that the need outstrips the means – and that may erode the entire system, forcing people to seek other strategies to ensure livelihood security and wellbeing (Miles 2007; Hydén 2013). When people's capacity to pool resources horizontally and share among themselves diminishes, assistance must be sought elsewhere. Increasingly such assistance is sought from vertical exchanges supported by the state, albeit through informal networks, thus advancing another trend in SSA where pooling, or cooperative exchange, serves to deepen political clientelism. The consequence is concentration of both power and wealth in the hands of a few male political leaders (Hoon 2002; Hydén 2013). For women in the LVB, significantly underrepresented in national and local political leadership positions, these recent developments may undermine individual agency and even restrict their choices of and access to the adaptive capacities – loans, farming education, drought resistant seeds or new land areas – necessary for coping with and adapting to increased climate risks in the future. Instead, access to these critical adaptive capacities may be reserved for those, predominately men, who already have personal relationships with the political patrons in power or have established social networks that may influence access to such political leaders.

The narrowing of the economy of affection is thus likely to have negative consequences for men and women alike. But this will apply more to some than others, as lack of adaptive capacities will leave them with limited options for engaging in any types of activities beyond instrumental action, i.e. coping with impacts rather than preventing them from taking place (Gabrielsson and Ramasar 2012). From an adaptation perspective, this means that most responses to the increased risks of climate uncertainty become based primarily on reactive and autonomous coping mechanisms, like resource diversion and reduced food intake, instead of autonomous and planned adaptation strategies which are more likely to increase overall livelihood security and wellbeing (Andersson and Gabrielsson 2012).

Women across the LVB who today have few resources to reciprocate beyond their labour power, especially female-headed households and/or those with many dependents, are finding themselves increasingly excluded from the reciprocal system, and must fend for themselves, with dire consequences. Widows are among those to suffer most from this exclusion, since they tend to be burdened already with many dependents to support but with weakened widow rights and security (Gabrielsson and Ramasar 2012). With limited options available to them, many women are thus increasingly involving themselves in exchanges that transcend the boundaries of the extended family. But this search for new support is associated with a higher degree of moral hazard, such as seeking incomes from prostitution and risking HIV infection (Fenio 2009). Paradoxically, the economy of affection that in the past was largely beneficial for rural livelihoods has today – because of outside socio-economic policies and global environmental changes, in combination with persistent gender inequality – become one of the underlying causes of why so many rural farmers in the LVB lack the adaptive capacities needed to reduce their vulnerability to climate variability and change.

Addressing the causes of vulnerability by improving women's adaptive capacities

Africa is considered the region where the 'adaptation deficit' (Osbahr 2007), i.e. the lack of explicit integration of livelihood adaptation to climate change and broader development issues, is most evident (Tschakert and Dietrich 2010). For that reason, it is of urgent importance to understand the constraints that the current gender regime and the narrowing of the economy of affection play in impeding people's capacities to pursue adaptation, if climate vulnerability on the continent is to be reduced.

In the LVB, considerable emphasis has been put on finding technological or economic tools and strategies to reduce climate impacts – as by optimizing planting with the use of mobile phones for seasonal forecasting, developing drought and flood-resistant seed varieties, or studying the economic mechanisms linked to carbon storage in soils and trees to mitigate carbon emissions (Gabrielsson 2012). This has often come at the expense of understanding how adaptive capacities may be improved among those who will use such tools and technologies. Certainly, all these activities and measures are important parts of the adaptation portfolio available to rural farmers in the LVB, but none of these strategies can succeed without a deeper understanding of the social context in which these strategies ultimately may be put to use.

This study of the LVB found signs of deliberate transformations taking place. These are indeed embedded in a social context, and they build on principles inherent in the economy of affection. Through collective efforts, widows in a few communities in the LVB have joined forces to adapt to increasing climate variability and change by working to improve their livelihoods and wellbeing. Their informal institutions, while still based on trust and mutual engagement, are also rooted in a collective culture of planning and saving, which has enabled them to pool labour, share risks, land plots and tools, and thus improve both food and income buffers by diversifying farm and non-farm incomes, while experimenting with new crops, business ventures and conservation of natural resources (Andersson and Gabrielsson 2012). Moreover, women in these groups have shown that deliberate transformations are possible if people can attain the power to access resources and decision-making; if they can draw on the power from the mutual support and collective solidarity generated among group members; and recognize the positive changes in individual attitudes, consciousness and confidence developed from their actions and outcomes (Kabeer 1999). Such empowerment has the potential to allow not only widows to adapt to climate variability and change – it may challenge the very structures and social norms that contribute to climate vulnerability or limit adaptive capacity in the first place.

What are the lessons here for the development of future climate-adaptation projects and policies in SSA? The findings discussed here highlight the importance of engaging more with local communities to understand their specific cultural contexts and conditions, to be able to identify avenues for change and agents of change. In theory this means a radical paradigm shift in how we approach and address adaptation on the African continent in the future, where gender empowerment must be a fundamental driving force in the development, selection and funding of specific adaptation projects targeting rural areas. In practice this means improving the adaptive capacities of men but even more so those of women, by focusing on improving the areas of their lives that currently divert attention and resources away from pursuing adaptation strategies that can respond to increased climate risks, as well as directly targeting areas that will encourage the adoption of sustainable agricultural production or diversification activities.

For instance, this could mean projects focused on improving and scaling up access to basic needs such as clean water and sustainable sanitation. Today, fetching water diverts much of women's time away from farming and potential business ventures; and unnecessarily large amounts of household incomes are spent on treating preventable water-related diseases. Projects could also target road construction and maintenance, to facilitate mobility to and from market places, educational facilities and health clinics. For women this is particularly important, because many are highly immobile and must depend on male modes of transport, like motorbikes. Greater mobility through the use of bicycles and better public transport, like buses and minibuses, would also enable women to have the opportunity to build social networks outside their own villages and give them access to financial institutions and educational facilities. Projects could also target education and training for farmers, particularly female farmers, who have rarely been included in farming extension training or educational programmes, even though they comprise half of all the farmers on the continent. Adaptation projects could also focus on narrowing the gender gap in local political leadership positions, by encouraging women to run for political office in their rural communities. Today's Kenyan and Tanzanian laws proclaim that political appointments are to be based on gender equality, but in reality the majority of rural communities lack female representation altogether. Increasing the political voice of women where they live could enable them to influence the future development of their communities and inspire other women to do the same. And lastly, projects could target the development of alternative local financial institutions that could enable individual as well as groups of farmers to save money in a safe way and take up loans with collateral based on non-fiscal securities. Such institutions could then facilitate the access to capital needed to invest in business ventures and agricultural equipment that would diversify farmers' incomes and increase food production. In particular, it could empower women to become financially independent of their husbands/sons/brothers/brothers-in-law, thereby also bolstering their decision-making power within their families.

If we are sincere about reducing climate vulnerability, we will need to increase women's adaptive capacities. To do that, we must commit ourselves to promoting radically different adaptation projects and policies in the future compared to those in the past. This new approach must be based on the actual needs and demands of people on the ground, instead of a supply-driven approach constructed around a foreign-made standard blueprint for *development as usual*, since that not only risks reproducing the conditions of the most vulnerable, but worse, coercing them into adopting strategies that may ultimately lead to maladaptive outcomes (Adger et al. 2012; Bassey 2012).

Conclusions: yes, gender matters

Drawing on research conducted among smallholders living in the Lake Victoria Basin (LVB) area, this chapter has shown that in order to reduce the climate vulnerability currently felt by millions of smallholder farmers across rural sub-Saharan Africa, it is first necessary to deal with the underlying causes of this vulnerability. This will require in-depth knowledge of the specific cultural context and circumstances, which only an expert in the social sciences can uncover through repeated visits to the study context and by using a wide range of data-collection methods.

From studying the social dimensions that delineate farmers' lives and livelihoods in the LVB, this chapter has shown how the gender regime that assigns gender-differentiated rights and responsibilities, combined with a moral economy based on imposed social obligations, has tremendous bearing on the disparities existing between women's and men's adaptive capacities to respond to greater climate uncertainty. The chapter further highlights the importance of a demand-driven approach to adaptation guided by gender-integrated knowledge, to ensure that the strategies and projects developed actually reach and are utilized by those in greatest need of such measures.

Gender *does* matter. If we are serious about addressing the real causes of climate vulnerability and contributing to a future that is guided by sustainability, it is neither ethically defensible nor economically responsible to ignore the role that gender plays in the lives and livelihoods of millions of human beings.

References

Adger, W.N., Barnett, J., Brown, K., Marshall, N. and O'Brien, K. (2012). 'Cultural dimensions of climate change impacts and adaptation'. *Nature – Climate Change*, DOI: 10.1038/NCLIMATE1666.

Agarwal, B. (1997). '"Bargaining" and gender relations: within and beyond the household'. *Feminist Economics*, 3(1), 1–51.

Andersson, E. and Gabrielsson, S. (2012). 'Because of poverty we had to come together – collective action as a pathway to improved food security in rural Kenya and Uganda'. *Journal of International Agricultural Sustainability*, DOI:10.1080/14735903.2012.666029

Bassey, N. (2012). *To Cook a Continent: Destructive Extraction and the Climate Crisis in Africa*. Oxford: Fahamu Books and Pambazuka Press.

Bryceson, D. (2002a). 'The scramble in Africa: reorienting rural livelihoods'. *World Development*, 30, 725–739.

Bryceson, D. (2002b). 'Multiplex livelihoods in rural Africa: recasting the terms and conditions of gainful employment'. *Journal of Modern African Studies*, 40(1), 1–28.

Cleaver, F. (2005). 'The inequality of social capital and reproduction of chronic poverty'. *World Development*, 33, 893–906.

Ellis, F. (2000). *Rural Livelihoods and Diversity in Developing Countries*. Oxford: Oxford University Press.

Ellis, F. and Freeman, H.A. (2005). *Rural Livelihoods and Poverty Reduction Policies*. London: Routledge.

Eriksen, S., Brown, K. and Kelly, P.M. (2005). 'The dynamics of vulnerability: locating coping strategies in Kenya and Tanzania'. *The Geographical Journal*, 171(4), 287–305.

Fenio, K.G. (2009). *Between Bedrooms and Ballots: The Politics of HIV's 'Economy of Infection' in Mozambique*. PhD Dissertation, University of Florida.

Francis, E. (1998). 'Gender and rural livelihoods in Kenya'. *Journal of Development Studies*, 35(2), 72–95.

Francis, E. (2000). *Making a Living – Changing Livelihoods in Rural Africa*. London: Routledge.

Gabrielsson, S. (2012). *Uncertain Futures – Adaptive Capacities to Climate Variability and Change in the Lake Victoria Basin*. PhD Dissertation, Centre for Sustainability Studies, Lund University, Sweden.

Gabrielsson, S. and Ramasar, V. (2012). 'Widows: agents of change in a climate of water uncertainty'. *Journal of Cleaner Production*, DOI:10.1016/j.jclepro.2012.01.034.

Gabrielsson, S., Brogaard, S. and Jerneck, A. (2013). 'Living without buffers – illustrating climate vulnerability in the Lake Victoria basin'. *Sustainability Science*, 8(2), 143–157.

Githeko, A. K. (2009). *Malaria and Climate Change*. Nairobi: Commonwealth Health Ministers' Update.

Gunga, S. (2009). 'The politics of widowhood and re-marriage among the Luo of Kenya'. *Thought and Practice: A Journal of the Philosophical Association of Kenya*, 1(1), 161–174.

Hoon, P. (2002). 'The verticalization of personal-reciprocal relationships: changes in the local political economy of Eastern Zambia'. Paper presented at the Annual Meeting of the American Political Science Association, Boston, MA, 29 August –1 September.

Hydén, G. (1980). *Beyond Ujamaa in Tanzania: Underdevelopment and an Uncaptured Peasantry*. Los Angeles, CA: University of California Press.

Hydén, G. (1983). *No Shortcuts to Progress: African Development Management in Perspective*. Berkeley, CA: University of California Press.

Hydén, G. (2007). 'Governance and poverty reduction in Africa'. *Proceedings of the National Academy of Sciences*, 104(43), 16751–16756.

Hydén, G. (2008). 'The economy of affection: why the African peasantry remains uncaptured', in I.N. Kimambo (ed.), *Contemporary Perspectives on African Moral Economy*. Dar es Salaam: University of Dar es Salaam Press.

Hydén, G. (2013). *African Politics in Comparative Perspective*. Cambridge: Cambridge University Press.

Kabeer, N. (1999). 'Resources, agency, achievements: reflections on the measurement of women's empowerment'. *Development and Change*, 30(3), 435–464.

Kizza, M., Rodhe, A., Xu, C.Y., Ntale, H.K. and Halldin, S. (2009). 'Temporal rainfall variability in the Lake Victoria Basin in East Africa during the twentieth century'. *Theoretical and Applied Climatology*, 98(1), 119–135.

Lee-Smith, D. (1997). *My House is My Husband*. PhD Dissertation, Lund Institute of Technology, Division of Architecture and Development Studies, Lund University, Sweden.

Mies, M. (1986). *Patriarchy and Accumulation on a World Scale – Women in the International Division of Labor*. London: Zed Books.

Miles, C. (2007). '"Because women *are* property": issues of gender, food security, property ownership, quasi-development and religion in sub-Saharan Africa'. UNU-WIDER Conference on Gender and Food Security, May 2007, Accra, Ghana.

Minot, N. (2010). Summary report, COMESA Policy Seminar on Variation in staple food prices: causes, consequence, and policy options, Maputo, Mozambique, 25–26 January. Washington, DC: IFPRI.

Mohan, G., Brown, E., Milward, B. and Zachs-Williams, A. (2000). *Structural Adjustment, Theory Practice and Impacts*. London: Routledge.

Morton, J.F. (2007). 'The impact of climate change on smallholder and subsistence agriculture' *PNAS*, 104(50), 19680–19685.

Njogu, K., Ngeta, K. and Wanjau, M. (eds). (2010). *Ethnic Diversity in Eastern Africa – Opportunities and Challenges*. Nairobi: Twaweza Communications.

O'Brien, K. (2012). 'Global environmental change II: from adaptation to deliberate transformation'. *Progress in Human Geography*, 36, 667–676.

O'Brien, K. and Leichenko, R. (2007). *Human Security, Vulnerability and Sustainable Adaptation*. Human Development Report Office, Occasional Paper 2007/9. New York: United Nations Development Programme.

Odada, E., Olago, D. and Ochola, W. (2006). *Environment for Development: An Ecosystems Assessment of Lake Victoria Basin Environmental and Socio-economic Status, Trends and Human Vulnerabilities*. Nairobi: United Nations Environment Programme.

Osbahr, H. (2007). *Building Resilience: Adaptation Mechanisms and Mainstreaming for the Poor*. Human Development Report Occasional Paper. New York: United Nations Development Programme.

Pelling, M. (2011). *Adaptation to Climate Change: From Resilience to Transformation*. London: Routledge.

Pretty, J., Toulmin, C. and Williams, S. (2011). 'Sustainable intensification in African agriculture'. *Journal of International Agricultural Sustainability*, 9(1), 5–24.

Rarieya, M. and Fortun, K. (2010). 'Food security and seasonal climate information: Kenyan challenges'. *Sustainability Science*, 5, 99–114.

Reid, P. and Vogel, C. (2006). 'Living and responding to multiple stressors in South Africa: glimpses from KwaZulu Natal'. *Global Environmental Change*, 16, 195–206.

Rocheleau, D., Thomas-Slayter, B. and Wangari, E. (eds). (1996) *Feminist Political Ecology: Global Issues and Local Experiences*. London: Routledge.

Smucker, T.A. and Wisner, B. (2008). *Changing Household Responses to Drought in Tharaka, Kenya: Vulnerability, Persistence and Challenge*. Oxford: ODI/Blackwell.

Thornton, P.K., Jones, P.G., Alagarswamy, G., Andresen, J. and Herrero, M. (2010). 'Adapting to climate change: agricultural system and household impacts in East Africa'. *Agricultural Systems*, 103, 73–82.

Toulmin, C. (2009). *Climate Change in Africa*. London: Zed Books.

Tschakert, P. and Dietrich, K.A. (2010). 'Anticipatory learning for climate change adaptation and resilience'. *Ecology and Society*, 15(2), 11.

Tsuruta, T. (2008). 'Between moral economy and economy of affection', in I.N. Kimambo (ed.), *Contemporary Perspectives on African Moral Economy*. Dar es Salaam: University of Dar es Salaam Press.

UNEP (2006). *Environment for development: an ecosystems assessment of Lake Victoria basin environmental and socio-economic status, trends and human vulnerabilities*. Odada, E., Olago, D. and W. Ochola eds. Nairobi: UNEP.

Wandiga, S. (ed.). (2006). *Climate Change Induced Vulnerability to Malaria and Cholera in the Lake Victoria Region – A Final Report*. Assessments of Impacts and Adaptations to Climate Change Project. Washington, DC: International START Secretariat.

Wenger, E. (1998). *Communities of Practice*. Cambridge: Cambridge University Press.

6

ADAPTATION TECHNOLOGIES AS DRIVERS OF SOCIAL DEVELOPMENT

Sara Trærup and Lars Christiansen

Introduction

Technology development and transfer is an area of increasing priority on the international agenda on adaptation to climate change. Whereas discussions of technologies had focused mainly on mitigation, technologies for adaptation have recently been brought squarely into the discussions (United Nations Framework Convention on Climate Change (UNFCCC) 2010). The heightened international focus on adaptation technology may have consequences for how, and how much, consideration is given to the social development dimensions of adaptation in the practical implementation of adaptation activities in developing countries.

There is general agreement in the recent literature that technology may play an important role in adaptation to climate change, but that its scope and effectiveness is often location-specific and depends on the broader development and socio-cultural context in which it is deployed (Agrawala and Broad 2002; Adger et al. 2007; Klein 2011; Practical Action 2011). Further, it is often argued that technologies fail to address the underlying stressors (like access to basic resources such as water, infrastructure and public facilities) to vulnerability to climate change (Klein 2011; Vincent et al. 2011). Olhoff (2014) notes that adaptation technologies may be only partially effective if they do not address other key aspects that contribute to vulnerability to climate change; they may be ineffective if they are not suited to local conditions; and that they may prove maladaptive (i.e. increase vulnerability) if implemented without recognition of relevant social and environmental processes. And Fankhauser, Smith and Tol (1999) and Tol et al. (2006) note that the risk and uncertainties of climate change pose barriers to the development as well as the adoption of certain technologies.

Recognizing that adaptation is not merely a matter of making adjustments to technical equipment, the understanding of technologies for adaptation can be expanded to include the organizational and social dimensions of adaptation as well. It has become common to distinguish three categories of technologies for adaptation: hardware, software and orgware (Boldt et al. 2012). Hardware refers to 'hard' technologies such as capital goods and equipment, including drought-resistant crops and new irrigation systems. Software refers to the capacity and processes involved in the use of technology, and covers knowledge and skills, including aspects of awareness-raising, education and training. Thirdly, there is the concept of orgware (Thorne et al. 2007), which relates to ownership and institutional arrangements of the community/organization where the technology will be used.

Several authors (Vincent et al. 2011; Klein 2011; Fida 2011) note that prioritization and application of adaptation technologies in developing countries have been heavily skewed towards 'hardware', with soft- and orgware receiving comparatively little attention, and that this bias is preventing sustainable and effective long-term adaptation. Based on new data from a large international capacity building programme, this chapter discusses early evidence of development implications from a focus on technologies in adaptation planning in developing countries, and tests the above argument against concrete data from the 25 study countries. The chapter also examines the underlying reasons why some technologies were selected above others, including a discussion of the criteria used in the national processes for prioritizing adaptation technologies, as well as the degree to which the technologies identified contribute to development priorities such as poverty reduction.

In particular, we ask:

- To what degree are hardware technologies systematically given priority over more behaviourally oriented soft- and orgware technologies?
- To what degree and in what ways do current adaptation technologies contribute to social development priorities?

The chapter begins with an overview of the current understanding of the concept of 'adaptation technology' and discussions on its application and implications. Building on this background the chapter continues with an introduction to the Technology Needs Assessment (TNA) data and methodology used in the analysis. Lastly, we present the results, discussing these with reference to the above questions, and offering some concluding reflections about technology choice for adaptation and relation to the poor.

Technology for adaptation

What is an adaptation technology?

Historically, limited attention has been given to adaptation technologies, and little operational experience is available from activities focusing specifically on adaptation technologies (UNFCCC 2006). The Intergovernmental Panel on Climate Change (IPCC) (2000), in its special report on Methodological and Technological Issues in Technology Transfer, defines technology as 'a piece of equipment, technique, practical knowledge or skills for performing a particular activity'. The *Handbook for Conducting Technology Needs Assessment for Climate Change* (United Nations Development Programme (UNDP) 2010), defines the concept of technologies for adaptation very generically as: 'All technologies that can be applied in the process of adapting to climatic variability and climate change'. A UNFCCC report on the development and transfer of technologies for adaptation to climate change proposes the following definition: 'the application of technology in order to reduce the vulnerability, or enhance the resilience, of a natural or human system to the impacts of climate change' (UNFCCC 2010).

As noted, it has become common practice to distinguish between three categories of technologies for adaptation: *hardware, software and orgware*. Hardware includes capital goods; software refers more to the capacities and processes involved in the use of the technology, and includes knowledge and skills, including aspects of awareness-raising, education and training. Additionally, adaptation methods and practices not normally considered as technologies, such as insurance schemes or crop rotation patterns, may also be characterized as software (UNFCCC 2006). The third distinction is equally important to the understanding of technologies for adaptation and their implementation: this is the concept of orgware, which relates to ownership and institutional arrangements of the community/organization where the technology will be put to use. This subdivision of technology shares characteristics with the concept of 'explicit' and 'tacit' knowledge increasingly applied in fields like economic geography and development economics to describe the complexities of knowledge-exchange processes. 'Tacit knowledge' is here defined as knowledge that cannot be codified but depends on learning by doing, and/or cultural and social contexts – in other words, it is dependent on social interaction (Gertler 2003). In this chapter, we apply a practical interpretation of hardware, software and orgware, as follows:

- Hardware: technologies that require the transfer and 'installation' of physical material from sources outside the targeted locality.
- Software: technologies that solely involve the transfer of knowledge and/ or practice.
- Orgware: technologies that involve the re-organization or establishment of social networks and/or institutions.

The logic of dividing adaptation technologies into these broad categories is illustrated by the general adaptation literature and by Agrawal (2010), who states that all adaptation occurs in an 'institutionally rich context and the success of adaptation depends on specific institutional arrangements', thereby underlining the importance of including orgware. Without local institutions, it can be far costlier for poor households to adapt sufficiently to climate change, since these institutions are enablers of the capacity of households and groups to deploy specific adaptation practices. Thus, according to Agrawal (2010) in facilitating any adaptation to climate change, institutions should be considered in terms of their role of determining vulnerability as the expression of power of different social groups, and in terms of the groups' ability to change and adapt in response to climate change or other external factors. Household adaptive capacity is closely related to the demand for, access to and use of information at the local level (Ribot and Peluso 2003). For example, those households in a village whose contacts and knowledge are based around the village will have less adaptive capacity in the face of climate exposure than households with networks that extend over a greater geographical range and connect with a wider variety of institutions (Adger 2003).

Previous TNAs of adaptation have accorded limited emphasis to further specifying the concept of technologies for adaptation. A review by Fida (2011) of existing TNAs (the 'top-up round') for adaptation reveals that, possibly as a result, countries do not distinguish between 'adaptation technologies' and 'adaptation measures', but use the terms interchangeably. There exists a broad range of different adaptation typologies, presented in various concepts and frameworks (see Biagini et al. 2014 for an overview). One such interpretation sees adaptation as also being a means of embracing and taking advantage of the new circumstances and conditions presented by changes. The perception of climate change adaptation within human systems has been described as 'the process of adjustment to actual or expected climate and its effects, in order to moderate harm or exploit beneficial opportunities' (IPCC 2012).

An optimal mix of technology types?

The technologies are available, but there remain other potential problems associated with the use of technology – especially hard technology – for climate adaptation, even if access to technologies were greatly improved (Klein 2011; Markandya and Galarraga 2011). Stand-alone technology, such as physical structures and equipment, is seldom sufficient in itself, without an enabling framework. In many cases, hardware will need to be combined with software and orgware to become adequately embedded in communities and thereby ensure the acceptance and ownership necessary for successful implementation (Agrawal 2010). An 'enabling environment' should be understood as the set of resources and conditions within which the technology and the target beneficiaries operate. For adaptation technologies, such conditions (or enabling environment elements) include relevant policies, human and organizational capacity building and appropriate infrastructures.

For example, in a situation where an adaptation technology seeks to reduce storm risks in a coastal area by building storm shelters, such shelters will be of little use without early warning system and communication infrastructures. The technology (storm shelters) is contingent on a communication infrastructure such as an early warning system, as well as awareness of and the skills necessary for using it: the early warning system is both an element of the enabling framework and an adaptation technology. Strengthening this enabling environment element (the communications infrastructure) would therefore contribute significantly to the effectiveness of storm shelters.

Previous experiences with TNAs have shown that the prioritization and selection of technologies for adaptation has been biased towards 'hard' technologies. In addition, assessments tend to be quite generic, with little attention to the details of national circumstances, including biophysical settings and the economic, institutional, legal and socio-cultural contexts involved. That indicates there is a special need for reconsidering technology options, as they may otherwise fail to support countries in adapting to climate change. Klein (2011) furthermore stresses that a narrow focus on technological hardware adaptation options may in some cases be detrimental to development and vulnerability reduction, particularly if there is a bias towards hard technologies. That is an observation supported by Markandya and Galarraga (2011) and Vincent et al. (2011) as well. Greater attention to soft technologies and framework conditions, including orgware is generally advocated. Fida (2011) analyses the process of TNAs for adaptation under the first phase of TNAs, the 'top-up round' from 1998 to 2008, with a focus on the challenges and lessons learned in countries that have developed TNAs for adaptation. To inform and improve the process of conducting future and ongoing TNAs, Fida (2011) explores how countries have interpreted the concept of technologies for adaptation, and the impact of this interpretation on the final outcome of the needs assessment for adaptation technologies. Most first-phase countries chose hard technologies for adaptation. Kossam (2011) draws several lessons on Malawi's experiences from the first phase of TNAs, showing how more soft and organizational components of technologies could help to improve the effectiveness of future TNAs, emphasizing capacity building, institutional continuity, and the importance of aligning TNA priorities with other national development objectives. Importantly, Vincent et al. (2011) note that first-phase TNAs were often too generic to provide sufficient detail on national contexts; moreover, by under-emphasizing the soft and organizational components of technologies relative to the hard components, one risks impeding effective adaptation to climate change.

Hardware cannot stand alone: soft- and orgware will need to be part of the 'technology package' applied for adaptation. Or, put differently: all technologies (and their successful implementation) consist of three interconnected elements (hardware, software and orgware); and the relative weight of each element in a specific development context depends partly on the characteristics of the technology (see discussion of agriculture and water below) and partly on management/political decisions.

Data and methodology

The analysis in this chapter is based on data from the Technology Needs Assessment (TNA) project,[1] 2010–2013. The project has provided targeted financial, technical and methodological support to assist countries from Africa, Asia, Latin America, the Caribbean and Eastern Europe in conducting TNAs. The project is a country-driven activity aimed at assisting developing countries in identifying and prioritizing technology needs for mitigating and adapting to climate change. Data on criteria for prioritizing technologies and the prioritized technologies were collected from national reports submitted to the TNA project 2010–2012. In all, 25 country reports were available for data collection: participant countries and geographical distribution are shown in Table 6.1.

During the project, countries have identified and prioritized adaptation sectors and adaptation technologies within the prioritized sectors. In most cases, countries have selected two sectors and three to four technologies per sector.

Classification of criteria

The countries participating in the TNA project identified criteria that should make it possible, in practice, to judge or measure how well a technology would score on these criteria. In some cases, for example for technologies with an impact on local planning issues, one approach to identifying criteria was to involve the parties concerned in the stage of identifying potential criteria. Additionally, relevant policies and other secondary information about relevant stakeholders were examined to derive criteria that would reflect their concerns. In some cases,

TABLE 6.1 Geographical distribution of countries participating in the TNA project

Region	Countries	No. of countries
Africa	Côte d'Ivoire, Ghana, Kenya, Mali, Mauritius, Morocco, Rwanda, Senegal, Sudan, Zambia	10
Asia	Bhutan, Cambodia, Indonesia, Mongolia, Sri Lanka, Thailand, Vietnam	7
Eastern Europe	Azerbaijan, Georgia, Kazakhstan, Republic of Moldova	4
Latin America	Costa Rica, Ecuador, El Salvador	3
Middle East	Lebanon	1
Total		25

where an identified criterion was very broad, such as 'environmental impacts', assessing technologies against this could prove difficult, even though the dimension of environmental impacts would be regarded as important. Because of this need for specific criteria, some of them were grouped or clustered into a few broad categories that involve separate and distinguishable dimensions of the overall objective for the prioritization exercise. Each of the criteria in a cluster was referred to as a sub-criterion. These sub-criteria should each address a single component of the overall problem. For the TNA project, this could mean grouping sub-criteria for adaptation technologies for dealing with the problem of unsustainable water use and management within the agricultural sector under the criterion of 'water management'.

Stakeholder consultations and working group sessions in each country used Multi-Criteria Analysis (MCA) to assign a weighting for each of the criteria, identifying criteria for prioritizing the sectors and technologies. Information on which criteria the various countries applied in their TNAs was collected from the 25 national TNA reports available. Although different groups may have had different perceptions of the exact meaning of some criteria, which could affect comparability, the data still provide a reasonable foundation for drawing comparisons and experiences as to the priorities of countries in making TNAs.

Classification of technologies

The technologies identified by the countries were classified into the categories of hardware, software and orgware, as described earlier. In practice, however, technologies often contain elements of more than one category, so a system of proportional weights was applied in the classification exercise. Each country prioritized between one and three sectors, and for each of the sectors two to five technologies were selected, yielding a total of 192 technologies from 25 countries.

Here it should be noted that the actual categorization of individual technologies based on the general categories presented above was necessarily a somewhat subjective exercise, which, beyond categorization based on technology titles, also included a detailed review of the technology description in the individual country reports. Thus, the same type of technology (e.g. 'Irrigation' or 'Drought-resistant crops') might involve several different activities aimed at overcoming barriers in the individual country, which in turn might push the balance towards hardware, or software. Lacking a formal methodology for quantifying the weights of technology types in the individual technology, this qualitative classification is currently the only possible approach for analysing the TNA data. Examples of technologies and how they were classified are shown in Table 6.2.

Identifying pro-poor technologies

With the objective of identifying the share of technologies prioritized for the TNA project, which would go into the category of being pro-poor, the

TABLE 6.2 Examples of practical technology classification and weighting in hardware, software and orgware

Technology	Hardware weight	Software weight	Orgware weight
Seawall and revetment (Indonesia – coastal zones)	1	0	0
Drip irrigation system (Mongolia – agriculture)	1	0	0
Agro-forestry (Zambia – agriculture)	0	1	0
Transfer of knowledge and skills to health personnel (Sri Lanka – health)	0	1	0
Organization of water users communities (Ecuador – water)	0	0	1
Provisional posts of emergency care and prompt rehabilitation during critical periods of heat waves (Moldova – health)	0	0	1
Reducing water leakages in water management facilities (Azerbaijan – water)	2/3	1/3	0
Adaptive co-management of watersheds (Costa Rica – water)	0	2/3	1/3
Decentralized early warning systems in coastal zone (Georgia – coastal zones)	1/3	1/3	1/3
Water metering in irrigation (Kazakhstan – water)	2/3	0	1/3
Drought-tolerant sorghum variety (Kenya – agriculture)	1/3	2/3	0

technologies were evaluated against the definition of pro-poor initiatives proposed by Ravallion and Chen (2003). According to this definition, a technology is considered pro-poor if it contributes to additional income generation or increased employment generation for people likely to be most affected by climate change. Recognizing that this definition is limited to economic poverty, the technologies were assessed against these benchmarks based on their descriptions in the national reports. A pro-poor technology could, for example, be one that targets employment of landless rural poor and provides stable income opportunities for seasonal workers. Whilst it would be desirable to analyse the longer-term effects of technologies on income generation and employment rates, that would require monitoring and evaluation data from implemented projects, which is not possible with the data currently available.

Results and discussion

Criteria applied in prioritizing adaptation technologies

The most widely used criterion for prioritizing the nationally identified adaptation technologies is the potential to reduce climate change vulnerability (Table 6.3), followed by costs of the technology and social-, economic- and environmental development implications. Several countries had only very general criteria and did not employ more specific indicators, whereas others went into greater detail,

TABLE 6.3 Criteria and weights for prioritizing technologies assigned by countries participating in the TNA project

Criteria	Weight			
	Average	*Min.*	*Max.*	*n*
Social development	0.25	0.12	0.42	18
Political and institutional stability	0.25	0.25	0.25	1
Water management (quality and accessibility)	0.22	0.17	0.33	3
Economic development	0.21	0.10	0.37	18
Environment development	0.21	0.09	0.33	18
Vulnerability reduction potential	0.20	0.10	0.44	22
Socio-economic development	0.20	0.13	0.33	4
Social suitability and acceptability to local population	0.19	0.11	0.33	5
Implementation feasibility	0.19	0.09	0.33	14
Cost (investment, annual operation and maintenance costs)	0.18	0.07	0.33	19
Ensure food security and the fight against poverty	0.14	0.11	0.27	2
Improving health	0.14	0.14	0.14	1
Capacity-building element	0.14	0.13	0.14	2
Women's participation in management	0.14	0.14	0.14	1
Technology maturity	0.13	0.13	0.13	1
Technology vulnerability to climate change	0.13	0.13	0.13	1
National priority	0.11	0.07	0.29	5
Total *n*				25
Number of criteria per country	5	3	7	

providing one or several indicators for each criterion. For economic impact, examples of criteria used include job creation, improving farmer income and ability to reinvest, and catalysing private investments. Very broad criteria, such as 'environmental impacts', could make it difficult to assess technologies against this, even though the dimension of environmental impacts would be important. Therefore some countries specified sub-criteria like 'biodiversity conservation' and 'contribution of the technology to protect and sustain ecosystem services', as with the economic criteria as exemplified above.

The 'social development' criterion was, when made more specific, evaluated against indicators such as impact on health, job creation and community involvement. Some criteria, like water management, are nevertheless highly specific. A criterion like 'political and institutional stability' seems very contextually contingent and was applied by only one country.

That the vulnerability criterion emerged as the most used criterion may not come as a surprise, although it is ranked only as number 6 in terms of the weighting attributed to the criterion, which reflects the relative importance of each criterion in comparison to the other criteria. It may also appear a bit misleading to have the 'political and institutional stability' criterion listed as one of the highest weighted criterion since it was used by only one country, whereas 'vulnerability' was applied by a full 22 of the 25 countries. When we take a closer look at the range of weights for each criterion, the 'social' and 'vulnerability' criteria show the greatest discrepancies in the range of weighting assigned by countries. Ranking seventh among the most used criteria is 'social suitability and acceptability to local population'. Stakeholders in one country who used this criterion in their prioritization process explained that the technology was evaluated against the extent to which it would be culturally and socially acceptable, including considerations of indigenous knowledge and practices. Similarly, another focus group said, in referring to this criterion, 'a good technology option must be accepted by the public and farmers for effective implementation'.

Only one country included 'women's participation in management' as a criterion. This was measured as the potential of the technology to enhance/increase the participation of women and other vulnerable groups in the planning, implementation and management of the system introduced by the technology.

Distribution among technology types – hardware, software and orgware

The distribution of technologies among the different technology types is shown in Figure 6.1. It would appear that the bias towards hardware in national adaptation planning noted by several authors is not prevalent in the data sets from the current TNA project. Participating countries do not seem to have any clear preference for hardware technology solutions to adaptation, but have

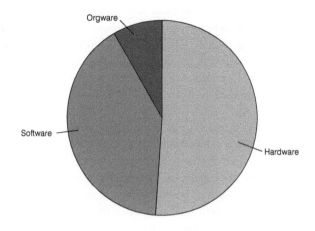

FIGURE 6.1   Distribution of 192 priority technologies identified in 25 TNA reports: hardware, software and orgware categories

considered and given priority to a wide range of software measures – improved management of soil, water and crops; restoration of ecosystems; improved extension services; implementation of community-level early warning and response systems; creation and support for water-user associations, etc. All the same, these measures are oriented to hard technology, rather than being social in nature. We also note the strong presence of hardware options like water harvesting, drought-resistant crops, drip irrigation, structural coastal defence, climate-proofing of roads, national-scale monitoring and early warning systems etc. in the portfolios of prioritized technologies.

In any case, this shows that current understandings and implementation of technologies for adaptation in developing countries are far from being as one-sided as found by previous studies based on earlier assessments of technology needs (Vincent et al. 2011; Klein 2011; Fida 2011). In turn, this indicates that introducing 'technology approaches' into adaptation and development practice will not necessarily lead to major changes in priorities or in the actual measures implemented compared to those that have emerged from earlier non-technology-focused adaptation priority assessments like National Adaptation Plans of Action (NAPAs) and National Communications. The reason for this may lie in the developments in approach and methodology which form the basis for country-level work in recent TNAs. More emphasis has been given to training and technical support of the country teams undertaking the assessments, by including sectoral guidebooks, for instance. Moreover, closer inspection shows that many of the technologies identified include elements of more than one of the main categories of technology, in some cases all three. The fact that it can be difficult to categorize a specific technology as belonging to one group or the other (see examples above) may indicate that many

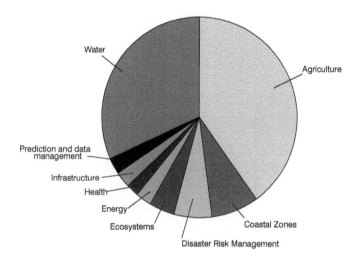

FIGURE 6.2   Sectoral distribution of 192 priority technologies identified in 25 TNA reports

developing countries recognize that adaptation is more than simply installing 'climate-proofed' infrastructure, but must also address underlying factors of vulnerability.

Further, the balance between software (40 per cent of total) and orgware (8 per cent) seems somewhat skewed. This is not necessarily a suboptimal balance: it might simply indicate that while countries take social organization of adaptation processes and the provision of 'institutional infrastructure' into consideration in the TNA process, their role in adaptation is generally seen as supportive to the functions of hardware and software, and is thus less represented in the final list of national priority technologies. We did not find in the literature any mention of proposed 'optimal levels' of orgware versus hard- and software, so it is difficult to conclude that orgware is underrepresented in the data sets. In general, however, giving low priority to orgware in the adaptation process entails clear risks. Social organization of adaptation processes (as opposed to individuals acting independently of each other) and efficient, capable and responsive institutions are crucial for ensuring that the deployment of other types of adaptation technologies (hard and soft) is both effective and socially sustainable.

Another striking aspect concerns sectoral distribution. Figure 6.2 provides an overview of sectoral distribution of all technologies identified in the TNA reports examined. It should be noted, however, that each country first identified one or more 'priority sectors' and then proceeded to identify only technologies pertaining to that particular sector. Thus, the distribution shown in Figure 6.2 is not the full picture of technology needs in the TNA countries: what it shows is that most countries identified water and agriculture among their priority sectors, which is consistent with previous findings from

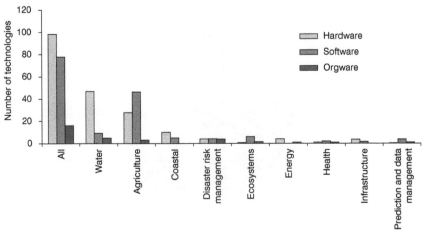

FIGURE 6.3 Distribution of hardware, software and orgware by individual sectors for the 25 countries

priority exercises like the TNA 'top-up round' and the development of NAPAs (UNFCCC 2009; Fida 2011).

The relative weight of hardware, software and orgware varies significantly when technologies within the individual sectors are compared (see Figure 6.3). In particular, the water technologies identified were significantly more 'hardware-intensive' (77 per cent hardware technologies) than with, for example, the agriculture sector (36 per cent hardware technologies). This difference is probably explained by the individual characteristics of each sector: technologies related to water tended to be supply-focused (as with water harvesting and storage from roofs, small dams and reservoirs to store run-off, desalinization, and restoration/construction of wells) rather than demand/management-focused (like water-user organizations or integrated watershed management). By contrast, the technologies identified for agriculture tended to be more complex and focused on resource management and integrating aspects of both hardware and software (increasing irrigation efficiency through improved management, developing and disseminating drought-resistant crops and cropping systems, implementing integrated agriculture systems such as agroforestry and mixed farming, improving extension services etc.). Only rarely were the agriculture technologies that were identified purely hardware-focused (e.g. investments in modern irrigation systems and terracing), and even then some level of changed practices or knowledge transfer would unavoidably be an integral part of the technology implementation (although this may not necessarily be stated in the documentation).

However, the deeper reasons for this fairly even balance between hardware and soft/orgware in the agriculture sector versus the water sector are not entirely clear. One explanation may simply be that the nature of the water sector is necessarily more focused on infrastructure and on ensuring the basic supply of a single critical resource, whereas agriculture by its very nature entails the management of more complex processes at the confluence of biophysical and socio-cultural systems. For instance, installing a water-harvesting system or deepening a well in a community faced with water shortages can 'solve' the problem without significant knowledge transfer or changes in behaviour of the vast majority of local water consumers, at least for the lifetime of the installed systems. By contrast, implementing a drought-resistant cropping system or agroforestry practices will necessarily have to involve some level of knowledge transfer and behavioural change for all those who use and implement the system on a daily basis (knowledge of how and when to sow seeds, how to manage plant growth, water inputs, weeds etc.). Simply providing drought-resistant seeds or tree seedlings to communities without further support is unlikely to facilitate the intended adaptation benefits.

Another explanation of the observed difference in the distribution of technology types in water and agriculture could relate to the guidance provided in the TNA guidebooks. The TNA project has produced several sectoral guidebooks for adaptation. These provide detailed descriptions and guidance for various key adaptation technologies in each sector – with the objective of providing a sound and comprehensive technical foundation for national discussions of adaptation options and their prioritization. The extent to which countries have based their work on the guidebooks is highly variable, however. Some have used the guidebooks' technology lists almost directly as input in their national prioritization exercises (as the sole technology option), whereas others have used them more indirectly as inspiration, while also identifying more specific national-level technology options not necessarily in line with the format of the guidebooks. In particular, countries in the first category were heavily influenced by the composition of the technology portfolios outlined in the guidebooks. Interestingly, the distribution of technology types (hard, soft, orgware) described in the guidebooks match quite well with distribution shown in Figure 6.3 (73 per cent and 36 per cent hardware for water and agriculture sector respectively, based on the same classification described above). An underlying reason for this difference in focus could be that the water guidebook was developed by a consultancy team of (primarily) engineers from a US university, whereas the agriculture guidebook was developed by a team of non-governmental organization (NGO) development practitioners (primarily from social science backgrounds) from Latin America. This is not to say that one approach is superior to the other – simply that professional background may well influence the selection of technology options.

A final point connected to the differences in technology approach for the water and agriculture sector is that the two sectors and their associated adaptation technologies are highly interrelated, as agriculture is by far the largest consumer of fresh water in most developing countries. A large share of the water technologies identified is fully or partly focused directly on the agriculture sector. The additional water supply facilitated by a 'hardware' water technology may therefore feed directly into (and in practice be co-implemented with) software agriculture technologies such as water-user associations, implementation of more drought-resistant cropping systems, etc. The integrated nature of many of the proposed water technologies related to the agriculture sector thus implies that the practical balance of hardware versus soft/orgware in water-technology implementation (and vice versa for agriculture technologies) may be more balanced than indicated by the distribution in Figure 6.3.

From the above discussion on water and agriculture it seems clear that, in order to draw general conclusions on technology intensity (the weight of hardware versus soft- and orgware) and the ensuing practical implications, one must first carefully consider that individual sectors may have very different inclinations as regards the 'optimal mix' of technology elements.

Proportion of technologies that has a pro-poor dimension

As noted, the objectives of the technologies prioritized by the participating countries are heavily dependent on national priorities. Among these objectives is being 'pro-poor' – but when can a technology be considered to be pro-poor? According to the definition provided by Ravallion and Chen (2003), a technology is pro-poor if it has an immediate effect on poverty reduction. Standard household surveys such as the Living Standards Measurement Study (LSMS), Demographic Household Survey (DHS) funded by United States Agency for International Development (USAID), and the Multiple Indicator Cluster Survey (MICS) developed by United Nations Children's Emergency Fund (UNICEF) include employment as an indicator in poverty measurements. Thus it seems reasonable to assume that technologies that support employment of the poorest population or contribute to capacity building for unskilled labour in the sectors where the poor find work can be characterized as having a pro-poor dimension. Seen in that way, many of the prioritized technologies in the TNA project can be classified as pro-poor.

Evaluating each of the technologies against the criteria that they should generate additional income or create increased employment opportunities for the poorest people, we find that 57 per cent of the technologies do fulfil this condition. The distribution of technologies with a pro-poor dimension (contributing to employment generation) among the different categories of technologies emerges as relatively equal with 53 per cent of the hardware, 57 per cent of the software and 53 per cent of the orgware technologies having a pro-poor dimension. Again, this shows that in current TNAs for adaptation to climate change there is not only a focus on large capital-intensive investments such as physical infrastructure projects, but also small-scale soft technologies that generate employment and capacity building, benefitting the poor and those with least resources. This finding indicates that TNAs can go hand in hand or be an integral part of other development initiatives supporting bottom-up approaches to initiating social development.

Conclusions

The chapter has investigated the empirical basis of adaptation technology preferences among developing countries. We find that earlier tendencies to give priority to 'hardware' technologies over software and orgware technologies are no longer predominant. This analysis of 25 TNAs shows that developing countries are well aware that hardware technology cannot stand alone. In many cases, the preferred technologies consisted of several components covering hard-, soft- and orgware. This further indicates that introducing 'technology approaches' into adaptation and development practice will not necessarily lead to major changes in priorities or in the actual measures implemented, compared to those shown in earlier non-technology-focused adaptation priority assessments such as NAPAs and National Communications.

Thus we see that countries are, to a large extent, already applying a wide approach to TNAs. Hardware adaptation measures involving capital-intensive, large, complex, inflexible technology and infrastructure are becoming integrated with approaches that involve behavioural soft- and orgware adaptation measures, such as natural capital, user organizations, community control, and appropriateness.

The chapter has also shown that the social development aspects of adaptation remain a high priority in technology-focused adaptation assessments and implementation strategies, such as those developed under the TNA project. Social criteria like 'social development', 'socio-economic development' and 'social suitability' have all been widely applied and given significant weight in the establishment of national priorities for adaptation technology. Similarly, we have seen that both software and orgware are in practice being accorded considerably more weight than foreseen by many, which in turn would tend to favour social elements of adaptation like resilience of local livelihoods, institutions and capacity building. Moreover, the analysis of social development attributes of selected technologies has indicated that many of these can be considered directly beneficial to social development, as they are beneficial to the poor; and that the focus in the practical application of technology frameworks is not so much on large capital-intensive investments as on smaller-scale technologies suited to community-level interventions and participation.

Further, the organizational component of technologies has a relatively low share of the total technology priorities identified, compared to hardware and software. There is little mention in literature of an 'optimal level' of orgware in adaptation. However, systematically according low priority to the orgware components of technologies entails the risk of creating ineffective adaptation processes where adequately adapting to climate change could prove far costlier, since institutions have been shown to enable the capacity of vulnerable households and groups to deploy specific adaptation technologies (Agrawal 2010). The social organization of adaptation processes and efficient, capable and responsive institutions are crucial for ensuring that the application of other types of adaptation technologies (hard and soft) is both effective and socially sustainable, also in a longer-term perspective. An important recommendation based on the findings of this chapter would thus be to step up efforts at including orgware as an integral part of adaptation technology planning, recognizing that hard-, soft- and orgware technologies are not mutually exclusive technology options.

Current proposals in TNA reports show that there is awareness that stand-alone technologies, such as physical structures and equipment, are seldom sufficient in themselves but need to be supported by an enabling framework – a point also recognized in development studies in general. An overly narrow focus on technological adaptation options may prove detrimental to development and vulnerability reduction, particularly if there is a bias towards hard technologies.

Lastly, this chapter has shown that work on transferring adaptation technologies needs to be based on recognition and understanding of the national socio-cultural, economic, political and institutional contexts in which they are to be implemented.

Note

1 More information available at: www.tech-action.org

References

Adger, W.N. (2003). 'Social capital, collective action and adaptation to climate change'. *Economic Geography* 79 (4), 387–404.
Adger, W.N., Agrawala, S., Mirza, M.M.Q., Conde, C., O'Brien, K., Pulhin, J., Pulwarty, R., Smit, B. and Takahashi, K. (2007). 'Assessment of adaptation practices, options, constraints and capacity', in M.L. Parry, O.F. Canziani, J.P. Palutikof, P.J. van der Linden and C.E. Hanson (eds), *Climate Change 2007: Impacts, Adaptation and Vulnerability: Contribution of Working Group II to the Fourth Assessment Report of the Intergovernmental Panel on Climate Change*, 717–743. Cambridge: Cambridge University Press.
Agrawal, A. (2010). 'Local institutions and adaptation to climate change', in R. Mearns and A. Norton (eds), *Social Dimensions to Climate Change*. Washington, DC: World Bank.
Agrawala, S. and Broad, K. (2002). 'Technology transfer perspectives on climate forecast applications'. *Research in Science and Technology Studies*, 13, 45–69.
Biagini, B., Bierbaum, R., Stults, M., Dobardzic, S. and McNeeley, S.M. (2014). 'A typology of adaptation actions: a global look at climate adaptation actions financed through the Global Environment Facility'. *Global Environmental Change*, 25, 97–108.

Boldt, J., Nygaard,I., Hansen, U.E. and Trærup, S. (2012). *Overcoming Barriers to the Transfer and Diffusion of Climate Technologies*. Roskilde, Denmark: UNEP Risø Centre.

Fankhauser, S., Smith, J.B. and Tol, Richard S.J. (1999). 'Weathering climate change: some simple rules to guide adaptation decisions'. *Ecological Economics*, 30 (1), 67–78.

Fida, E. (2011). 'Experiences in conducting Technology Needs Assessment (TNAs) for adaptation from non Annex I countries under the "top up" phase', in L. Christiansen, A. Olhoff and S. Trærup (eds), *Technologies for Adaptation: Perspectives and Practical Experiences*. Roskilde, Denmark: UNEP Risø Centre.

Gertler, M.S. (2003). 'Tacit knowledge and the economic geography of context or, the undefinable tacitness of being (there)'. *Journal of Economic Geography* 3, 75–99.

IPCC (2000) Bert Metz, Ogunlade Davidson, Jan-Willem Martens, Sascha Van Rooijen and Laura Van Wie Mcgrory (eds). *Methodological and Technological Issues in Technology Transfer*. Cambridge: Cambridge University Press.

IPCC (2012). 'Glossary', in *Managing the Risk of Extreme Events and Disasters to Advance Climate Change Adaptation. A Special Report of Working Groups I and II of the Intergovernmental Panel on Climate Change*, 555–564. Cambridge: Cambridge University Press.

Klein, R. (2011). 'Adaptation: more than technology', in L. Christiansen, A. Olhoff and S. Trærup (eds), *Technologies for Adaptation: Perspectives and Practical Experiences*. Roskilde, Denmark: UNEP Risø Centre.

Kossam, F. (2011). 'Synergies between technology needs assessment and national adaptation plan of action in Least Developed Countries: A case study for Malawi', in L. Christiansen, A. Olhoff and S. Trærup (eds), *Technologies for Adaptation: Perspectives and Practical Experiences*. Roskilde, Denmark: UNEP Risø Centre.

Markandya, A. and Galarraga, I. (2011). 'Technologies for adaptation – an economic perspective', in L. Christiansen, A. Olhoff and S. Trærup (eds), *Technologies for Adaptation: Perspectives and Practical Experiences*. Roskilde, Denmark: UNEP Risø Centre.

Olhoff, A. (2014). 'Adaptation in the context of technology development and transfer'. *Climate Policy* DOI: 10.1080/14693062.2014.873665.

Practical Action. (2011). Briefing paper: Technology for adapting to climate change. Retrieved from http://weadapt.org/knowledge-base/community-basedadaptation/technology-and-adaptation.

Ravallion, M. and Chen, S. (2003).'Measuring pro-poor growth'. *Economics Letters* 78 (1), 93–99.

Ribot, J.C. and Peluso, N.L. (2003). 'A theory of access'. *Rural Sociology* 68 (2), 153–181.

Thorne, S., Kantor, K. and Hossain, I. (2007). 'Community based technology solutions: adapting to climate change'. Cape Town: SouthSouthNorth. Retrieved from http://www.preventionweb.net/files/9545_Community.pdf

Tol, R.S.J., Bohn, M., Downing, T.E., Guillerminet, M., Hizsnyik, E., Kasperson, R. and Yetkiner, I.H. (2006). 'Adaptation to five metres of sea level rise'. *Journal of Risk Research* 9, 467–482.

United Nations Development Programme, UNDP (2010). *Handbook for Conducting Technology Needs Assessment for Climate Change*. New York: UNDP.

United Nations Framework Convention on Climate Change, UNFCCC (2006). *Application of Environmentally Sound Technologies for Adaptation to Climate Change*. Bonn: UNFCCC.

United Nations Framework Convention on Climate Change, UNFCCC (2009). *Support Needed to Implement National Adaptation Programmes of Action (NAPAs)*. Bonn: UNFCCC.

United Nations Framework Convention on Climate Change, UNFCCC (2010). *Report of the Conference of the Parties on its Sixteenth Session, held at Cancun from 29 November to 10 December 2010, Addendum, Part Two: Action taken by the Conference of the Parties.* Bonn: UNFCCC.

Vincent, K., Joubert, A. and Cull, T. (2011). 'Technology needs for adaptation in southern Africa: customizing responses to different country contexts', in L. Christiansen, A. Olhoff and S. Trærup (eds), *Technologies for Adaptation: Perspectives and Practical Experiences*. Roskilde, Denmark: UNEP Risø Centre.

7

MULTILEVEL GOVERNANCE AND COPRODUCTION IN URBAN FLOOD-RISK MANAGEMENT

The case of Dar es Salaam

Trond Vedeld, Wilbard Kombe, Clara Kweka Msale and Siri Bjerkreim Hellevik

Introduction

African coastal cities are highly vulnerable to climate risks such as floods, but they also have high potential for reducing risks and enhancing resilience, provided they are well governed. The worst affected are typically the urban poor, who tend to live in informal settlements or 'slums' – along rivers, in low-lying coastal zones or in former marshlands.

The study reported here was designed as an in-depth study of how urban flood-risk management is integrated in multilevel governance, flood risks being considered a local manifestation of climate risks. Based on interviews with local and central decision-makers, we analyse the structure and processes and challenges of multilevel governance of flood risks across the territory of Dar es Salaam, a typical large coastal city in Africa.

The focus is particularly on the capabilities of the city municipality as regards *vertical steering and coordination* and how multilevel governance (as prescribed and practised) serves to enable or obstruct high citizen participation in planning and input into local management of flood risks and coproduction. We wished to learn more about how urban authorities facing extreme financial constraints and various urban development challenges have started to integrate adaptation in policy and governance when these authorities are not even able – or willing – to meet a set of basic service demands, such as for drainage, piped water, low-cost housing and other services. Hence, we focus on how key *social dimensions* are tackled, and how these relate to potentials of adaptation and resilience.

Given the multiple challenges facing urban authorities, the empirical data collection focused on the integration of adaptation in three key sectors and related actors/agencies: urban planning (strategic, land-use and development planning); water resources management (flood-risk and storm-water management, sewerage, water supply); and disaster-risk management (Rauken et al. 2014; Roberts and O'Donoghue 2013; Bicknell et al. 2010).

The chapter contributes new insight into the relationship between multilevel adaptation governance, coproduction and resilience – a subject that to limited degree has been dealt with in research on climate-change adaptation in Africa (see Carmin et al. 2012; Cartwright et al. 2012; Ziervogel and Parnell 2012) or elsewhere (Bulkeley 2013; Bicknell et al. 2010).

Adaptation and climate-risk management are important at all levels of government and governance and across sectors (Betsill and Bulkeley 2007). Moreover, since the impacts of climate change will have local variations, and adaptive capacity will vary across socio-political and institutional settings, a significant share of flood-risk management needs to take place at local levels – the municipal and community levels. This is in line with observations by Elinor Ostrom (among others) that key management decisions in resource management should be made as close as possible to the scene of events and the actors involved (Ostrom 2005).

In the case of Dar es Salaam, we find that the city and sub-city levels are severely constrained in capacity for self-governance and provisioning by multilevel governance. The municipality lacks appropriate mandate and support from the central state to build own capacity for adaptation and coordination of local actors, such as pursuing transitional adaptation to meet future climate extremes (or transformative actions). The institutional barriers facing city municipality and sub-city level actors in responding to climate change are deep-seated and exacerbated by constraints in available finances, resources and technologies at all levels. This stands in contradiction to the 'place-bound' character of both adaptation and flood-risk management: high capacity is required at the local level to ensure fast and adequate response to an emergency situation or an extreme climate event (Bicknell et al. 2010; Douglas et al. 2010). These findings are supported by other studies from urban Africa, reflecting general problems of poverty, financial constraints and institutional deficiency (Roberts and O'Donoghue 2013; UNISDR 2012; Ziervogel and Parnell 2012; Vedeld et al. 2012; Booth 2011).

The problems of integrating climate-change adaptation into urban governance are not unique to Africa. Such challenges are also observed in countries with higher adaptive capacity and resilience, as in Scandinavia and elsewhere in Europe (Hanssen et al. 2013; Bulkeley 2010). Moreover, there are several African cities – Durban and Cape Town for example – where important actions towards adaptation have been taken in planning and sector work, even in the absence of firm national policy directions and central support (Roberts and O'Donoghue 2013; Ziervogel and Parnell 2012). Such action is typically explained as response to the experiences of specific hazards and risks like floods, often combined with the efforts of individual champions who have been exposed to international climate-adaptation programmes and new knowledge, as in Saint Louis in Senegal (Vedeld et al. 2012). This may also be a result of more genuine autonomous action by entrepreneurial planners who have recognized the need to address climate risks on a broad scale, as in Durban (Roberts and O'Donoghue 2013).

Overall, our findings resonate with the call in the international literature for a stronger mandate and more resources to the city and sub-city levels for adaptation and response to future climate risks – to be provided by a more supportive national government that will take responsibility at central and regional levels (Bicknell et al. 2010; Satterthwaite et al. 2010). This would enhance the power, authority and legitimacy of the municipality to act on climate change. It is the *city government* that needs to bring coherence to agendas that in the past have been addressed without coordination, as with development, climate-change adaptation and disaster-risk management (Bulkeley 2013 and 2010; Satterthwaite 2011).

Analytical framework – assumptions about multilevel governance

Our analytical framework brings together theories from *multilevel governance, coproduction and related network governance theory*, and *resilient cities*.

Analytically, we delimit our analysis to the study of how traditional state command-and-control forms of governance in *vertical coordination* (hierarchical steering) are combined with or enable more soft forms of governing where government officials actively enable (or obstruct) high levels of citizen participation in local adaptation and flood-risk management, through forms of *coproduction* (Ostrom 1996 and 2005). This is perceived as a key governance challenge in Tanzania, as the state has remained a relatively dominant actor in urban governance and is not considered particularly participatory in its approaches to service delivery (Kiunsi 2013; Vedasto and Mrema 2013; Vedeld et al. 2012; Kombe and Kreibich 2006; Keyssi 2002). Especially at local level, we analyse the integration of adaptation in local governance and, hence, in *horizontal coordination* (Kern and Alber 2009; OECD 2009; Peters 2008).

Resilience

Resilience has risen to prominence within academic and political discourses on climate change as a means for understanding and managing complex systems (including cities) confronted by climate risks and uncertainties ('wicked problems') (Satterthwaite and Dodman 2013; Welsh 2013). Within the literature on climate adaptation, the resilience discourse is linked with contemporary governmental and governance discourses about the sharing of responsibilities between state and non-state actors for risk management, and conditions for change towards a new, more sustainable system state. This inherently normative stand relates to discussions about transitional adaptation and transformation (Pelling 2011). Cities as systems need to be assessed with regard to their resilience, capacity to act or adapt, and transformation. The integration of adaptation into government and governance across sectors, levels and scales is critical to long-term resilience (Bulkeley 2013; Satterthwaite and Dodman 2013; Pelling 2011). A key academic puzzle, however, relates to how such change can come about, whether through collaboration and coproduction and constructive public management of conflicts and differences, or through political resistance and action (Welsh 2013).

We argue that the focus on resilience is useful for understanding most urban contexts confronted with external risks. In the climate literature, 'resilience' has been explained as 'capacities to withstand or recover from all direct and indirect impacts of climate change' (Satterthwaite and Dodman 2013:292; Pelling 2011). It is fruitful to employ a broad and 'transformative' definition of resilience that opens up for 'improvements of basic structures and functions' (cf. IPCC 2012). From an adaptation perspective, we will then need to understand what and who must become more resilient within the city at different levels and scales. According to Satterthwaite and Dodman (2013), first, individuals and citizen groups and their assets need to become resilient. Second, their resilience requires support from resilient systems: from sector services, built and natural systems, and local institutions. Third, the arrangements of government and multilevel governance in urban areas need to be flexible, responsive and properly resourced with both financial and technical capacities, to ensure that these systems operate in resilient and sustainable ways. And finally, the politico-administrative system needs to be genuinely responsive to the priorities and needs of all residents.

There exist a wide range of complementary adaptation and disaster-risk management approaches that can enhance resilience and reduce exposure and vulnerability to (flood) risks from climate extremes and disasters. Such approaches are in part overlapping. The distinction between the two concepts or policy fields is not made clear in the literature (IPCC 2012). Adaptive measures to enhance resilience to flood risks (before, during or after an extreme climate event) might involve reducing vulnerability; preparation, response and recovery; transfer or sharing risk; reducing exposure; and transformation (IPCC 2012; Satterthwaite et al. 2010; Adger et al. 2009). By *integration of adaptation and climate-risk management* into policy and governance, in this study we look for highly specific measures, decisions or actions taken within multilevel governance and policy to enhance *a more resilient city at municipal and community levels* – inspired by key elements of the Ten Essentials for Making Cities Resilient (UNISDR 2014), namely:

- a city climate-action strategy in place (enabling a broad approach across sectors)
- organizational homes with resources that function in responsive manners (e.g. to enhance coproduction)

- coordination mechanisms (vertical and/or horizontal)
- early warning systems and emergency response systems
- land-use principles that are enforced
- operational resettlement programmes
- drainage and storm-water infrastructure in place
- sound watershed and environmental management to ensure drainage or buffers for storm water.

Multilevel governance, coproduction and network governance

The focus on *multilevel governance* captures the interplay between actors, levels and sectors of government in addressing complex and cross-cutting public policy challenges ('wicked problems'), as well as the interface of government officials with citizen groups and private actors (in coproduction or disengagement and conflict) (Bulkeley 2013; Osborne 2010, Peters 2008; Betsill and Bulkeley 2007; Ostrom 2005; Bache and Flinders 2004). *Network governance* theory is an element of multilevel governance and has been applied mainly in studies of Western democracies and developed countries (Sorensen and Torfing 2014 and 2009; Weber and Khademian 2008); more recently within the field of adaptation to climate change (Bulkeley 2013 and 2010; Pelling 2011; OECD 2009). The related concept and theory of *coproduction* has to greater degree than network governance informed studies on service delivery in *developing* countries (Ostrom 2005). *Coproduction* is defined as 'the process through which inputs used to produce a good or service are contributed by individuals who are not "in" the same organization' (Ostrom 1996:1074).

In this chapter, we apply theory from these areas to explain the integration of adaptation in urban governance (or lack of such), while we also draw implications from the case-study analysis for governance and coproduction theory and for the conceptual discussions about resilience and resilient cities. The integration of climate adaptation policies is assessed with the help of a multilevel governance framework (see Bulkeley 2013; Kern and Alber 2009). We refer to ideal modes of governance which relate to a specific set of processes and techniques that municipal authorities deploy: municipal self-governing, provisioning, regulation and enabling. Beyond these, both state and private/civil society actors interact and condition municipal actions from above and from below, through multilevel government or governance arrangements. In Africa there are many variants of 'community' or 'public–private' modes of governing at the local level (Crook and Booth 2011; de Sardan 2011). Each of these processes relies on different forms of governing capacity or powers, mandates and resources for pursuing climate policies in governance (Betsill and Bulkeley 2007).

Methodology

The research methods involve a combination of primary and secondary data collection and analysis. We conducted semi-structured interviews with citizens and decision-makers at various levels and scales (19 interviews) – with planners, policy-makers and practitioners working across various policy sectors (planning, environment, disaster-risk management, water resources). Each interview lasted between one and two hours. In addition to the individual interviews, we engaged stakeholders in selected focus groups. Interviews were combined with reviews of policies, urban plans and institutional and organizational arrangements (e.g. GOT 1999, 2004a, 2004b, 2077a, 2007b, 2011a, 2011b). Two local case studies were selected at ward/sub-ward levels within Kinondoni Municipality to study community and local-level responses, local governance and forms of coproduction in climate-risk management. The case studies illustrate issues related to participation and co-management of flooding and water resources in informal settlements that are exposed and vulnerable to different kinds of floods. Suna is subject to high-magnitude river floods; Bonde la Mpunga to more localized flash floods. Different types of floods mobilize different kinds of responses and institutions. The inclusion of local researchers and PhD candidates on the research team helped in validating findings. We also drew on findings from other Climate Change and Urban Vulnerability in Africa (CLUVA) research activities, for example on risks and vulnerability to floods (CLUVA 2014).

Drivers and barriers

The extent to which different modes of governance are actually deployed and have been successful is the result of a wide range of factors that can act as both drivers and barriers to achieving urban climate-change responses or resilience. The literature distinguishes three sets of factors in particular: *institutional, political* and *socio-technical* (see Bulkeley 2013); the latter set includes *ecological factors* as well (Ostrom 2005).

Institutional factors shape the capacity of urban institutions (formal and informal) – as prescribed and practised – to respond to or withstand risks, or improve a system's resilience – concerning matters like organizational arrangements and operations, knowledge, financial resources, and allocation of responsibilities between levels and actors (e.g. for coproduction or 'community' governance) (Bulkeley 2013; Ostrom 2005 and 1996). Regarding the constraints of *multilevel governance*, we investigate how the *state* at national and regional levels work – through (hierarchical) steering and coordination – to balance powers and enable or constrain adaptation of city and sub-city level actors through processes related to the *decentralization* and *devolution of* key functions and resources of the public sector; the *delegation* of public authority (for instance, to civil society or private markets); and the *de-concentration* of public authority and tasks to regional state bodies or a variety of (semi-) autonomous corporations or agencies (Manor 2011; Peters 2008; Vedeld 2003). Moreover, *financial and other resources* are considered particularly critical for local governance in low-income countries like Tanzania. *Socio-technical and ecological factors* relate to the ecosystem context, social and demographic conditions (including urbanization trends and change in settlement patterns), and urban landscapes or morphologies.

Dar es Salaam – the case study

Brief background

Dar es Salaam, the largest city in Tanzania and its main economic centre, has a population of close to 4 million people and an annual growth rate of about 4.4 per cent – a doubling in less than ten years. The city has experienced a series of floods arising from smaller rivers and lack of drainage as well as coastal flooding in recent years (Ardhi 2011). Mean annual rainfall is about 1100 mm, in two rainy seasons, frequently through heavy cloudbursts. CLUVA's analysis of extreme rainfall events, based on climate data projected up to 2050, indicates an increase in the frequency of extreme events, but a reduction in intensity and a limited increase in rainfall. Flood impacts are projected to increase, but this is mainly due to the growing concentrations of people in flood-prone areas (CLUVA 2014). The city has experienced various floods (as well as droughts) over the past three decades; and smaller or larger floods have become annual events since the turn of the millennium. In 2011, flash floods after heavy rains killed over 40 people and displaced thousands, destroying houses and assets across the city.

Like many large cities in sub-Saharan Africa, Dar es Salaam is faced with rapid population growth and continuous market-led settlement of people in risk-exposed and underserviced areas, as exemplified by the two local case studies of Suna and Bonde la Mpunga. The failure of the urban authorities to meet the basic service needs of the population across the city can be seen from the fact that only 11 per cent have access to sewerage, 25 per cent to piped water, and more than 90 per cent continue to rely on pit latrines and informal systems of sewerage (Vedeld et al. 2012). Key governance problems for the city relate to the lack of provisioning for strategic city planning and land management, and the lack of land-use regulation and enforcement (Vedasto and Mrema 2013; Ardhi 2011; UN-Habitat 2010 and 2009). Moreover, the long-term degradation of green environment, combined with weak storm-water management, lack of sewerage systems and solid waste management, have gradually exacerbated the impacts of flooding in low-lying areas with limited natural or formal drainage. Coastal flooding and erosion is a further key issue (John et al. 2012; Mng'ong'o 2005). It is in the context of these different climate-change risks, together with the multiple challenges of providing services and development to a rising population, that the urban authorities have started to respond to climate-change adaptation and to flood risks more systematically.

Multilevel governance and barriers to municipal capacity

The multilevel governance structure critically constrains municipal capacities for autonomous self-governance and provision of key services and infrastructure, in particular at the local level (ward/sub-wards). Tanzania has basically a three-tier government structure characterized by a strong unitary state with de-concentrated services at a regional level, a relatively autonomous yet weak municipal level, and an even weaker regional elected level (with fairly recently established regional councils and weak administrative capacity). However, the regional *state administration* has key mandates in strategic urban planning, coordination of services, land management, enforcement of land-use zoning and resettlement of flood-risk prone families through Regional Secretariat and Regional/District Commissioners (RC/DC). Two of the key ministries that intervene or invest in urban development are the Prime Minister's Office for Regional Administration and Local Government (PMO-RALG) and the Ministry of Lands, Housing and Human Settlement Development (MLHHSD). PMO-RALG provides policies on decentralization and control of deployment of human resources of the municipality. MLHHSD is the 'custodian' of all land in Tanzania, and is central to urban land management and enforcement, since land is defined as state-owned. MLHHSD has also taken charge of developing the new Dar es Salaam Master Plan (2010–2030) (Moss and Happold 2012) (see Figure 7.1).

A key constraint across all sectors and levels is the lack of financial and other resources for operations and enforcement (also at state levels and with public service corporations). This can be seen in the limited overall annual budgets for the three city municipalities of the city, Kinondoni Municipality included. The annual budget represents only about €31 per capita, whereas budgets at sub-ward levels are only about €1–2 per capita per year (PMO-RALG 2012). By contrast, a typical Norwegian municipality would have an annual budget per capita of approximately €5000 (Satterthwaite and Dodman 2013). Beyond the general budget for fire and rescue services, there are no specific budget allocations for adaptation or disaster-risk management. Financial resources are even more constraining at ward and sub-ward levels, where funding goes mostly to cover the running costs of a small office, with very limited funding for the ward/sub-ward development plans. One planner in the Ministry of Lands explained, the 'ward in their development plans do prepare a list of priority development activities but finances for these are very limited' (interview, MLHHSD decision-maker/planner, 4 June 2012). Key urban development programmes are mostly funded directly by central government agencies, public enterprises or by external partners (donors).

Knowledge and capacity within the multilevel governance structure is often enhanced by various long-standing ties that urban officials and municipal politicians have had with networks, international agencies and bilateral partners. Moreover, important networks involving local and international researchers

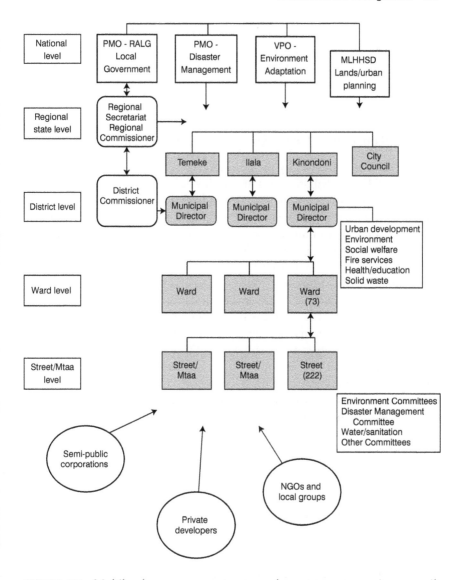

FIGURE 7.1 Multilevel governance structure: key state actors, city council, municipality and key private/semi-public actors and non-state actors (authors' construct)

at, for instance, ARDHI University, Tanzani (School of Urban and Regional Planning) has been reinforced through the CLUVA project (CLUVA 2014). The city is associated with ICLEI's Africa climate adaptation initiatives, the World Mayors' Council on Climate Change, the Clinton Foundation, the C40 Mayors' initiative on climate change, United Nations Office for Disaster Risk Protection (UNISDR)/Global Facility for Disaster Risk Protection (GFDRR) Resilient Cities Campaign, and the EU Adaptation to Climate Change in

Coastal Dar es Salaam project. Many of these networks and agencies have come with funding for smaller and a few larger adaptation projects (policy studies, risk assessments, workshops), but with relatively limited outreach, except for investment programmes funded by the World Bank on upgrading (Kiunsi 2013; Vedeld et al. 2012).

Municipal government: complex structure and weak mandate

Beyond the constraints set by the state level government, the organizational structure of Dar es Salaam city municipality is complex and multi-layered, suffering from evident structural deficiencies in terms of both vertical communication and engagement of sub-city levels and citizens, and horizontal communication. The municipality is composed of a complex four layered structure (see Figure 7.1). The city itself is headed by the Dar es Salaam City Council (DCC) and sub-divided into three autonomous municipal councils (or municipalities): Kinondoni (531 km^2), Ilala (210 km^2) and Temeke (652 km^2). The City Council lacks powers and resources to undertake substantive coordination among the municipalities. Kinondoni Municipality includes almost half the population of the city, and most of its high-income residential areas. Each municipality is divided into wards (73 wards in total) and sub-wards or Mtaas (222 in total). However, the three municipalities tend to govern with limited regard for the City Council and its mandated role as regards coordination. It would appear that municipal officials act as if they are accountable upwards to some of the state ministries, and to a lesser degree downwardly accountable to the wards/sub-wards or the people they are meant to serve (Vedeld et al. 2012; Kombe and Kreibich 2006; Keyssi 2002). Moreover, the municipalities (here: Kinondoni Municipality) are responsible for a rather limited set of services, such as development planning, strategic planning, fire services, solid waste collection, health/education, social welfare, and environmental management. The city as such falls under the Dar es Salaam region, which is headed by the Regional Commissioner.

Centralized adaptation and disaster-risk management

Centralization also characterizes adaptation as a policy field. There is no substantive institutional 'home' mandated for either adaptation or disaster-risk management with the Dar es Salaam City Council or the municipality which can build knowledge and coherence between these two agendas and key planning and service operations (indicated as critical by Solecki et al. 2011; Birkmann and von Teichman 2010). This greatly affects the capacity of the municipality to self-govern within its territory, and provide, regulate or enable these policy areas at community levels.

Responsibility for *climate change adaptation* is located within the Ministry of the Environment of the Vice President's Office. A national strategy for climate change was established in 2007 (NAPA 2007); the new National Climate Change Strategy (2012) institutes a national steering committee and highlights a set of adaptation measures that might be taken across different sectors. However, neither the old nor the new strategy provides guidance for urban adaptation, beyond some general suggestions as to what is required regarding improving urban human settlements and enforcement of land-use zoning, and possible relocation of flood-affected communities (Kiunsi 2013). As adaptation is located with the Ministry of the Environment, which has limited field staff at a lower level, adaption for all practical purposes does not appear well integrated in policy or practice at local levels. For example, environmental staff at state or municipal levels is either not in place, or awareness about climate change adaptation is low, as shown by our interviews. Climate change is perceived as a distant threat mostly related to (global) mitigation issues (Kiunsi 2013). With the assistance of CLUVA researchers, the municipality has, however, recently shown interest in developing a city Climate Action Plan.

Disaster-risk management as a formal policy sector is older and more firmly established than climate change adaptation. The agenda is vested with the Department of Disaster Management in the Prime Minister's Office. The department has only nine staff members to cover the whole nation, and is located within the city. A Disaster Relief Coordination Act was prepared in 1990/1991 (Becker 2011). The most recent national strategy on disaster-risk management (DRM) was approved in 2004, inspired by the process related to signing of the Hyogo Framework of Action (2005). Most actions in both domains have been pioneered from the Vice President's Office and Prime Minister's Office and lack coordination in practice between the Commissioner level and Municipal Directors, as became evident with emergency operations during extreme flooding in 2011 (according to several interviewees, e.g. interview with ward representative, September 2012, and our own observations). The emergency response during the 2011 flood in Suna relied heavily on assistance from the Red Cross country office located in Dar es Salaam. '…the military and the police were called upon and were present during the event. [but] they did not have the required operational equipment such as life jackets, vehicles, blankets, first aid. They only contributed human resources'; further, 'officials at the ward level during the flood were mostly confused and did not help much' (interview with Red Cross official, 5 June 2012).

Urban planning – market-led expansion of informal settlements

Flood-risk issues have not been well integrated in urban planning in the case-study areas, and land-use planning is conducted with little active local involvement (Vedeld et al. 2012; Kombe and Kreibich 2006; Keyssi 2002). Our fieldwork shows that public officials to limited degree encourage active citizen inputs into local development planning, land-use planning and coordination in the local management of flood risks, water resources and land. Expansion of housing in the informal areas we studied is mostly unplanned. Local development planning at ward/sub-ward levels generally involves drawing up 'wish' lists of relatively insignificant local development projects that tend to end up not being funded.

There are land-use zones identified as prone to flood hazard and not to be settled or built on, such as in Bonde la Mpunga and Suna, identified in the Master Plan from 1979. But this is not respected in practice by the local people or by government officials. There are few or no specific legal covenants for planning or for building codes (for example in the NAPA 2007). An old zoning rule in the Master Plan stipulates that no house may be built closer than 60 m to a river or from the coastline (tourist hotels exempted). But according to a planner in MLHHSD 'this is not adhered to ... take the example of Suna'. Even so, this rule has been kept in the new Master Plan; this shows, according to this planner that 'the new Master Plan does consider climate-change issues' (interview, MLHHSD decision-maker/planner, 4 June 2012). However, this reference to flood-risk zones, based on some recent maps, is a relatively minor reflection of the climate-change issue (Kiunsi 2013; Moss et al. 2012; URT 2011).

Overall, the combined state–municipal planning system has not been successful as regards strategic planning or with detailed land-use planning and management (Herslund et al. 2012; Vedeld et al. 2012; Kombe and Kreibich 2006). Close to 80 per cent of the residents of Dar es Salaam live in unplanned or informal settlements, generally lacking such infrastructure and services as storm drains and basic sanitation facilities. CLUVA researchers have identified some 20 of the total 150 informal settlements in the city as extremely vulnerable to flooding, given current rainfall and social patterns (Kiunsi 2013; John et al. 2012). As noted, expansion of housing in informal areas is mostly unplanned. The Master Plan was prepared without much citizen or private-sector participation, as is also generally the case with land-use plans (Vedeld et al. 2012; Kombe and Kreibich 2006). For example, one senior urban planner in MLHHSD commented that the MLHHSD took over master planning from the City Council, arguing that the municipality 'is not technically very strong' and 'does not have the budget' to do the work. 'Everything regarding the Master Plan is done by the Ministry.' He reported that the municipalities 'only have one or two engineers and planners, and lack capacity and competence and finance' (interview, MLHHSD planner, 5 June 2012).

Unsuccessful integration and weak coproduction in flood-risk management

The case of Bonde la Mpunga shows that public agencies and officials are not capable of encouraging or mobilizing high levels of citizen input into the local management of flood risks and related land-use conflicts. Bonde la Mpunga is an informal, underserviced settlement of some 12,000 people, situated in a low-depression and waterlogged wetland area prone to flooding. This is an old settlement in an unplanned area that has gradually expanded, partly by expansion through often 'illegal' settlements by local people on adjacent floodplains subject to flooding, partly by the construction of middle-class houses and shops/offices. The area is bisected by a local river and was designated as hazard land in the 1979 Master Plan. Two storm-water channels pass through the area (Kiunsi 2013). About 450 low-income houses are flooded each year; negative impacts include damage to homes and assets, disruption of local services (schools), temporary relocation, overflow of latrines, and various health issues (John et al. 2012). As Bonde la Mpunga is located close to the beach and the commercial centre of Dar es Salaam (5 km) and shopping malls, it has become increasingly attractive to private investors.

A key governance issue arose some years ago when the central government allowed private developers to construct middle-class houses and new commercial buildings on the high-value land adjacent to the settlement – in violation of the original Master Plan, which had defined the areas as hazardous marshlands to be protected. The new buildings were constructed in such a way that they blocked natural drainage, and forced floodwater into the houses of many of the original low-income residents. Local people protested about this development through the media, local demonstrations and by mobilizing local politicians. Most of the key agencies relevant to flood-risk management (planning, water resources, sewerage, disaster-risk management) have been absent as regards everyday management of these local flood-risk issues. In contrast, both government and private developers have engaged in the promotion of the middle-class housing projects. Occasionally, the central government has sent urban planners and water engineers to engage in dialogue, but no shared solution acceptable to the local population has been found. The interventions of various state and municipal agencies in local affairs have resulted in conflicts and mutual disengagement, not coproduction. There are, for example, no plans for providing sewerage facilities for the informal area (interview 5 June 2012).

In this regard, the local people have been met with an ambivalent government agency (MLHHSD) that has been less concerned about 'good governance' and local demands, and more responsive to private business and middle-class housing concerns. According to one person from MLHHSD,

> wrong decisions have been made on transfer of hazardous land to commercial area and residential area … Wealthy people have constructed houses in the wetlands and changed flooding patterns, and poor people suffer. This was not allowed according to the Master Plan. Still, the developers were given permits; now there is a need to demolish some houses and do better drainage.
>
> (interview, MLHHSD planner, 4 June 2012).

Local communities formed a local flood-risk management committee to further their case with the local authorities and the PMO, with some support from the sub-ward/ward and a few non-governmental organizations (NGOs) (although NGOs are not numerous in the area, and there are relatively few civil society associations). This community action led to the construction of a local storm-water drainage canal by the private developer that reduced the flooding problems, but did not resolve the underlying issues.

Community action can work both ways in terms of strengthening local resilience. On the one hand, local people have mobilized collectively and individually to address flooding and resolve related land and water resources issues. Individual households have engaged in the maintenance of drains and protecting houses and assets by raising their doorsteps, cleaning and digging new drains, hanging household assets from ceiling boards, and collecting solid waste that may block natural drains. When a flood is in the making, the people call local authorities on cell phones on an ad hoc basis. They temporarily relocate from the submerged areas to higher-lying areas or to local school buildings. There are also sub-committees of the sub-ward with responsibilities for water and sanitation. On the other hand, the people themselves also undermine resilience by settling in vulnerable areas, as well as by dumping solid waste in drains or emptying pit latrines before or during the rainy season, engendering health issues.

Both case-study areas (Bonde and Suna) show that enforcement of land-use zoning is weak or ambivalent, allowing for continuous growth of new informal settlements. Since poor people have few options other than to settle in these areas, the areas are subject to a market-led informalization with limited regard for rules and regulations (Kombe and Kweka 2012; Vedeld et al. 2012). Local 'Big Men' are involved in these informal land transactions, often in violation of land-use zoning principles. Several respondents suggested a stronger role for the sub-ward/Mtaa and ward levels in land-development planning and control – a statutory role they do not have today. They are mostly involved in local planning concerning minor development projects, not in land allocations and management (Vedasto and Mrema 2013; Kombe and Kreibich 2006). According to a senior planner in the Ministry of Lands, 'due to the lack of enforcement capacity with higher level authorities, the Mtaa should be given the power to guide development and control' (interview, MLHHSD planner, 5 June 2012).

The problem of enforcing land-use zoning is compounded by political factors. Following the 2011 flood in the Suna settlement, the government decided on a plan to resettle many of the flood-affected households, with support from the United Nations Human Settlements Programme (UN-Habitat). However, residents came together to form a local political bureau of CCM, the main political party, to resist what was perceived as 'forced' resettlement. This shows how local people in informal settlements establish protection through ties to political representatives to secure tenure and houses, against the aims of the central government administration (interview with ward representative,

September 2012; interview 4 June 2013 with official in Disaster Management Office, PMO). Such 'political patronage' also shows the ambivalence of the government in dealing with informality: administrators seek to move people; politicians engage to protect them.

Discussion

Lack of integration of adaptation and climate-risk management

Climate change adaptation – narrowly defined – remains a fairly nascent agenda and is not well integrated in planning and governance at the municipal or community levels in Dar es Salaam. Adaptation is addressed only indirectly in the draft city Master Plan; however, it may become a more integrated element in municipal governance thanks to the recent interaction with CLUVA researchers on a new city *Climate action plan* (Kombe et al. 2013). Basically, disaster-risk management is a national and regional state-anchored agenda, and the municipalities are little involved in disaster preparedness or direct coordination of emergency responses. Flood-risk management interfaces with all the sectors discussed in this study. Given the many public and private actors involved, it has remained a fragmented agenda as regards municipal provision and regulation. As a policy area, flood-risk management has several institutional homes and is not well defined or coordinated at municipal levels in planning and development.

The city has – often in concert with state agencies – executed a set of smaller (incremental) adaptation activities and projects on climate change. But these initiatives have only to a very limited degree involved the provision of long-term adaptation programmes, or substantive investments or active attempts at regulating local action and enabling active involvement of residents or the private sector towards transformative action.

Complex interaction of institutional, financial and political factors

A complex combination of institutional and other factors places particular constraints on effective city and sub-city level climate-risk governance in Dar es Salaam. We argue that barriers to the provisioning of services and enabling of participation can be found in the historically centralized location of responsibilities for urban development with state agencies and ineffective multilevel governance, with limited devolution to local authorities, lack of financial resources, weak commitment to participation, and other political factors that undermine coproduction. Additional related factors include the complexities of the multi-layered city government, lack of clarity in division of roles between (regional) state bodies and the municipal agencies, lack of relevant institutional 'homes' for adaptation with city authorities, ambivalence in the enforcement of plans and laws and local encounters; and, finally, institutional fragmentation across sector lines (see Vedeld et al. 2012). At the root of these problems is the inability of urban authorities to govern inequality and informality in land management and provide low-cost housing in secure sites as part of the urban change processes: a lack of capability to tackle *social dimensions*.

Public officials from different urban development agencies are ambivalent in their responses and do not always act in concert with the political system. Planners and water engineers tend to discourage or not actively encourage local contributions to service delivery and flood-risk management. This undermines trust and has major negative implications for the mobilization of local resources and possible synergies in development (Sorensen and Torfing 2014; Osborne 2010; Ostrom 1996). We see the failure of public officials to enhance *coproduction within the system of multilevel governance* as a decisive factor in explaining the weak integration of adaptation and flood risks in municipal governance at city and community levels.

We also hold that the relative efficiency in local participation and thus in coproduction depends on a certain *community capacity and agency*, as measured, for instance, in terms of the density of local associations or social organization at the sub-ward levels (Vedeld et al. 2012; Ostrom 2005). Although the density of NGOs did not seem high, we found various types of local-level community groups, with possibly untapped time and resources, which are not mobilized actively and systematically by local officials today. Community involvement in adaptation is an essential part of any process that seeks to build resilience or to overcome forms of structural inequalities (Bulkeley 2013). Especially regarding cities in developing countries, many have stressed the importance of local governance for management of water and land, and development – not least given the extreme financial constraints faced by governments (Satterthwaite 2011; Bicknell et al. 2010; Ostrom 1996). For example, de Sardan (2011) has identified at least eight modes of local governance in countries in West Africa (see also Booth 2011; Crook and Booth 2011; Crook 2010).

We argue that political factors should be taken into consideration when analysing the integration of flood-risk management in local governance. Political factors are important for explaining why and how people are allowed to settle in unplanned and risky sites. However, political factors impact in different manners, and can work both against the interests of local people (more floods, land loss) and in support of their interests (protection of land and assets). This may indicate that political factors become decisive once *important* decisions are on the agenda about the governance of local conflicts, or when decisions are to be taken about important infrastructural investments aimed at addressing climate vulnerability and inequality (Bulkeley 2013; Pelling 2011). But political factors need not be a decisive factor for getting incremental adaptation going, as the case of Durban in South African has shown (Roberts and O'Donoghue 2013).

Finally, the municipality of Kinondoni is operating under extreme financial constraints at city and sub-city levels. Financial constraints are most pronounced at the ward and sub-ward levels. The availability of financial and other resources is obviously critical for municipal capacity to provide services and enable coordinated infrastructural development at local level. That said, the availability of resources per se may not necessarily be what explains governance approaches to adaptation. Also, in the multilevel governance system, constraints are related to what the state does or does not do in terms of enabling the municipality or directly contributing to urban investments and development. (See comparison between Dar es Salaam and Saint Louis (Senegal) in Vedeld et al. 2012.)

Implications for theory on resilience, coproduction and multilevel governance

The experiences reported from Dar es Salaam indicate that *resilience* as a concept can be useful for identifying important factors that might define a 'resilient city' and what needs to become resilient from a 'systems' perspective (UNISDR 2014): individuals, communities and their assets supported by local institutions, municipal services, multilevel governance and the political system (Satterthwaite and Dodman 2013). We have seen how the capabilities of local residents and communities depend crucially on services (including ecosystem), financial flows, and processes that originate from outside their boundaries and jurisdictions. Hence, resilience should be considered as a process, more than an outcome. We find the concept of resilience a useful complement to adaptation, as it indicates a capacity not only to withstand shocks but also to recover from potentially unexpected events. However, resilience should be defined more broadly than often implicit in the climate literature, with its narrow notion of 'bouncing back' to some previous system state or maintenance of prior structures after a shock (Bulkeley 2013:148). Resilience must include scope for improvements in basic structures and functions if it is to serve to point towards a way forward, beyond incremental adaptation to transitional adaptation and transformation (IPCC 2012). This is captured in the disaster-risk management literature in the focus on disaster-risk *reduction* and on the need to 'build back better' (Satterthwaite and Dodman 2013).

Cities and urban communities need to be assessed with regard to *resilience*, the *capacity to act* and deliberately change or adjust urban development (adaptation), and *transformation* (Pelling 2011). Conceptually, resilience should reflect more than the first level of adaptation, as suggested by Pelling (2011:69). Resilience should be open towards the second level of adaptation related to *transitional adaptation*, which is defined as targeting reform in the design and application of governance and service systems (Pelling 2011). As such, resilience can become a means for understanding and managing complex change processes. However, resilience also has its limitations. For instance, it would not cover the third level of adaptation, *transformation*, which, according to Pelling (2011) refers to more radical or progressive changes within society. And indeed, transformation in political, institutional and cultural systems is required in order to tackle the more structural causes of vulnerability and inequality, and meet future climate-risk challenges (Bulkeley 2013; O'Brian 2012; IPCC 2012). In Dar es Salaam, the current structures and functions of the multilevel governance systems act as major barriers to effective governance and constructive dialogue between officials and citizens, and coproduction in flood-risk management and sustainable development. The multilevel governance context, as well as other institutional barriers, will need to change radically if the goal is to enable more active participation in local planning and local capacity to act on climate risks.

Hence, there are limitations to resilience as an analytical concept, both as utilized in the academic literature (Welsh 2013) as well as a policy goal for 'resilient cities' as promoted by UNISDR (2014). The Ten Essentials provide limited guidance for cities on how more precisely to govern the resilience agenda, for example whether to embark upon a vertical approach and a few sectors, or employ a broad-based horizontal approach (Roberts and O'Donoghue 2013). Nor does resilience offer guidance on how to deal with political and key institutional factors that often intervene to condition government and governance responses. Resilience focuses more on 'what' needs to change or adapt, and is less developed in terms of understanding governance and the interplay of state and non-state actors.

The concept of *coproduction* (in multilevel governance) can provide a fruitful framework for analysing the governance context and understanding how to go about managing climate risks and related service production and local development. Coproduction has in particular been utilized to understand vertical relationships, like how public officials interact with the people, but also conditions for horizontal coordination. 'Coproduction is one way that synergy between what a government does and what citizens do can occur' (Ostrom 1996:1080; see also Cleaver 2012; Tendler 1997).

Coproduction here is closely related to the emphasis in New Public Governance (NPG) on public–private and civic collaboration through networks and partnerships and social innovation in the public sector (Sorensen and Torfing 2014). NPG moves beyond the New Public Management literature to focus on how collaboration between, for example, government and non-government actors – defined as 'the constructive management of differences' – can drive public innovation and change in relationships. In Dar es Salaam, despite some encouragement among street-level bureaucrats to mobilize people in emergency situations, the overall workings of the state–municipal system in planning and flood-risk management generally discourage local contributions to flood-risk management, or collaboration and coproduction in service delivery.

In conclusion, compared to the debate on multilevel governance in Western democracies, which tends to emphasize constraints related to knowledge sharing and horizontal coordination among key state and non-state actors for tackling 'wicked problems', we find in Dar es Salaam more deep-rooted structural issues to effective governing of climate risks, related to vertical steering and coordination issues. These issues reflect a broader 'institutional crisis' in public service delivery in Tanzania and the magnitude of diverse urban governance challenges facing the urban authorities, which distracts attention away from adaptation and related environmental issues in local governance and politics. The new dialogue on a city climate-action plan with CLUVA researchers (Kombe et al. 2013) may serve to promote a more coherent approach to climate risks and adaptation.

References

Adger, N., Lorenzoni, I, and O'Brien, K. (2009). *Adapting to climate change: thresholds, values, governance*. New York: Cambridge University Press

Ardhi (2011). *Dar es Salaam case study. Climate change, disaster risk and the urban poor: cities building resilience for a changing world*. Dar es Salaam: Ardhi University

Bache, I. and Flinders, M. (2004). *Multilevel governance*. Oxford: Oxford University Press

Becker, P. (2011). Scoping study for capacity development in disaster management between Tanzania and Sweden, April–July 2011, DMD, OPM, Tanzania and MSB, Sweden. Lund University. Open access, http://lup.lub.lu.se/luur/download?func=do wnloadFile&recordOId=2295000&fileOId=2295001, accessed 15.2.2014

Betsill, M. and Bulkeley, H. (2007). 'Looking back and thinking ahead: a decade of cities and climate change research'. *Local Environment*, 12(5), 447–456

Bicknell, J., Dodman, D. and Satterthwaite, D. (eds) (2010). *Adapting cities to climate change. understanding and addressing the development challenges*. London: Earthscan Climate

Birkmann, J and von Teichman, K. (2010). 'Integrating disaster risk reduction and climate change adaptation: key challenges – scales, knowledge, and norms'. *Sustainable Science*, 5, 171–184

Booth, D. (2011). 'Introduction: working with the grain?' The Africa power and politics programme. *IDS Bulletin*, 42(2), 1–10

Bulkeley, H. (2010). 'Cities and the governing of climate change'. *Annual Review of Environment and Resources*, 35, 229–253

Bulkeley, H. (2013). *Cities and climate change*. London: Routledge

Carmin, J., Anguelovski, I. and Roberts, D. (2012). 'Urban climate adaptation in the Global South: planning in an emerging policy domain'. *Journal of Planning Education and Research*, 32(1), 18–32

Cartwright, A., Parnell, S., Oelofse, G. and Ward, S. (eds) (2012). *Climate change and the city scale: impacts, mitigation and adaptation in Cape Town*. Oxford: Routledge/Earthscan

Cleaver, F. (2012). *Development through bricolage: rethinking institutions for natural resources management*. London: Routledge/Earthscan

CLUVA (2014). homepage. Available at http://www.cluva.eu/, accessed 10.3.2014

Crook, R.C. (2010). 'Rethinking civil service reform in Africa: "islands of effectiveness" and organisational commitment'. *Commonwealth and Comparative Politics*, 48, 479–504

Crook, R.C. and Booth, D. (eds) (2011). 'Working with the grain? Rethinking African governance'. *IDS Bulletin*, 42(2): iii–iv, 1–101

de Sardan, J.-P. (2011). 'The eight modes of local governance in West Africa', in R.C. Crook and David Booth (eds), 'Working with the grain? Rethinking African governance', *IDS Bulletin*, 42(2): 22–31.

Douglas, I., Alma, K., Magenta, M., McDonnell, Y., McLean, L. and Campbell, J. (2010). 'Unjust waters. Climate change, flooding and the urban poor in Africa', in J. Bicknell, D. Dodman and D. Satterthwaite (eds), *Adapting cities to climate change: understanding and addressing the development challenges*. London: Earthscan Climate

GOT (1999). The Land Act No. 4 of 1999 Dar es Salaam: Government of Tanzania

GOT (2004a). The National Disaster Management Policy. Government of Tanzania

GOT (2004b). Dar es Salaam City Profile. Dar es Salaam: Government Publishers

GOT (2007a). Land Use Planning Act 2007. Government of Tanzania.

GOT (2007b). National Adaptation Programme of Action (NAPA). Government of Tanzania

GOT (2011a). Report on the Hyogo Framework of Action. Government of Tanzania

GOT (2011b). Urban Development Management Policy. Government of Tanzania

Hanssen, G., Mydske, P.K. and Dahle, E. (2013). 'Multilevel coordination of climate change adaptation: by national hierarchical steering or by regional network governance'. *Local Environment*, 18(8), 869–887

Herslund, L., Lund, D.H., Yeshitela, K., Workalemahu, L., Kombe, W. and Keyssi, A.G. (2012). *Strategic measures and recommendations on two cities: Dar es Salaam and Addis Ababa.* CLUVA deliverable 3.7, http://www.cluva.eu, see CLUVA 2014

Hyogo Framework for Action (2005). 'Hyogo Framework for Action 2005–2015: Building the resilience of nations and communities to disasters', World Conference on Disaster Reduction 18–22 Jan., Kobe, Japan, United Strategy for Disaster Reduction (UNISDR), http://www.unisdr.org/2005/wcdr/intergover/official-doc/L-docs/Hyogo-framework-for-action-english.pdf, accessed 8.3.2014

IPCC (2012). *Managing the risks of extreme events and disasters to advance climate change adaptation.* A special report of Working Groups I and II of the Intergovernmental Panel on Climate Change (IPCC). Cambridge: Cambridge University Press

John, R., Mayunga, J., and Kombe, W. (2012). 'Preliminary findings on social vulnerability assessment in the selected cities'. Internal CLUVA report (D5.4). Ardhi University-ARU, Dar es Salaam

Kern, K. and Alber, G. (2009). 'Governing climate change in cities: modes of urban climate governance in multilevel systems', in OECD, *Competitive cities and climate change*, OECD Conference Proceedings (Milan, 9–10 October, 2008), 171–196

Keyssi, A.G. (2002). *Community participation in urban infrastructure provision, servicing informal settlements in Dar es Salaam.* PhD Thesis, SPRING Publication Series no. 33, University of Dortmund

Kiunsi, R. (2013). 'The constraints on climate change adaptation in a city with large development deficit: the case of Dar es Salaam', *Environment and Urbanization*, 25, 321–333

Kombe, W. and Kweka, C. (2012). *Institutional analysis for climate change in Dar es Salaam City.* CLUVA deliverable WP5. http://www.cluva.eu, see CLUVA 2014

Kombe, W., Keyssi, A., Kassenga, G. and Shemdoe, R. (2013). *City local climate action plan 2014-2020 of African cities facing climate change.* ARDHI University, CLUVA deliverable D5.7. http://www.cluva.eu, see CLUVA 2014

Kombe, W.J. and Kreibich, V. (2006). *Governance of informal urbanization in Tanzania.* Dar es Salaam: Mkuki Na Nyota Publishers

Manor, James (2011). *Perspective on decentralization.* Working Paper no. 3, ICLD, Visby: Swedish International Centre for Local Democracy

Mng'ong'o, O. (2005). *Browning process: the case of Dar es Salaam.* PhD Thesis. Royal Institute of Technology, School of Architecture and Built Environment, Stockholm.

Moss, D, and Happold, B. (2012). 'Afri Arch, BuroQ (2012) Dar es Salaam Master plan 2030'. Preliminary Draft, Dar es Salaam

NAPA (2007): *Tanzania: National Adaptation Plan for Action.* Dar es Salaam: Government Publishers

National Climate Change Strategy (2012). *National climate change strategy 2012.* Environment Division, Vice President's Office. Dar es Salaam:Government Publishers

O'Brian, K. (2012). 'Global environmental change II: from adaptation to deliberate transformation'. *Progress in Human Geography*, 36(5): 667–676

OECD (2009). *Competitive cities and climate change.* OECD Conference Proceedings, Milan, 9–10 October, 2008

Osborne, S. (2010). 'Introduction: the (new) public governance: a suitable case for treatment?', in S. Osborne (ed), *The new public governance: emerging perspectives on the theory and practice of public governance.* Oxford: Routledge

Ostrom, E. (1996). 'Crossing the great divide: coproduction, synergy, and development'. *World Development*, 24(6), 1073–1087

Ostrom, E. (2005). *Understanding institutional diversity.* Princeton, NJ: Princeton University Press

Pelling, M. (2011). *Adaptation to climate change: from resilience to transformation.* London: Taylor & Francis

Peters, B.G. (2008). *The two futures of governing. Decentering and recentering processes in governing.* 114 Reihe Politikwissenschaft/Political Science Series. Wien: Institut für Höhere Studien

PMO-RALG (2012). Annual budgets for Tanzanian municipal councils. http://beta. pmoralg.go/tz/lginformation/monotor1a.php, accessed 15.11. 2012

Rauken, T., Mydske, P.K. and Winsvold, M. (2014). 'Mainstreaming climate change adaptation at the local level'. *Local Environment: International Journal of Justice and Sustainability*, doi: 10.1080/13549839.2014.880412

Roberts, D. and O'Donoghue, S. (2013). 'Urban environmental challenges and climate change action in Durban, South Africa'. *Environment and Urbanization*, 25(2), 299–319

Satterthwaite, David (2011). 'Editorial: why community action is needed for disaster risk reduction and climate change adaptation'. *Environment & Urbanization*, 23(2), 339–350

Satterthwaite, D. and Dodman, D. (2013). 'Editorial. Towards resilience and transformation for cities within a finite planet'. *Environment and Urbanization*, 25(2), 291–98

Satterthwaite, D., Huq, S., Pelling, M., Reid, H. and Lankao, P.R. (2010). 'Adapting to climate change in urban areas: the possibilities and constraints in low- and middle-income nations', in J. Bicknell, D. Dodman and D. Satterthwaite (eds), *Adapting cities to climate change. Understanding and addressing the development challenges.* London: Earthscan Climate

Solecki, W., Leichenko, R. and O'Brien, K. (2011). 'Climate change adaptation strategies and disaster risk reduction in cities: connections, contentions, and synergies'. *Current Opinion in Environmental Sustainability*, 3(3): 135–141

Sorensen, E. and Torfing, J. (2009). 'Making governance networks effective and democratic through metagovernance'. *Public Administration*, 87, 234–258

Sorensen, E. and Torfing, J. (2014). 'Enhancing social innovation by rethinking collaboration, leadership and public governance', Paper presented at *Social Frontiers. The next edge of social innovation research*, 14 and 15 November, 2013, Glasgow Caledonian University

Tendler, J. (1997). *Good governance in the tropics.* Baltimore, MD: Johns Hopkins University Press

UN-Habitat (2009). *Tanzania: Dar es Salaam city profile.* Nairobi: UN-Habitat

UN-Habitat (2010). *Citywide action plan for upgrading unplanned and unserviced settlements in Dar es Salaam.* Nairobi: UN-Habitat

UNISDR (2012). *Making cities resilient report.* Geneva: UNISDR

UNISDR (2014). 'The 10 essentials for making cities resilient', http://www.unisdr.org/campaign/resilientcities/toolkit/essentials, accessed 8.3.2014

URT (2011). 'New draft urban development and management policy', unpublished, Dar es Salaam: Government of Tanzania

Vedasto, R.V. and Mrema, L.K. (2013). 'Architectural perspectives on informalization of formal settlements: case of Sinza Neighbourhood in Dar es Salaam'. *Online Journal of Social Science Research*, 2(6), 151–172

Vedeld, T. (2003). 'Democratic decentralisation and poverty reduction: exploring the linkages'. *Forum for Development Studies*, 2, 159–203

Vedeld, T., Kombe, W., Kweka-Msale, C., Ndour, M.N., Coly, A. and Hellevik, S. (2012). *Report on planning system and government structure in 2 cities* (Dar es Salaam and Saint Louis), Scientific report, CLUVA, http://www.cluva.eu/deliverables/CLUVA_D3.1.pdf, accessed 10.3.2014

Weber, E.P. and Khademian, A.M. (2008). 'Wicked problems, knowledge challenges, and collaborative capacity building in network settings'. *Public Administration Review*, 68(2), 334–349

Welsh, M. (2013). Resilience and responsibility: governing uncertainty in a complex world. *Geographical Journal*, doi:10.1111/geoj.12012

Ziervogel, G. and Parnell, S. (2012). 'South African coastal cities: governance responses to climate change adaptation', in A. Cartwright, S. Parnell, G. Oelofse and S. Ward (eds), *Climate change and the city scale: impacts, mitigation and adaptation in Cape Town*. Oxford: Routledge/Earthscan

8

CAN LINKING SMALL- AND LARGE-SCALE FARMERS ENHANCE ADAPTIVE CAPACITY?

Evidence from Tanzania's Southern Agricultural Growth Corridor

Jennifer West

Introduction

A central question in the adaptation–development nexus is if and how agricultural investments that are undertaken as part of general development efforts can enhance the adaptive capacity of smallholder farmers and rural communities in the context of climate change. There is growing recognition that agricultural investments that include smallholder farmers as part of a core business strategy may provide broad social and economic benefits (World Bank 2013; Vermeulen and Cotula 2010). However, little is known about how particular agricultural investment models affect the adaptive capacities of rural households and communities. Tanzania provides an illustrative case of some of the challenges that must be addressed if agricultural investments targeting smallholder farmers are to support climate adaptation. Tanzania's National Adaptation Programme of Action (NAPA) and National Climate Change Strategy identify agriculture as the sector of the economy that is most vulnerable to climate change, with agriculture and food security being priority arenas for adaptation efforts (URT 2012b; URT 2007). At the same time, Tanzania is seeking to modernize and transform its agricultural sector through major initiatives that aim to attract greater private sector investment in the country's agricultural sector.

The Southern Agricultural Growth Corridor of Tanzania (SAGCOT) is a prominent example of these initiatives. SAGCOT, which forms the policy context for the discussion in this chapter, aims to set a benchmark for sustainable and responsible agricultural investment and development in Africa, and has attracted wide attention nationally and internationally (Jenkins 2012). A flagship programme of the Tanzanian government's *Kilimo Kwanza* (Agriculture First) strategy for increasing private-sector investment in the agriculture sector, SAGCOT's goals are 'to deliver rapid and sustainable agricultural growth, with major benefits for food security, poverty reduction and reduced vulnerability to climate change' (AgDevCo and Prorustica 2011: foreword). In its efforts to target smallholder farmers, SAGCOT is promoting outgrower (OG) schemes – a form of contract farming (CF) that links independent smallholder farmers to a large, centralized processing unit or commercial farming operation through contracts that specify one or more conditions of crop production and marketing (Little and Watts 1994). OG schemes have been established in various African, Asian and Latin American countries over the past 50 years and have enjoyed wide popularity among governments, donors and multilateral development agencies for their perceived potential to deliver development benefits to smallholder farmers and rural communities (Tyler and Dixie 2013). In combining small- and large-scale farming, OG schemes offer an alternative to an agricultural development approach that favours *either* large-scale commercial agriculture, *or* smallholder production. However, the literature is divided as to whether OG schemes represent an opportunity or a threat for smallholder farmers, rural communities and the environment (Oya 2012: 4). This chapter extends the literature on OG schemes and contract farming by exploring *how OG schemes can support the adaptive capacities of smallholder farmers and rural communities to climate variability and change in the context of ongoing development challenges, opportunities and constraints.*

How agricultural investments can support smallholder farmers' adaptive capacity is a pertinent question for governments, donors and investors seeking to promote agricultural development in Tanzania. Tanzania's agricultural production is dominated by smallholder production (Hella et al. 2011). More than 80 per cent of the population relies on agriculture for food security, income and employment (URT 2012a). Smallholder farmers and rural areas face numerous development challenges associated with poor health status, low life expectancy, malnutrition, food insecurity, limited employment opportunities, poverty, low producer prices, and lack of access to reliable infrastructure, information and services (UNDP 2013; Paavola 2003). Climate variability and change represent an additional source of uncertainty in this context (Paavola 2008). The projected impacts of climate change in Tanzania include a warming in the mean temperature of 1.5–5°C by 2100 (depending on the emissions scenario), with greater relative warming during dry seasons compared to wet seasons and in inland areas compared to coastal regions of the country (Watkiss et al. 2011). Changes in the onset and duration of the rainy seasons, and the incidence and intensity of drought and heavy rainfall, are already observed by farmers around the country, and are expected to affect irrigation potential, agricultural productivity and hydropower production in the future (URT 2012b; URT 2007). Smallholders are recognizing and responding to climate variability and change, although they face barriers and limits to adapting (Sanga 2013; Mongi 2010; Mary 2009).

Conceptual framework

To answer the research question, the chapter draws on literatures on CF and OG schemes, and adaptive capacity. In the literature on climate change, adaptive capacity, together with exposure and sensitivity to climatic risks, are central components of vulnerability (Smit and Wandel 2006). Vulnerability varies between and among individuals, regions, sectors and social groups and over time due to differences in social, economic, environmental and institutional conditions, and the distribution of assets, resources and entitlements in society (IPCC 2007). The term 'adaptive capacity', as applied in this chapter, refers to the capacity of individuals, households, communities and the wider socio-ecological systems of which they are a part to adjust to, and thrive, in the face of uncertainties. It includes the ability to deal with immediate 'surprises' and long-term risks, climatic and otherwise, as well as the capacity to seize opportunities, recognizing that people do not respond to climate variability and change in isolation from other processes of change (IPCC 2014). The interplay between participation in OG schemes and adaptive capacity is explored in relation to seven factors: economic resources; risk management; technology; information and skills; infrastructure; institutions; and equity. These factors are broadly referred to as 'determinants' of adaptive capacity in the climate change literature (Keskitalo et al. 2011; Smit and Wandel 2006; Eakin and Lemos 2006; Yohe and Tol 2002; Smit and Pilifosova 2001). They also resonate with the literature on CF and OG schemes, which suggests that successful OG schemes promote local development and smallholder welfare by increasing household incomes (Bellemare 2012; Barrett et al. 2012; Miyata et al. 2009; Warning and Key 2002); by enhancing access to agricultural markets, inputs, technology and training (Abebe et al. 2013); by reducing production and marketing risks (Glover and Kusterer 1990); by strengthening equity, transparency and trust in OG relationships (Kirsten and Sartorius 2002; Glover 1987); and by contributing to local development through investments in jobs, infrastructure and services (Tyler and Dixie 2013; Poulton et al. 2008). Below I outline these factors in more detail and describe the ways in which they are operationalized in this chapter.

Access to economic resources can enhance households', communities' and societies' abilities to withstand and recover from climatic shocks and undertake investments to adapt to climate change (Eakin and Lemos 2006). I operationalize this determinant by assessing whether and how OG production contributes to or undermines the *stability, diversity,* and *flexibility* of participating households' agricultural incomes. 'Risk management' refers to the process of managing and spreading risks, and includes both formal (e.g. commercial insurance) and informal channels (Yohe and Tol 2002). In OG schemes, the estate (the buyer) normally assumes the marketing risks while the smallholder producer assumes the production (including climate) risks (Glover and Kusterer 1990). I assess how OG schemes are affecting smallholders' adaptive capacity by discussing how participation in OG schemes affects the agricultural production and the marketing risks that farmers face. Access to appropriate technologies (e.g. early warning systems, improved crop varieties) can enhance adaptive capacity by expanding farmers' response options in the face of uncertainties – but it may also result in 'lock-ins' that lead to maladaptation (Barnett and O'Neill 2010). The term 'information and skills' includes factors such as literacy, education, training, communication networks and knowledge dissemination forums (Eakin and Lemos 2006). There is increasing recognition that co-production of knowledge and collaborative and iterative learning processes, as opposed to top-down transfers of information and technology, are needed for effective adaptation (Tschakert and Dietrich 2010). For example, while scientific and 'expert' knowledge is necessary to develop improved rice varieties that are high yielding or can withstand drought, knowledge of farmers' production circumstances and preferences is needed to select breeding materials with features – such as aroma and cooking qualities – that farmers value (Kafiriti et al. 2003). I operationalize these two determinants by asking whether the technologies, information and skills promoted by OG schemes are considered locally relevant and appropriate, and whether they promote two-way flows of information and collaborative learning, experimentation and adaptation. Investments in physical infrastructure such as roads, wells, hospitals, schools and markets can enhance a community's adaptive capacity by improving health, income and access to employment, resources and services (Eakin and Lemos 2006). However, infrastructural investment may be vulnerable to climatic risks, such as flash flooding (Keskitalo et al. 2011). I explore the extent to which OG schemes are investing in infrastructure that is adapted to current and future climate variability and change. 'Institutions' are the formal and informal structures, rules and incentives that govern individual, collective and societal behaviour (Ostrom 1990; North 1990). They play a key role in shaping adaptive capacity by mediating the barriers and incentives for accessing and using resources (Gupta et al. 2010). OG schemes are considered an 'institutional innovation' (Glover 1987) in which smallholder farmers enter into agricultural production and marketing partnership with large estates, formalized in a written contract. I explore the formation and role of smallholder OG associations and the role of institutional dynamics outside OG schemes in shaping smallholder farmers' bargaining power vis-à-vis the large estates. Equity is a concern that cuts across the determinants. It is closely connected to formal and informal institutions, which are subject to power relations and that structure the ways in which entitlements to adaptation resources such as financial and social capital, technology and information are allocated in society (Eakin and Lemos 2006). I outline how OG schemes are influencing equity at the community level by examining which households are participating in OG schemes, and why, and how access to land and water is negotiated and contested within and beyond the schemes.

Research methods and study area

The fieldwork informing this chapter was undertaken during five visits to Tanzania totalling 15 months in the period October 2010 to April 2013. Research focused on two OG schemes in Morogoro Region – one, Kilombero Plantations Limited (KPL), producing rice; the other, Mtibwa Sugar Estates (MSE), producing sugarcane – and two communities located adjacent to these schemes (see Table 8.1). Morogoro Region is characterized by high agricultural potential, relatively good backbone infrastructure (outside the rainy season), and generally adequate rainfall compared to other parts of the country (Environmental Resources Management Limited 2013; AgDevCo and Prorustica 2011). Both OG schemes are located in flat valleys/floodplains (250–350 metres above sea level) bordering wetlands at the foot of mountain ranges that form part of the Eastern Arc Mountain chain, a recognized global hotspot for biodiversity (Frontier Tanzania 2009). KPL and MSE schemes were chosen due to their location within the SAGCOT region, and because initial field investigations identified rice and sugarcane as having strategic potential to contribute to national development efforts through import displacement. Research explored what factors are important for understanding the contribution of OG schemes to adaptive capacity at the household and community levels. The author lived and conducted research in and near the two study sites throughout the fieldwork. A mixture of qualitative and quantitative methods was employed to collect data, including participatory observation of farming activities; key informant interviews with OG farmers, livestock keepers, estate personnel and a range of actors in the public, private, donor, non-governmental organization (NGO), civic and research sectors; and group discussions and participatory rural appraisal exercises with male and female farmers in the two communities. Semi-structured interviews ($n=142$) with OG and non-OG households of different wealth categories were conducted in two villages to gain insight into farmers' views of MSE and KPL estates, the OG schemes, and wider farming systems and livelihoods. A review of policy documents relating to SAGCOT and national climate and agriculture policies, and the author's participation in meetings in villages and with Tanzanian researchers and policy-makers, donors, private-sector actors and agricultural development practitioners, helped to contextualize and triangulate the data collected through formal and informal interviews and observations.

Assessing the contribution of OG schemes to adaptive capacity

In this section, I describe how the two OG schemes are shaping adaptive capacity at the household and community levels in relation to the seven determinants of adaptive capacity described above.

TABLE 8.1 Overview of Mtibwa Sugar Estate and Kilombero Plantations Limited Outgrower Schemes

Key variables	Mtibwa Sugar Estate[1]	Kilombero Plantations Limited[2]
OG crop sown	Sugarcane	Rice
Other crops grown by farmers	Rice, maize, sunflower, pigeon pea, pumpkin, vegetables	Maize, cassava, sweet potato, banana, watermelon, vegetables
District	Mvomero	Kilombero
Estate size (hectares)	6000 (5400 in use[3])	5000
Number of outgrowers	3500	1200 (scaling up to 4500 in 2013)
Number of households interviewed	50 (29 OG/21 non-OG)	92 (57 OG/35 non-OG)
Current ownership structure	Private (domestic: Super Group of Companies)	Public–Private (Agrica,[4] RUBADA,[5] Norfund,[6] Swefund, Capricorn[7]), International
Past ownership structure	Government parastatal	Joint venture between the Governments of Tanzania and North Korea.
Outgrower scheme initiated	1996/1997	2011/2012
Rainfall pattern, climate trends and key climate stressors identified	Bimodal rainfall pattern. Two main rain seasons: March–May (Masika) October–December (Vuli) Decreasing rainfall in the Vuli season;[8] Periodic rainfall shortages in the Masika; flooding in the Vuli; disappearance of the Vuli rains and increasingly unreliable rainfall patterns reported by farmers	Unimodal rainfall pattern Reliable rainfall in the main rain season (December–May) Periodic flooding[9] Unreliable onset of the main rains, increasing temperatures and increasing crop and livestock pests and diseases were reported by farmers
Sample population for household interviews	Lungo village (185 households)	Mkangwalo village (ca. 1300 households): Kidete, Mgudeni, Ilole and Idulike sub-villages
Sampling methods	Purposive: OG and non-OG farming households of different wealth categories	Purposive: OG and non-OG farming households and households of different wealth categories

Notes

1 Background information on Mtibwa Sugar Estate can be found on the Sugar Board of Tanzania webpage: http://www.sbt.go.tz/index.php/factories

2 More information on KPL is available at: http://www.agrica.com/html/project1.html

3 See: Mtibwa Sugar Estates Limited 2009.

4 See the Agrica webpage: http://www.agrica.com/html/background.html

5 The Rufiji Basin Development Authority (RUBADA) is a corporate body established by the Act of Parliament No: 5 of 1975. The Authority is charged with multi-sectoral responsibility for promoting, regulating, coordinating and facilitating sustainable and balanced long-term ecological and socioeconomic development activities in the sectors of energy, agriculture, fisheries, forestry, tourism, mining, industry, transport and environment in the basin. The basin covers ca. 177,000 sq.km of land (about 20 per cent of Tanzania's land) and 30 per cent of runoff water.

6 Norwegian Investment Fund for Developing Countries.

7 Information on Capricorn and other KPL investors can be found at: http://www.agrica.com/html/investors.html

8 Mtibwa Sugar Estate Daily Rainfall records 1952–2012, unpublished data set analysed by the author.

9 A major flood occurred at Kilombero on April 19, 2011, prior to the onset of fieldwork. The flood rendered the main road from Ifakara to KPL estate impassable for a month, destroyed crops and pastures, and left several families in neighbouring villages homeless.

Economic resources

OG production is one of a portfolio of agricultural and livelihood strategies pursued by OG households in both communities. Among interviewed OG households, rice and sugarcane are cultivated *in addition to* crops that are grown by non-OG households. Both OG and non-OG farmers grow rain-fed lowland rice and maize, and a vareity of crops including sunflower, cassava, pigeon pea, cowpeas, bananas, pumpkin, and indigenous and improved vegetables for home consumption and sale. Many OG and non-OG households in Lungo village keep livestock, and poorer households in both communities engage in petty trading activities connected to local natural resources, such as fishing, brick production, production of local brew, and selling vegetables and snacks from local food stands. Better-off farmers also engage in processing and sale of crops to larger towns within the district. The ability to diversify economically and gain access to a broader range of income sources is an important component of adaptive capacity for dealing with uncertain production environments (Eriksen et al. 2005; Mortimore and Adams 2001; Ellis 1998). In the literature on OG schemes, diversification of income sources is also associated with enhanced bargaining positions for farmers, higher overall income levels and reduced exposure to risks (Glover 1990: 308).

The MSE OG scheme also enhances adaptive capacity by providing *stability* to participating households' incomes. Although at the time of the fieldwork, OG farmers and associations claimed that there was a widespread problem of farmers converting their cane fields to other crops due to low prices and late cane payments (see also: Assess Consulting 2011; Matango 2006), observations over the course of the fieldwork indicated that they continued to grow cane. Several factors explain this. Once it has been established, sugarcane, a perennial crop, requires less labour compared to rice, which is an important cash crop in the area. According to farmers, it is also more drought-tolerant than rice, and provides some income security for elderly, sick and female-headed households with a shortage of labour power to devote to labour-intensive farming activities. However, this security function may be compromised by adverse weather conditions that disrupt cane harvesting and delivery to the factory, as discussed under the section on 'risk management'. The labour requirements for cane cultivation complement those employed for growing food and cash crops, as sugarcane harvesting and early weeding of the ratoon[1] crop normally takes place between July and December, outside the main rainy season in which food (maize, rice) crops are sown. Cane payments, which arrive as a lump sum, also perform a savings role, enabling farmers to pay for large expenditures such as school fees and home improvements.

In contrast to sugarcane, rice provides a degree of *flexibility* to household incomes. Rice stores well as paddy (unmilled grain), compared to maize and other legumes. It can be consumed or traded for maize, or saved and sold in small quantities throughout the year, as household food and cash needs arise. The rice variety that KPL promotes in its OG scheme is a publically bred, semi-aromatic, high-yielding, short-stature rice variety called 'SARO 5'[2] (Kanyeka 2005). This variety matures more quickly[3] than farmers' traditional rice varieties, which are tall and aromatic, and preferred for their cooking qualities and price premium in local markets, but which are photoperiod-sensitive and can be grown only in the main rainy season (Kafiriti 2003). The SARO variety regularly functions as a 'hunger food' because it can be grown and harvested before the tall varieties have matured, and at a time when rice prices are normally higher in the local market, giving farmers an option to sell, rather than consume, the rice and obtain cash (see also: Mwaseba et al. 2007). Participation in OG schemes thus enhances smallholder households' adaptive capacity by contributing to income diversification, stability and flexibility.

OG schemes and smallholder risk management strategies

The data do not support the view that participation in OG schemes directly lowers production or marketing risks for smallholder farmers, but there are indications that it may do so in the context of the wider production systems in which OG production takes place. In principle, the fact that smallholder farmers in both OG schemes produce crops on contract for an agreed price should reduce the marketing risks that they face. However, no strong evidence was found for this in practice. This is partly explained by the fact that the marketing situation for sugarcane at MSE is one of monopsony: MSE is the sole local buyer (Matango 2006). While the price of OG cane is agreed and fixed ahead of the harvesting, the price specified in the contract is conditional on the sugar content, or 'rendement', of the cane, which is reduced during periods of heavy rainfall (Tarimo 1998). Sugarcane is highly perishable; and once it has been harvested, heavy machinery and nearby processing facilities are required to process it (Tarimo 1998). During the 2011 cane harvesting season at MSE, heavy rainfall over a 24-hour period led to a situation where the cane harvesting machinery could not enter farmers' fields, trucks got stuck in the mud or broke down, and the sugarcane delivered to the factory on lorries contained sand that was uprooted along with the cane due to the wet conditions. This led to factory breakdowns and closures that caused additional delays to the harvesting schedule. Some of the cane that had been cut deteriorated and eventually rotted in the fields, resulting in a total loss for several farmers in Lungo. Other farmers received low payments due to the low sugar content in the cane that was delivered late to the factory. According to OG farmers, such losses are not insured; they must be borne by individual farmers. Thus, production and marketing risks for sugarcane are intertwined. On the other hand, since there is no other local buyer for the sugarcane that farmers produce, it cannot be concluded that the MSE OG scheme increases marketing risks for farmers.

In contrast to sugarcane, rice has vibrant local and regional markets, with numerous participants and transactions along the value-chain (European

Cooperative for Rural Development 2012; Mwaseba et al. 2007). KPL estate sells the rice that it purchases from smallholder farmers onwards at domestic (spot) market prices to buyers in Dar es Salaam, where it is marketed to domestic rice consumers. Domestic rice prices in Tanzania vary widely within and between years (Hella et al. 2011). The existence of a parallel local market and the volatility of domestic rice prices make it difficult for KPL to 'get the price right' in negotiating a price with OG farmers. The existence of a parallel local rice market is clearly advantageous for smallholder farmers, as it gives them greater bargaining power in relation to price negotiations with KPL. The downside for KPL is that it faces the possibility of farmers reneging on contracts and side-selling to the local market. This point is illustrated by the fact that in the 2012/2013 season, OG farmers negotiated a contract price for rice that was upward of what KPL had initially offered in farmers' favour, due to the existence of the parallel local market for rice, where prices were higher than those agreed previously in the contract.[4] However, households with adequate resources may prefer to take part in, rather than avoid, the seasonal price variations for rice, in order to increase their incomes. Participating in an OG scheme that involves a fixed price for rice may be less attractive to these households. Government efforts to discourage 'hoarding' of rice by lifting the ban on imports of rice when consumer prices become too high – as occurred in early 2013 – serve to heighten both the production and the marketing risks for farmers who are net sellers rice and 'bank' on the prices rising. The effect is both direct, in lowering producer prices, and indirect, in that it creates disincentives for future investments in rice farming (see Hella et al. 2011). Interviews with farmers and key informants at KPL indicated that rice imports in early 2013 had a distinctly negative impact on small- and large-scale rice producers, as well as local rice traders, who responded by stockpiling rice, to avoid having to sell at very low prices. Anecdotal evidence suggests that MSE also engages in stockpiling during periods of sugar imports, to avoid selling when sugar prices are low. The findings thus do not support the view that participation in OG schemes lessens the marketing risks for smallholder farmers. Smallholders and large estates alike face marketing risks that are to various extents connected to macro-level policy decisions.

However, there is some evidence that growing the contracted crops reduces smallholders' production risks in relation to the wider farming system. OG farmers at MSE explained that sugarcane is more drought-tolerant than rice. Drought and lack of sufficient moisture during the main growing season are particular concerns in relation to rice and maize, both of which are key food crops in Lungo. Growing sugarcane thus enables farmers to spread the production risks associated with food crops. In Kilombero, farmers grow a local version of the 'short' rice variety that KPL is promoting, to mitigate the impacts of late rains and seasonal flooding on their agricultural production. This variety was distributed as relief seed by the government in 2011 in the wake of widespread flooding in villages near KPL. When faced with flooding, rice farmers in Mkangawalo are able to adapt the timing, location and methods of planting rice, dig channels to drain fields, employ or hire oxen for ploughing, plant quick-maturing varieties, and plant rice gradually over several months. Farmers' production strategies contrast markedly with those of KPL estate, which relies on heavy machinery, only one rice variety, and faces logistical constraints connected to coordinating planting and harvesting over large areas in the event of flooding. Thus, it is farmers' existing rice production strategies, rather than the existence of the estate per se, that lower the production risks facing farmers. However in cases where OG farmers receive agricultural credit via the estate and repayment is tied to the crop (instances of this were found in both schemes), farmers may bear increased production risks. KPL, in cooperation with local banks and a microcredit institution, provided loans to eligible farmers for production purposes at the start of the 2011/2012 season, with the agreement that it would be repaid by a set quantity of rice of the specified variety after harvest. When prices dropped in 2013 due to the government's decision to import rice, several farmers reported difficulties in repaying the production loans they had obtained under the programme. Thus, accessing credit for crop production in a context of climatic and or market volatility may be a risky undertaking for some farmers.

Provision of technology, information and training through OG schemes

The fact that participation in OG schemes does not directly lower production or marketing risks for smallholders raises the question of whether farmers participate for other reasons. The possibility for smallholder farmers to gain access to agricultural technology, extension services and training was evident at both MSE and KPL. At the time of the fieldwork, KPL estate, in cooperation with the United States Agency for International Development (USAID) and financing from Norfund, was training 1200 farmers in the System of Rice Intensification (SRI). SRI is a set of principles for rice production that has garnered international attention due to claims that it dramatically increases smallholder rice yields, and reduces inputs (mainly of seed and water) through wider spacing of rice plants, alternate wetting/drying of rice fields, use of fewer seedlings/seeds, and careful selection of seed (Glover 2011; McDonald et al. 2006; Dobermann 2004; Stoop et al. 2002). SRI is actively promoted within SAGCOT and internationally as a climate-smart agricultural technology (EcoAgriculture Partners 2012). OG farmers at KPL who were interviewed as part of the research were very pleased with the SRI training they were receiving. Follow-up visits and interviews with smallholder farmers indicated that some had begun to experiment and adapt components of the training, such as the spacing principles and transplanting young seedlings, to their traditional, tall varieties, indicating that the skills learned through participation in the OG schemes have application and usefulness beyond the scheme itself. However, some participants noted that SRI is more labour-intensive and 'expensive' compared to traditional rice cultivation practices, which are based on broadcasting seed, as opposed to direct seeding or making a nursery and then transplanting rice. According to KPL personnel and extension staff, the additional costs of planting, and of weeding, due to wider plant spacing, should be offset by the higher yields that farmers can obtain using SRI methods. However, it is not clear whether farmers adopt SRI as an entire 'package', or instead select elements that suit their farming systems and circumstances – as observed by other studies of rice technology adoption in Tanzania (Mwaseba et al. 2006). One of the central tenets of the SRI principles as originally conceived is farmer adaptation and experimentation (Stoop et al. 2002). However, the author's observations of and participation in SRI trainings at KPL indicate that SRI is promoted as a 'package' to be adopted, rather than adapted, by smallholder farmers. For example, both rice seed and fertilizer are supplied to farmers as part of the production loan extended under the SRI scheme, the latter through a partnership with the fertilizer company, YARA. However, discussions with farmers and extension staff indicated that soil fertility is generally high in the area, raising the question of whether inorganic fertilizer is actually needed.

At MSE, no formal system of providing farmers with access to inputs such as seed and fertilizers exists, even though the estate is well connected to national and international sugar research activities, and produces certified cane seed. Until 2012, OG and non-OG farmers in both schemes could access fertilizer through a government-sponsored seed and fertilizer subsidy for rice and maize. However, the scheme required farmers to contribute a minimum amount of cash, which limited the possibility for poorer households to participate. Many farmers and key informants also noted that these inputs often arrived too late, and several farmers in Lungo emphasized that fertilizing cane fields would lead to destruction of the soils in their area. OG farmers in Lungo reported that difficulties in accessing good seed cane and in securing loans for production in the absence of timely cane payments constrained their ability to invest in their cane farms, which in turn directly contributed to poor cane harvests. While farmers can acquire cane seed 'on loan' from MSE, they explained that the process is bureaucratically cumbersome, and the cost of seed cane is deducted from farmers' cane profits. Fear of losing a seed crop to drought or flooding leads farmers in Lungo to prefer sourcing seed from their own farms or from their neighbours.

At Mtibwa, government extension officers trained and financed under a joint European Union (EU)–Tanzania sugarcane cooperative initiative are tasked with helping smallholders improve their cane production through the establishment of farmer field schools and block farms linked to the donor-funded extension initiative.[5] In addition to piloting 'block farms' – where farmers pool their land and share production costs and profits – this initiative has been lobbying for the construction of smallholder irrigation schemes in several villages.[6] However, the economic feasibility and social acceptability of block farming and smallholder irrigation schemes for cane are not clear. During a focus group discussion with sugarcane farmers in Lungo, farmers rejected outright the idea of block farming. They explained that it would not be feasible in their area, due to the scattered location of sugarcane farms, and differences in soil quality, topography and farmer management practices, which could bring down overall cane quality and prices for farmers, should they choose to pool their land. Key informants indicated that smallholder irrigation schemes would be beneficial to farmers, but were likely to induce farmers to grow rice, rather than sugarcane, due to its greater profitability. These observations indicate that while OG schemes may serve to enhance smallholder farmers' access to technologies, inputs, training and skills, there is room for improving the top-down manner of training in some cases, which fails to consider farmers' existing knowledge, experience, risk management portfolios and production concerns. However, given the weaknesses and bottlenecks in the existing public agricultural extension system, OG schemes and the public and private investment that they attract constitute an important opportunity to build on for enhancing smallholder farmers' agricultural production and adaptation options.

Infrastructure

Both estates inherited worn-down infrastructure on acquiring them from the government (Coleman 2011; Mtibwa Sugar Estates Limited 2009; Halcrow Consulting 1995). KPL was originally demarcated and partially developed under North Korean–Tanzanian cooperation and lay idle for several decades before being put into production by KPL in 2008. The owners have invested in new farming equipment, a state-of-the-art rice mill, and a pilot pivot irrigation system that enables it to run at full capacity. Both MSE and KPL have contributed to maintaining roads on the estates, thereby improving accessibility to farmers' cane fields, and to local markets and public transport. Villages and towns located near the estates have expanded to provide additional services and employment to the growing permanent and transient workforces associated with the OG schemes. Both estates have financed the construction of schools and health clinics for local populations, and generated opportunities for casual and permanent employment on the estate. KPL voluntarily pays into a yearly community development fund that is divided proportionally among the three villages immediately bordering the farm, according to how much land they 'lost' when the original boundaries of the farm were again put into production (Kayonko 2011; Coleman 2011). Because the estate was originally demarcated in the 1980s and was never fully developed, a number of farmers and pastoralists had moved onto the farm in the ensuing years. The new management took care when relocating people to compensate farmers and pastoralists with cash settlements (payment for standing crops) and land, as well as constructing new homes for those affected by the relocation (Kayonko 2011; Coleman 2011). Investments in the two OG schemes have thus contributed to positive spillover effects on local economic development. While these investments are laudable, the research suggests that investments in schooling, road and irrigation infrastructure at KPL are vulnerable to existing climate variability and change. Periodic flooding makes the seasonal road to the estate impassable, and in 2011, forced its closure for two months, cutting off access to fuel and equipment supplies (Coleman 2011). According to households in Mgudeni, a sub-village of Mkangawalo, the estate's drainage infrastructure aggravated the impacts of the 2011 flooding, leading to inundation of farmers' homes, fields and the school that had been constructed with KPL community development funds. Moreover, KPL's profitability depends on harvesting two rice crops per year (NORAD 2013: 96). This will require irrigation from a river whose water-flow varies seasonally and which according to irrigation experts, like other rivers in the Kilombero Valley, is already being affected by climate change (Mavere 2012). These findings show that MSE and KPL OG schemes have been enhancing communities' adaptive capacities by investing in infrastructure that can improve households' access to healthcare services, education and markets. However, these investments will need to take into account the projected impacts of climate variability and change, and plan accordingly.

Institutions

OG schemes consist of a range of formal and informal relations, rules and incentives, not least the contract itself, which defines the formal production-marketing relationship between smallholders and large estates. In addition to functioning as institutions in their own right, KPL and MSE OG schemes foster new institutions, as well as being impacted by informal institutions, market mechanisms and formal institutions at higher levels. While the contract defines the formal production and marketing relationship between smallholders and the two estates, the existence of KPL and MSE and the possibility for farmers to engage in contract production has promoted the development of OG associations that provide various benefits for smallholder farmers. These benefits include the possibility of participating in agricultural training, accessing extension advice, and enhanced voices for smallholders in negotiations with the estates, as well as being able to engage in political lobbying at higher levels.

At both KPL and MSE, the bargaining position of OG associations vis-à-vis the estate is clearly important in determining whether the OG contract is in smallholders' favour. As shown in previous sections, the existence (or absence) of alternative markets for the contracted crops plays a key role in determining farmers' bargaining power. The existence of a parallel local market for rice where rice prices were higher than those in the contract enabled OG farmers to re-negotiate the contractual price in their favour. At MSE, the monopsony market for cane and the absence of an alternative buyer leave farmers in a decidedly weaker position when it comes to price negotiations. OG cane prices at MSE lag behind those of its closest competitor in Kilombero District. Farmers must either accept the price that MSE offers, or convert their cane fields to other crops – an expensive and risky undertaking, as sugarcane is a perennial crop with high initial investment costs. According to OG farmers and key informants at MSE and Kilombero Sugar Company Ltd (KSCL), price differences between the two estates are due to differences in the managements' attitude towards OG farmers, the milling efficiency of the factories, and the fact that KSCL estate has no capability to expand in size, but must rely on increased production of cane from smallholder OGs for profitability. In contrast, MSE has acquired a new 30,000-hectare concession of land from the government, which it plans to develop partially for irrigated cane production.

However, in both cases, the OG associations provide benefits to smallholders that extend beyond their role in price negotiations with the estates. KPL has deliberately fostered the development of farmers' organizations through its SRI training and establishment of SRI demonstration plots and farmers' groups down to the sub-village level. Farmers have also received training in how to organize and register their SRI associations, and have held elections for the village and the Apex level SRI association to represent farmers' interests in contractual negotiations with the estate. Regular interactions with farmers during the course of these trainings and elections indicated that they greatly valued the group cooperation and social camaraderie fostered through the SRI training and demonstration plots. Farmers mentioned the 'motivating' role of these groups, the learning and sharing that they encouraged, the individual and group pride that they instilled, and the social ties among participants. At MSE, two different OG associations represent farmers' interests in contract negotiations with the estate. Among OG households in Lungo, husbands and wives commonly maintain separate memberships in these two associations, in order to facilitate switching between them, should their performance decline in the eyes of the farmer. These same associations are responsible for harvesting and delivering farmers' cane crops to the factory, and delivering cane payments from MSE to farmers. At the time of the fieldwork, the OG associations at MSE were actively engaged in lobbying the Mvomero District Commissioner to allow construction of a smaller cane factory that could compete with MSE, with the goal of raising the producer price in smallholder farmers' favour. This issue was taken all the way to the president, and discussed in the national parliament.

These findings show that OG schemes do not operate in an institutional vacuum. They interface with formal and informal institutions at the local level and with market mechanisms and policies at higher levels – most notably related to agricultural marketing but also indirectly, in the case of land-use and agricultural investment policies. While many of the institutional dynamics that ultimately affect OG crop prices are beyond smallholders' ability to control, OG associations enhance the adaptive capacities of smallholder farmers by helping to build social capital and cooperative ties among farmers, and strengthening their ability to lobby politically for their interests and rights at higher levels.

Equity dimensions at community and scheme levels and beyond

The need to consider whether and how development interventions enhance or undermine equity within and across communities is highlighted in the literatures on agricultural investment, contract farming and climate adaptation (World Bank 2013; Silici and Locke 2013; Eriksen et al. 2011; Vermeulen and Cotula 2010; Thomas and Twyman 2005; Adger et al. 2004; Warning and Key 2002; Little and Watts 1994). OG investments in infrastructure, markets, and agricultural inputs and technologies may help to overcome constraints to agricultural development and poverty reduction in rural areas and enhance local adaptive capacity. Yet, because OG schemes link very different sets of actors, they also carry the potential to create dependency and widen economic inequalities within and between communities and households (Porter and Phillips-Howard 1997; Little and Watts 1994). This may be problematic because development interventions that ignore existing power relations and social inequalities risk exacerbating the vulnerabilities and processes of social, political and economic marginalization (Eriksen et al. 2007).

Space considerations do not permit a full discussion of the equity issues surrounding the allocation of power and access to resources within the two communities studied here, and the ways in which OG schemes interact with these dynamics. However, several points can be mentioned. First is the question of who participates in and benefits from the two OG schemes. At KPL, farmers participating in the SRI training and OG scheme represent a mixture of small-, medium- and large-scale women and men farmers, with a greater participation by small and medium, compared to large farmers.[7] The stipulation for participation in the scheme is that farmers have access to ½ acre of land, and that they grow the contracted variety, using SRI principles. However, OG farmers in Lungo to a large degree represent the founding members of the community who were relocated from the Kilimanjaro region to the village in the early 1970s under the government's villagization policy.[8] Farmers were at this time allocated plots within a village sugarcane farm. These plots were later redistributed to farmers. Since then, the value of sugarcane plots has increased, making it difficult for farmers who moved to Lungo after villagization, and whose families are not among the original inhabitants, to acquire a sugarcane farm. This point is illustrated by the fact that ownership of a sugarcane farm was considered a sign of wealth by sub-village leaders and farmers during wealth-ranking of households in Lungo (West 2011).

A second factor that affects the potential for OG schemes to contribute to adaptive capacity at the community level is existing competition over land and water resources. While KPL and MSE estates have both existed for some time, increasing immigration into the region by farmers and livestock-keepers in both communities is leading to growing pressures on land and water resources. Conflicts between farming and livestock-keeping interests abounded in both locations at the time of the fieldwork, some of which resulted in loss of lives and/or imprisonment. These conflicts are a microcosm of a much larger and pervasive dilemma at the national level that has yet to be adequately addressed (HAKIARDHI 2009). Whether and how livestock-keepers will benefit from investments in the OG scheme and agricultural investments in SAGCOT, and in Tanzania more generally, is thus an important question. The establishment of the Wami-Mbiki Wildlife Management Area whose borders pass near Lungo, and MSE's recent acquisition of a new, 30,000-hectare land concession from the government, may aggravate conflicts over land and water in future. The anticipated deforestation and need for irrigation that the new MSE concession will require raises issues of rights to adaptation resources such as land and water, and indicates that there is potential for OG schemes to contribute to maladaptation at community and landscape levels (Barnett and O'Neill 2010). Rather than suggesting that OG schemes reduce social, economic or environmental inequalities in participating communities in either the short or the long term the findings suggest that greater efforts are needed to empower marginalized groups, and to lower the entry costs to enable poorer households to participate in OG schemes. Since equity is fundamentally a development concern, stronger state involvement is needed to ensure that the benefits of OG schemes are equitably distributed and that access to and control over land and water resources are governed in a transparent, sustainable and equitable manner.

Conclusions

The research presented in this chapter shows that agricultural investments that link large- and small-scale farmers can enhance the adaptive capacities of smallholder farmers and communities in various ways: by contributing to household income diversification, stability and flexibility; by enhancing access to technologies, inputs, training and skills that widen farmers' production choices; by investing in physical infrastructure that enhances community and household access to healthcare services, education and markets; and by helping to build social capital and cooperative ties between farmers, and strengthening their ability to lobby collectively for their interests and rights. The investments made by KPL and MSE have also attracted financing and initiatives from the government and from third parties. The spillover effects have been broadly beneficial for rural households and communities. Tellingly, non-OG farmers who were interviewed, including lower-income households, expressed their desire to participate, indicating that farmers perceive that there are welfare benefits to be gained from participating in OG schemes.

However, the evidence does not suggest that participation in OG schemes directly lowers smallholder farmers' production or marketing risks. This suggests that smallholder farmers may participate in OG schemes for reasons that have less to do with risk management, and more to do with the ancillary benefits available under the schemes. Neither do the findings show that the OG schemes serve to reduce social, economic or environmental inequalities in participating communities. This suggests that greater efforts are needed to empower marginalized groups, and lower the entry costs for poorer households to participate and that stronger state involvement is needed to ensure that the benefits of OG schemes are equitably distributed.

The research also uncovered various ways and cases in which OG schemes have missed opportunities to enhance adaptive capacity, or are potentially undermining it. Promoting top-down agricultural training approaches that fail to incorporate local knowledge, extending agricultural credit to smallholders who produce under rain-fed conditions, and undertaking investments in areas where there is high competition over land and water resources and where road and irrigation infrastructure is vulnerable to existing climate variability and change are notable examples. These findings suggest that further investments in OG schemes should prioritize two-way learning processes in OG schemes; promote cooperation between the public and private sectors and civil society; lobby for greater equity, transparency and sustainability in land and water use; and seek to expand the benefits, while mitigating the potential risks to smallholders of participating in OG schemes for smallholder farmers and rural communities.

Notes

1 A new shoot that grows from near the root or crown of sugarcane, after the old growth has been cut back.
2 Also known as TXD306.
3 In roughly 90 days, compared to 120 or more for traditional varieties.
4 Thobias Sijabaje, RI Manager at KPL, personal communication 2013.
5 N. Mkula, National OG Coordinator, Sugar Board of Tanzania, personal communication, 2012.
6 M. Mgogo, Tanzanian Sugar Board Zonal Coordinator for sugar farming, personal communication, 2012.
7 Unpublished records of participants in SRI and loan training activities; participatory observation in loan trainings, key informant discussions with estate personnel, extension officers and farmer interviews.
8 Under the period of state socialism in Tanzania referred to in Kiswahili as *Ujamaa*.

References

Abebe, G. K., J. Bijman, R. Kemp, O. Omta and A. Tsegaye (2013). 'Contract farming configuration: Smallholders' preferences for contract design attributes'. *Food Policy* 40(0): 14–24.

Adger, W. N., N. W. Arnell and E. L. Tompkins (2004). 'Successful adaptation to climate change across scales'. *Global Environmental Change* 15: 77–86.

AgDevCo and Prorustica (2011). Southern Agricultural Growth Corridor of Tanzania Investment Blueprint. http://www.sagcot.com/resources/downloads-resources/

Assess Consulting (2011). *Environmental Audit Report on Mtibwa Sugar Factory In Lukenge Village, Mtibwa Ward, Turiani Division, Mvomero District in Morogoro Region.* Dar es Salaam, Tanzania: 91.

Barnett, J. and S. O'Neill (2010). 'Maladaptation'. *Global Environmental Change* B(2): 211–213.

Barrett, C. B., M. E. Bachke, M. F. Bellemare, H. C. Michelson, S. Narayanan and T. F. Walker (2012). 'Smallholder participation in contract farming: Comparative evidence from five countries'. *World Development* 40(4): 715–730.

Bellemare, M. F. (2012). 'As you sow, so shall you reap: The welfare impacts of contract farming'. *World Development* 40(7): 1418–1434.

Coleman, C. (2011). Agrica: Setting the standard for rice farming in East Africa. Powerpoint presentation held at KPL headquarters during President Kikwete's visit on October 8, 2011.

Dobermann, A. (2004). 'A critical assessment of the system of rice intensification (SRI)'. *Agricultural Systems* 79(3): 261–281.

Eakin, H. and M. C. Lemos (2006). 'Adaptation and the state: Latin America and the challenge of capacity-building under globalization'. *Global Environmental Change* 16(1): 7–18.

EcoAgriculture Partners (2012). The SACOT Greenprint: a Green Growth Investment Framework for the Southern Agricultural Growth Corridor. http://www.sagcot.com/resources/downloads-resources/

Ellis, F. (1998). 'Household strategies and rural livelihood diversification'. *Journal of Development Studies* 35(1): 1–38.

Environmental Resources Management Limited (2013). SAGCOT Environmental and Social Management Framework, Dar es Salaam: SAGCOT. http://www.sagcot.com/news/newsdetails/artikel//re-disclosure-of-environmental-and-social-management-framework-for-sagcot/

Eriksen, S., P. Aldunce, C. S. Bahinipati, R. D. A. Martins, J. I. Molefe, C. Nhemachena, K. O'Brien et al. (2011). 'When not every response to climate change is a good one: Identifying principles for sustainable adaptation'. *Climate and Development* 3(1): 7–20.

Eriksen, S. E. H., R. J. T. Klein, K. Ulsrud, L. O. Næss and K. O'Brien (2007). Climate change adaptation and poverty reduction: key interactions and critical measures. GECHS Report 2007:1 ISSN: 1504-5749.

Eriksen, S. H., K. Brown and P. M. Kelly (2005). 'The dynamics of vulnerability: Locating coping strategies in Kenya and Tanzania'. *Geographical Journal* 171(4): 287–305.

European Cooperative for Rural Development (2012). Rice Sector Development In East Africa: 72.

Frontier Tanzania (2009). Social Surveys in the Kilombero Valley: A preliminary report. Society for Environmental Exploration, UK: 122.

Glover, D. (1987). 'Increasing the benefits to smallholders from contract farming: Problems for farmers' organizations and policy makers'. *World Development* 15(4): 441–448.

Glover, D. (1990). 'Contract farming and outgrower schemes in East and Southern Africa'. *Journal of Agricultural Economics,* 41(3): 303–15.

Glover, D. (2011). 'The system of rice intensification: Time for an empirical turn'. *NJAS – Wageningen Journal of Life Sciences* 57(3–4): 217–224.

Glover, D. and K. C. Kusterer (1990). *Small Farmers, Big Business: Contract Farming and Rural Development.* London, Macmillan.

Gupta, J., C. Termeer, J. Klostermann, S. Meijerink, M. van den Brink, P. Jong, S. Nooteboom and E. Bergsma (2010). 'The Adaptive Capacity Wheel: A method to assess the inherent characteristics of institutions to enable the adaptive capacity of society'. *Environmental Science & Policy* 13(6): 459–471.

HAKIARDHI (2009). The changing terrain of land use conflicts in Tanzania and the future of a small producer. Land Rights Research and Resources Institute (HAKIARDHI) Institute. Dar es Salaam, Tanzania.

Halcrow Consulting (1995). Report on the potential for a BOT mechanised rice project in Tanzania. Sir William Halcrow & Partners Limited, UK.

Hella, J. P., R. Haug and I. M. Kamile (2011). 'High global food prices – crisis or opportunity for smallholder farmers in Tanzania?' *Development in Practice* 21(4–5): 652–665.

IPCC (2007). Climate Change 2007: Impacts, Adaptation and Vulnerability. Contribution of Working Group II to the Fourth Assessment Report of the Intergovernmental Panel on Climate Change. O. F. C. M. L. Parry, J. P. Palutikof, P. J. van der Linden and C. E. Hanson. Cambridge University Press, Cambridge: 976.

IPCC (2014). *Climate Change 2014: Impacts, Adaptation, and Vulnerability. Part A: Global and Sectoral Aspects. Contribution of Working Group II to the Fifth Assessment Report of the Intergovernmental Panel on Climate Change.* Field, C.B., V.R. Barros, D.J. Dokken, K.J. Mach, M.D. Mastrandrea, T.E. Bilir, M. Chatterjee, K.L. Ebi, Y.O. Estrada, R.C. Genova, B. Girma, E.S. Kissel, A.N. Levy, S. MacCracken, P.R. Mastrandrea, and L.L. White (eds.). Cambridge: Cambridge University Press.

Jenkins, B. (2012). *Mobilizing the Southern Agricultural Growth Corridor of Tanzania.* Cambridge, MA, The CSR Initiative at the Harvard Kennedy School.

Kafiriti, E. M., S. Dondeyne, S. Msomba, J. Deckers and D. Raes (2003). 'Coming to grips with farmers' variety selection. The case of new improved rice varieties under irrigation in South East Tanzania'. *Tropicultura* 21(4): 211–217.

Kanyeka, Z. L., J. M. Kibanda, S. C. Msomba and H. Tusekelege (2005). SARO 5: An emerging high yielding and profitable rice cultivar in Tanzania. *Tanzania Agricultural Research and Training Newsletter.* Dar es Salaam, Tanzania, Ministry of Agriculture Food Security & Cooperatives, Department of Research & Training xix: 14–16.

Kayonko, J. (2011). External review and audit implementation of Environmental and Social Management plan and Resettlement Action Plan for Mngeta Farm, Kilombero Valley, Kilombero District, Morogoro Region, Tanzania. Dar es Salaam, Tanzania: Green Tanzania Environmental Consultants Limited: 29.

Keskitalo, E. C., H. Dannevig, G. Hovelsrud, J. West and Å. Swartling (2011). 'Adaptive capacity determinants in developed states: Examples from the Nordic countries and Russia'. *Regional Environmental Change* 11(3): 579–592.

Kirsten, J. and K. Sartorius (2002). 'Linking agribusiness and small-scale farmers in developing countries: Is there a new role for contract farming?' *Development Southern Africa* 19(4): 503–529.

Little, P. D. and M. J. Watts (1994). *Living Under Contract : Contract Farming and Agrarian Transformation in Sub-Saharan Africa.* Madison, WI: University of Wisconsin Press.

Mary, A. L. and A. E. Majule (2009). 'Impacts of climate change, variability and adaptation strategies on agriculture in semi arid areas of Tanzania: The case of Manyoni District in Singida Region, Tanzania'. *African Journal of Environmental Science and Technology* 3(8): 206–218.

Matango, R. (2006). Mtibwa Outgrowers Scheme: A model for smallholder cane production in Tanzania. UNCTAD Expert Meeting: 'Enabling small commodity producers in developing countries to reach global markets'. Palais des Nations, Geneva: 33.

Mavere, P. A. (2012). Water Officer, Rufiji Basin Water Office, Ifakara Field Office. Personal communication.

McDonald, A. J., P. R. Hobbs and S. J. Riha (2006). 'Does the system of rice intensification outperform conventional best management?: A synopsis of the empirical record'. *Field Crops Research* 96(1): 31–36.

Miyata, S., N. Minot and D. Hu (2009). 'Impact of contract farming on income: Linking small farmers, packers, and supermarkets in China'. *World Development* 37(11): 1781–1790.

Mongi, H., A. E. Majule and J. G. Lyimo (2010). 'Vulnerability and adaptation of rain fed agriculture to climate change and variability in semi-arid Tanzania'. *African Journal of Environmental Science and Technology* 4(6): 371–381.

Mortimore, M. J. and W. M. Adams (2001). 'Farmer adaptation, change and 'crisis' in the Sahel'. *Global Environmental Change* 11: 49–57.

Mtibwa Sugar Estates Limited (2009). Company Brief. Unpublished internal document.

Mwaseba, D. L., R. Kaarhus, F. H. Johnsen, A. Z. Mattee and Z. S. K. Mvena (2007). 'Rice for food and income: Assessing the impact of rice research on food security in the Kyela and Kilombero districts of Tanzania'. *Outlook on Agriculture* 36(4): 231–236.

Mwaseba, D. L., R. Kaarhus, F. H. Johnsen, Z. S. K. Mvena and A. Z. Mattee (2006). 'Beyond adoption/rejection of agricultural innovations: Empirical evidence from smallholder rice farmers in Tanzania'. *Outlook on Agriculture* 35(4): 263–272.

NORAD (2013). Evaluation of Norway's Bilateral Agricultural Support to Food Security. Annex 5: In-depth case study reports. Evaluation Department. Oslo, Norwegian Agency for Development Cooperation.

North, D. C. (1990). *Institutions, Institutional Change and Economic Performance*. Cambridge, Cambridge University Press.

Ostrom, E. (1990). *Governing the Commons: The Evolution of Institutions for Collective Action*. Cambridge, Cambridge University Press.

Oya, C. (2012). 'Contract farming in sub-Saharan Africa: A survey of approaches, debates and issues'. *Journal of Agrarian Change* 12(1): 1–33.

Paavola, J. (2003). Vulnerability to climate change in Tanzania: sources, substance and solutions. Inaugural Workshop of Southern Africa Vulnerability Initiative (SAVI). Maputo, Mozambique.

Paavola, J. (2008). 'Livelihoods, vulnerability and adaptation to climate change in Morogoro, Tanzania'. *Environmental Science & Policy* 11(7): 642–654.

Porter, G. and K. Phillips-Howard (1997). 'Comparing contracts: An evaluation of contract farming schemes in Africa'. *World Development* 25(2): 227–238.

Poulton, C., G. Tyler, P. Hazell, A. Dorward, J. Kydd and M. Stockbridge (2008) 'All-Africa review of experiences with commercial agriculture: Lessons from success and failure'. Background paper for the Competitive Commercial Agriculture in Sub-Saharan Africa (CCAA) Study. Washington: World Bank. Accessed 10.06.2013 at: http://siteresources.worldbank.org/INTAFRICA/Resources/257994-1215457178567/CCAA_Success_failure.pdf

Sanga, G. J., A. B. Moshi and J. P. Hella (2013). 'Small scale farmers' adaptation to climate change effects in Pangani River Basin and Pemba: Challenges and opportunities'. *International Journal of Modern Social Sciences* 2(3): 169–194.

Silici, L. and A. Locke (2013) 'Private equity investments and agricultural development in Africa: Opportunities and challenges'. FAC Working Paper 062. Bright: Futures Agricultural Consortium.

Smit, B. and O. Pilifosova (2001). Adaptation to climate change in the context of sustainable development and equity. Climate Change 2001: Impacts, Adaptation, and Vulnerability – Contribution of Working Group II, *Third Assessment Report of the*

Intergovernmental Panel on Climate Change. Cambridge, UK, Cambridge University Press: Chapter 18.

Smit, B. and J. Wandel (2006). 'Adaptation, adaptive capacity and vulnerability'. *Global Environmental Change* 16: 282–292.

Stoop, W. A., N. Uphoff and A. Kassam (2002). 'A review of agricultural research issues raised by the system of rice intensification (SRI) from Madagascar: Opportunities for improving farming systems for resource-poor farmers'. *Agricultural Systems* 71(3): 249–274.

Tarimo, A. J. P. and Y.T. Takamura (1998). 'Sugarcane production, processing and marketing in Tanzania'. *African Study Monographs* 19(1): 1–11.

Thomas, D. S. G. and C. Twyman (2005). 'Equity and justice in climate change adaptation amongst natural-resource-dependent societies'. *Global Environmental Change* 15(2): 115–124.

Tschakert, P. and K. A. Dietrich (2010). 'Anticipatory learning for climate change adaptation and resilience'. *Ecology and Society* 15(2): 11.

Tyler, G. and G. Dixie (2013). Investing in agribusiness: a retrospective view of a Development Bank's investments in agribusiness in Africa and Southeast Asia and the Pacific. Agriculture and environmental services discussion paper; no.1. Washington, DC: World Bank.

UNDP (2013). Human Development Report 2013. The rise of the South: human progress in a diverse world. Canada, Gilmore Printing Services Inc.: 203.

URT (2007). National Adaptation Programme of Action (NAPA). Vice President's Office, Division of Environment. Accessed July 31, 2013 at: http://unfccc.int/resource/docs/napa/tza01.pdf: 52.

URT (2012a). *AGSTATS for food security. Volume 1: The 2011/12 Final Food Crop Production Forecast for 2012/13 Food Security.* Dar es Salaam: Ministry of Agriculture Food Security and Cooperatives.

URT (2012b). *National Climate Change Strategy*, Dar es Salaam: Division of Environment, Vice President's Office.

Vermeulen, S. and L. Cotula (2010). *Making the Most of Agricultural Investment: A Survey of Business Models that Provide Opportunities for Smallholders.* London/Rome/Bern: IIED/FAO/IFAD/SDC.

Warning, M. and N. Key (2002). 'The social performance and distributional consequences of contract farming: An equilibrium analysis of the Arachide de Bouche Program in Senegal'. *World Development* 30(2): 255–263.

Watkiss, P., T. Downing, J. Dyszynski and S. Pye et al. (2011). The economics of climate change in the United Republic of Tanzania. Report to the Development Partners' Group and the UK Department for International Development. Published January 2011. Accessed 5 November 2013 at: http://economics-of-cc-in-tanzania.org/.

West, J. (2011). Unpublished field notes, Lungo Village.

World Bank (2013). *Growing Africa: Unlocking the Potential of Agribusiness.* Washington, DC: World Bank.

Yohe, G. and R. S. J. Tol (2002). 'Indicators for social and economic coping capacity—moving toward a working definition of adaptive capacity'. *Global Environmental Change* 12(1): 25–40.

9

ADAPTATION SPINOFFS FROM TECHNOLOGICAL AND SOCIO-ECONOMIC CHANGES

Julie Wilk, Mattias Hjerpe and Birgitta Rydhagen

Introduction

Societies are continuously evolving through technological and socio-economic changes. Some of these changes are planned or at least anticipated within the broader goals of development aid (Soubbotina and Sheram 2000). Local, national and international authorities strive to foster increased wellbeing in vulnerable households through planned interventions, such as job creation, subsidies and grants, although they do not always succeed in meeting their targeted aims. These interventions unfold in a continuously fluctuating context, together with large-scale globalization trends, such as urbanization, institutional and societal change and the spread of information and communication technology (ICT). All these phenomena, planned as well as unplanned, influence individuals, households and communities through a complex chain of events in contextualized environments (see e.g. Eriksen et al. 2011). Moreover, such changes shape and form the vulnerability of people and places, as well as their ability to develop effective adaptive strategies in response to these changes. To our knowledge, few scholars have scrutinized the potential opportunities for climate change adaptation arising from the *unplanned* impacts of changing socio-economic processes and major globalization trends, like ICT.

This chapter is based on the premise that technological and socio-economic trends with a potential for enhancing local adaptation strategies continually arise, but are often overlooked and consequently under-utilized. We focus on the unplanned effects that stem from such changes and that have potential to enhance climate adaptation efforts. We use the term *spinoffs* to refer specifically to these effects. O'Brien (2012) holds that researchers often assume that people have limited opportunities to effect change. She argues for more research on deliberate transformation where critical reflection and integration of knowledge from multiple sources are key components. The spinoff concept advances this by underscoring the opportunities for tapping into possible benefits from ongoing societal changes. We examine spinoffs along two dimensions: 1) whether they are *orchestrated*, stemming primarily from organized development programmes or government interventions, or *opportunity-driven*, arising from unplanned processes emerging from larger-scale changes; and 2) whether they are primarily induced by *technological* or by *socio-economic* changes. Although spinoffs may affect the adaptive capacity of local communities positively and/or negatively, our focus is on positive examples.

Spinoffs may emerge from orchestrated programmes aimed at improving socio-economic conditions. For instance, women's empowerment programmes are based on a broad developmental perspective that links enhanced opportunities and wellbeing for women with poverty reduction. Self-help groups (SHGs) are widespread in rural Asia and Africa, for promoting micro-credit for women and enabling them to undertake livelihood-generating enterprises. Besides access to credit, SHGs can generate positive spinoffs, like greater confidence and self-worth, and community inclusion (see Kabeer 2001), and improved water management skills that reduce vulnerability to climate change (Jonsson and Wilk 2014). On the other hand, several less positive aspects associated with SHGs have also been noted, for instance increased tension, anxiety and stress about making repayments, or when non-governmental organizations (NGOs) use shaming women as a tactic to increase loan repayments (Ahmed et al. 2001); also, that the narrow SHG focus on income may constrain women's empowerment by failing to promote change in underlying social factors (Izugbara 2004). SHGs may also further marginalize those women who cannot meet the membership requirements. Thus, despite the positive aspects of SHGs, they can never replace the need for equal legal rights and government intervention in oppressive gender relations but only complement them.

An example of an opportunity-driven, technological spinoff can be seen in the widespread use of mobile (cellular or cell) phones, even in the poorest households (e.g. Hahn and Kibora 2008). Such phones can provide opportunities for networking and information sharing and early notice of upcoming events ranging from drought to job opportunities. Studies have also noted the negative effects on poorer households, for instance that people sometimes sacrifice travel or buying food to pay the service costs (Diga 2008). Lifestyle changes can also lead to opportunity-driven, socio-economic spinoffs as incomes increase and the world population becomes increasingly urbanized. During periods of rapid economic growth, rising purchasing power creates numerous new markets for products and services. Even poorer households can become consumers in these emerging markets as their incomes rise and/or they become producers of goods and services that meet new demands (Wilk et al. 2014). Lifestyle-induced changes can indirectly, but significantly, enhance adaptive capacities as households change or diversify their agricultural techniques. For instance, shifting to organic production allows farmers to reap benefits from increasing environmental awareness among consumers; shifting to new crops, like grapes for wine production, can provide access to consumers with newly acquired habits. Households can also alter their livelihood base by, for instance, starting tourism-based activities or delivering services to more affluent neighbours. Nevertheless, with changes new pitfalls may also emerge. If households become heavily dependent on tourism-based profits, they are also vulnerable to fluctuating tourist numbers or degraded environments (see Gössling et al. 2002). Further, there are negative environmental, climate and health effects from some new habits related to increased material wellbeing, such as higher meat consumption (Steinfeld et al. 2006; Micha et al. 2010) and private car use. The ways in which households respond to changing societal demands can make them better or worse off in terms of climate adaptation.

This chapter explores the spinoff concept in three cases in rural areas of developing countries undergoing rapid economic growth. Our intention is to promote the recognition and use of spinoffs from current and upcoming trends that have potential for creating and enhancing climate adaptation strategies in low-income households. This spinoff approach is innovative in that it frames climate-related externalities within this dimensional framework; it enables analysis of induced changes regardless of prior intentions; and it illustrates how opportunities for achieving substantial positive differences can stem from various types of innovations.

Exploring adaptation spinoffs

Households face multiple stresses that can affect them in a myriad of ways (O'Brien and Leichenko 2000): their vulnerability is inherently dynamic and contextually determined (Vogel and O'Brien 2004). This also concerns households' adaptive responses. A South African study (Maponya and Mpandeli 2012) showed that the same piece of information may induce different responses depending on context, need and opportunity. Whereas resource-rich farmers refined and improved their irrigation schemes after receiving drought warnings, resource-poor farmers covered their crops to reduce evaporation. There is no single road to vulnerability reduction (see Brock 1999), and changing contexts must continually be addressed in day-to-day management, not as isolated once-off exercises (see Hjerpe and Glaas 2012).

As Leichenko and O'Brien (2002:3) note, rapid economic and institutional changes are 'exposing many rural regions to the impacts of globalization and climate change, with new sets of winners and losers emerging in the process'. The *double exposure* framework (O'Brien and Leichenko 2000) addresses both climate and socio-economic stressors in order to assess vulnerability and adaptive responses. Most research in this area has focused on climate-sensitive activities and locations facing fairly dramatic social or institutional stresses, such as structural adjustment programmes (see Eakin 2005). If we accept that global change is one of the major factors shaping the vulnerability and livelihood opportunities of households (see O'Brien and Leichenko 2000), then it is imperative that local adaptive responses are compatible with these changes (Eriksen et al. 2011). Moreover, since vulnerability is nested in these changes (Adger et al. 2009), it is affected through substantial feedbacks and linkages that negatively affect the poorest countries and households to a greater degree (Mattoo and Subramanian 2009).

Supporting and promoting climate adaptation strategies for resource-poor households involves mainstreaming them with other policies, including development aid. Climate change scholars and policy-makers underscore the need to nurture synergies and avoid, where possible, ill-informed trade-offs and conflicts between climate change- and development policies and objectives (Klein et al. 2005; Smit and Wandel 2006; Sharma and Tomar 2010; Román and Hoffmaister 2012). This is challenging: whereas short-term coping activities normally fit within the time frame of a development project, the planning and execution of longer-term adaptation strategies may fall outside (Janetos et al. 2012). Responses to climate change can be seen as prime opportunities for promoting alternative pathways – for instance through organic agriculture, water harvesting and rapid public transport. Sustainable adaptation in many instances calls for entirely new societal structures, innovations and mindsets than what current development programmes are based upon. As Román and Hoffmaister (2012) point out, developing countries may not need to reduce their greenhouse gas (GHG) emissions, but they could select developmental paths that avoid increased emissions or even reduce them.

The spinoff term as used here – to refer to externalities with the potential for improving adaptation to the impacts of climate variability and change – is related to other concepts in recent literature. *Co-benefits* are 'a potentially large and diverse range of collateral benefits that can be associated with climate change mitigation policies in addition to the direct avoided climate impact benefits' (Bollen et al. 2009:5). They include effects from other policy goals, but the term commonly does not include new responses that arise after a policy has been implemented. *Maladaptation* refers to changes that achieve a positive outcome but concurrently lessen adaptive capacity for other outcomes. For example, converting mangroves to shrimp farms increases farmers' incomes but also heightens their vulnerability to coastal hazards (Adger 2003). Fazey et al. (2011) describe maladaptive trajectories of change as dynamic processes and responses of individuals and communities to societal changes that, when combined, act to create negative effects. On the Solomon Islands, for instance, communities that previously were affluent in subsistence resources are now negatively stressed due to population increase and planned interventions focusing on monetary gain. Spinoffs encompass the unintended effects of planned or responsive actions, but also of unplanned, opportunity-driven trends that have a potential for positively affecting the adaptive capacities of local communities to climate-related phenomena.

TABLE 9.1   The three spinoff cases placed in the two-dimensional classification framework

		Spinoff stemming from:	
		Technological change	Socio-economic change
Spinoff stemming from:	Orchestrated change		The empowerment case
	Opportunity-driven change	The ICT case	The lifestyle case

A framework for categorizing spinoffs

We categorized spinoffs according to a two-dimensional framework describing whether they stem primarily from orchestrated or opportunity-driven changes, or from technological or socio-economic changes (Table 9.1). While insufficient from an empirical perspective, this allows a simple analysis of different types of spinoffs.

The first dimension of the framework maps whether the emerging change has arisen from planned or organized development initiatives, or from opportunities arising from more general unplanned societal change. As Biggs (2008:40) has highlighted and we reiterate, there is a long tradition of learning from development successes, but this strand of research often '(1) gives a privileged position to the idea that "successful" development comes about primarily as a result of planned development, (2) places undue attention on attributing causation to outside actors and funders, and (3) portrays development as a gradual process that goes through stages', that may or may not be linear. Emphasizing principles rather than prescriptions of innovation, it is often rewarding to distinguish between *orchestrated* and *opportunity-driven* innovation trajectories (Biggs 2008; Hall et al. 2007). Orchestrated changes are often initiated and catalysed by state actors on the national or regional level in a top-down manner, but are implemented by various grassroots development organizations. In the context of climate change adaptation, Seidl and Lexer (2013:461) hold that 'climate change adaptation needs to balance between anticipating expected future conditions and building the capacity to address unknowns and surprises'. This implies that any recommendations for capitalizing on spinoffs would require attention to the capacity to detect and respond to what is currently uncertain. Opportunity-driven changes give prominence to responses taken by private actors. Tompkins and Eakin (2011) have elaborated on private and public actor provision of adaptation goods, noting that the individuals who bear the costs are seldom the same as those who benefit, particularly over time. They therefore suggest encouraging private production of public adaptation goods by social appeal, financially incentivizing local action or implementing adequate regulation.

The second dimension of the framework distinguishes whether the spinoff is primarily related to a technological or socio-economic change. It is widely recognized that for a technological intervention to have a lasting effect on development it needs to be accompanied by changes in the social sphere, for instance by institutional modifications. For the purposes of this framework, a spinoff will primarily be seen as a consequence of either technological or socio-economic phenomena, although it is often difficult to separate the two.

Cases

Empirically, this chapter builds on work in research projects based in agricultural communities in which the authors were principal researchers. The project aims all related to assessing vulnerability and water resource management in the context of climate change (Andersson et al. 2013; Wilk and Jonsson 2013; Wilk et al. 2014). While the specific research questions and methods of the projects differed, all dealt with the responses of rural households to climate and socio-economic change. The study areas were located in large developing countries undergoing rapid economic and/or social change: India, South Africa, and China (Table 9.2). We have labelled the cases as *empowerment, ICT*, and *lifestyle*, according to the primary factor driving the spinoff. Each case exemplifies one of the four types of spinoffs in the classification framework. Our empirical data do not include the fourth type, which most closely resembles traditional aid through orchestrated technological change. This could be investigated in future research. Examples include rainwater harvesting- or water and sanitation systems that bring water to households but also create opportunities for establishing small local businesses and industries. Despite commonalities in terms of activities and targeted groups, the three cases presented here differ in terms of climatic conditions, farming systems and institutional setup. However, they provide sufficiently heterogeneous empirical data for assessing the usefulness of the spinoff concept for greater recognition of emerging opportunities for improving local adaptive capacity to climate-related phenomena.

The *empowerment* case describes an orchestrated, socio-economic spinoff. In a three-year participatory research project in Madhya Pradesh, India, group exercises, rural appraisal and semi-structured interviews were designed and conducted to establish a Water Prosperity Index. Community members identified and ranked issues that they felt contributed most to successful water management (Wilk and Jonsson 2013).[1] The case presented here explores the role of empowerment in women's SHGs for strengthening their adaptive capacity to handle water-related issues by increasing self-confidence and heightening problem-solving skills (Wilk and Jonsson 2013; Jonsson and Wilk 2014).

The *ICT* case takes up an opportunity-driven, technological spinoff in South Africa. A three-year participatory research project employing semi-structured interviews with 44 farmers, group exercises, and modelling of water resources vulnerability to economic globalization and climate change showed that

TABLE 9.2 Key features of the three spinoff cases

	The empowerment case – an orchestrated, socio-economic spinoff	The ICT case – an opportunity-driven, technological spinoff	The lifestyle case – an opportunity-driven/ orchestrated socio-economic spinoff
Location	A rural community in Madhya Pradesh, India	Rural areas in Kwazulu-Natal, South Africa	Rural areas in Xinjiang, China
Target group	SHG members, primarily smallholder farmers	Commercial and smallholder farmers	Farmers with diverse agricultural methods, crops and land tenure
Research activity	Participatory compilation of a community Water Prosperity Index	Participatory climate impact modelling	Climate adaptation efforts among farmers
Orchestration	Establishment of SHGs to improve women's economic situation	None by outside actors	Creation of policies to raise rural incomes, to counteract urbanization
Spinoff catalyst	Empowerment	Use of cellphones to fight forest fires and stock theft	Urbanized lifestyle induced demand for tourist activities and healthy, organic food
Impact on climate adaptive capacity	Increased capacity to solve water-related problems, confidence to participate in meetings and voice opinions	Access to technology and social networks for knowledge sharing and early warning	Increased ability to tap into new sources of income or livelihoods

wildfires and stock theft were the two main problems shared by commercial farmers and smallholders alike (Andersson et al. 2013; Wilk et al. 2013).[2] The case describes the potential emerging from the spread of cellphones among local small-scale farmers, enabling them to join fire-fighting networks that could reduce community climate vulnerability.

The *lifestyle* case concerns an opportunity-driven, socio-economic spinoff. A two-year research project on agricultural vulnerability to socio-economic and climate change among a diverse set of farmers in Xinjiang, China, included semi-structured interviews with 50 farmers with various agricultural practices and types of land tenure.[3] It showed that the growing number of high-income urban households has created a demand not only for more varied types of food, such as organically grown mushrooms and vegetables, but also for other services such as tourist activities (Wilk et al. 2014). The case examines the spread of urbanized lifestyle-induced changes in agricultural techniques, crops and livelihood sources, and explores their potential for decreasing climate vulnerability.

The empowerment case

Despite possible negative effects that need to be proactively avoided when initiating and running women's SHGs, such groups have the potential to trigger far-reaching benefits. These include countering negative emotions related to poverty such as shame, insecurity, fear and depression (Brock 1999); greater mobility based on their identities as group members, beyond their homes and communities in order to collaborate with other women (Tesoriero 2006); and the creation and enhancement of empowerment, capability, citizenship and participation in democratic processes. Study results from one community in central India showed that local women perceived capacity as a key factor in successful water management. In a participatory exercise they ranked it as second highest (after access) of the five factors in the Water Prosperity Index: Resources, Access, Use, Capacity and Environment (Wilk and Jonsson 2013).

In the research study, the concept of *capacity* included self-confidence, problem-solving and social capital, illustrated by speaking and/or leading meetings, holding a position in an organization, participating in mixed-gender meetings, participating in training programmes, disseminating information from training programmes, and travelling to the district and state capitals. The women associated these skills and activities with their SHG membership. Thus they saw the SHGs as a strong forum for empowerment, through their experiences of regular savings practices, and belonging to an institution that had economic resources and a voice in the community. These SHG-related assets were also found to make SHG participants better water managers, and to heighten their adaptive capacity to meet new, climate-related water challenges (Jonsson and Wilk 2014). Greater self-confidence enabled them to speak at gender-mixed meetings; and, with improved problem-solving skills, they contacted and interacted with local government officials about problems such as broken or declining flows in hand-pumps.

The ICT case

Cellular telephones are one form of ICT that have become very widespread among all ages and societal classes. Although their use was first confined mainly to wealthier people, by 2010 60 per cent of the population in sub-Saharan Africa had cellphones. While the first to start using cellphones were primarily male, educated, young, well-off and urban users, secondary adopters include young and old, rich and poor, urban and rural (Aker and Mbiti 2010). One advantage of cellphones is their availability in areas that previously lacked telephones, as mobile coverage leapfrogged landlines. Reliance, however, on cellphones requires steady transmission, electricity for charging, and affordable airtime. All three are more likely to be problematic in rural, poor and sparsely populated areas (Watts 2008). The use of cellular phones for leisure purposes might also divert limited economic resources from strategic agricultural inputs like fertilizers, pesticides or equipment. In Uganda people were found to sacrifice travel or food purchases to pay phone service costs (Diga 2008). Nevertheless the use of cellphones has brought new opportunities for improving the livelihoods and wellbeing of vast numbers of people. The multi-purpose nature of cellphones has opened up many possibilities beyond leisure communication, such as getting information on job opportunities and crop prices, and receiving automatic messaging as reminders to take medicines on schedule (Aker and Mbiti 2010). They are also useful as early warning devices: they reduce the need to travel to the nearest communication post, thus speeding up communication as well as response actions (Andersson et al. 2009).

In a recent South African study, commercial farmers noted the importance of their cellphone networks for combating the disastrous effects of wildfires (Wilk et al. 2013). The recent spread of cellphones among smallholders offers great potential for including them in such networks, thereby covering large tracts of land previously excluded. As societal divisions in South Africa have historically limited inter-racial meeting places, networks that can include commercial as well as smallholder farmers are practically non-existent. Cellphone networks provide opportunities for long-range communication between these two groups that could ease contact. As wildfires are projected to increase in the area in the future due to higher ambient temperatures, including smallholders in the fire-fighting cellphone networks could heighten the adaptive capacity of the community at large.

The lifestyle case

In the 1980s, de-collectivization in China began to distribute rights to households, creating an agricultural system consisting of millions of individual household farms where farmers could lease land for up to 15 years (Ostwald et al. 2007). Agricultural markets were established, where individual farmers are free to sell their produce as they choose. In the province of Xinjiang, this led to a shift from cotton production to more diversified agriculture. Concurrently China in general and Xinjiang in particular have experienced recent rapid economic growth, particularly in urban areas.

According to household interviews in Xinjiang, the new food habits of the growing urban middle class, including organically grown products, meat and wine, as well as an interest in leisure activities, have rapidly increased prices as well as market demand (Wilk et al. 2014). The interest in tourism and travel has been growing among all but the poorest of farmers, making local people not only producers but also consumers of tourist services. Interviewees also explained that subsidies and favourable tax reductions have been offered to facilitate the transition from monoculture farming and herding to alternative tourism-based or augmented livelihood sources.

Many farmers have begun to tap into the opportunities stemming from such societal changes (Wilk et al. 2014). Farmers noted that rural inhabitants, mainly herdsmen, have diversified their livelihoods to include tourism operations, such as restaurants, tented accommodation, horseback riding, trekking tours, and transportation services. Competition for grazing land is becoming intense due to the rising demand for meat, and land scarcity is likely to be aggravated by higher temperatures. By diversifying their livelihoods to include tourist activities, herdsman can reduce their vulnerability to climate change. Further, cultivators have begun with new crops (e.g. mushrooms, and grapes for wine production), as well as different production methods, like growing vegetables through specialized greenhouse-based organic agriculture. Some of these new activities have potential to make farmers less sensitive to climate variation and change, as with mushrooms and vegetables grown in greenhouses where farmers can regulate temperatures and be protected from weather events like hail (by covering the crops or burning straw to mitigate cold spells). Crop changes can either reduce or increase sensitivity to climate variation and change, depending on which crops are introduced. By growing a variety of crops instead of relying on cotton or other monocultures, they can reduce their vulnerability. Currently, however, greenhouses are often heated with inefficient fossil fuels that contribute to GHG emissions. Intensive cattle raising has also emerged as a response to the growing demand for meat; this can strengthen adaptive capacity through higher incomes, but also brings higher GHG emissions and greater exposure to livestock diseases (Steinfeld et al. 2006).

The new agricultural initiatives in the lifestyle case show that farmers take both price and climate into account in their livelihood choices. They show great flexibility in choosing crops, crop varieties and buyers for their produce – all key factors in high adaptive capacity. Government support through subsidies can direct livelihood activities towards activities that are more, or less, climate-appropriate. Subsidizing organic vegetables at the expense of meat production may, for example, help to curb the demand for meat, although this is not a simple matter. Support to mixed farming (such as livestock herding as well as crop cultivation) or non-farming (such as tourist-based businesses) activities has enabled Xinjiang farmers to diversify their livelihood bases and increase their incomes. Such pluri-activity is likely to reduce vulnerability (Rigg 2005). Despite tourist instability in recent years because of ethnic upheavals as well as rainy summers, farmers said that their incomes were nevertheless more stable than when based solely on pastoralism, given the area's climate extremes and increasing grassland degradation.

Discussion

The three spinoff cases show how unplanned effects from technological and socio-economic changes are being used, or could be used, by socially vulnerable groups for dealing with climate-related challenges. In addition to the opportunities that arise directly from top-down development policies, utilizing the spinoff potential could bring into play a new type of development, whereby adaptive capacity is heightened through social innovations that emerge within the local communities themselves. Social activators (empowerment), ICT (cellular telephones), capitalization on new lifestyle changes (consumer demands) or other emerging trends could feed into positive feedback loops and enhance adaptive capacity to climate change.

As socio-economic changes are so complex, the causes and effects are rarely unidirectional. Many links in cause–effect chains will in turn further influence the need to reinforce and develop adaptation strategies for meeting the challenges of a warmer world. While one phenomenon can be said to lead to a particular spinoff, such as tourism leading to new livelihood opportunities, the subsequent changes could also be seen as the effects of alternate factors or combinations of them. In the lifestyle case, some farmers chose to grow strawberries, not only for income from passing tourists, but also because it was less labour-intensive. The same case also highlights the two-way directionality of causes and effects. The decreased vulnerability stemming from greenhouse cultivation, where crops receive greater protection from climate extremes, can serve to increase incomes. This in turn makes it possible for farmers to visit restaurants or overnight accommodation or buy organic food that augments incomes for other 'converted' farmers. Farmers who cannot invest in greenhouses need to find other alternatives for reinforcing their climate adaptation. The adaptive capacity of farmers must also be continually re-evaluated as conditions change and they engage in new livelihood activities and response strategies.

However, capitalizing on emerging societal demands through new livelihood activities will not automatically promote positive spinoffs. The lifestyle case shows that entering new markets for products or services may involve various management and/or technological choices or practices. These will in turn affect the source and degree of household exposure to climate impacts and adaptive capacity as well as contributions to other global issues. For example, the budding market demand for wine in western China may induce farmers to increase their grape production through additional cropped areas. While current water resources may support this, glacier meltwater is projected to diminish in some areas as future temperatures rise. Further, livestock raising can enhance farmers' incomes, but in a long-term global perspective, increased meat consumption threatens sustainable land use and increases GHG emissions. Serving locally produced and organic food at newly opened restaurants is considered an environmentally friendly, low-emission pathway. But, as the local consumer base expands to include tourists from farther away, even international destinations, increased emissions from travel will be counterproductive to the higher adaptive capacity to respond to climate change effects gained by livelihood diversification. Especially problematic is the situation when the negative spinoffs are not immediately apparent or simple to remedy, or where significant positive and negative effects emerge from the same phenomenon. The various steps in the value chain need to be evaluated separately to make such pitfalls visible (Román and Hoffmaister 2012).

Efforts at adapting to climate change, whether they are internally-, government- or CBO/NGO-driven, will benefit from identifying and utilizing existing social structures, local organizations and initiatives. SHGs that are based on existing groups, including informal ones, have been found to be more successful than those created specifically for a new scheme (Omorodion 2007). The ICT case shows that commercial farmers already successfully use cellphones to convey information on the spread of wildfires. New social media may also be required to promote positive spinoffs such as forums for information exchange and communication that include smallholders. In programmes that encourage vulnerable groups to pursue wage-earning activities or engage with decision-makers and a broader circle of community members, socio-economic features like SHGs, forums and networks can be important as spinoff capitalization spaces. Infrastructural features can also be important, such as the construction of new roads that could link tourists with formerly remote dwellers. Research on inclusive innovation in East Africa (e.g. Kjellqvist et al. 2013) showed that comparatively slow and locally based changes are best suited in development contexts, as poor households are usually restricted to joining slower stepwise processes. A local market for tourism and organic food, as in the livelihood case, illustrates such a process where poorer households are being integrated through a gradual, small-scale approach.

As climate change progressively impacts on various aspects of society, a mind-shift is needed among planners, politicians and development workers. Open-mindedness, creative thinking and flexibility (O'Brien 2012) are required to recognize social innovations and take advantage of them in the short as well as long term. This will entail devising and promoting adaptation measures for dealing not only with current climate variability but also probable future climates. Development workers should reflect on how climate change will impact on their region, and they need to understand adaptation as much more than merely reacting to negative conditions. An important starting point is to acknowledge that communities and households, and especially poor ones, are not passive but rather highly dynamic and adaptive. Recognition should also be given to the many socio-economic and technological spinoffs that already exist and are being used in local communities, although perhaps not in all households and not necessarily specifically for climate adaptation. It is important to recognize and analyse existing and emerging spinoffs to determine how to best support or introduce them in climate adaptation activities in low-income households.

Lessons can be learnt from efforts at introducing gender equality and environmental sustainability in development projects and government policy. It has become evident that gender and environmental sustainability need internal expertise as well as widespread recognition within organizations in order to have a positive influence on policies and practice (Derbyshire 2012). Likewise, while advocates who focus on specific aspects of climate change are necessary, adaptation should be concurrently mainstreamed in existing organizational structures. As noted by Janetos et al. (2012), there is a real risk that climate change will be added on as a problem, rather than mainstreamed as a central consideration that needs to be addressed in development policies and practice in a similar manner as gender issues.

Opportunity-driven and locally initiated development and adaptation need more recognition (see Biggs 2008). Development initiatives can – given the proper foresight – recognize and interpret spinoffs in order to take advantage of potential opportunities, or at least mitigate or not re-enforce any negative effects. The capacity to identify and effectively use spinoffs will vary between levels and contexts. It is advantageous if national political agendas can recognize and support adaptation potentials from emerging spinoffs. However, it can be difficult for organizations to achieve this, because the same phenomena are likely to manifest differently depending on the local setting. Recognizing spinoffs requires ongoing, conscious open-minded appraisal of new technological and socio-economic phenomena, and weighing of their advantages, disadvantages and potential uses. Before new initiatives are undertaken informed but reflective pre-studies should be performed to avoid or at least seek to counter possible maladaptation. Extra attention should be paid to ensuring that measures that give rapid short-term gains do not compromise longer-term adaptive capacity. Moreover, community members cannot afford to deal with climate change adaptation separately from other aspects that affect their livelihoods – and this applies also to supporting structures including governments and NGOs. A new approach is needed, one that can more quickly recognize and utilize emerging phenomena that support sustainable climate adaptation in locally relevant ways.

Conclusions

The three cases in this chapter have illustrated some emerging positive spinoffs that can lessen problems, improve livelihoods and enhance sustainable adaptation strategies. Identifying other examples requires good insight into what people are doing, especially the poor. Simple investigations can help to determine how the effects of societal changes may be used to create or reinforce climate change adaptation strategies, especially among the poor. Any promoted spinoffs would also need to be 'climate-proofed' to enhance low-emission and sustainable options according to current climate variability and future climate projections.

Three key messages have emerged from the cases examined here:

1   evaluate and utilize widespread societal changes that have the potential to reduce climate vulnerability
2   capitalize on new societal demands to promote and support low-emission livelihood opportunities and
3   support empowerment initiatives that can boost local adaptive capacity for handling climate-related impacts.

Recognition of existing societal groups (such as SHGs and farmers' associations), emergent technologies (such as cellphones), and new lifestyle choices (such as healthy foods and tourism) that show potential for enhancing or creating new climate adaptation options are strong starting points for understanding what is working and why. The utilization of spinoffs may be either self-organized or externally initiated but, as Eriksen and O'Brien (2007) point out, sustainable climate adaptation must be context sensitive. Government interventions and NGO projects need to take global climate effects as well as poverty reduction agendas into consideration when designing locally relevant adaptation measures for vulnerable groups. As previously noted in the lifestyle case: despite the positive effects for farmers' livelihoods and their adaptive capacity to climate-related issues stemming from intensified livestock raising, new tourism and food habits may also contribute to increased GHG emissions.

To what degree can spinoffs be facilitated and enabled by government policy? More creative, adaptive and opportunistic policies are needed, emphasizing the enabling role as well as the envisioning capacity of government agencies. Furthermore, our cases have shown that spinoffs can manifest themselves differently depending on the local context, and are thus likely to require policies and support at or close to that level. Organizations operating at this level are probably best equipped for assessing adaptation measures, contexts and spinoff potentials.

Both public and private organizations could play a facilitating role for spinoffs, depending on the type of spinoff and the context. For instance, in the ICT case the farmers themselves possess the platform, whereas the government agencies could intervene by coordinating access to fire alerts and setting up more inclusive emergency phone lists to bridge the gap between socio-economic segments. In the empowerment case, both NGOs and the state are involved in facilitating SHGs, which shows that different actors can play a positive role in heightening adaptive capacity through positive spinoffs. This supports the findings of Tompkins and Eakin (2011) who note that, since the effects of adaptation spinoffs occur in a local context, it is advantageous to involve a set of public and private actors that can collectively play an enabling role at that level. Further, it is more important to incentivize the use of spinoffs than to prescribe specific adaptation measures. This case also shows that there is no general blueprint for responsibility, as roles are likely to differ according to context. Study of changing trends and their potential adaptation spinoffs by public or private actors will require open, ongoing dialogue and interaction with local communities to be successful.

Lastly, the cases show how vulnerable groups can take advantage of spinoffs that are being successfully used by others. In some instances this can mean enabling them to access new technology, knowledge or organizational forms. Spinoff successes cannot be applied in new areas in a standard cookie-cutter fashion. They should serve to inspire and highlight possibilities. The 'development as usual' approach, with top-down measures often applied with no consideration, acknowledgement or use of local social innovation, ignores a wealth of opportunities for instigating or strengthening low-emission adaptation measures for vulnerable groups.

Notes

1 Detailed descriptions of the methods used can be found in Wilk and Jonsson (2013) and Jonsson and Wilk (2014).
2 Detailed descriptions of the methods used can be found in Andersson et al. (2013) and Wilk et al. (2013).
3 Detailed description of the methods used can be found in Wilk et al. (2014).

References

Adger, W.N. (2003). 'Social aspects of adaptive capacity', in J.B. Smith, R.J.T. Klein and S. Huq (eds), *Climate change, adaptive capacity and development*, 29–49. London: Imperial College Press.

Adger, N., Eakin, H. and Winkels, A. (2009). 'Nested and teleconnected vulnerabilities to environmental change'. *Frontiers in Ecology and the Environment*, 7(3), 150–157.

Ahmed, S.M., Chowdhury, M. and Bhuiya, A. (2001). 'Micro-credit and emotional well-being: experience of poor rural women from Matlab, Bangladesh'. *World Development*, 29(11), 1957–1966.

Aker, J.C. and Mbiti., I. (2010).'Mobile phones and economic development in Africa'. *Journal of Economic Perspectives*, 24(3): 207–232.

Andersson, L., Wilk, J., Graham, P. and Warburton, M. (2009). *Local assessment of vulnerability to climate change impacts on water resources in the Upper Thukela River Basin, South Africa – Recommendations for adaptation*. Climatology No 1, Norrköping: SMHI.

Andersson, L., Wilk, J., Graham, P. and Warburton, M. (2013). 'Design and test of a model-assisted participatory process for the formulation of a local climate adaptation plan'. *Climate and Development*, 5(3), 217–228.

Biggs, S. (2008). 'Learning from the positive to reduce poverty and increase social justice: institutional innovations in agricultural and natural resource research and development'. *Experimental Agriculture*, 44, 37–60.

Bollen, J., Guay, B., Jamet, S. and Corfee-Morlot, J. (2009). *Co-benefits of climate change mitigation policies: literature review and new results*, Economics Department Working Paper No. 693. Paris: OECD.

Brock, K. (1999). 'It's not only wealth that matters – it's peace of mind too: a review of participatory work on poverty and ill-being', Paper prepared for the Global Synthesis Workshop, Consultations with the Poor, World Bank, Washington, DC mimeo, July.

Derbyshire, H. (2012). 'Gender mainstreaming: recognising and building on progress. Views from the UK Gender and Development Network'. *Gender and Development*, 20(3), 405–422.

Diga, K. (2008). 'Mobile cell phones and poverty reduction: technology spending patterns and poverty level change among households in Uganda', presented at workshop on the Role of Mobile Technologies in Fostering Social Development, Sao Paulo, Brazil, 2–3 June.

Eakin, H. (2005). 'Institutional change, climate risk, and rural vulnerability: cases from Central Mexico'. *World Development*, 33, 1923–1938.

Eriksen, S., Aldunce, P., Bahinipati, C.S., Martins, R.D., Molefe, J.I., Nhemachena, C., O'Brien, K., Olorunfemi, F., Park, J., Sygna, L. and Ulsrud, K. (2011). 'When not every response to climate change is a good one: identifying principles for sustainable adaptation'. *Climate and Development*, 2, 7–20.

Eriksen, S. and O'Brien, K (2007). 'Vulnerability, poverty and the need for sustainable adaptation measures'. *Climate Policy*, 7(4), 337–352.

Fazey, I., Pettorelli, N., Kenter, J., Wagatora, D., and Schuett, D. (2011). 'Maladaptive trajectories of change in Makira, Solomon Islands'. *Global Environmental Change*, 21, 1275–1289.

Gössling, S., Borgström Hansson, C., Hörstmeier, O. and Saggel, S. (2002). 'Ecological footprint analysis as a tool to assess tourism sustainability'. *Ecological Economics*, 43, 199–211.

Hahn, H.P. and Kibora, L. (2008). 'The domestication of the mobile phone: oral society and new ICT in Burkina Faso'. *Journal of Modern African Studies*, 46(1), 87–109.

Hall, A., Pehu, E. and Rajaahti, R. (2007). *Enhancing agricultural innovation: how to go beyond strengthening research systems*. Agriculture and Rural Development Department, Washington, DC: World Bank.

Hjerpe, M. and Glaas, E. (2012). 'Evolving local climate adaptation strategies: incorporating influences of socio–economic stress'. *Mitigation and Adaptation of Strategies for Global Change*, 17(5), 471–486.

Izugbara, C.O. (2004). 'Gendered micro-lending schemes and sustainable women's empowerment in Nigeria'. *Community Development Journal*, 39(1), 72–84.

Janetos, A.C., Malone, E., Mastrangelo, E., Hardee, K. and de Bremond, A. (2012). 'Linking climate change and development goals: framing, integrating, and measuring'. *Climate and Development*, 4(2), 141–156.

Jonsson, A. and Wilk, J. (2014). 'Opening up the Water Poverty Index: co-exploring capacity for community water management'. *Society and Natural Resources*, Advance online manuscript DOI:10.1080/08941920.2013.861553

Kabeer, N. (2001). 'Conflicts over credit: re-evaluating the empowerment potential of loans to women in rural Bangladesh'. *World Development*, 29(1), 63–84.

Kjellqvist, T., Rydhagen, B. and Trojer, L. (2013). 'Inclusive innovation processes – experiences from Uganda and Tanzania', submitted for publication *to African Journal of Science, Technology, Innovation and Development*.

Klein, R.J.T., Schipper, E.L.F. and Dessai, S. (2005). 'Integrating mitigation and adaptation into climate and development policy: three research questions'. *Environmental Science and Policy*, 8(6), 579–588.

Leichenko, R. and O'Brien, K. (2002). 'The dynamics of rural vulnerability to global change: the case of southern Africa'. *Mitigation and Adaptation Strategies for Global Change*, 7, 1–18.

Maponya, P. and Mpandeli, S. (2012). 'Climate change adaptation strategies used by Limpopo Province farmers in South Africa'. *Journal of Agricultural Science*, 4(12), 39–47.

Mattoo, A. and Subramanian, A. (2009). *Criss-crossing globalization: uphill flows of skill-intensive goods and foreign direct investment*. Working Paper 09-7, Peterson Institute for International Economics, Washington, DC.

Micha, R., Wallace, S.K. and Mozaffarian, D. (2010). 'Red and processed meat consumption and risk of incident coronary heart disease, stroke, and diabetes mellitus: a systematic review and meta-analysis'. *Circulation*, 121(21), 2271–2283.

O'Brien, K. (2012). 'Global environmental change II: from adaptation to deliberate transformation'. *Progress in Human Geography*, 36(5), 667–676.

O'Brien, K. and Leichenko, R. (2000). 'Double exposure: assessing the impacts of climate change within the context of economic globalization'. *Global Environmental Change*, 10, 221–232.

Omorodion, F.I. (2007). 'Rural women's experiences of micro-credit schemes in Nigeria: case study of Esan women'. *Journal of Asian and African Studies*, 42(6): 479–494.

Ostwald, M., Simelton, E., Chen, D. and Liu, A. (2007). 'Relation between vegetation changes, climate variables and land use policy in Shaanxi Province, China'. *Geographical Annals*, 89(A4): 223–236.

Rigg, J. (2005). 'Poverty and livelihoods after full-time farming: a South-East Asian view'. *Asia Pacific Viewpoint*, 46(2), 173–184.

Román, M. and Hoffmaister, J.P. (2012). 'Climate and development: the potential for climate co-benefits in the Mozambican rice sector'. *Climate and Development*, 4(3), 219–233.

Seidl, R. and Lexer, M.J. (2013). 'Forest management under climatic and social uncertainty: trade-offs between reducing climate change impacts and fostering adaptive capacity'. *Journal of Environmental Management*, 114, 461–469.

Sharma, D. and Tomar, S. (2010). 'Mainstreaming climate change adaptation in Indian cities'. *Environment and Urbanization*, 22(2), 451–465.

Smit, B. and Wandel, J. (2006). 'Adaptation, adaptive capacity and vulnerability'. *Global Environmental Change*, 16, 282–292.

Steinfeld, H., Gerber, P., Wassenaar, T., Castel, V., Rosales, M. and de Haan, C. (2006). *Livestock's long shadow: environmental issues and options*. Rome: FAO.

Soubbotina, T.P. and Sheram, K.A. (2000). *Beyond economic growth: meeting the challenges of global development*, Washington, DC: World Bank.

Tesoriero, F. (2006). 'Strengthening communities through women's self help groups in South India'. *Community Development Journal*, 41(3), 321–333.

Tompkins, E.L. and Eakin, H. (2011). 'Managing private and public adaptation to climate change'. *Global Environmental Change*, 22(1), 3–11.

Vogel, C. and O'Brien, K. (2004). 'Vulnerability and global environmental change: rhetoric and reality'. AVISO – Information Bulletin on Global Environmental Change and Human Security, 13, available at: http://www.gechs.org/publications/aviso/13/index.html.

Watts, L. (2008). 'The future is boring: stories from the landscapes of the mobile telecoms industry'. *Twenty-First Century Society*, 3(2), 187–198.

Wilk, J., Andersson, L. and Warburton, M. (2013). 'Adaptation to climate change and other stressors among commercial and small-scale South African farmers'. *Regional Environmental Change*, 13(2), 273–286.

Wilk, J., Hjerpe, M., Yang, W. and Fan, H. (2014). 'Farm-scale adaptation to extreme climate and rapid economic transition'. *Journal of Environment, Development and Sustainability*. DOI:10.1007/s10668-014-9549-2

Wilk, J. and Jonsson, A. (2013). 'From water poverty to water prosperity: a more participatory approach to studying local water resources management'. *Water Resources Management*, 27(3), 695–713.

10

SUSTAINABLE ADAPTATION UNDER ADVERSE DEVELOPMENT?

Lessons from Ethiopia

Siri Eriksen and Andrei Marin

Introduction

Afar pastoralists manage their livelihoods in one of the hottest and driest environments on Earth. At the same time, they face rising temperatures and more frequent droughts induced by climate change, as well as increasing socio-economic and political pressures on pastoral lifestyles. Adaptation and development are closely intertwined for the Afar of Ethiopia, illustrating the importance of identifying adaptation approaches that can contribute to social sustainability, equity and justice on the ground. In the climate change literature, there are increasing calls for new types of development that are not mere adjustment to practices, technologies and institutions *within* the current development regime, but which instead address the shortcomings of current development pathways (see O'Brien 2012). In this chapter, we draw on the case of Afar pastoralists in Ethiopia to examine how *sustainable adaptation*, a concept that focuses specifically on development–adaptation interactions and on addressing the vulnerability of the poor (Eriksen and O'Brien 2007), can be broadened to transform development pathways.

Most adaptation policies and measures have been formulated as part of dominant (and often unquestioned) development approaches, reinforcing 'development as usual'. Despite some promising work on community-based adaptation (Sabates-Wheeler et al. 2008), many local and national adaptation plans of action are often sectoral, top-down, technical or risk-reduction measures (such as new agricultural technologies or flood protection measures) focused on avoiding physical or monetary damage, human injuries and death from extreme events (Vincent et al. 2013; Nightingale this volume). In addition, many interventions initially designed as local development projects have later been re-labelled 'adaptation' (McGray et al. 2007). Ireland and Keegan (2013) describe how development actors use the term adaptation 'malleably and through the constructs of pre-existing approaches and concepts of development' (p. 225). Adaptation research and policy have generally lacked fundamental reflection on what overall development approach such measures represent – for example, whether the approach is based on modernization assumptions, or on explicitly addressing dependency relations and inequities. Instead, there has been a 'development as usual' approach, operating on the assumption that 'more development' will necessarily reduce vulnerability, without critical examination of whether this will lead to ineffective or counterproductive measures (Klein et al. 2007), or how poverty and vulnerability differ, and whose vulnerability is to be addressed. This is highly problematic, since some types of development may actually reinforce inequities and vulnerability, and constitute a root cause driving the climate change problem (Brooks et al. 2009; Eriksen 2013; St Clair and Lawson 2013).

An alternative approach to adaptation can build on critical development theories that underscore the primacy of using a political conceptualization of sustainability. Often emphasizing the importance of including equity, scale and human rights in the analysis of sustainability (Adams 2001), such theories recognize sustainable development as an intrinsically political process. This process entails negotiating what kinds of socio-environmental arrangements we wish to produce, how this can be achieved, what sorts of natures we wish to inhabit (Swyngedouw 2007) and whose development goals are heeded (Munck 1999).

We conceive development pathways as sets of relations and processes that create a trajectory of socio-economic change toward (often covert) development goals that may encompass environmental, economic or social objectives. Such pathways entail more or less specific visions of the 'destination' and the 'route' to reach it, which may refer to changes in technologies, regulations, political doctrines, economic models or value systems. Development pathways refer to societal (national or sub-national level) rather than household-level trajectories.

Sustainable development pathways have previously been described in local contexts (Adams 2001), but sustainability has only recently started to inform climate change adaptation policy. Despite increasing calls to shift towards more sustainable development pathways and the emerging literature exploring the potential pathways for such change (Berkhout et al. 2009; Steffen et al. 2011; Westley et al. 2011; O'Brien and Sygna 2013; O'Brien 2013), not enough is known about how this can be achieved in practice in the context of climate change.

In this chapter, we examine empirical evidence related to the four normative principles associated with sustainable adaptation as developed by Eriksen et al. (2011) and further described below. Then we focus on the local context of Afar pastoralists in Ethiopia to see what sustainable adaptation may look like in practice. This empirical research allows us to develop a deeper conceptual understanding (described in the scetion on 'Transforming development') of what adaptation means in terms of interventions, actions and change, and how it relates to development pathways. Our analysis emphasizes the potential of climate change adaptation to be not merely 'mainstreamed' into existing development paradigms, but to actually transform development paradigms and practices. We propose adding a fifth normative principle of sustainable adaptation that focuses on the empowerment of vulnerable groups.

A sustainable adaptation framework

Distinguishing between *weak* and *strong* sustainability illuminates the danger of 'mainstreaming' climate change adaptation into business-as-usual development models. The concept of weak sustainability is based on the idea that technology can remove any environmental constraints that limit constant economic expansion, consistent with ecological modernization, market environmentalism and technocratic approaches to development that form the 'dominant force in mainstream sustainable development' (Adams 2001:110). It relies on the assumption that crises can be avoided by applying technological or procedural innovations (Hajer 1996), making small changes to the conventional development model of growth-based capitalism.

In contrast, strong sustainability is less optimistic about the potential for technology to overcome ecological constraints, for example due to lack of knowledge and means to correct environmental consequences of unsustainable practices in a timely and efficient way (Douthwaite 1999). In addition, if ecological modernization principles imply ordering nature to suit human ends by rational planning, then it is important to reflect on the social construction of the nature to be ordered and on the diversity and political aspects of 'human ends' and 'rationality'. This requires discussing 'developmentS' (in the plural) as a way of regaining the political dimension of sustainability (Munck 1999; Swyngedouw 2007). We hold that such approaches are also necessary when analysing adaptation to climate change and its interrelations with societal development pathways.

Sustainable adaptation is an approach to climate change adaptation that emphasizes the importance of development pathways built on strong sustainability. The term is based on an understanding of adaptation not as a single formal (or informal) measure but as a process involving the interaction between decisions and practices by many actors to manage climate change as a part of multiple socio-environmental changes facing them (Eriksen 2013). Therefore, sustainable adaptation is not a matter of identifying one specific 'sustainable' practice or action, but of developing a set of actions that can contribute to socially and environmentally sustainable development pathways. Its conceptual underpinnings draw heavily on a contextual vulnerability approach (O'Brien et al. 2007), which describes vulnerability as an interaction between contextual conditions (socio-economic, technical, institutional and biophysical), the processes that shape these conditions (political, institutional, social and economic structures and changes, in addition to climate variability and change), and people's and societies' responses to change. Early elaborations of 'sustainable adaptation' built on the recognition that altering the conditions under which climate change occurs, addressing the social and environmental processes driving vulnerability, and enabling people to better respond to changes are central to reducing the vulnerability of the poor (Eriksen and O'Brien 2007).

Later elaborations of sustainable adaptation formulated four normative principles (explained in greater detail in Eriksen et al. 2011 and in the section on 'Principles of sustainable adaptation: development pathways, vulnerability and adaptation in Afar' below) aimed at equity and environmental criteria, linking sustainable adaptation more closely to recent discussions of transformative change (Pelling 2010; O'Brien 2012; Kates et al. 2012). O'Brien (2012: 671) argues for the need for fundamental shifts in societal systems, including 'transformation of energy and agricultural systems, financial systems, governance regimes, development paradigms, power and gender relations, production and consumption patterns, lifestyles, knowledge production systems, or values and world-views' in order to achieve sustainable development.

Transformation and sustainability have been explored theoretically and empirically, especially within resilience research (Westley et al. 2011); however, such approaches have been criticized for ignoring the political aspects of social change (Cote and Nightingale 2011). In contrast, recent elaborations of sustainable adaptation focus specifically on the political – that is, on conflicts of interests and decision-making processes (Eriksen et al. 2011). Changes of a political nature are required in order to change governance systems that control the access to and use of resources, adjust development priorities, and empower local decision-making. Sustainable adaptation is hence aligned more closely to traditions in political ecology and political economy, investigating the processes that create exclusion and inequity (Adams 2001). It forms part of a wider *deliberate* transformation process, where actions are undertaken purposefully, in order to influence future change towards more sustainable pathways, including reducing emissions and vulnerability (Eriksen 2013). It is argued that the potential to alter development pathways lies in the fact that every decision (or non-decision) is in essence political – overtly or covertly favouring certain interests or objectives over others.

Studying sustainable adaptation in Afar

The study reported here was conducted in the Afar region of north-eastern Ethiopia. The region is the fourth largest in Ethiopia (100,860 km^2), with an estimated population of 1.4 million people, and is one of the poorest regions in the country (Macro International Inc. 2008). Average rainfall is less than 300 mm/year (Viste et al. 2012), measured at only 202 mm/year (1982–2011) at Dubti, the nearest rainfall station to our sites. Moreover, the region is one of the hottest inhabited places on Earth, with temperatures sometimes exceeding 50°C (Davies and Bennett 2009). Temperature increases associated with climate change may restrict adaptation in the future (Sherwood and Huber 2010).

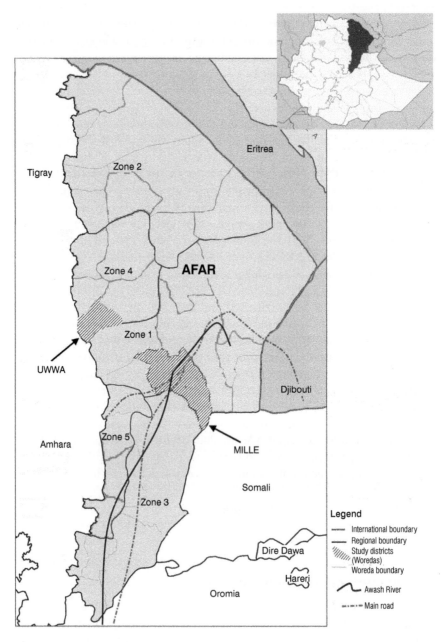

FIGURE 10.1 Map of Ethiopia, showing the two study districts (Uwwa and Mille); inset: Ethiopia's regions

More than 80 per cent of the population in the Afar region relies on livestock (camels, cattle, goats, sheep and donkeys) for their main livelihood (Davies 2006; FDRE 2008), based on a mobile, flexible utilization of seasonal pastures (Davies and Bennett 2009). The livestock and their products (meat, milk and butter) are used for subsistence and trade.

Two districts were selected for data collection in Afar (see Figure 10.1): Mille (pop. 79,000) and Uwwa (pop. 47,000). The two are similar in terms of pastoral livelihoods and frequent exposure to drought, but Mille is close to the Awash River and farming schemes, whereas Uwwa is situated on the drier plains. A dam and plantation are large-scale development interventions prominent in Mille, but there has been very little intervention or even non-governmental organization (NGO) presence in Uwwa.

The Mille site is located on the banks of the river, upstream from a dam, and is described by the Afar as *kallo* or 'wet', a riverside area that supports agro-pastoralists as well as pastoralists. Interviews in Mille were conducted in a relatively settled village with permanent housing, a characteristic partly attributable to a banana plantation that was in operation during the Derg regime (1974–1987). Mille illustrates some of the dramatic changes to the vulnerability context caused by development schemes. Since the plantation closed, the local people have been forced to migrate more with their animals than formerly. The nearby Dubti and Ayssaita districts are also home to a large sugar-cane plantation (60,000 ha) based on irrigation provided by the (2009) damming of the Awash River at Tendaho. An unintended consequence of the dam has been dramatic flooding that has threatened livestock, grazing, farmland and possessions (as in 2010 and in 2012). The Mille site is also exposed to conflict with the pastoralist clan Issa Somali. While such conflicts are nothing new, they have intensified recently – an issue increasingly affecting grazing, security and livelihoods in large parts of south-eastern Afar and forming part of recent political developments in Ethiopia (Ali 2008; Hagmann and Mulugeta 2008).

Uwwa is part of the vast semi-dry grazing lands (*duka'a*) in the west of the region, where herds mass-migrate for pasture when the rains come. Interviews in Uwwa were carried out in four villages. The population is much more dispersed and mobile than in Mille, relying on pastoralism to a greater extent.

Four group discussions were conducted with elders (male), women, administrators and youth (male and female) in each site. Topics covered were extreme weather and other important events, long-term changes, development and institutions, and social interactions. The overview acquired from group discussions was complemented with in-depth information gathered in 20 key informant interviews at each site. Respondents were selected with the help of local key informants in order to represent a balanced range of socio-economic characteristics (men/women, young/old, rich/poor, including households regarded as vulnerable). The local interviews were carried out in 2010 during a severe drought.

Principles of sustainable adaptation: development pathways, vulnerability and adaptation in Afar

The sustainable adaptation approach grew out of an awareness that climate adaptation can have unintended negative effects on people and the environment, and that there is a need to think critically about what types of adaptation are desirable (Eriksen et al. 2011). It recognizes that the term 'sustainable' may be used to green-wash and de-politicize any type of adaptation (Brown 2011). To deal with this, and based on empirical evidence from various cases, Eriksen et al. (2011) formulated four normative principles for adaptation approaches that can contribute to socially and environmentally sustainable development:

1   Recognize the context for vulnerability, including multiple stressors
2   Acknowledge differing values and interests affecting adaptation outcomes
3   Integrate local knowledge into adaptation responses
4   Consider potential feedbacks between local and global processes

In this section, we illustrate how these principles have been operationalized for our analysis of the Afar case.

Principle 1: understanding the vulnerability context

A key challenge in developing sustainable adaptation approaches is to distinguish the root causes of vulnerability and how they can be addressed. Principle 1 is concerned with the underlying processes that lead to the appearance of contextual vulnerability conditions and the inability to respond to change and shocks (O'Brien et al. 2007). Our material shows that although the vulnerability context in Afar appears closely connected to extreme weather events like drought and floods, and climatic changes over time, in fact it is fundamentally driven by multiple environmental and social processes.

As is common for pastoralists in many parts of the world (see Marin 2008; 2010), mobility and trade are the cornerstones of Afar pastoralists' adaptive capacity, allowing the flexible re-organization of herds and income sources. Our informants consistently describe how consecutive droughts have led to great livestock losses, many families being unable to replenish their stock. They identified the recent decades' decreasing livestock herds, and the related shifts from cattle and camels to goats and sheep, as a proximate cause of declining adaptive capacity. Five key informant interviews in each site specifically explored in depth how families had coped with recent climatic events (drought in Uwwa; drought and flood in Mille). A recurrent concern in both sites was how a decline in livestock numbers was making it difficult for individual families to cope with drought while also aggravating vulnerability at community level, as few people now had enough livestock to be able to assist others. In Uwwa, the sale of livestock and migration to find pasture were the key drought strategies practised by all five respondents. They also described how other households in the community had lost all their livestock and had to move in with relatives. Those who still had many livestock (including camels to carry goods), and sons to lead the herds to several places, were seen as relatively less vulnerable. Women (especially if pregnant) and children were considered most vulnerable because they were often unable to migrate with the animals. Several informants described how children fell ill due to poor nutrition. In Mille, several informants had also lost animals, but remittances and salary were more common as coping strategies in addition to migrating with the livestock. Some households had received food aid, although this was not commonly mentioned as a coping strategy.

Even if some people managed relatively better, animal losses were high also among the better-off households, who lost livestock to weakness and disease while migrating. Thus, although vulnerability was socially differentiated, animal loss appeared near universal, threatening the foundations of the pastoralist system. For example, a Mille herder (of average wealth) reported: 'Before [the environmental changes] I had 50 camels, 200 goats and 30 cattle. Now I am left with 2 camels and 20 goats.'

The in-depth interviews revealed that declining herds were often associated with closely interlinked processes of changes in climatic and rangeland conditions. More severe weather events, in particular less rain and higher temperatures that led to droughts, were seen as directly contributing to the decline in pasture production and water availability.

Analysis of precipitation between 1971 and 2011 (Viste et al. 2012) shows that although there is no overall trend of declining rainfall for the Afar region, recent years have been some of the driest of the past 40 years, and spring droughts have occurred more frequently during the past decade. An Uwwa pastoralist recounted: 'I have noticed how the environment is getting drier. Drought used to be every 8 years – now it is one after the other. It means we have to migrate all the time.' This indicates that even if overall precipitation may not be decreasing, higher temperatures may increase evapotranspiration and hence aridity.

According to Mille respondents, increasingly hot summers are also leading to less regeneration of trees. Trees are used as alternative sources of fodder for browsing livestock (camels, goats and sheep) in times of drought. Some indigenous tree species which are important sources of food and fodder during drought, such as *Dobera glabra*, are now threatened in many areas (Tsegaye et al. 2007). Dam-induced floods and cutting trees for charcoal were also reported to lead to a decline in trees. Uwwa informants were similarly concerned that the combined effects of drought and cutting of trees seem to have led to preferred tree species being replaced by invasive species that are not valuable as fodder (e.g. *Prosopis juliflora*), supporting previous observations by Shiferaw et al. (2004).

These environmental factors have been compounded by developmental and political processes, undermining pastoral livelihoods and strategies to manage environmental variability and producing a harsh vulnerability context. In Mille, our key informants mentioned conflict with the neighbouring Issa groups and floods due to the recent Tendaho dam among such processes. The dam had been constructed to provide irrigation services for large areas cultivated with sugar cane and maize, now partly converted to cotton because of soil salinization. Most Mille respondents had been directly affected by the flooding, as dam waters flooded back up the river (up to 35 km) washing away houses, inundating grazing lands, depleting forests and farmlands, sweeping away livestock and leaving families split up and stranded for days. In Uwwa, key threats to the pastoralist way of life included an acute lack of infrastructure such as veterinary services, water provision and schools, as well as increased migration that led to conflict with Amhara farmers.

These processes form part of Afar-wide trends: lack of support and necessary services for pastoralist livelihoods as well as a consistent loss of key rangeland resources. In particular, drought grazing areas have been lost to development schemes, settlements and to neighbouring groups (such as the Issa, a Somali clan neighbouring the Afar in the east) over the past decades, making droughts harder to survive (Kassa 2001; Ali 2008; Behnke and Kerven 2013). In large parts of Afar, including Mille, important grazing areas on the eastern side of the Awash River are increasingly unsafe as a result of conflicts with the Issa. Although mutual raiding with some deaths and loss of livestock is not new, the character of the conflict is described by respondents in Mille as having changed, making it less manageable for the Afar, as shown by these two statements:

> Before it was pastoralist against pastoralist but now the Issa are well equipped and organized by backing – it is now a politics to take the land.
>
> (woman, 45 years)

> Before it looked like the Issa were looking for resources, for animals, but now it is totally changed to a political mission.
>
> (man, 28 years)

In order to understand the vulnerability context, local conflicts must be set in the context of national political structures, including the system of ethnic federalism. After the Federal Democratic Republic of Ethiopia (FDRE) regime took over in 1991, the government divided the country into nine ethnically based administrative regions (Hagmann 2005). Several studies describe how, since 1991, political power and access to resources have become linked to control over territory by an ethnic group or clan (Vaughan 2006; Ali 2008; Hagmann and Mulugeta 2008). Ethnicity is used to lay political claims to pastures, especially in borderlands (Lenaerts et al. 2014). Hence, land use is changing towards domination by one group over land, rather than the interaction and fluidity required in pastoral migratory strategies in the face of variable climate and grazing patterns.

While pastoral livelihoods were becoming less viable in both sites, the strategies into which many were being pushed served to reinforce processes that generated vulnerability. In Uwwa, persistent drought and lack of alternative sources of water and grazing forced people to increase mobility. This in turn contributed to conflict with the Amhara farmers, and loss of animals and human lives. Traditionally strong social interactions with neighbouring highlander groups may be changing as pastoral livelihoods come under pressure (Simonsen 1996; Tesfay and Tafere 2004; Tafere 2006; Lenaerts 2013). An important response to loss of herds during drought was increase in trade through peaceful interaction with the Amhara and other neighbouring groups, in both Mille and Uwwa markets. However, our interviews in Mille revealed that this was not unproblematic since markets were unreliable, especially during drought. Uwwa residents also expressed that their economic context was deteriorating: the prices of consumer goods (food, clothing, etc.) had been rising dramatically more than sales prices of animal products. In Mille, an important drought response among some Afar was to allow Amhara to cut trees for charcoal production in return for a share of the income. Several informants saw this as a major cause of rangeland degradation and loss of fodder trees critical for pastoralists.

The case of the Afar shows the importance for adaptation of understanding how various processes at different scales create vulnerability, such as the processes that act to undermine adaptive capacity for pastoral livelihoods. In the Afar context, a *sustainable adaptation approach* would involve measures targeted at the key drivers of vulnerability, including the underlying causes of conflict and livestock loss, as well as measures to strengthen the fluidity on which livelihoods depend, such as access to grazing in time of drought. Careful consideration of how development interventions, such as constructing a dam, affect local livelihoods and vulnerability is critical in order to avoid measures that feed into development pathways that push groups like pastoralists into poverty. The equity and poverty dimensions of sustainable adaptation cannot be addressed unless the choices about development futures are also confronted – a dimension further explored in principle 2 below.

Principle 2: differing values and interests affect adaptation outcomes

The processes described above have led to a development pathway for the Afar that is detrimental to adaptive capacity, to the environment (negative effects on rangelands) and to social relations (e.g. with neighbouring groups): quite the opposite of the goals of sustainable adaptation. It could be seen as an unintended outcome of societal changes (contrasting with deliberate transformation) resulting from conflicting values and interests – between pastoralists who value their lifestyles and a government that sees cultivation as more 'modern'– as well as variation and changes in values within and between groups. The second normative principle of sustainable adaptation focuses on the different values and interests present in adaptation, and how they are negotiated through social and power relations.

Much of the conflict of values and interests can be traced back to the Ethiopian government's development strategy that emphasizes 'modernization' through settled agriculture. This view is in stark contrast with the livelihoods and lifestyles preferred by the local population. When five key informants in each site were asked about their favoured way of life, all said that they wanted to be pastoralists (and if possible increase their herd size), indicating that this is the main ambition among young and old alike. A Mille respondent who had lost most of his livestock explained: 'I'd prefer to be a pastoralist – but due to the challenges if we get equipment like water pumps from the government, I would try to do farming.' Several respondents saw government plans as promoting a settled lifestyle, and felt that this government orientation, combined with all the other changes, would force them to become farmers. According to one key informant in Mille, the government was actively settling people by allocating to each a half-hectare of land for cultivation on the banks of the Awash River.

A deliberate government prioritization of cultivation has resulted in the enclosure of land for farming in the Awash valley (Gedamu et al. 1999), with a government crop extension package contributing to over 4000 ha of land being converted to small-scale agriculture, mainly for maize and vegetables (Afar State Adaptation Plan of Action 2010:24). Farming is currently a minor activity among the Afar in our study sites (Afar State Adaptation Plan of Action 2010). However, the transition from pastoralism to agriculture forms part of a general development strategy for pastoral areas in Ethiopia, based on the fact that the government puts a very different value on pastoralism than do the pastoralists themselves (Gedamu et al. 1999; Kassa 2001; Tesfay and Tafere 2004; Hagmann and Mulugeta 2008; Behnke and Kerven 2013).

Importantly, values and interests can also vary *within* the local communities, with the government pathway being embraced by some members. Values and interests may also vary between different government and other formal policy-making institutions, though this is not investigated here. Kassa (2001) has described how in other areas of Afar, when floodplain lands are set aside for farming, the incomes from farming go to a few individuals, whereas the costs (loss of key drought grazing areas) must be borne by the entire community. This de facto privatization of land is often accepted locally because it profits an influential member of the community, often someone who is highly educated or a clan/political leader (Behnke and Kerven 2013).

Of course, farming can constitute a form of community diversification of incomes and adaptation of livelihood systems in the face of declining herds and grazing lands. However, increasing local inequities and loss of dry-season grazing severely diminish the adaptive capacity of the community. Further, as farming (including irrigation farming) is so heavily dependent on rainfall, such a development may mean greater sensitivity to drought and floods. Although rangeland productivity may decline with climate change (Ericksen et al. 2013), a shift to livestock production may prove more viable than cultivation in semi-arid areas (Jones and Thornton 2009). Irrigation is not necessarily a sustainable pathway in the face of climate change and increased incidence of drought (Cooper et al. 2008); in the Afar region it is often less profitable and more environmentally damaging than pastoralism (Behnke and Kerven 2013).

Closer study of values and interests in Afar reveals that many changes that drive vulnerability form part of specific development pathways and associated notions of developments that have highly differentiated and in part negative effects. Development pathways are the result of particular values and the power relations through which different interests are negotiated. Powerful actors (such as the government) see pastoralism as less valuable than cultivation, making it difficult to secure support for pastoralist interests in development decisions. Although both Mille and Uwwa districts have received government food aid and some NGO attention (e.g. from Médecins Sans Frontières and APDA), much of the support that would engender effective systems of support for restocking and ensure viable mobility is sorely missing. This modernization-led development pathway has had the most direct effects in Mille, where the Tendaho dam was seen as a threat to local interests: the benefits were not apparent to our interviewees, while the negative effects were immediate and dramatic: flooding. In both Mille and Uwwa, indirect effects of the modernization pathway have been the loss of grazing land, long-term herd decline and the perceived need to shift from their preferred lifestyle – pastoralism – to farming.

Such developments reinforce perceptions among our informants that they are not consulted in development plans. When discussing development interventions, all key informants said that they felt they had no influence, and that they were not represented by local politicians who could influence such decisions. A real risk is that inequitable power relations (locally as well as between central government and local communities) and prejudicial processes of resource appropriation (land in particular) can be reinforced and exacerbated if adaptation policy measures involve disbursement of development funds through these same power structures.

In contrast to a blanket application of modernization strategies, sustainable adaptation approaches would consider multiple development pathways. Interventions would need to represent and negotiate diverse values and interests, and address inequitable power relations and political marginalization. In Afar, sustainable adaptation would ensure that key decisions prioritize pastoralism as part of a diverse set of livelihoods, and that key grazing areas are not converted to agriculture or other development schemes. Instead, interventions might include the provision of services that would make it easier for pastoralists to tackle the combined onslaught of drought and disease (through services like veterinary facilities, water-harvesting structures, assistance to re-stocking after drought, and/or mobile health and education units).

Principle 3: integrate local knowledge into adaptation responses

The importance of local knowledge is closely linked to the principle of recognizing differential and competing interests and how they are negotiated in adaptation. Knowledge and problem understanding shape the solutions that are formulated; hence, integrating local knowledge is important for empowering vulnerable groups and furthering diverse local values and needs – not least the adaptive capacity of the community as a whole in the face of dominant development discourses.

In Ethiopia, unfavourable attitudes to pastoralism and distrust in the abilities of pastoralists to adapt are contradicted by recent evidence of the ability of pastoralists (in Borana state) not only to shift from seasonal planning to long-term visions of sustainability, but also to reduce inequity and conflict and upgrade traditional rangeland management systems with relevant external information (Reid et al. 2013).

People in Mille and Uwwa hold detailed environmental knowledge codified in collective memory of the past, involving strategies and practices for managing variability that have been tried out for generations. Climatic events in recent Afar history are recalled both by the elders and key informants and given symbolic local names that reflect the multitude of contextual conditions that create them. For example, the 2007 drought in Mille was called *Laa sele* ('cattle are finished') and *Baggexo* ('diarrhoea'), an event where drought, conflict and disease converged and 83 people died; and the 2010 famine was called *Yeden lee* ('the tying of the water'), signifying flooding from the dam.

Local knowledge, traditional forecasts and customs/moral codes of conduct (often combined with formal climate information such as government flood and drought warnings) are critical to dealing with environmental variability. In Afar, teams of scouts are regularly sent out to other areas to observe the state of the rangelands, the effects of rainfall and the suitability for grazing. There are specific rules for most types of natural resource use: for instance the cutting of live trees is forbidden, as is grass-cutting on communal land. Clans also have a tradition of setting aside grazing land for difficult times and of preventing over-grazing. This system regulates interaction between clans and households in the use of common grazing areas. However, such rules come under pressure when droughts are severe; in addition, with marginalization and destitution, people are forced to migrate further, using up emergency grazing areas and cutting trees. The 2004 drought in Mille was called *Arkakis*, 'scattered', reflecting how drought forced the people to migrate; and the 2008 event in Uwwa was called *Goad maale*, 'cut by the axe'. Moreover, a recent study indicates that the practice of Afar traditional law is declining as a result of the deterioration of pastoralist lifestyles, the displacement of pastoralists and disrupted clan land-use boundaries (APDA 2010). Customary laws appear to be weakened by the fact that they operate in parallel with the formal law system rather than being supported by the formal system.

Building adaptation measures on local problem understanding, strategies to manage climatic events and customary law is important to ensure livelihoods as well as the environmental integrity central to sustainable adaptation. However, although Ethiopia's current climate change *National Adaptation Plan of Action* (NMA 2007) mentions that collaboration of local people is desired, it fails to indicate how their representation in key decisions or planning could be strengthened. Despite formal acknowledgement of 'capacity building and institutional strengthening of the local community' as a general adaptation option across sectors, the specific adaptation measures identified in the *Plan of Action* as relevant to pastoralism emphasize de-stocking, restricting free-range grazing and promoting stall feeding, as well as introducing mixed farming and irrigation schemes (pp. 40–41). This attitude toward pastoralism is reflected also in the recent Afar state *Programme of Plan on Adaptation to Climate Change* (Biru et al. 2010). Although this state programme recognizes that 'most adaptation strategies adopted by pastoral communities are crucial' (p. 58) in building resilience against climate change, it promotes investment in irrigation agriculture and other (non-pastoral) livelihoods as a long-term adaptation strategy (p. 60), reconfirming the deep-seated divergence of values and interests, as well as the marginalization of local knowledge in decision-making. By contrast, a sustainable adaptation approach would focus on building up formal mechanisms that give local knowledge real power and influence in decision-making, including more dynamic modes of policy formulation with multiple local interests continuously evaluated and negotiated in light of considerations of communal adaptive capacity and changing vulnerability contexts.

Principle 4: consider potential feedbacks between local and global processes

This normative principle builds on the recognition that actions by one group may affect others. Previous analyses of local–global linkages in sustainable adaptation (e.g. Eriksen et al. 2011) have focused on how adaptation in one place may lead to increased carbon dioxide (CO_2) emissions or threaten environmental integrity at higher spatial scales (local-to-global linkages). What the Afar situation highlights is the importance of including an analysis of how groups and individuals are *affected by* and respond to global scale processes (global-to-local linkages). For example, the process of large-scale land investments appears to influence the allocation of large tracts of land to industrial irrigation agriculture in Afar. Another important insight is that the need for CO_2 mitigation in high-emission societies, resulting in high demand for biofuels, may redistribute large land areas for biofuel production (such as sugar cane in Afar), with unexplored effects on local adaptive capacity. Therefore, efforts to strengthen adaptation in developing countries cannot be delinked from global processes of mitigation and Western models of development. This insight challenges the current simplistic integration of adaptation into development aid and underlines the need to ensure that adaptation funding is not incapacitated by donor-led mitigation strategies. Sustainable adaptation approaches must therefore include local adaptation efforts as part of a larger strategy for producing global development pathways that can act to reduce global emissions – including changes in trade systems, consumption patterns and technologies.

Transforming development

The previous section has shown some practical implications of the four normative principles of sustainable adaptation in an Ethiopian context. In this section, we apply these findings to show that a different conceptualization of the adaptation process is required to achieve sustainable adaptation pathways. Such pathways are predicated on negotiated strong sustainability goals of social equity and environmental integrity, as compared to the conceptualization that underlies a model of 'development as usual' focused on modernization.

The 'development as usual' conceptualization of adaptation rests on the assumption that appropriate policy interventions aimed at observed climate threats will result in successful mitigation and adaptation (Figure 10.2a). Here, adaptation is conceived as emerging from policy interventions that focus on adjustments in technology, management or governance systems, without changing the underlying social and political systems. Our analysis contradicts this assumed adaptation pathway, and shows that sustainable adaptation requires political change to ensure that a central role in formal strategies is accorded to local understanding of climatic events and how they can be managed. A sustainable adaptation approach acknowledges that decisions are made by a whole range of actors in addition to policy-makers. Rather than being restricted only to formal policy-led adaptation and mitigation measures (Figure 10.2a), negotiated decisions lead to diverse actions that permeate daily life and economic sectors, including livelihood strategies, shifting practices and technology adoption, infrastructure and service provision, natural resource management, investments, development projects, and formal adaptation and mitigation projects, as illustrated in Figure 10.2b.

Adaptation in the 'development as usual' conceptualization, is an outcome of the past and current decisions of a few policy actors based on implicit or unquestioned development goals or understandings. In Afar, modernization is an implicit development goal or paradigm that drives decisions toward uncontested development destinations. Shove (2010) argues that such de-politicization helps to enable governments to structure options and possibilities actively, including unsustainable economic institutions and ways of life. In the 'development as usual' conceptualization of adaptation, the role of development goals and values – and how they are negotiated through social and political relations to reach particular decisions that favour some interests over others – is not recognized. In our view, adaptation can become more sustainable if the sets of power relations and political processes inherent in choosing

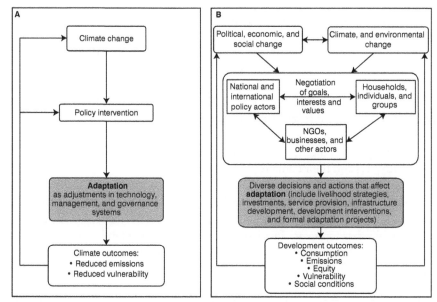

FIGURE 10.2   The conceptualizations of adaptation used in a) 'development as usual' and b) sustainable development pathways

development goals are made overt and explicit, as indicated in Figure 10.2b. In a 'development as usual' conceptualization of the adaptation process, adaptation and mitigation actions lead to climate outcomes, that in turn influence rates of climate change and formal policy responses required. A sustainable adaptation conceptualization recognizes that development outcomes more broadly influence political, economic and social change in addition to climate and environmental change, forming part of a dynamic societal context. Adaptation is hence understood as a broader societal process. In contrast, the 'development as usual' conceptualization of adaptation leaves out many elements that are critical for achieving more sustainable development pathways.

Yet, simply acknowledging the political nature of development and adaptation is not enough. It is also necessary to acknowledge that the current 'development as usual' pathway, based on perpetual economic growth and unlimited use of resource and energy throughput (Beddoe et al. 2009), acts to alter environmental processes at the systemic level and threatens the entire global socio-ecological system (Westley et al. 2011; Steffen et al. 2011). The case of Afar shows how processes related to a modernization-related development pathway generate vulnerability and inequity (principles 1 to 3), in turn also related to global development pathways (principle 4). What is required, therefore, is a model of development as a societal transformation driven by common goals negotiated among broad interests (Beddoe et al. 2009; O'Brien and Sygna 2013). A major question is nevertheless how and to what extent common societal sustainability goals can be achieved (Shove and Walker 2007; Manuel-Navarrete 2010).

Our study has shown fundamental differences in the power of various categories of agents (e.g. the Afar herders versus top-level bureaucrats and policy-makers who determine the national modernization pathway). It also indicates that these power differences between 'recipients' and designers of development models and adaptation plans are structural, and need to be tackled. Therefore, our findings lead us to conclude that an additional, fifth, normative principle is needed for sustainable adaptation:

> Principle 5: empower vulnerable groups in influencing development pathways and their climate change outcomes.

This principle emphasizes that sustainable adaptation must go beyond discrete local actions, and instead significantly influence the formation of pathways to equitable development. Precisely because Afar vulnerability contexts are fundamentally driven by development pathways, it will be impossible to achieve equity and environmental sustainability through a narrow focus on ameliorating the outcomes of climate change vulnerability.

Sustainable adaptation pathways require a focus on decisions, practices and actions as elements of particular *development* outcomes (rather than just *climate* outcomes) – including emission levels, consumption patterns, wellbeing, environmental integrity, equity and poverty. Such outcomes vary in space and time, and may yield 'unintended' outcomes (Eriksen and Selboe forthcoming). It is therefore illusory to approach adaptation as a neat process that can be planned and implemented through a top-down strategy like modernization. Adaptation must be recognized and analysed as part of political development processes. Livelihoods in Afar are being transformed through the interaction between environmental change, development interventions, and local adaptation strategies, with greater vulnerability as an unintended outcome. A sustainable adaptation pathway would involve a transformation of relations, with priority accorded to local practices, interests, knowledge and problem understandings as part of (debated) development goals and paradigms.

Conclusions

The Afar case study presented here has shown how the four normative principles of sustainable adaptation can be employed empirically to illuminate how deep-seated social structures and development pathways may constrain the ability to adapt. It also points to the changing and political character of these structures, and their dependence on the evolving nature of development pathways. Even when adaptation is to some extent negotiated, if it is based on structures and processes that ignore the four principles of sustainable adaptation, the result may be greater vulnerability and inequity for already vulnerable groups. With Young (2010), we argue that those who suffer from structural injustices by having their opinions and visions excluded from adaptation plans and general development pathways should be accorded priority in planning processes. This is not only because such actors are in danger of being impacted more severely by climate change, but also because they will often have unique insights into the sources and impacts of injustice, significant interest in changing the current situation, and determination for proposing alternative solutions. Our analysis indicates that this is indeed the case with Ethiopian pastoralists.

What the Afar case underscores is that the voices of the vulnerable should have special political influence in deciding not only adaptation strategies but also development strategies more generally. This is an important insight and a routinely missed opportunity of analyses that argue for the mainstreaming of adaptation *into* existing development plans. It is, we contend, the development plans themselves that need to be adjusted to adaptation strategies that draw on the views and experiences of vulnerable groups. This reflects the arguments of development theorists that we need multiple alternative development pathways based on a 'dialogue of equals' (Tucker 1999), and takes the idea further by proposing that such equality is in fact possible only by 'tilting the negotiation table' to favour the vulnerable – which is the focus of our proposed fifth normative principle of sustainable adaptation. The severity and urgency of the climate problem, as well as the availability of significant international financial support for adaptation (such as the Green Climate Fund), offer important opportunities for influencing general development pathways toward courses that can be conducive to strong sustainability and adaptation. However, this can be achieved only if the donor countries that contribute to adaptation funds take political responsibility toward achieving this goal.

Acknowledgements

This chapter is based on a study funded by the Norwegian NGO 'Development Fund' and conducted in collaboration with APDA, Afar Pastoralist Development Association who carried out the data collection. The full study was published as a Development Fund report entitled 'Pastoral Pathways'. The current chapter represents further theoretical and empirical development of this work. Thanks to Lutgart Lenaerts, Noragric, for assisting with rainfall data. We are also grateful to anonymous reviewers as well as Lenaerts for comments on an earlier draft.

References

Adams, W.M. (2001). *Green Development Environment and Sustainability in the Third World*, London: Routledge.
Afar State Adaptation Plan of Action (2010). *Afar National Regional State Programme of Plan on Adaptation to Climate Change*, Environmental Protection Authority of the Federal Democratic Republic of Ethiopia. http://www.epa.gov.et/Download/Climate/Regional%20Climate%20Change%20Adaptation%20Programmes/Afar%20National%20Regional%20State%20%20Climate%20Change%20Adaptation%20program.pdf (accessed February 2014).

Ali, H.H. (2008). *Historical Perspectives of the Afar and Issa-Somali Conflict in North-Eastern Ethiopia*. MSc thesis, Department of International Environment and Development Studies, Norwegian University of Life Sciences, Ås.

APDA (Afar Pastoralist Development Association) (2010). *Environmental Protection in the Hands of Traditional Leadership – Preparation Phase*. Report written 20 July 2010. Oslo: Development Fund.

Beddoe, R., Costanza, R., Farley, J., Garza, E., Kent, J., Kubiszewski, I., Martinez, L., et al. (2009). 'Overcoming systemic roadblocks to sustainability: The evolutionary redesign of worldviews, institutions, and technologies'. *Proceedings of the National Academy of Sciences*, 106(8): 2483–2489.

Behnke, R. and Kerven, C. (2013). 'Counting the costs. Replacing pastoralism with irrigated agriculture in the Awash Valley,' in A. Catley, J. Lind and I. Scoones (eds), *Pastoralism and Development in Africa. Dynamic Changes at the Margins*. London and New York: Routledge/Earthscan, pp. 57–70.

Berkhout, F., Angel, D. and Wieczorek, A.J. (2009). 'Sustainability transitions in developing Asia: Are alternative development pathways likely?' *Technological Forecasting & Social Change*, 76, 215–217.

Biru, A.A., Eshete, A.B., Mahmud, A.M., Mohammed, A.A., and Terefe, A.B. (2010). *Afar National Regional State Programme of Plan on Adaptation to Climate Change*. http://www.epa.gov.et/Download/Climate/Regional%20Climate%20Change%20Adaptation%20Programmes/Afar%20National%20Regional%20State%20%20Climate%20Change%20Adaptation%20program.pdf (accessed October 2013).

Brooks, N., Grist, N. and Brown, K. (2009). 'Development futures in the context of climate change: Challenging the present and learning from the past'. *Development Policy Review*, 27(6), 741–765.

Brown, K. (2011). 'Sustainable adaptation: An oxymoron?' *Climate and Development*, 3(1): 21–31.

Cooper, P.M.J., Dimes, J., Rao, K.P.C., Shapiro, B., Shiferaw, B. and Twomlow, S. (2008). 'Coping better with current climatic variability in the rain-fed farming systems of sub-saharan Africa: An essential first step in adapting to future climate change?' *Agriculture, Ecosystems and Environment*, 126 (1/2), 24–35.

Cote, M. and Nightingale, A. (2011). 'Resilience thinking meets social theory: Situating social change in socio-ecological systems (SES) research'. *Progress in Human Geography*, 36(4), 475–489.

Davies, J. (2006). 'Capitalisation, commoditisation and obligation among Ethiopia's Afar pastoralists'. *Nomadic Peoples* 10(1), 29–52.

Davies, J. and Bennett, R. (2009). 'Livelihood adaptation to risk: Constraints and opportunities for pastoral development in Ethiopia's Afar region'. *Journal of Development Studies*, 43(3), 490–511.

Douthwaite, R. (1999). 'Is it possible to build a sustainable world?' in R. Munck and D. O'Hearn (eds), *Critical Development Theory*, London: Zed Books, pp. 157–177.

Ericksen, P., de Leeuw, J., Thornton, P., Said, M., Herrero, M. and Notenbaert, A. (2013). 'Climate change in Sub-Saharan Africa. What consequences for pastoralism?' in A. Catley, J. Lind and I. Scoones (eds), *Pastoralism and Development in Africa. Dynamic Changes at the Margins*, London and New York: Routledge/Earthscan, pp. 71–82.

Eriksen, S. (2013). 'Understanding how to respond to climate change in a context of transformational change: The contribution of sustainable adaptation', in L. Sygna, K. O'Brien and J. Wolf (eds), *Changing Environment for Human Security: Transformative Approaches to Research, Policy and Action*. London: Earthscan, pp. 363–374.

Eriksen, S. and O'Brien, K. (2007). 'Vulnerability, poverty and the need for sustainable adaptation measures'. *Climate Policy*, 7, 337–352.

Eriksen, S., Aldunce, P., Bahinipati, C., Martins, R., Molefe, J., Nhemachena, C.R., O'Brien, K., et al. (2011). 'When not every response to climate change is a good one: Identifying principles for sustainable adaptation'. *Climate and Development*, 3(1), 7–20.

Eriksen, S. and Selboe, E. (forthcoming). 'Transforming towards or away from sustainability? How conflicting interests and aspirations influence local adaptation', in K. O'Brien and E. Selboe (eds), *The Adaptive Challenge of Climate Change*, Cambridge: Cambridge University Press.

FDRE (2008). *Summary and Statistical Report of the 2007 Population and Housing Census. Population Size by Age and Sex.* Federal Democratic Republic of Ethiopia, Population Census Commission, Addis Ababa.

Gedamu, F., Kassa, G., Ado, S. and Bibiso, B. (1999). *Pastoralism in the Afar Region of Ethiopia.* ALARM Working Paper No. 9, Centre for Basic Research, Kampala.

Hagmann, T. (2005). 'Beyond clannishness and colonialism: Understanding political disorder in Ethiopia's Somali Region, 1991–2004'. *Journal of Modern African Studies*, 43(4), 509–536.

Hagmann, T. and Mulugeta, A. (2008). 'Pastoral conflicts and state-building in the Ethiopian lowlands'. *Afrika Spectrum*, 43(1), 19–37.

Hajer, M.A. (1996). 'Ecological modernisation as cultural politics', in S. Lash, B. Szerzynski and B. Wynne (eds), *Risk, Environment and Modernity: Towards a New Ecology*, London: Sage, pp. 246–268.

Jones, P.G. and Thornton, P.K. (2009). 'Croppers to livestock keepers: Livelihood transitions to 2050 in Africa due to climate change'. *Environmental Science and Policy*, 12(4), 427–437.

Ireland, P. and Keegan, P. (2013). 'Climate change adaptation: Challenging the mainstream', in L. Sygna, K. O'Brien and J. Wolf (eds), *Changing Environment for Human Security: Transformative Approaches to Research, Policy and Action*. London: Earthscan, pp. 224–233.

Kassa, G. (2001). 'Resource conflicts among the Afar in North-East Ethiopia', in M.A.M. Salih, T. Dietz and A.G.M. Ahmed (eds), *African Pastoralism: Conflict, Institutions and Government.* London: Pluto Press, pp.145–171.

Kates, R.W., Travis, W.R. and Wilbanks, T.J. (2012). 'Transformational adaptation when incremental adaptations to climate change are insufficient'. *PNAS*, 109(19), 7156–7161.

Klein, R.J.T., Eriksen, S., Næss, L.O., Hammill, A., Robledo, C. and O'Brien, K. (2007). 'Portfolio screening to support the mainstreaming of adaptation to climate change into development'. *Climatic Change*, 84(1), 23–44.

Lenaerts, L., Breusers, M., Dondeyne, S., Bauer, H., Haile, M. and Deckers, J. (2014). '"This pasture is ours since ancient times": An ethnographic analysis of the reduction in conflicts along the post-1991 Afar–Tigray regional boundary'. *The Journal of Modern African Studies*, 52, 25–44.

Macro International Inc. (2008). *Ethiopia Atlas of Key Demographic and Health Indicators, 2005.* Calverton, MD. http://pdf.usaid.gov/pdf_docs/PNADM636.pdf (accessed 7 June 2011).

Manuel-Navarrete, D. (2010). 'Power, realism, and the ideal of human emancipation in a climate of change'. *WIREs Climate Change*, 1, 781–785.

Marin, A. (2008). 'Between cash-cows and golden calves: Adaptations of Mongolian pastoralism in the "age of the market"', *Nomadic Peoples*, 12(2): 75–101.

Marin, A. (2010). Riders under storms: Contributions of nomadic herders' observations to analysing climate change in Mongolia', *Global Environmental Change*, 20(1): 162–176.

McGray, H., Hammill, A. and Bradley, R. (2007). *Weathering the Storm: Options for Framing Adaptation and Development.* WRI Report. World Resources Institute, Washington.

Munck, R. (1999). 'Deconstructing development discourses: Of impasses, alternatives and politics', in R. Munck and D. O'Hearn (eds), *Critical Development Theory*, London: Zed Books, pp. 196–210.

NMA (National Meteorological Agency) (2007). *Climate Change National Adaptation Programme of Action (NAPA) of Ethiopia*. http://unfccc.int/resource/docs/napa/eth01.pdf (accessed October 2013).

O'Brien, K. (2012). 'Global environmental change III: From adaptation to deliberate transformation'. *Progress in Human Geography*, 36(5), 667–676.

O'Brien, K. (2013). 'Global environmental change (III): Closing the gap between knowledge and action'. *Progress in Human Geography*, 37(4): 587–596.

O'Brien, K. and Sygna, L. (2013). 'Responding to Climate Change: The Three Spheres of Transformation'. *Proceedings of Transformation in a Changing Climate, 19–21 June 2013*, Oslo, Norway. University of Oslo. ISBN: 978-82-570-2000-1.

O'Brien, K.L., Eriksen, S., Schjolden, A. and Nygaard, L.P. (2007). 'Why different interpretations of vulnerability matter in climate change discourses'. *Climate Policy*, 7, 73–88.

Pelling, M. (2010). *Adaptation to Climate Change: From Resilience to Transformation*. London: Routledge.

Reid, H., Faulkner, L. and Weiser, A. (2013). *The Role of Community-Based Natural Resource Management in Climate Change Adaptation in Ethiopia*. IIED Climate Change Working Paper 6. London: IIED.

Sabates-Wheeler, R., Mitchell, T. and Ellis, F. (2008). 'Avoiding repetition: Time for CBA to engage with the livelihoods literature?' *IDS Bulletin*, 39(4), 53–59.

Sherwood, S. and Huber, M. (2010). 'An adaptability limit to climate change due to heat stress'. *PNAS*, 107, 9552–9555.

Shiferaw, H., Teketay, D. and Nemomissa, S. (2004). 'Some biological characteristics that foster the invasion of Prosopis juliflora (Sw.) DC. at Middle Awash Rift Valley Area, north-eastern Ethiopia'. *Journal of Arid Environments*, 58(2), 135–154.

Shove, E. (2010). 'Beyond the ABC: Climate change policy and theories of social change'. *Environment and Planning A*, 42, 1273–1285.

Shove, E. and Walker, G. (2007) 'Caution! Transitions ahead: politics, practice, and sustainable transition management', *Environment and Planning A* 39 (4): 763-770.

Simonsen, G. (1996). *The Wossama Afar. A Study of Natural Resource Management of a Pastoral Group in North-Eastern Ethiopia*. Master's thesis, Department of International Environment and Development Studies, Norwegian University of Life Sciences, Ås.

St Clair, A. and Lawson, V. (2013). 'From poverty to prosperity: Addressing growth, equity and ethics', in L. Sygna, K. O'Brien, and J. Wolf (eds), *Changing Environment for Human Security: Transformative Approaches to Research, Policy and Action*. London: Earthscan, pp. 203-215.

Steffen, W., Persson, A., Deutsch, L., Zalasiewicz, J., Williams, M., Richardson, K., Crumley, C., et al. (2011). 'The Anthropocene: From global change to planetary stewardship'. *Ambio*, 40, 739–761.

Swyngedouw, E. (2007). 'Impossible "sustainability" and the postpolitical condition', in R. Krueger and D. Gibbs (eds), *The Sustainable Development Paradox. Urban Political Economy in the United States and Europe*, London: The Guilford Press, pp. 13–40.

Tafere, K. (2006). *Indigenous Institutions of Conflict Resolution among the Ab'ala Afar of North-Eastern Ethiopia*. Social Anthropology Dissertation Series No. 11. Addis Ababa: Addis Ababa University.

Tesfay, Y. and Tafere, K. (2004). *Indigenous Rangeland Resources and Conflict Management by the North Afar Pastoral Groups in Ethiopia.* Drylands Coordination Group Report No. 31, Oslo.

Tsegaye, D., Balehegn, M., Gebrehiwot, K., Haile, M., Gebresamuel, G., Tilahun, M. and Aynekulu, E. (2007). *The role of garsa (Dobera glabra) for household food security at times of food shortage in Abaàla Wereda, North Afar: Ecological adaptation and socio-economic value.* Drylands Coordination Group Report No. 49, Oslo: Drylands Coordination Group.

Tucker, V. (1999). 'The myth of development: A critique of a Eurocentric discourse', in R. Munck and D. O'Hearn (eds), *Critical Development Theory. Contributions to a New Paradigm,* London: Zed Books, pp. 1–27.

Vaughan, S. (2006). 'Responses to ethnic federalism in Ethiopia's Southern Region', in D. Turton (ed.), *Ethnic Federalism: The Ethiopian Experience in Comparative Perspective.* Oxford; Ohio University Press, Athens, OH; and University of Addis Ababa Press, Addis Ababa: James Currey, pp. 181–207.

Vincent, K., Næss, L.O. and Goulden, M. (2013). 'National level policies versus local level realities – Can the two be reconciled to promote sustainable adaptation?', in L. Sygna, K. 'Brien, and J. Wolf (eds), *Changing Environment for Human Security: Transformative Approaches to Research, Policy and Action.* London: Earthscan, pp. 126-134.

Viste, E., Korecha, D. and Sorteberg, A. (2012). 'Recent drought and precipitation tendencies in Ethiopia'. *Theoretical and Applied Climatology.* DOI 10.1007/s00704-012-0746-3.

Westley, F., Olsson, P., Folke, C., Homer-Dixon, T., Vredenburg, H., Loorbach, D., Thompson, J., et al. (2011). 'Tipping toward sustainability: Emerging pathways of transformation', *Ambio,* 40(7): 762–780.

Young, I.M. (2010). *Responsibility for Justice.* Oxford: Oxford University Press.

11

THE ROLE OF LOCAL POWER RELATIONS IN HOUSEHOLD VULNERABILITY TO CLIMATE CHANGE IN HUMLA, NEPAL

Sigrid Nagoda and Siri Eriksen

Introduction: understanding vulnerability to climate change and food security

For effective adaptation to climate change, the complexities inherent in vulnerability must be understood and its fundamental driving forces dealt with (Watts and Bohle 1993; Ribot 1995; O'Brien et al. 2007; Eriksen et al. 2011; O'Brien 2011). An important aspect of these complexities is the fact that the causes of vulnerability vary between individuals, groups, areas and over time, and cannot easily be related to simple climatic characteristics (Handmer et al. 1999; Cannon et al. 2003; Huq et al. 2004; O'Brien et al. 2004; Ribot 2010). These insights have emerged against the backdrop of development and food-security interventions that have often focused on agricultural production, food distribution, and material assets in the face of climate-triggered events – although, under some conditions, these interventions may even exacerbate vulnerability (Barrett and Maxwell 2004; Sperling et al. 2004; Adhikari 2008). A major question emerging in climate change research is what is required if adaptation is to address the vulnerability context, and transform – rather than perpetuate – the developmental patterns that have created vulnerability in the first place (O'Brien 2011).

Vulnerability is a dynamic state, since the contextual conditions that comprise vulnerability are always changing (Eriksen et al. 2005; O'Brien et al. 2007). These conditions are driven by multiple processes that include shifting market conditions, conflicts, political marginalization and environmental changes (Ribot 1995; Eriksen and Silva 2009). Hence, in order to deal with vulnerability effectively, it is particularly important to understand the social dynamics at the local level that lead to differential levels of vulnerability between people and over time, and how these dynamics relate to societal processes of change, including national policies and development paths.

A focus on food security not only provides an opportunity for critically examining the nexus between adaptation and development policies, it can also serve as a starting point for empirically observing the local manifestations of vulnerability. Food insecurity and vulnerability are closely linked (Yaro 2004). Household food insecurity can therefore be used as an indicator of the outcome of the inherent state of vulnerability, which is often seen as a 'state of susceptibility to harm from exposure to stresses associated with environmental and societal change and from absence of capacity to adapt' (Adger 2006, p. 268). Although food insecurity can only provide an indication of vulnerability at a given time, it can serve as a useful starting point for gaining insights into which strategies for managing changes are available to whom, as well as the various motivations and objectives behind choosing particular strategies when faced with stress (Yaro 2004; O'Brien 2011).

Entitlements and sustainable livelihood frameworks (Sen 1981; Chambers and Conway 1991) describe food security in terms of the variation in entitlements and livelihood resources constituted by various types of assets (social, physical, economic, human and natural capital), but have limited value for explaining complex vulnerability dynamics. For example, they do not address the reasons behind the lack of entitlements or access to assets (Leach et al. 1997; Yaro 2004). In order to understand how to address vulnerability, it is therefore necessary to go beyond a focus on assets and access to resources, and to grasp how social and power relations operate in practice in local-level strategies for managing multiple stressors, including how this dynamic shapes vulnerability patterns over time.

Social and power relations play an important role in how people manage multiple changes that face them simultaneously, including weather events and changing climate conditions (Leichenko and O'Brien 2002; Nyborg et al. 2008; Eriksen and Lind 2009; Eriksen and Selboe 2012). Power is often used to enhance one's entitlement to resources by legitimizing (or delegitimizing) access to resources through social advantages (Bourdieu 1985; Watts and Bohle 1993; Ribot 1995; Adger and Kelly 1999; Tarrow 1998; O'Brien et al. 2008; Manuel-Navarrete 2012), hence influencing the coping and adaptive strategies of individuals and groups differently (McLaughlin and Dietz 2008). Similarly, actor-oriented approaches to rural development posit that the perception and strategies of different actors are fundamentally shaped by power, agency and knowledge (see Long 1992).

In this chapter, we examine the dynamics of vulnerability in rural households, and in particular the influence of local power relations on vulnerability patterns. We investigate how these relations create differential vulnerability outcomes as manifested in food insecurity through a case study of Humla, a remote and chronically food-insecure district in far north-western Nepal. Nepal is particularly well-suited as a case for examining the adaptation–development nexus. It is among the world's poorest countries, with an estimated 41 per cent rate of stunting in children below five years (World Food Programme 2012), and is also considered highly vulnerable to climate change (Jianchu et al. 2007;

Chhetri and Pandey 2009; Ministry of Environment of Nepal 2010; NPC 2010). Observations of climate conditions over the past century in South Asia reveal increasing temperatures in the Himalayan region and important seasonal changes in precipitation along with fewer but more intense precipitation events over the next 100 years (Christensen et al. 2013). Climate change and variability are expected to further worsen the food-security situation of small-scale farmers (Chaudhary et al. 2006), prompting humanitarian organizations to scale up their interventions (Oxfam 2009; World Food Programme 2009).

Our empirical analysis shows, first, that climate-change vulnerability cannot be seen as a simple product of traditional agricultural indicators at village level, since it encompasses various livelihood strategies at the household level as well. Second, we investigate how various social and political relations are central in determining access to strategies to secure food, thus driving differential vulnerability patterns. Finally, our analysis focuses on how stress situations, such as drought, influence dependency relations between those who have food and those who do not. Our findings indicate that deepening dependency between people is a key element in the local vulnerability dynamic because greater social inequities within and among villages aggravate the vulnerability of the poor. Understanding this dynamic has critical implications for how the humanitarian and development communities can approach solutions to the joint problems of food insecurity and adaptation to climate change, and effectively reduce the vulnerability of the poor.

Our analysis challenges the 'development as usual' approaches of governments and humanitarian organizations that distribute food and seeds in response to food insecurity in poor countries such as Nepal (Adhikari 2008), instead of addressing social relations and the distribution of power. With increasing attention and international funding being directed to climate-change adaptation in poor and food-insecure areas (Tanner and Mitchell 2008; Agrawal and Perrin 2009), it is particularly important that policies and actions be formulated on the basis of a sound understanding of the causes of vulnerability.

Studying vulnerability and food security in Humla

The study focuses on the mountainous district of Humla in far north-western Nepal, bordering Tibet in the north (Figure 11.1). Humla is one of the poorest districts in Nepal, as indicated by its very low Human Development Indicator (UNDP 2007 in Mission East 2010; Sanders 2010; Citrin 2012). Large parts of the district are regularly classified as highly food insecure (DFSN 2010). This situation may be worsened by climate change, which is likely to lead to increased incidence of heavy rainfall events during summer and less rain and snow during winter (NCVST 2009; Christensen et al. 2013). Practical consequences for small farmers in the study area may include higher risks of landslides, difficulties in predicting sowing time and decreased water availability (Eriksson et al. 2009; Oxfam 2009).

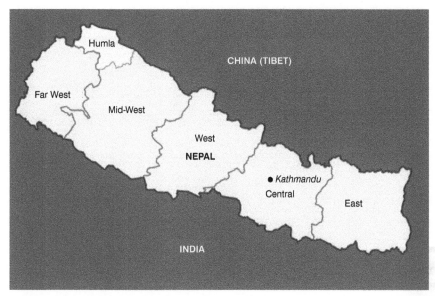

FIGURE 11.1   District of Humla (Map of the Foundation Nepal, http://www.foundation-nepal.org/content/map)

Humla is characterized by its physical remoteness as there is no road access to the district. The headquarters, Simkot, which lies at about 3000 metres above sea level (masl), is linked with two towns further south by a very unreliable small plane system, and is otherwise about one week on foot from the nearest road to the south. Humla is politically marginalized as well: the presence of the state outside Simkot is very limited, a situation further aggravated by the decade of civil war that ended with the overthrow of the monarchy in 2006.

Humla is divided into two ecological regions: Upper Humla in the north, bordering Tibet; and Lower Humla in the south, characterized by villages at lower elevations with a warmer climate and land better suited for agriculture than in Upper Humla. Data collection focused on three villages belonging to these two ecological regions and with different social structures: Khaagaalgaon and Syaandaa in Upper Humla and Khankhe in Lower Humla (Figure 11.2). All three are situated on relatively steep mountain slopes facing east[1] with access[2] to water through small rivers and nearby forests. Agriculture is mainly rain-fed, with small land holdings. While subsistence agriculture, animal husbandry and trade are the dominant livelihood strategies, the three villages differ in terms of livelihood strategies, food security, ethnicity, castes and social structure, as outlined in Table 11.1.

The first village, Khaagaalgaon, is situated at 2808 masl, about four days' walk from the Tibetan border and six to seven hours' walk from Simkot. The village has around 75 households (Roy 2010) and is inhabited by the Lama ethnic group, a Buddhist, Tibetan-speaking people. The Hindu caste system is not practised. In addition to agriculture and livestock, Khaagaalgaon villagers

FIGURE 11.2 Location of case study sites in Humla District

base their livelihood on trade in non-timber forest products (NTFP), *furu* (a wooden cup used by Lamas and Tibetans for tea), grains, rice and salt, with Tibet and southern regions. Living conditions observed during fieldwork appeared relatively better than in the two other villages, with most households having improved cooking stoves and functioning sanitary facilities. In addition, the child mortality rate reported during interviews was much lower than in the other villages (see Table 11.1).

The second and the third case-study villages are inhabited by Nepali-speaking people where the Hindu caste system is a predominant aspect of the social structure. These villagers depend mainly on agriculture and livestock, in addition to some trade in NTFP and with rice and grain. Syaandaa has about 152 households (Roy 2010) and is situated on a mountain ridge at an elevation of 2747 masl (ibid.), a few hours' walk from Khaagaalgaon. The third village, Khankhe, is situated in Lower Humla, two to four days' walk to the south of Simkot, at an elevation of around 1700 msal, and is home to around 94 households (own data). While Syaandaa is inhabited mostly by people belonging to the Chhetri-Byansi group, a high caste in the Hindu caste system, the inhabitants of Khankhe are divided into two castes: the Dalits, low-caste groupings, and the higher-caste Thakuri. Poverty in Syaandaa and Khankhe is more pronounced than in Khaagaalgaon, and sanitation facilities are poor or non-existent. In Syaandaa, almost all households interviewed had lost at least one child under the age of one year, and some families had lost as many as six children.

TABLE 11.1   Characteristics of the three villages studied, Humla district

Villages	Khaagaalgaon	Syaandaa	Khankhe
Religion	Buddhist	Hindu	Hindu
Caste/ethnic group	Lama	Chhetri/Byaansi	Thakuri, Dalit
Persons per household	7*	8.6*	7.2
Child mortality per household	0.2	1.4	0.9
Food security**	Moderately food-insecure	Highly food-insecure	Highly food-insecure
Main livelihood strategies	Agriculture, trade	Agriculture, trade, wage labour	Agriculture, trade, wage labour, migration, food aid
Main crops cultivated	Buckwheat, millet, barley, potatoes, seasonal vegetables	Buckwheat, millet, barley, wheat, potatoes, seasonal vegetables	Rice, millet, barley, wheat, corn, seasonal vegetables
Main livestock	Yaks, yak/cow hybrids, horses, sheep, goats	Yaks, yak/cow hybrids, horses, sheep, goats	Cows, buffalo, sheep, goats

Data based on fieldwork 2010–2011 except for those denoted with an asterisk based on Roy (2010) and with two asterisks that are based on DFSN (2010).

Field studies were conducted over a three-year period from August 2008 to July 2011. A total of 68 semi-structured and 52 key informant interviews covering quantitative and qualitative data were carried out within the three villages. In addition, seven focus group interactions, including with Dalits, Thakuri, women, very poor and elders, were undertaken. In each village, households were ranked into four wealth categories. The semi-structured interviewees were selected as randomly as possible (through a list of household heads) in an attempt to get fairly equal representation of the different divisions (wards) within the villages and of each wealth category in each village.[3]

Although food security is formally defined as a 'situation that exists when all people, at all times, have physical, social, and economic access to sufficient, safe, and nutritious food that meets their dietary needs and food preferences for an active and healthy life' (Food and Agriculture Organization 2002, Chapter 2), people's perception of what constitutes food security and insecurity may vary. To capture perceptions of food insecurity, we measured food insecurity by asking interviewees if they felt that their household had access to enough food to live a healthy life. As such, this is a contextualized (reflecting in part the past history of aid, political motivation and sense of identity as vulnerable or self-sufficient) rather than an absolute measure of food availability and consumption and is used as a starting point for analysing the causes of vulnerability.

Vulnerability patterns and dynamics

Food security, livelihood strategies and differential vulnerability patterns

Vulnerability, reflected here as food insecurity outcomes or households' perceived persistent ability to access sufficient food, is highly differentiated both between and within villages (Figures 11.3 and 11.4). Informants relate food insecurity mostly to seasonal and inter-annual variations in weather conditions; but our analysis also shows that food security is a result of the complex interactions of diverse livelihood strategies and that various social and political relations are central in determining access to these strategies and thus driving differential vulnerability patterns.

Food insecurity is most intense around February/ March when food stocks have been depleted after the October/November harvest and the snow still prevents people from travelling to Tibet to buy food. A second period of stress for food-insecure households is in May/June, also between harvest times. The analysis of household data identified changing climatic conditions, with decreasing rain in Lower Humla, more unpredictable precipitation in Upper Humla, and less snow during winter, as a major stress factor for most households. In Khankhe, lack of rain has been considered an increasing problem for the past eight to ten years, while in the two villages of Upper Humla unpredictability of rain is reported to have created challenges for the past five years. Observations related to changes in precipitation are in line with the expected impacts of climate change in the region (Ministry of the Environment of Nepal 2010).

However, the severity of stress due to climatic variability is perceived differently among the three villages, as well as by different households within the same village. In the relatively food-secure village of Khaagaalgaon, the unpredictability of rain was not viewed as a main concern for food security,

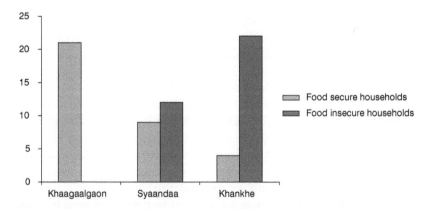

FIGURE 11.3   Number of semi-structured interviews in the three villages categorized into food-secure and food-insecure households

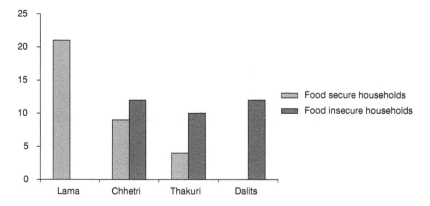

FIGURE 11.4 Number of semi-structured interviews in the three villages categorized into food-secure and food-insecure households related to castes and/or social group

while in Syaandaa and Khankhe, where only 23 per cent and 15 per cent of the interviewees respectively consider themselves food secure, the impacts of changing rainfall patterns are perceived as much more severe.

Interestingly, even though subsistence agriculture and livestock are the main livelihood strategies, agricultural production or access to agricultural assets are not necessarily the main determinants of vulnerability on the village level. Analysis of the quantitative interview data shows that while households in Khaagaalgaon and Syaandaa have on average similar production levels[4] (7.5 quintals per year), their food-security situations are very different. Similarly, non-food-secure households in Khankhe cultivate plots quite similar in size to those of food-secure households in Khaagaalgaon (4.5 haal[5] versus 4 haal, respectively).

This does not mean that access to agricultural assets is unimportant; however, it can be meaningfully understood only when seen as part of the larger vulnerability context at the household level. Analysis of the differences between households within the villages reveals important social inequities related to land access in the villages that are most food insecure; and that social, political and economic relations of exclusion, as represented in the caste system, are particularly powerful in explaining food insecurity.

In Khankhe, all of the households belonging to the lowest caste (Dalits) consider themselves food insecure, while 29 per cent of the higher caste (Thakuris) report food security throughout the year. An average Dalit household in Khankhe produces less than one third of the food, and has only about half as many livestock, as an average Thakuri household (9 versus 16 animals respectively). The better-off also have on average (median) five times as much land as the Dalits (16 haal versus 3.5 haal respectively). In Syaandaa, while all villagers belong to the same caste (Chhetri), food-secure households on average cultivate larger areas, produce more food and have more livestock than food-insecure households. In contrast, in Khaagaalgaon, differences between poor households and better-off ones related to land area are minimal (4.5 haal for better-off and poor households). The type of land to which households have access is very important. Lack of access to quality land (i.e. land with irrigation, less steep land and/or land near the village) is more prevalent among food-insecure households, especially Dalits, and it makes them even more vulnerable to unpredictable rainfall or animals eating their plants. As one Dalit woman said, 'why should we work on our [bad] fields, since it doesn't rain they no longer produce any food anyway'.

Social structures, such as caste, determine not only access to land (quantity and quality), but also access to other (non-agricultural) livelihood strategies. In order to explain vulnerability at the household level it is necessary to look beyond the linear impacts of climate variability on traditional agricultural indicators. People use a range of livelihood and social strategies to manage what are in effect interactions between climatic and other social and environmental stressors and not one single climate stressor. According to household interviews, important stress factors in addition to climatic variability and change include lack of quality land, lack of manpower, lack of manure, failing trade, and high taxes to be paid to the Community Forest Groups in southern areas when sheep and goats are brought to graze during the winter.

The villagers in all three locations said that those with the most diverse livelihood options were the least vulnerable to climate variability. Very few households in Humla can produce enough food for the whole year, and most combine various strategies to access food. Trade is by far the second most important livelihood strategy after agriculture and livestock, as this allows households to purchase food at the Tibetan border or to buy subsidized rice from the Nepal Food Corporation (NFC). As one better-off informant in Khankhe explained, 'Without trade we would be poor.' Another, in Syaandaa, stated that without the market of Thaklakot in Tibet, 'there would be no village'.

However, capacity to engage in trade varies greatly between villages and between households. Trade is most important in the village of Khaagaalgaon. Families here have almost twice as high incomes from trade as do households in Syaandaa and nine times as much as the average Dalit household in Khankhe (a median of NR 92,700, NR 50,000 and NR 10,000[6] respectively). Within the three villages, the difference is also striking: some families would make more than NR 200,000, while poor families reported incomes of less than NR 10,000 per year.

These differences in trade between and within villages can be explained partly by socio-cultural and geographical characteristics (see for example Fisher 1987; von Fürer-Haimendorf 1988), but also by the strength of networks and personal relations. All informants still consider access to political and social networks as essential for success in trading. Consequently, as is the case with access to land, trade is mostly concentrated in the hands of better-off families and households from high castes, leaving behind those with fewer resources and low-caste families that lack the necessary connections.

Role of social networks and power relations in vulnerability dynamics

Social status and access to social and political networks, including trading networks, are important in explaining the distribution of vulnerability in the study area, and form an integral part of the vulnerability context of the households. In this section, we discuss how social and power relations influence households' access to land, trade or development advantages – and, in turn, local vulnerability dynamics.

In Upper Humla, access to trade networks within and outside the district is a major factor distinguishing the better-off from the poorer families. For trader families of Khaagaalgaon, almost all had one or more family member living in Kathmandu. In Lower Humla, where households engage less in trade, interviews reveal that high priority is given to networking with political parties, local decision-makers and development/humanitarian organizations. Those active in political parties are mostly men from more prosperous Thakuri families; none of the Dalit households consider themselves part of political networks. A Thakuri informant of Khankhe put it this way: 'We must engage in politics so that we do not remain poor' and a Dalit said: 'We do not engage in politics because we are not heard, and so we remain poor.'

Likewise, many informants regard lack of access to quality land and other resources as determinants of vulnerability that are caused by unequal power relationships. Dalit interviewees in particular recounted many instances of 'elite capture' and oppression, where unequal access to land and water, as well as lack of education and information about development work and decision-making processes, were seen as major barriers to improving their livelihoods. Limitations and stress caused by the oppression of one group by another (Dalits versus Thakuri; men versus women; poor versus better-off) was clearly expressed by most Dalits, poor and women during informal interviews, but the sensitivity of this topic is shown by the fact that this was not mentioned in formal household interviews.

Nevertheless such unequal power relations were frequently referred to and observed during fieldwork. For example, some better-off households in Khankhe had access to improved varieties of wheat and rice from the District Agriculture Development Office, but none of the Dalits interviewed. The Dalits explained this by the fact that they have no lands suited for the improved seed varieties and had received no information from the authorities about the seeds. One Dalit recounted how he, hearing that the local authorities were providing irrigation systems to some villagers, applied – but that high-caste families (Thakuri) with fields close to the river blocked his application. Another Dalit described how government funds earmarked for the improvement of Dalit livelihoods never arrived, as the Dalits had not been aware of the existence of such funds. A similar narrative from the village of Syaandaa came from a poor old man: 'We [the poor] do not get to know what the development organizations do in our village – those who benefit from these organizations are always the same few educated people.' His comment was supported by several other informants, who stressed the importance of having an education and a good social network in order to obtain benefits from external interventions.

Most food-insecure households mentioned the lack of schooling, in particular among women and Dalits, as a key barrier to their active participation in village political life. Among Dalits in Khankhe, only three people (of the 16 households interviewed) had more than six years of schooling. By comparison, at least twice as many children from Thakuri households and better-off households in Syaandaa and Khaagaalgaon had completed between six and ten years of schooling, in some cases more.

We also noted a pronounced gender dimension to the power dynamics that contributed to food insecurity. Education is much less common for girls. No Dalit girls in Khankhe had more than six years of schooling, and only a few families in the three villages – most of them better-off – prioritize girls' education. Women, especially in Syaandaa and Khankhe, pointed out that they were often excluded from decision-making processes and were overloaded with work. This prevented them from taking proper care of the children (such as breast feeding), and created important health problems. Women rarely participate in meetings on the village and regional level where local development issues are discussed; it was widely held that they did not have to go, since they were represented by their husbands. These gender dimensions to the local power dynamics act as a contributing factor to vulnerability in the villages, a point supported by other studies, such as Thomas-Slayter and Bhatt (1994), Nelson and Stathers (2009) and Nightingale (2011).

Entrenched inequities and dependencies

An important aspect of the dynamics of vulnerability is the tendency for highly unequal social and power relations, in combination with chronic food insecurity, to reinforce dependencies and inequities. Focus group discussions and individual informal interviews reveal how fewer livelihood options and unequal power relations aggravate existing vulnerabilities, whereas some of the better-off may even improve their position through a crisis situation. As one interviewee in Khankhe put it, 'those who had food before also have food now, but those who did not have enough food before have even more problems now that the rains have stopped'. This statement is supported by household interviews findings that most of the very poor consider that their wellbeing has remained the same or worsened over the past ten years. By contrast, most of the relatively prosperous households feel that their wellbeing has improved over the last decade – due mainly to the increase in small trade – indicating that differential access to livelihood options is leading to increasing inequities. These findings are supported by other studies that have highlighted the linkages between vulnerability, power and social inequities (Chambers and Conway

1991; Watts and Bohle 1993; Blaikie et al. 1994; Ribot 1995; Adger and Kelly 1999; Yaro, 2004; O'Brien et al. 2008; Pelling 2008; Eriksen and Lind 2009).

Dependency relations are a critical part of the dynamic that reinforce differences in vulnerability between households. Borrowing food, money and seeds from the better-off in the village or villages nearby is the most common response to acute food shortage. The system of creditor and lender constitutes an essential informal network where the poorer and food-insecure households owe money (or food) to a few relatively well-off households. Food-insecure households often report having relatively large debts compared to food-secure households – some up to NR 200,000 (about USD 2400) – which is a lot of money for poor households that typically report annual incomes of less than NR 20,000). In addition, men from poor households engage more in daily labour to repay the debt, thus spending less time on agricultural production, and adding this task to the women's burden. For example, one very poor family in Syaandaa owed more than NR 100,000 (approximately USD 1200) to a better-off family due to loans taken over several years to buy food and clothes. The latter family took half of the lands of the poor family as a mortgage to recover the money. This left the poor family with barely enough land to produce food for about four months of the year. Moreover, whatever money the husband earned through daily labour went directly to the creditors, restricting any chances to invest in education for the children and/or small trade. Next time their harvest failed they would have no option but to increase their debt to the local creditors even more.

Among various social networks, the *lagi* system,[7] a feudal arrangement similar to a patron–client relationship (or a form of bonded labour), is still practised in Humla, with Dalits having to work a certain number of days each year for 'their' *lagi* Thakuri families in exchange for food. These bonds are inherited, and although Dalits may have more freedom compared to a few years ago, this system is still much in use. About 60 per cent of the Dalits interviewed report that they turn to their 'Thakuri *lagi*' for food during crisis. In return for this support, the Dalits are expected to work for the *lagi's* household on a regular basis. However, most Dalits consider the help they could receive from the *lagi* system unreliable, since the Thakuri *lagis* might be unwilling or unable to provide them with sufficient food in times of crisis. The dependency inherent in this system is shown by the fact that if a Dalit has not already done a favour for his/her Thakuri *lagi* in the past, he/she has, in practice, no legitimate claim for assistance in time of crisis. For example, in the course of our fieldwork we observed how a Dalit man asked for food at a Thakuri house, but was turned down because he had not collected firewood for them. There were also a few cases where Thakuri and Dalits mutually helped each other, exemplifying the diversity of social relations. For example, one Dalit reported that he had been helped by his Thakuri *lagi* to sort out a dispute with the Maoists during the war.

The power and social relations represented by social networks – whether the deeply entrenched caste system in Lower Humla or the more informal creditor–

lender system in Upper Humla – become consolidated and tightened in time of crisis. Households with access to political and/or trading networks rely heavily on these, while households that lack access to networks outside their village typically borrow food and/or money from fellow villagers as their main coping strategy, thereby further constraining the possibilities of diversifying their livelihoods. The result is a deepening of the dependency and inequity between those who have access to networks and those who do not.

However, even if power relations produce and reinforce vulnerability in food-insecure households, these relations are not static. There are indications that in some cases traditional power relations are being challenged and new livelihood opportunities created. Discrimination against Dalits in Hindu societies and social exclusion and marginalization of certain groups, including women, have been practised for centuries in Nepal (Levine 1987; Bista 1994; Cameron 1995; DFID and the World Bank 2006; Khadka 2009). Such oppression and marginalization have been historically linked with practices of social hierarchies and land distribution in rural western Nepal, but have also been challenged through recent political changes and movements, not least the ten-year Maoist insurgency that called for abolition of the caste system. Several informants were of the opinion that systematic oppression, in particular of Dalits, is less of a problem today than it used to be. As one elderly Dalit woman put it 'We are still very poor but at least they [Thakuri] cannot threaten us anymore' – or as a Thakuri informant put it furiously when his *lagi* [Dalit] did not come to work: '*Mero lagi* [Dalit] *Thulo Maanche baisakyo*' ('My [Dalit] *lagi* has become a Big Man now').

As the local economy has become monetized and more diversified, and as the uncertainty of rain has led small farmers to diversify their livelihood strategies, more households turn to small trade as a source of income to access food. Indeed, while the traditional trading system in the region, the salt trade with Tibet, used to be dominated by a few powerful traders (von Fürer-Haimendorf 1988; Bishop 1990), informants say that trading systems today are more diversified (mostly with NTFP) and involve more small traders. This shift has occurred mainly in the course of the past decade or so, and may have challenged some traditional power relations as more households now have cash incomes. However, it also appears that the relatively better-off households have benefited the most from these new opportunities.

Conclusions: implications for adaptation and challenging 'development as usual'

This chapter, based on case studies from north-western Nepal, has shown that understanding the dynamics of local social and political processes is essential for explaining differential vulnerability among households. While local power structures enable some people and/or groups to adapt better to stresses like climate change by creating and/or exploiting political and social opportunities, the same power structures also effectively act as barriers for other households seeking better ways of adapting to the new, changing situation. This finding is consisted with McLaughlin and Dietz (2008, p. 106): 'adaptation by some actors can and often does entail increased vulnerability for others'. Our study adds to these insights by demonstrating that social and power relations also can create a dynamic of deepening dependency and inequity when households are faced with stress. We argue therefore that greater emphasis should be placed on understanding and challenging local power dynamics in order to effectively reduce the vulnerability of the poor when seeking to tackle food security and vulnerability to climate change.

In the case of Humla, 'development as usual' is represented by measures that address vulnerability and food security as an outcome of low and unreliable agricultural production in the face of climatic stressors. Consequently, a main focus of the humanitarian actors in recent decades has been on distributing food and seed to vulnerable households and villages to improve their food security. We would argue that this approach is fundamentally flawed as a strategy to reduce vulnerability in the long term. Our study has shown that networks and power relations influence agricultural production as well as access to other livelihood strategies, including trade. Thus, seeking to address the production gap solely by distributing food does not deal with the underlying drivers of vulnerability.

Instead of challenging structural relations, current development and aid interventions in Humla appear to be embedded in the local power dynamic, in part reinforcing inequities and vulnerability. For instance, most interviewees held that, in order to benefit from aid, one needed to have the right contacts in district headquarters, in addition to some cash and other resources. Similar findings from western Nepal have been reported by Adhikari (2008) and Bishokarma (2010).

Nevertheless, relations are not static. They can be challenged, and new livelihood options can be created, shifting the patterns of vulnerability. For example, in Humla, education targeting low castes and girls should be considered as part of a comprehensive approach to break down intra- and inter-village power relations, so as to reduce the vulnerability of the poorest. In all three villages studied here, measures to improve decision-making access for the most vulnerable could help address the dynamic that now exacerbates inequities. The case of Humla has demonstrated some opportunities for formal measures that can act to strengthen local strategies, reduce dependencies and contribute to 'adaptation as *un*usual'. Such adaptation would affect not only how people can manage climatic variability and change, but development pathways more widely. Challenging relations, inequities and dependencies as part of adaptation measures would contribute to driving what Eriksen et al. (Chapter 1, this volume) describe as deliberate transformation, which, they argue, is required as a contrast to 'development as usual'.

However, for development organizations that have to work with and within existing structures and institutions, there remains a fundamental dilemma as those very same structures may act as major barriers to challenging important drivers of vulnerability. Tackling these social hierarchies and power structures, locally or nationally, can be highly controversial, and even considered outside the mandate of most humanitarian organizations. A critical area for future research will involve identifying the space for manoeuvre available for altering current approaches, so as to address key drivers of vulnerability and challenge 'development as usual' in practice. How are the values and hierarchies that legitimize current power relations enacted? And how may they shift over time as part of adaptation efforts aimed at deliberate transformation? These are issues particularly relevant to Nepal, where poverty, inequities and vulnerability are prevalent – but can be highly important also in other contexts (including wealthy countries), where power relations determine which adaptation decisions are made and how vulnerability is distributed within the population.

Notes

1 The village of Khaagaalgaon faces slightly more to the north than do Syaandaa and Khankhe, resulting in more shade in Khaagaalgaon and greater capacity to retain humidity in the soil.
2 Because of the lack of meteorological data on temperature, precipitation and environmental situation in the area, informants' perceptions as well as own observation are the main sources of information.
3 In Khaagaalgaon and Syaandaa, however, some of the selected respondents were absent, leading to a slight overrepresentation of interviewees from the higher wealth categories.
4 Because the quantitative information was in some cases based on estimates rather than measurements, they are used only to illustrate the relative variation between households, groups and/or villages, and not in absolute terms.
5 The area cultivated is presented using the local measurement system, as this is most precise and meaningful locally. The *haal* (1 haal = approx. 0.128 hectares, according to Bishop 1990) corresponds to the number of days used to plough the land with the buffalo/yak hybrid.
6 USD 1 = NR 86.1 (Nepali Rupees) at the time of the fieldwork.
7 The term varies from village to village.

References

Adger, W.N. (2006). 'Vulnerability'. *Global Environmental Change* 16, 268–281
Adger, W.N. and Kelly, P.M. (1999). 'Social vulnerability to climate change and the architecture of entitlements'. *Mitigation and Adaptation Strategies for Global Change* 4, 253–266
Adhikari, J. (2008). *Food crisis in Karnali: a historical and politico-economic perspective.* Kathmandu: Martin Chautari
Agrawal, A. and Perrin, N. (2009). 'Climate adaptation, local institutions and rural livelihoods', in W.N. Adger, I. Lorenzoni and K.L. O'Brien (eds). *Adapting to climate change: thresholds, values, governance.* Cambridge: Cambridge University Press, pp. 350–367
Barrett, C. and Maxwell, D. (2004). *Food aid after fifty years: recasting its role.* London: Routledge

Bishokarma, M. (2010). *Action in food crises: the influence of food aid on the livelihoods of Nepalese small-scale farmers in Mugu*. Master thesis. Geographisches Institut der Rheinischen Friedrich-Wilhelms-Universität Bonn

Bishop, B. (1990). *Karnali under stress: livelihood strategies and seasonal rhythms in a changing Nepal Himalaya*. Chicago, IL: University of Chicago Press

Bista, D.B. (1994). *Fatalism and development. Nepal's struggle for modernization*. Hyderabad: Sangam Books (Patna: Longman Orient, first edition 1991)

Blaikie, P.M., Cannon, T., Davis, I. and Wisner, B. (1994). *At risk: natural hazards, people's vulnerability and disasters*. London: Routledge

Bourdieu, P. (1985). 'The social space and the genesis of groups'. *Theory and Society* 14(6), 723–744

Cameron, M. (1995). 'Transformations of gender and caste divisions of labor in rural Nepal: land, hierarchy, and the case of untouchable women'. *Journal of Anthropological Research* 51(3),215–246

Cannon, T., Twigg, J. and Rowell, J. (2003). *Social vulnerability, sustainable livelihoods and disasters*. Report to the Department for International Development (DFID), Conflict and Humanitarian Assistance Department and Sustainable Livelihoods Support Office. London: DFID

Chambers, R. and Conway, G. (1991). *Sustainable rural livelihoods: practical concepts for the 21st century*. IDA Discussion paper 296. Brighton, UK: Institute of Development Studies

Chaudhary, R.P., Aase, T.H., Vetaas, O.R. and Subedi, B.P. (2006). *Local effects of global changes in the Himalayas: Manang, Nepal*. University of Bergen, Tribhuvan Univerisity, funded by NUFU/ SIU (The Norwegian Centre for International Cooperation in Higher Education

Chhetri, M.P. and Pandey, R. (2009). 'Effects of climate change in Nepal: time for policy to action'. Nepal Center for Disaster Management (NCDM), Department of Planning, Nepal and Disaster Preparedness Network (DPNet), Nepal

Citrin, D. (2012). 'The anatomy of ephemeral health care: 'health camps' and short-term medical voluntourism in remote Nepal'. *Studies in Nepali History and Society* 15(1), 27–72

Christensen, J.H., Krishna Kumar, K., Aldrian, E., An, S.-I., Cavalcanti, I.F.A., de Castro, M., Dong, W., Goswami, P., Hall, A., Kanyanga, J.K., Kitoh, A., Kossin, J., Lau, N.-C., Renwick, J., Stephenson, D.B., Xie, S.-P. and Zhou, T. (2007). ' Climate phenomena and their relevance for future regional climate change', in T.F. Stocker, D. Qin, G.-K. Plattner, M. Tignor, S.K. Allen, J. Boschung, A. Nauels, Y. Xia, V. Bex and P.M. Midgley (eds), *Climate Change 2013: The Physical Science Basis. Contribution of Working Group I to the Fifth Assessment Report of the Intergovernmental Panel on Climate Change* Cambridge, UK: Cambridge University Press, pp. 1271–1308

DFID and the World Bank (2006). *Unequal citizens. Gender, caste and ethnic exclusion in Nepal*. London: Department for International Development/Washington, DC: World Bank

DFSN (2010). 'Food Secure Phase Classification Map of Humla, reporting period January–March 2010, Outlook period April–June 2010', District food security network, Nepal food security monitoring system NeKSAP. Kathmandu: Ministry of Agricultural Development, National Planning Commission and United Nations World Food Programme

Eriksen, S., Brown, K. and Kelly, P.M. (2005). 'The dynamics of vulnerability: locating coping strategies in Kenya and Tanzania'. *Geographical Journal* 171(4), 287–305

Eriksen, S. and Lind, J. (2009). 'Adaptation as a political process: adjusting to drought and conflict in Kenya's drylands'. *Environmental Management* 43, 817–835

Eriksen, S. and Silva, J. (2009). 'The vulnerability context of a savanna area in Mozambique: household drought coping strategies and responses to economic change'. *Environmental Science and Policy* 12, 33–52

Eriksen, S., Aldunce, P., Bahinipati, C.S., D'Almeida Martins, R., Molefe, J.I., Nhemachena, C., O'Brien, K., Olorunfemi, F., Park, J., Sygna, L. and Ulsrud, K. (2011). 'When not every response to climate change is a good one: identifying principles for sustainable adaptation'. *Climate and Development* (1), 7–20

Eriksen, S. and Selboe, E. (2012). 'The social organisation of adaptation to climate variability and global change: the case of a mountain farming community in Norway'. *Applied Geography* 33(1), 159–167

Eriksen, S., Inderberg, T.H., O'Brien, K. and Sygna, L. (2014). 'Introduction. Development as usual is not enough', in T.H. Inderberg, S.H. Eriksen, K. O'Brien and L. Sygna (eds). *Climate change adaptation and development: changing paradigms and practices.* London: Routledge, pp. 1–18

Eriksson, M., Jianchu, X., Shrestha, A.B., Vaidya, R. A., Nepal, S. and Sandströmm, K. (2009). *The changing Himalayas: impact of climate change on water resources and livelihoods in the Greater Himalayas.* Lalitpur, Nepal: ICIMOD

Fisher, J.F. (1987). *Trans-Himalayan traders: economy, society and culture in northwest Nepal.* Berkeley, CA: University of California Press, 1986

Food and Agriculture Organization, FAO (2002). *The state of food insecurity in the world 2001.* Rome: FAO

Fürer-Haimendorf, C. von (1988). *Himalayan traders: life in highland Nepal.* New Delhi: Times Book International/London: John Murray (original edition London: St Martins, 1975)

Handmer, J.W., Dovers, S. and Downing, T.E. (1999). 'Societal vulnerability to climate change and vulnerability'. *Mitigation and Adaptation Strategies for Global Change* 4, 267–281

Huq, S., Reid, R., Konate, M., Rahman, A., Sokona, Y. and Crick, F. (2004). 'Mainstreaming adaptation to climate change in least developed countries (LDCs)'. *Climate Policy* 4, 25–43

Jianchu, X., Shrestha, A., Vaidya, R., Eriksson, M. and Hewitt, K. (2007). *The melting Himalayas – regional challenges and local impacts of climate change on mountain ecosystems and livelihoods.* Lalitpur, Nepal: International Centre for Integrated Mountain Development (ICIMOD)

Khadka, M. (2009). *Why does exclusion continue? Aid, knowledge and power in Nepal's community Forestry Policy Process.* PhD dissertation, The Hague: International Institute of Social Studies

Leach, M., Mearns, R. and Scoones, I. (1997). 'Environmental entitlements: a framework for understanding the institutional dynamics of environmental change'. *IDS Discussion Paper* 285

Leichenko, R. and O'Brien, K. (2002). 'The dynamics of rural vulnerability to global change: the case of Southern Africa'. *Mitigation and Adaptation Strategies for Global Change* 7, 1–18

Levine, N. (1987). 'Caste, state, and ethnic boundaries in Nepal'. *Journal of Asian Studies* 46(1), 71–88

Long, N. (1992). 'Introduction', in N. Long and A. Long (eds). *Battlefields of knowledge: the interlocking of theory and practices in social research and development.* London: Routledge

Manuel-Navarrete, D. (2012). 'Entanglements of power and spatial inequalities in tourism in the Mexican Caribbean', desigualidades.net Research Network on Interdependent Inequalities in Latin America, Working paper, No. 17

McLaughlin, P. and Dietz, T. (2008). 'Structure, agency and environment: toward an integrated perspective on vulnerability'. *Global Environmental Change* 18, 99–111

Ministry of Environment of Nepal (2010). *National Adaptation Programme of Action (NAPA) to climate change.* Kathmandu: Government of Nepal

Mission East (2010). *A review of vulnerability hazard and disaster in Southern Humla.* April 2010 available from ICIMOD (http://www.icimod.org/?opg=977&q=2322)

NCVST (2009). *Vulnerability through the eyes of vulnerable: climate change induced uncertainties and Nepal's development predicaments.* Institute for Social and Environmental Transition–Nepal (ISET–N), Nepal, Climate Vulnerability Study Team (NCVST) Kathmandu

Nelson, V. and Stathers, T. (2009). 'Resilience, power, culture, and climate: a case study from semi-arid Tanzania, and new research directions'. *Gender and Development* 17(1), 81–94

Nightingale, A. (2011). 'Bounding difference: intersectionality and the material production of gender, caste, class and environment in Nepal'. *Geoforum* 42, 153–162

NPC (2010). *Food security atlas of Nepal.* Food Security Monitoring Task Force, National Planning Commission, Government of Nepal

Nyborg, I., Jalalludin, A. and Gotehus, A. (2008). *Exploring rural livelihoods in Afghanistan: a study of 10 villages in Dai Kundi Province.* Noragric Report No. 40. Ås: Department of International Environment and Development Studies, Norwegian University of Life Sciences

O'Brien, K.L. (2011). 'Global environmental change: from adaptation to deliberate transformation'. *Progress in Human Geography* 35, 542–549

O'Brien, K., Leichenko, R., Kelkar, U., Venema, H., Aandahl, G., Tompkins, H., Javed, A., Bhadwal, S., Barg, S., Nygaard, L. and West, J. (2004). 'Mapping vulnerability to multiple stressors: climate change and globalization in India'. *Global Environmental Change* 14, 303–313

O'Brien, K.L., Eriksen, S., Nygaard, L. and Schjolden, A. (2007). 'Why different interpretations of vulnerability matter in climate change discourses'. *Climate Policy* 7, 73–88

O'Brien, K.L., Sygna, L., Leichenko, R.M., Adger, W.N., Barnett, J., Mitchell, T., Schipper, L., Tanner, T., Vogel, C. and Mortreux, C. (2008). *Disaster risk reduction, climate change adaptation and human security.* Report prepared for the Royal Norwegian Ministry of Foreign Affairs by the Global Environmental Change and Human Security (GECHS) Project, *GECHS Report* 2008:3, ISSN: 1504–5749

Oxfam (2009). *Even the Himalayas have stopped smiling. Climate change, poverty and adaptation in Nepal.* Report Summary, Kathmandu, Nepal

Pelling, M. (2008). 'The vulnerability of cities to disasters and climate change: a conceptual introduction', in H.G. Brauch, U.O. Spring, C. Mesjasz, J. Grin, P. Kameri-Mbote, B. Chourou, P. Dunay and J. Birkmann (eds). *Coping with global environmental change, disasters and security.* Berlin: Springer

Ribot, J. (1995). 'The causal structure of vulnerability: its application to climate impact analysis'. *GeoJournal* 35(2), 119–122

Ribot, J.C. (2010). 'Vulnerability does not just fall from the sky: toward multi-scale pro-poor climate policy', in R. Mearns and A. Norton (eds). *Social dimensions of climate change: equity and vulnerability in a warming world.* Washington, DC: World Bank

Roy, R. (2010). *Contribution of NTFPs [Non-Timber Forest Products] to livelihood in Upper Humla, Nepal*. PhD thesis. Asian Institute of Technology. School of Environment, Resources and Development, Pathumthani , Thailand

Sanders, C. (2010). 'Getting more greens from the greenhouse: opportunities for adoption in remote regions of Nepal. *Contributions to Nepalese Studies* 37(2), 249–260

Sen, A. (1981). *Poverty and famines: an essay on entitlement and deprivation*. Oxford: Oxford University Press

Sperling, L., Remington, T., Haugen, J.M. and Nagoda, S. (2004). *Addressing seed security in disaster response: linking relief with development*. Cali, Colombia: International Center for Tropical Agriculture (CIAT)

Tanner, T. and Mitchell, T. (eds). (2008). Special issue: 'Poverty in a changing climate'. *IDS bulletin*, 39(4) September, Brighton: IDS

Tarrow, S. (1998). *Power in movement: social movements and contentious politics*. Cambridge: Cambridge University Press

Thomas-Slayter, B. and Bhatt, N. (1994). 'Land, livestock, and livelihoods: changing dynamics of gender, caste, and ethnicity in a Nepalese village'. *Human Ecology* 22(4), 467–494

Watts, M.J. and Bohle, H.G. (1993). 'The space of vulnerability: the causal structure of hunger and famine'. *Progress in Human Geography* 17, 43–67

World Food Programme (2009). *The future of food. Creating sustainable communities through climate adaptation*. Food For Thought Series. United Nations World Food Programme. Issue 2, December 2009, United Nations World Food Programme, WFP

World Food Programme (2012). *Country Programme Nepal 200319 (2013–2017)*. Rome: WFP

Yaro, J.A. (2004). 'Theorizing food insecurity: building a livelihood vulnerability framework for researching food insecurity'. *Norwegian Journal of Geography* 58(1), 23–37

12

A SOCIONATURE APPROACH TO ADAPTATION

Political transition, intersectionality, and climate change programmes in Nepal

Andrea J. Nightingale

Introduction: adaptation for whom?

This chapter explores the challenges to adaptation posed by political instability, through a brief qualitative account of climate change programmes in Nepal. Fragile political contexts are assumed to be at greater risk from climate change in part because of changes in resources, and in part because of the lack of robust institutions (Raleigh and Urdal 2007). Responses put forward have included securitization (militarization and border controls), and the promotion of development in at-risk areas to reduce the threat of violence (Dalby 2009). However, this chapter shows how current 'development-as-usual' approaches to the promotion of adaptation are inadequate in conflict settings. Using a feminist political ecology lens to illuminate inequality and the 'socioecological' contexts through which climate change and contentious politics collide, I demonstrate how adaptation programmes need to attend to the links between society–nature and power. The main argument is that adaptation *for whom* is more important than the present emphasis on *how* to adapt. Using material from national and local levels, this chapter shows how adaptation processes cannot be conceived separately from politics: these processes need to be recognized as developing and unfolding within already-politicized relationships and networks. Such networks range from contentious local politics to global aid relations, requiring adaptation programmes to take a broader look at how, where and with what consequences they seek to assist people in developing countries to adapt.

The Nepal case study is particularly suited for critically interrogating current approaches to adaptation. Nepal has long been the recipient of aid funding for natural resource management programmes, and its participatory forestry and conservation projects are seen as models of best practice globally (Ojha et al. 2008). Most have now been re-branded as 'climate change adaptation and mitigation' programmes with a stronger techno-engineering emphasis, making lessons gleaned from this shift instructive for Nepal as well as other contexts. My analysis shows that it is not the quantities and qualities of resources and services that determine the ability of people to adapt: rather I find that those with greater social and political power can harness negative changes in resources and services to their own benefit, and thus shape adaptation outcomes. As such, the chapter explores how adaptation questions are less about techno-engineering schemes and more about attention to social relations and 'socionature' issues. It shows that the current approach to planning is too static to allow the kinds of renegotiations that are required in order to address social inequalities within the core of adaptation programmes.

Various discourses and programmes have been emerging to tackle both climate adaptation and mitigation at the 'Third Pole' (the Himalayas). For example, 'Readiness' efforts for Reducing Emissions from Deforestation and Degradation (REDD+), a mitigation programme aimed at sequestering carbon in forests, emphasizes benefit sharing, diversification of livelihood opportunities and other social programmes that can easily be classified as 'adaptation'. Nepal has developed a National Adaptation Plan of Action (NAPA), among other climate-specific plans. While these efforts purport to tackle the 'new' challenges posed by climate change, in many respects they mirror the development efforts of the past 30 years.

In addition to climate change, there are the many political challenges presently facing Nepal. In 2006, a popular movement unseated the monarchy and brought the Maoist People's War to an end. The insurgency (1996–2006) was an ideologically driven movement that sought to overturn the monarchy and entrenched feudal relations that date back to at least the 17th century (Hutt 2004). Since 2006, the political transition has been characterized by unpredictability and power struggles. This instability has also impacted upon the functioning of environmental governance, most notably at the national level, where key officials are often moved on a monthly basis and have limited authority. Many of the new programmes for natural resource management that were enacted in the 1990s have been disrupted. Thus resource and socio-political change are not separate processes. Rather, the approach adopted here helps to shed light on how climate change and political transition are inextricably bound together in shaping the overall trajectory of socionatural change.

Further, the feminist political ecology approach employed draws attention to the processes through which social inequalities are maintained, such that climate change produces differential impacts within societies. Other feminist work on gender and climate change has stressed the potentially disproportionate impacts on women due to their household roles and to violence against women (MacGregor 2009; Arora-Jonsson 2011). My analysis departs from this work in using feminist theory to explain how gender and other social relations can serve to create vulnerabilities, *and* serve as a point of friction through which resources are struggled over. This kind of analysis draws out the multi-scalar and multi-dimensional aspects of 'adaptation'. Such a conceptualization demands that we pay attention to social justice, not because of disproportionate impacts on women, but because it is impossible to produce durable adaptation programmes without accounting for socionatures and power.

Thus, a feminist approach attends to more than simply gender, but rather seeks to capture 'intersectional' social relations that shape the operation of power, and in this case, the way adaptation is conceived, implemented and enacted on the ground (Nightingale 2011). Intersectionality refers to the ways in which forms of social difference (race, class, gender, disability, among other identities) 'add up' to circumscribe how people see themselves and how they are seen in the social milieu, leading to various forms of discrimination or privilege (Butler 1997). In relation to environment, feminist political ecologists have further argued that not only does intersectionality shape access to, control over, knowledge of and distribution of resources (Rocheleau, Thomas-Slayter, and Wangari 1996), struggles over social difference are also played out in relation to environmental management (Sundberg 2003). Issues of how to 'participate' and what constitutes 'adaptation' are predicated upon ideas of inclusion, justice and equity, all of which have been shown to be strongly shaped by gender (MacGregor 2009). I go a step further and show how climate adaptation programmes themselves are instrumental in promoting particular ideas of inclusion, justice and equity; ideas highly contested in the current setting. Indeed, struggles over social identity and inclusion are at the very centre of political unrest. As such, adaptation programmes need to be understood as produced within and as part of fragile state politics – rather than fragile politics derailing well-designed adaptation programmes.

The analysis lends insights into both who is most at risk from climate change, and how climate change can become an opportunity for social change. The hope is that the context of rapidly shifting resources can be used to foster greater deliberation, inclusion, and realistic democratic processes that take inequality as a starting point rather than an externality that requires management. I argue that whether adaptation occurs or not will be the outcome of contestations over such relations, regardless of how well the plans are formulated.

In what follows, I first sketch my 'socionatural' theorization, followed by an outline of Nepal's climate adaptation plans and their relationship to contentious politics. I then probe Nepal's NAPA, Local Adaptation Plan of Action (LAPA) and related documents, as well as ethnographic data on the political transition at different scales to illustrate the ways that climate change and political transition intersect. The conclusion draws into question the adequacy of the current conceptualization of adaptation as 'moderating harm and capitalizing on benefits' for the challenges ahead. Rather, more emphasis needs to be placed on social inequalities and how they shape the design and implementation of adaptation programmes.

The case study is based on research done between 2005 and 2013 on the political transition in Nepal and forestry governance. Mixed qualitative methods were employed: more than six months of participant observation in rural areas on resource management and everyday politics (user-group meetings); over two months of consultancy work for international donor organizations in Nepal, which provided insights into current objectives, strategies and programmes related to climate change and forestry management; key informant interviews with forestry professionals at national, regional and local levels within the government, donor organizations and civil society; content analysis of key documents including the NAPA, LAPA and Climate Change Strategy documents; and use of the 'grey' literature published by donors working in Nepal and globally on these questions.

A socionatural approach to climate justice

Increasingly, the literature on climate adaptation focuses on ethics and distributional justice: who should pay, and how populations will be differently impacted (Eriksen et al. 2011; Thomas and Twyman 2005). While rarely explicitly mentioned, this work suggests that adaptation questions are less about techno-engineering schemes and more about attention to social relations and 'socionature' issues. Socionature theorists argue that the distinctions commonly drawn between 'social' change (adaptation) and 'natural' change (climate) are both ontologically incorrect and conceptually unhelpful (Castree and Braun 2001). If we instead begin from a relational understanding of socionature, we see that climate change is as much social as natural; similarly, adaptation cannot occur without causing further environmental change.

Climate change is socionatural in that humans cause greenhouse gas emissions, which drive atmospheric change. But climate change is also social because our understanding of it cannot exist outside the social milieu. The instruments developed to monitor change, the theories and computer models we build are all social artefacts, designed and accepted as 'true' by humans. Thus our comprehension of climate change is thoroughly social. This is not to suggest that climate change is not 'real', but rather to attract attention to the implications of *how* we frame the problem.

Furthermore, the political ecology and hazards literatures have shown that when faced with natural disasters, local consequences are unpredictable and carry with them a host of social justice issues (Ribot 2010; Turner and Robbins 2008). Disasters can be an opportunity for more powerful members of communities to profit, or 'luck' may in fact spare some of the most vulnerable while afflicting the more affluent. Thus, when planning for responses to climate change, attention to such distributional justice questions – both of impacts and potential benefits – need to be at the centre of adaptation planning (Eriksen et al. 2011).

The current literature on climate justice is slippery. It is difficult to find fault with the emphasis on vulnerability and how institutions need to be designed in order to distribute resources fairly and protect the poorest of the poor from climate change impacts (Adger et al. 2009). Yet, what is missing is a pathway beyond vulnerability. How exactly does one go about designing 'inclusive' institutions given the evidence that intersectional social differences play out *within* institutions? This chapter contributes to creative development alternatives by using feminist political ecology to hold contentious politics in view while thinking through adaptation challenges.

Nepal's NAPA and LAPA

Like other developing countries, Nepal received international donor support for writing its NAPA (GON/MoE 2010). Nepal's plan provides a baseline assessment of vulnerabilities based on known biophysical conditions and identifies seven priority areas for adaptation efforts including forestry and biodiversity, disaster management, water, and urban issues (encompassing water and energy concerns); note the focus on biophysical and technical domains. A key purpose of the NAPA is to ensure that all development programmes take climate change into consideration. In line with the Intergovernmental Panel on Climate Change (IPCC), 'adaptation' is defined as direct responses to perceived environmental change that moderate harm or capitalize on possible benefits (Klein et al. 2007, p. 750). 'Adaptation', is thus framed to be positive, but I suggest this masks important questions about adaptation for whom, at what cost and with what distributional justice consequences.

The publication of Nepal's NAPA was closely followed by the LAPA and its training manual, as well as a Climate Change Strategy document and the climate-finance focused Pilot Programme for Climate Resilience (PPCR). All these documents were produced by the Ministry of the Environment, in collaboration with other ministries, top-level government officials, and international consultants.

The development of the NAPA mirrored that of other developing countries, but it was unique in assembling a multi-stakeholder design group, including representatives from different political parties and civil society groups and relevant international donor-supported projects. This was done to lend legitimacy to the process in the context of political transition. The NAPA team conducted 'transect walks' to consult with communities across the range of the country's topographical zones. Nepal's plans are considered some of the best globally (Wiseman and Pandit Chhetri 2011), but coordination between the plans has been limited – the PPCR, for example, is not linked to the LAPA and has a different office within the Ministry of Environment.

Nepal's experience served to transform how United Nations Framework Convention on Climate Change (UNFCCC) processes are translated into other contexts, however. During the NAPA meetings, a Nepalese employee of an international donor suggested the scale of planning was flawed. He argued the real action for change occurs at the grassroots. He recounted to me, 'I said, "why are we talking about NAPA? We should be talking about LAPA, we need a local adaptation plan of action!'" He attributed his belief in the grassroots to his experience with community forestry in Nepal, a programme that empowers communities to govern forests. The idea was rapidly embraced, and now has been instituted elsewhere, including Pakistan and several states within the USA, although as yet there is no global UNFCCC mandate for LAPAs.

In keeping with a grassroots focus, the LAPA policy was developed based on the results of several pilot projects (drinking water, irrigation, agriculture). Yet despite this extensive consultation and grassroots learning, the concept of LAPA still assumes that adaptation planning must come from 'above' and that ordinary people lack the knowledge, skills and resources for adaptation. As another Nepalese employee of an international donor project who was closely involved in LAPA piloting remarked when we were discussing how the LAPA piloting engaged local people, 'ultimately, LAPA is also top-down'.

After an 18-month process, Nepal's NAPA was published in 2010 (available for download on the web in 2011), with the LAPA process beginning immediately afterwards (ADB 2012; GON/MoE 2010, 2011b, 2011a). The release was delayed due to internal political concerns and instability – government bureaucrats were moved frequently, leading to a lack of authority – yet the documents themselves are devoid of explicit consideration of the political transition. As I explore in more detail below, I suggest that this absence is not simply an oversight. Rather it is the result of both the internal situation in Nepal, but also a framing of climate change adaptation that is unable to account for competing visions of 'moderating harm and capitalizing on benefits'. Perhaps most significantly, the Nepal experience indicates that far more attention should be paid to adaptation *for* whom and at what cost for others within globally supported planning processes. In Nepal we see very clearly how some people are able to capitalize upon changes in resources, at the expense of others.

Political instability, intersectionality and environmental change

The apolitical framing of the NAPA and LAPA documents contrasts with the messy politics that lay behind their delay (and, indeed, everyday life in Nepal) in the period when they were written (2008–2011). Almost every sphere of life became increasingly politicized, with party politics cementing patronage and violence as the norm (International Crisis Group (ICG) 2011). In Nepal's NAPA, the political transition is mentioned only as a reason to immediately implement the plans, and it does not appear at all in the LAPA strategy document. There is no analysis of how political instability might shape the success of the proposals. Interestingly, people involved told me that the decision to sidestep contentious politics was made to avoid delays. However, political instability clearly presents many challenges for adaptation, as well as providing justification for their urgency.

Nepal's politics have been wracked with competition for power between the main political parties, causing three Constitution writing deadlines to be missed. Even after the elections in November 2013, there is an increasing sense that national leaders are more concerned with capturing power and resources than accountability to their electorate. Most significantly for environmental governance, contestations over ethnicity and community are central to on-going political instability. A large number of ethnic movements have emerged, demanding a bigger stake in the state. Similar to historical trends, these groups splinter as new identities and demands are made (Thapa 2004), reflecting a key driver of Nepalese politics, *aphno maanche* ('your own people'). *Aphno maanche* is a patronage system with long historical roots. People seek to have 'their own people' in positions of power, as it is through such personal connections that people gain access to resources (Dahal 2008). I elaborate further on this below in relation to the NAPA and LAPA, but here it is important to recognize how the vast majority of Nepalese interpret political representation literally. Groups seek to have their names written into the Constitution and their *aphno maanche* in key positions of power.

Nepal's environmental instability is seen as one of several underlying causes of conflict and vulnerability – and, as I show here, these causes intersect. Temperatures in the Himalayas are projected to rise much higher than the global average (IPCC 2007), triggering significant glacial melting and changes in the monsoon pattern, threatening agriculture and water resources throughout South Asia and China/Tibet (Regmi 2009). In fact, predictions of climate catastrophe harken back to the 'crisis on a Himalayan scale'. This 'Theory of Himalayan Degradation' (Ives and Messerli 1989) led to major donor investments in the natural resource and forestry sectors, resulting in the implementation of several conservation areas and bilateral community forestry programmes. Programmes to address climate change are thus part of a long line of interventions designed to 'rescue' the Himalayas and the wider region from impending environmental doom. Such antecedents are highly relevant not only because climate-focused development efforts are incorporated into on-going work in the natural resource sector, but also because these earlier programmes have shaped how people receive new ones.

Probing programmes from this angle draws into question the framing of adaptation within Nepal's NAPA and particularly the more detailed LAPA training manuals (ADB 2012; GON/MoE 2011b). Adaptation responses are assumed to derive from environmental change. Using a generic definition of climate sensitivity, the District Level training manual states: '*Socio-economic impacts* (for the bigger part) follow biophysical impacts and affect socio-economic development, e.g. reduced access to ser-vices [sic] due to damaged infrastructure or losses in tourism due to shoreline erosion' (Nepal is landlocked and thus has no shoreline) (ADB 2012, p. 50, italics in original). Further,

> The LAPA vulnerability assessment explicitly recognizes the role of resources and services in building adaptive capacity. This approach *combines* a top-down assessment that helps identify the status and quality of services

and resources at the ward level, with a bottom-up assessment that helps identify the extent to which vulnerable communities and households can access these resources and services.

(ADB 2012, p. 58, italics in original)

While not explicitly stated, extrapolating from the more detailed methodologies of vulnerability assessment (Olmos 2001), I interpret 'services' to refer to environmental services as well as infrastructure like bridges, dams, roads and communication networks.

Nepal's plans are thus progressive in the sense that they take seriously the need to engage the grassroots and build programmes by merging national and local perspectives and concerns. However, when absolute quantities and qualities of resources and services are assumed to determine the ability of people to adapt, it masks how those with greater social and political power can harness negative changes in resources and services for their own benefit. Political instability radically compounds this problem due to the lack of accountability and authority to distribute and govern resources at all levels. Struggles for authority over development programmes and distribution of resources are how politics is played in the transitional period (Nightingale and Ojha 2013) – with climate adaptation programmes potentially at the very centre of these dynamics.

While most climate programmes have yet to be fully implemented, I can cite two examples that indicate how politics are paramount in determining outcomes. First, one member of a benefit-sharing REDD+ pilot scheme stated, 'because there is so much money, it is changing the power balance within our user-group. This is causing problems.' Second, schemes intended to improve access to resources intersect with household relations. A programme used local labour to build an irrigation water tank in exchange for food. Our research found that some people claimed one day's rice rations after working 1–2 hours a day. Further, men who volunteered then claimed their work was done and refused to participate in agricultural and social reproductive activities required for household subsistence (Nightingale and Rankin 2012). Consequently women's work burdens increased.

These examples show that adaptation responses to changes in resources are not socially and politically neutral, but are bound up in (locally specific) (re) configurations of power (Nightingale 2006; Peluso 2009). In the first instance quoted, the infusion of money into the user group caused political factions to align so as to control these new resources. My informant made it clear that she had been excluded from a leadership position due to her gender and her political affiliation. She held that the additional money coming from the REDD+ project motivated the dominant political party to control key positions. This example is consistent with my previous research (Nightingale 2006) and shows how social differences (gender, caste, political party membership) 'add up' to present particular kinds of exclusions and inclusions.

In the second case, a programme aimed at key aspects of vulnerability – food shortages and lack of irrigation water – had the unintended consequence of creating a vulnerability differential within households. Women found they benefited minimally from the scheme, and their workload increased. In these examples, social differences are not fixed, but are performed and contested in everyday life. In terms of climate adaptation, this means that assumptions about men's and women's adaptive capacity, as well as tasks they undertake in order to adapt, have significant consequences for how social and power relations will change.

Furthermore, in adaptation programmes, struggles over power are not simply social justice questions. Which stakeholders and institutions are considered 'right' are strongly shaped by gender and intersectionality, with tangible environmental outcomes. Disempowered members of forest management committees break rules to exert power, or more powerful members break rules with impunity due to the inability of others to control their actions. I have witnessed all of these at work in Nepal (Nightingale 2005, 2006). As regards climate adaptation, it is essential to understand how adaptation programmes can serve as a context for people to control diminishing resources, gain access to new resources and exclude others, or to gain social power by controlling distribution – all of which have ecological consequences and thus implications for long-term adaptation. As such, these 'localized' relations have socioecological implications well beyond individuals, households and communities. The process of natural resource management is therefore a key site wherein social inequalities are contested and reinforced, again drawing into question whether it is *resources* that drive adaptation needs, or if it is social power relations.

Given these precedents, it is disquieting that (apolitical) community-based groups are proposed as solutions to most adaptation and distribution concerns in the NAPA and LAPA documents. Only watershed and regional habitat networks are defined as scales that require oversight by government Ministries 'at the appropriate level' (GON/MoE 2010, p. 33). Nevertheless, in some respects the promotion of community-based adaptation is a progressive response to questions of equity and justice in Nepal. This emphasis certainly derives in part from Nepal's exemplary record in promoting community resource governance. However, intersectionality cannot be ignored, and participation itself becomes another site of contest over social power. Well-functioning community forestry user groups, for example, reflect community inequalities, causing conflict over management and environmental change to erupt in unpredictable ways (Nightingale 2005; Thoms 2008); true inclusion remains elusive.

While not challenging the need for local control, I do question the efficacy of participatory approaches when they are framed outside contentious politics. Local user groups as well as regional and national governance programmes are hotly contested in the political transition; they are key sites where 'development' is occurring but also where the patterns of political patronage and violence are cemented. Careful attention to intersectionality is required, along with how such relationships are mapped out on the ground, if adaptation programmes are to be adequately responsive to fragile political contexts.

I am therefore troubled that Nepal's NAPA document reflects the current dynamics around intersectionality and political representation (*aphno maanche*) in only two contexts. First, in keeping with the history of Nepal's development priorities, a female consultant produced a 'gender analysis', outlined in Annex 5 of the document. Gender is only mentioned twice in the entire document outside the annex, despite being listed as a 'cross cutting theme'. The annex mentions several 'extra' risks to women, including sexual violence and increased workloads caused by diminishing water supplies and productive resources. How gender relations of power are contested and (re)produced within resource governance is not captured by such an analysis. Ironically, the politics behind the document reflects this point. A key informant told me that neither the gender consultant nor top-level women within the relevant ministries were asked to comment on the final document – an omission which serves to reinforce the marginalized position of women within Nepal's national bureaucracy. The LAPA Strategy summary document does not mention gender at all and has remarkably few references to 'marginalized groups', even though the LAPA was developed through an explicitly bottom-up process.

Cultural politics is also evident in the extensive consultation done for the NAPA, including 'youth, foresters, indigenous communities and disaster risk reduction networks' (GON/MoE 2010, p 16). This may seem a rather unexpected set of interest groups, but it reflects current political factions mixed with a techno-bureaucratic bias in resource governance (Nightingale and Ojha 2013). The document also promotes multi-level networks of resource users, 'good governance' and institution building across environmental sectors. A defining feature of 'good governance' in Nepal is careful record-keeping and the presence of women and ethnic minorities on management committees and in leadership roles. Consistent with this logic, the LAPA emphasizes bottom-up consultation in terms of vulnerability and capacities, conjoined with top-down mechanisms of response and resources.

Despite the implicit emphasis on social inclusion, there is no sense of how the different layers of the bureaucracy and civil society will interact. The entire LAPA process begins at the district level and identifies vulnerable village development committees (municipalities) and wards within them. However, district boundaries will change radically in the near future as the currently undefined federal structure unfolds. Such issues are deeply embedded within contestations over intersectional inequalities. Cultural identity struggles feature in virtually every sphere of governance, with the goals seeming to be political recognition and access to livelihood benefits through political patronage. Such contestations have profound consequences for adaptation *and* democracy building. Control over territory and exclusive rights to representation (e.g. consultation for the NAPA) underpin many of their demands. And, since contentious politics are not acknowledged within the policy documents, we may question how these plans will manage to cope with this volatile context.

The problematic nature of these static policy documents is recognized within Nepal by a small group of professionals. As one Nepalese intellectual reflected on his experience within the LAPA writing team, 'the document does not open up space for revision and negotiation'. He said the team was able to 'epistemologically recognize vulnerability as contextual and shifting', but that when vulnerability maps were produced, only he and another colleague were able to 'recognize that the maps are not absolute, but need to be designed to be dynamic' (my paraphrase). This lack of official recognition of vulnerability as dynamic is exacerbated by the mechanisms through which adaptation programmes are implemented by the state. As another Nepalese development professional remarked, '[for state bureaucrats] policy is not policy documents, it is letters from their immediate boss, [and those letters] must come with a budget code'.

The silence around the political transition was not limited to the actual written document. Several people who had participated in NAPA meetings indicated that politically sensitive issues were deliberately avoided. One explained that different political positions – such as favouring one form of resource governance over another – are closely identified with political parties in Nepal today, and many professionals were unwilling to reveal their political alliances in such a public context. Another indicated that when politically charged issues emerged, the facilitators and chair reminded the group that their job was to produce a technical strategy document, not to address politics.

My analysis, however, suggests that if attention to gender and intersectional social differences that underpin vulnerability and resource distribution practices were placed in the centre of adaptation concerns, questions of politics, power and the *means* through which social and political reproduction occurs would need become the 'priority areas'. Techno-engineering approaches, while useful in constructing infrastructure and ensuring technology transfer, also provide more opportunity for inequitable distribution of and control over resources. The groups seen to be the most worthy of 'consultation' are able to assert their 'rights' and 'knowledge' over that of others – in the Nepal case, this has generally meant high-caste Hindu males. Priority areas focused on biophysical resources (forests, biodiversity, energy, water) mask how those sectors are the product of specific social struggles. The quality, quantity and location of biophysical resources are inherently produced out of socionatural processes that shape which resources are considered vital, as well as the best mechanisms for and the actors assumed to have the right knowledge and skills to manage them. It is these processes that shape adaptation needs and adaptive capacity.

Conclusion

Adaptation must be understood as a *socionatural political process*, one that both constitutes and is derived from the trajectory of social–political change. There is a growing recognition that adaptation is not free from ethical and political concerns. Yet, within this recognition is the assumption that politics need to be considered in order to ensure that the adaptation process is not derailed by messy political contests. However, the analysis in this chapter has shown how politics *constitute* adaptation – from the most abstract conceptions in policy documents, to the implementation of plans on the ground. Climate adaptation strategies need to tackle their political nature straight on, rather than sidestepping these issues by referring to 'good governance'.

Nepal's climate adaptation documents all start with the assumption that absolute quantities and qualities of resources and services determine the ability of people to adapt. Gender is assumed to be relevant for the lives of individual women – climate change puts them at risk, physically and mentally, from greater workloads and increased sexual violence – heightening their vulnerability. I have shown, however, how gender and intersectionality shape the very process of adaptation planning itself. The expertise brought to bear on evaluating the hazards, and the techno-engineering solutions prioritized, all entail assumptions about who the right stakeholders are and who needs to be 'consulted'. Without close attention to gender and intersectionality, these stakeholders and experts are overwhelmingly composed of 'expert' men. Over-emphasis on the biophysical drivers of adaptation and techno-engineering fixes also masks how more powerful members of communities and nations can mobilize negative changes in resources and services to their own benefit. Therefore, I argue that less attention should be placed on techno-engineering schemes, and more on intersectional power relations when devising adaptation plans.

The NAPA and LAPA propose that cooperative, locally based user groups need to be empowered to manage their resources. This emphasis on community solutions opens up some possibility for placing intersectional power relations in the centre of adaptation planning, as a deliberative tool for thinking through social inequalities and injustice. Nepal has been at the forefront of promoting participatory resource governance, and many programmes have attempted to tackle equity issues. However, such efforts have not managed to overcome equity concerns; moreover, the political transition is now cementing, rather than challenging, forms of patronage as a 'normal' way of conducting business. Nepal's climate-change documents are silent on questions of resource control and the fundamentally contested nature of the institutions that shape adaptation efforts. Who is included in these efforts and how this serves to empower or retrench social relations will shape the adaptive capacity of individuals and the nation. The NAPA and LAPA documents, framed outside politics and without provisions for dynamic revisions, are unlikely to prepare Nepal to cope with the challenges of climate change.

The focus on institutions and communities as apolitical entities is not new to climate-change adaptation policies, but it is surprising in the context of Nepal's current political unrest, where questions of community inclusion are *the* issues being contested. Equity issues become de-politicized through 'consultation', 'ensuring gender sensitivity' and techno-engineering fixes. The case examined here shows, however, how development projects such as natural resource management are important contexts within which national and global ideas of resource distribution, democracy, development and climate change are taught. Such learning is not uncontested. As my other research shows, local people assert their own ideas of distributive justice, democracy and development as they engage in or resist the activities promoted – including climate adaptation programmes (Nightingale and Rankin 2012).

What emerges from this analysis is a recognition that adaptation programmes align citizens in particular relationships with each other ('cooperation') and the state ('local capacity for response') with highly significant implications for democracy, post-conflict state building and the long-term trajectory of politics, not only in Nepal but also in countries across the globe. As many of the countries projected to suffer most from climate change are also experiencing varying degrees of political violence, a more realistic approach to resource governance that places intersectional struggles in the centre of adaptation concerns is required.

Recommendations

- Adaptation documents need to be produced in a manner that invites revision and a dynamic understanding of climate change as well as vulnerability. One mechanism is to build a regular revision process into the policies, as well as conceptualizing adaptation as responding to unpredictability.
- An analysis of how political instability might shape the success of the proposals is required. A multi-scalar, multi-sectoral analysis of the barriers (and possibilities) for environmental governance created by contested politics is needed in each context.
- Climate-change strategy documents must recognize that social, political and cultural dynamics are equally important as biophysical dynamics in shaping the trajectories of adaptation possibilities. Questions of politics, power and the *means* through which social and political reproduction occur need to be 'priority areas'.
  - Inequality and contested politics should be taken as starting points rather than externalities that require management.
  - The documents should allow for competing visions of 'moderating harm and capitalizing on benefits'.
  - Adaptation programmes should evaluate contestations over social and political inclusion, and assume that dynamic contests will shape how programmes are implemented.

- Adaptation strategy documents should explicitly understand that access to, distribution of and control over resources are constrained primarily by political–economic factors and not biophysical ones. This can shift the focus to political mechanisms to ensure inclusion and distributional justice, rather than institutions, infrastructure and engineering.
- In addition to evaluating quantities and qualities of resources and services when mapping vulnerability, LAPA and NAPA programmes need to include a dynamic understanding of wider political economic relations that shape how people are able to access those resources. Such analyses are available in the vulnerability literature but have not been adequately applied to climate-change contexts.

- The (re)negotiations of power relations that are inherent to resource-governance contexts can be used as an opportunity for fostering greater deliberation, inclusion and realistic democratic processes – if their contested, unequal and dynamic nature is placed in the centre of institution building.

References

ADB. 2012. 'Nepal: Strengthening capacity for managing climate change and environment–district level training toolkit on climate change and environmental management.' In *TA 7173-NEP*, 199. Kathmandu: Asian Development Bank for Government of Nepal, Ministry of Environment, Science and Technology.

Adger, W. Neil, Suraje Dessai, Marisa Goulden, Mike Hulme, Irene Lorenzoni, Donald R. Nelson, Lars Otto Naess, Johanna Wolf and Anita Wreford. 2009. 'Are there social limits to adaptation to climate change?' *Climatic Change* 93:335–54.

Arora-Jonsson, Seema. 2011. 'Virtue and vulnerability: Discourses on women, gender and climate change.' *Global Environmental Change* 21(2):744–51. doi: http://dx.doi.org/10.1016/j.gloenvcha.2011.01.005.

Butler, Judith. 1997. *The psychic life of power.* Stanford, CA: Stanford University Press.

Castree, Noel, and Bruce Braun. 2001. *Social nature: Theory, practice and politics.* Oxford: Blackwell.

Dahal, Dilli Ram. 2008. 'The "mahadeshi" people: Issues and challenges of democracy in the Nepal terai.' In *Local democracy in south asia: Microprocesses of democratization in nepal and its neighbours,* edited by David N. Gellner and Krishna Hachhethu, 128–49. Delhi: Sage.

Dalby, Simon. 2009. *Security and environmental change.* Malden, MA: Polity Press.

Eriksen, Siri, Paulina Aldunce, Chandra Sekhar Bahinipati, Raphael D'Almeida Martins, John Isac Molefe, Charles Nhemachena, Karen O'Brien, et al. 2011. 'When not every response to climate change is a good one: Identifying principles for sustainable adaptation.' *Climate and Development* 3(1):7–20.

GON/MoE. 2010. 'National adaptation plan of action to climate change.' Kathmandu: Ministry of Environment, Government of Nepal.

GON/MoE. 2011a. 'Adaptation to climate change: NAPA to LAPA.' Kathmandu: Ministry of Environment, Government of Nepal.

GON/MoE. 2011b. 'The LAPA framework local adaptation plans for action: Summary steps and key actions.' Kathmandu: Climate Adaptation Design and Piloting–Nepal project team, Ministry of Environment, Government of Nepal.

Hutt, Michael. 2004. *Himalayan "people's war": Nepal's maoist rebellion*. London: C. Hurst and Co.

International Crisis Group (ICG). 2011. 'Nepal: Identity politics and federalism.' In *Asia Report*. Kathmandu and Brussels.

IPCC. 2007. *Climate change 2007 – the physical science basis*. Edited by Intergovernmental Panel on Climate Change, *Working Group I contribution to the fourth assessment report of the IPCC*. Cambridge: Cambridge University Press.

Ives, Jack D., and Bruno Messerli. 1989. *The Himalayan dilemma. Reconciling development and conservation*. London and New York: The United Nations University and Routledge.

Klein, R.J.T., S. Huq, F. Denton, T.E. Downing, R.G. Richels, J.B. Robinson, and F.L. Toth. 2007. 'Inter-relationships between adaptation and mitigation. Climate change 2007: Impacts, adaptation and vulnerability.' In *Contribution of Working Group II to the Fourth Assessment Report of the Intergovernmental Panel on Climate Change*, edited by M.L. Parry, O.F. Canziani, J.P. Palutikof, P.J. van der Linden and C.E. Hanson, 745–77. Cambridge, UK.

MacGregor, Sherilyn. 2009. 'A stranger silence still: The need for feminist social research on climate change.' *The Sociological Review* 57:124–40. doi: 10.1111/j.1467-954X.2010.01889.x.

Nightingale, Andrea J. 2005. '"The experts taught us all we know": Professionalisation and knowledge in Nepalese community forestry.' *Antipode* 34(3):581–604.

Nightingale, Andrea J. 2006. 'The nature of gender: Work, gender and environment.' *Environment and Planning D: Society and Space* 24(2):165–85.

Nightingale, Andrea J. 2011. 'Bounding difference: The embodied production of gender, caste and space.' *Geoforum* 42(2):153–62.

Nightingale, Andrea J., and Hemant R. Ojha. 2013. 'Rethinking power and authority: Symbolic violence and subjectivity in Nepal's terai forests.' *Development and Change* 44(1):29–51. doi: 10.1111/dech.12004.

Nightingale, Andrea, and Katharine Rankin. 2012. 'Peace building from the grassroots? The practices and challenges of local democracy in Nepal.' Research report. http://www.geos.ed.ac.uk/homes/anightin/Landscapes/brief.html: University of Edinburgh.

Ojha, Hemant R., N. Timsina, C. Kumar, B. Belcher, and M. Banjade. 2008. *Communities, forests and governance: Policy and institutional innovations from Nepal*. India: Adroit Publishers.

Olmos, Santiago. 2001. 'Vulnerability and adaptation to climate change: Concepts, issues, assessment methods.' In *Climate Change Knowledge Network Foundation Paper*, 21. International Institute for Sustainable Development.

Peluso, Nancy Lee. 2009. 'Rubber erasures, rubber producing rights: Making racialized territories in West Kalimantan, Indonesia.' *Development & Change* 40(1):47–80. doi: 10.1111/j.1467-7660.2009.01505.x.

Raleigh, Clionadh, and Henrik Urdal. 2007. 'Climate change, environmental degradation and armed conflict.' *Political Geography* 26(6):674–94.

Regmi, M.R. 2009. 'Climate change issues of Nepal: Challenges and perspectives for future generations.' *Progress in Environmental Science and Technology* 2:67–8.

Ribot, Jesse C. 2010. 'Vulnerability does not just fall from the sky: Toward multi-scale pro-poor climate policy.' In *Social dimensions of climate change: Equity and vulnerability in a warming world*, edited by Robin Mearns and Andrew Norton. Washington, DC: The World Bank.

Rocheleau, Diane, Barbara Thomas-Slayter, and Esther Wangari. 1996. *Feminist political ecology: Global issues and local experiences*. New York: Routledge.

Sundberg, Juanita. 2003. 'Conservation and democratization: Constituting citizenship in the Maya Biosphere Reserve, Guatemala.' *Political Geography* 22(7):715–40.

Thapa, Deepak. 2004. *A kingdom under siege: Nepal's Maoist insurgency, 1996-2004.* London: Zed Books.

Thomas, David S. G., and Chasca Twyman. 2005. 'Equity and justice in climate change adaptation amongst natural-resource-dependent societies.' *Global Environmental Change Part A* 15(2):115–24.

Thoms, Christopher A. 2008. 'Community control of resources and the challenge of improving local livelihoods: A critical examination of community forestry in Nepal.' *Geoforum* 39(3):1452–65. doi: 10.1016/j.geoforum.2008.01.006.

Turner, B.L., and Paul Robbins. 2008. 'Land-change science and political ecology: Similarities, differences, and implications for sustainability science.' *Annual Review of Environment and Resources* 33(1):295–316. doi: doi:10.1146/annurev.environ.33.022207.104943.

Wiseman, Katie, and Raju Pandit Chhetri. 2011. 'Minding the money: Governance of climate change adaptation finance in Nepal.' Research Report 52. Oxford: Oxfam.

13

INFLUENCING POLICY AND ACTION ON CLIMATE-CHANGE ADAPTATION

Strategic stakeholder engagement in the agricultural sector in Tanzania

Kassim Kulindwa and Baruani Mshale

Introduction

Although scientific research on climate-change impacts on the agricultural sector in Africa is accumulating, applying the results to improve adaptive capacity, especially among smallholder farmers, still lags behind. This is evidenced by the increases in climate-change impacts on agricultural productivity (see e.g. UNEP 2011; Hepworth 2010; Ziervogel and Zermoglio 2009; Fischer et al. 2005; Mendelsohn 2000). Some scholars have argued that this research–policy disconnect is a result of misalignment in the timing and duration needed to undertake proper research, versus the need to deliver policy recommendations, resulting in slow and incomplete processes of translating scientific evidence into appropriate policies in developing countries (see e.g. Aaserud et al. 2005; Hennink and Stephenson 2005; Hanney et al. 2003; Stephenson and Hennink 2002; Walt 1994). Others hold that poor communication between researchers and policy-makers further widens the science–policy gap, particularly as regards dissemination after the research project has ended. On the one hand, policy-makers contend that scientific information is usually presented in academic formats that are inaccessible to them; on the other hand, researchers feel that policy-makers lack understanding and respect for research, and that this limits the use of research in policy formulation (Hennink and Stephenson 2005; Stephenson and Hennink 2002). Yet others have argued that although the publication of research findings is important, this is generally not sufficient to change policy and practice (Aaserud et al. 2005; O'Brien and Vogel 2003). As O'Brien and Vogel explain, '...even if perfect forecasts were disseminated in an optimal manner, there remain significant factors constraining their use and thus limiting their value' (2003:18). Several authors (Vogel and O'Brien 2006; O'Brien and Vogel 2003; Ingram et al. 2002; Broad and Agrawala 2001; Roncoli et al. 2001, 2000) have identified these constraints as relating to social inequities, market forces, political instability and civil strife – gender inequality and social exclusion, limited options available to farmers including credit, alternative seeds, draft power, irrigation and land availability.

There are indeed many factors that limit effective linkages between research and policy. Here we focus on the politics of interactions and the role of power relations and interests in encouraging (or discouraging) collaborative production and application of scientific knowledge in the making of climate-change adaptation polices and plans in the agricultural sector. We ask whether participation and interaction involving relevant actors in the research process can help to narrow the gap between research to policy and action for improved adaptation to climate change. Our chapter analyses the interactions between researchers, policy-makers and smallholder farmers during initial research design, developing policy plans from research findings, and implementing actions resulting from this interactive policy process.

Theoretical and analytical framing

We employ a 'three-lens' framework (Naess et al. 2011; IDS 2011; Chinsinga et al. 2011; IDS 2006; Keeley and Scoones 2003) to provide an analytical design for how participatory action research could be combined with policy-process design and application in improving adaptation to climate-changes impacts in agriculture. This framework consists of three elements, or lenses: actors/organizations, narratives/evidence, and politics/interests. The first element involves identifying the actors/organizations involved in the policy process and, in our case, in the participatory research process aimed at providing scientific research evidence. Second, narratives are storylines that help to identify competing ways of viewing a particular policy problem and provide understanding of a range of interests (Naess et al. 2011). Examining the interaction among relevant actors helps to make clear the underlying power dynamics and how actors go about negotiating the inclusion of their interests in the research and policy process. This means power[1] relations in the research process need to be acknowledged (Naess et al. 2011; Chinsinga et al. 2011; IDS 2006). The analysis can therefore provide entry points for identifying policy spaces: 'moments, opportunities and channels where citizens can act to potentially affect policies, discourses and decisions and relationships that affect their lives and interests' (Gaventa 2006:26).

Using this framework enables sequential analysis covering the three elements: first, identification of actors and putting them into appropriate categories (e.g. researchers, policy-makers across multiple governance levels, and policy implementers, including smallholder farmers); second, identification and analysis of the narratives and evidence/arguments deployed by actors in making claims; and third, identification and analysis of interests and politics of the various actors and how such interests influence the arguments put forward and the actions taken.

The three-lens framework facilitates analysis of how various actors and organizations engage in the processes of generating information and planning for adaptation to climatic-change impacts in agriculture (Naess et al. 2011; IDS 2011; Chinsinga et al. 2011; IDS 2006). Using this framework, we can explore how various actors make and shape policy through narratives and their interests and position of power (or lack of such), while being constrained by them at the same time (IDS 2006). Studying these processes is crucial for understanding how research evidence is generated and interpreted by the various actors, and how they in turn use it to achieve their own goals.

Keeley and Scoones (2003) describe policy processes as incremental, complex and non-linear, encompassing actors with different views and discourses, networks and power relations. Similarly, interactive research models recognize the non-linearity of policy development processes, which can be complex, protracted and with a multitude of actors and interests (Hanney et al. 2003). These models therefore require a longer time frame for research utilization (Stephenson and Hennink 2002). The interactive model design involves a range of interactions between researchers and policy-makers throughout the research process, and exposes each party to the other's world (Hennink and Stephenson 2005). According to Hanney et al. (2003), research is less likely to be used if there is no interaction across the interface between producers and users of knowledge. Interactive research can therefore provide a more realistic view of the researcher–policy-maker interface.

Case description

We use the case of a Participatory Action Research (PAR) conducted by researchers from the Sokoine University of Agriculture (SUA), in Morogoro, Tanzania, titled 'Managing Risk, Reducing Vulnerability and Enhancing Agricultural Productivity under a Changing Climate'. This PAR project was implemented in Same District in north-eastern Tanzania, funded by the International Development Research Centre (IDRC), Climate Change Adaptation in Africa (CCAA) 2006–2012 programme (SUA 2009). The authors were not part of the PAR project team; they had a separate research team which was part of a Department for International Development (DFID)/IDRC funded Research to Policy for Adaptation (RPA) project that aimed at investigating the processes and outcomes of the interactive PAR project using the three-lens framework. This chapter reports the results.

The RPA project was also conducted in Same District, a semi-arid area in the Western Pare Lowlands on the western side of the Pare Mountain ranges, in the Kilimanjaro region. The district covers an area of approximately 5,730 square km, located between longitude 37°55' E and 40°15' S, and has a population of 202,235 (Kulindwa 2011). Same District is already experiencing erratic and declining annual rainfall amounts and drought, projected to intensify over the next 50–100 years (URT 2003). Most people in the area engage in smallholder rain-fed mixed-crop farming and livestock-keeping practices. Maize, beans, lablab beans (*lablab purpureous*), green vegetables and other crops are cultivated. Coping strategies vary between groups, making some more vulnerable than others (Eriksen and Lind 2009). Strategies include planting early-maturing seeds and drought-resistant crops, migration by cattle-keepers in search of water and fodder outside the district, selling off livestock, seeking employment opportunities in town, reducing the frequency of meals and the amounts eaten, and increased dependency on non-timber forest products such as charcoal-making, wild fruits and bush meat. However, these strategies are by no means adequate to sustain the communities. Without effective planned adaptation strategies, Same farmers will continue to be severely affected by climate-change impacts, given the situation of pre-existing socio-economic stresses and other factors.

The PAR project was based on the assumption that conjoining research and policy processes could help to foster social transformation by ensuring that research findings and recommendations reach the relevant stakeholders in time, and in usable formats. The PAR researchers explained that although local farmers do undertake various autonomous adaptation strategies, the effectiveness of such strategies is increasingly limited due to a range of factors, including lack of timely and reliable weather forecasts concerning rainfall. PAR researchers then sought to find ways that could enable farmers to know and act according to weather conditions in a timely and effective manner.

In this chapter we use the results of the RPA to focus solely on the interactions between the various actors participating in the PAR project, arguing that the politics of interaction are as important as the accuracy of information delivered. It is not our intention to evaluate the scientific validity of the PAR findings or the relevance of policy recommendations: what we aim to demonstrate is the importance of multi-stakeholder engagement in influencing social transformations among targeted audiences.

Methodology

Because the PAR project involved interaction between researchers from Sokoine University and national actors in Dar-es-Salaam and sub-national actors in Same District, we conducted repeated semi-structured interviews and focus group discussions with actors, from village to national levels. These interviews were combined with an extensive review of documents, and observation techniques. The semi-structured interviews used guiding themes on actor interests, knowledge, perceptions and roles in the design and application of climate-change adaptation strategies for agriculture. Interviews also sought to elucidate what the roles and responsibilities of other actors should be – for instance, we asked farmers to explain what they wanted the district government authorities and researchers to do, to enable more effective responses to climate-change impact. Following these individual interviews with selected actors of each category, we organized focus group discussions that brought several actors together. Focus group discussions held in Same District were attended by selected smallholder farmers, traditional weather forecasters, PAR researchers, representatives from a non-governmental organization (NGO) and from Same District Government Office. In these discussion groups we facilitated a joint evaluation of the various PAR activities. In total we interviewed and conducted discussion groups with 32 individuals at the village, district and national levels.

One village, Bangalala, was selected. Here we interviewed a group of six farmers who were working with PAR researchers to implement recommended actions from the interactive research project. In Bangalala we interviewed five traditional weather forecasters and the village agricultural extension officer, who were also part of the PAR project at the local level. At the district level we interviewed representatives from an NGO called Same Agricultural Improvement Project (SAIPRO), one supplier of agricultural inputs, the head of the Tanzanian Meteorological Agency (TMA)'s Same station, and several officials at district government offices. At the national level we interviewed two PAR researchers from SUA, seven officials from the Ministry of Agriculture, Food Security and Cooperatives, including the director of policy and planning, the director of the food security unit, the head of the environmental unit, a climate-change specialist in the food security unit, one senior economist in the food security unit, a principal agricultural and environmental protection officer. Other national-level actors interviewed included the Senior Environmental Officer and Assistant Coordinator in the National Adaptation Plan of Action (NAPA) in the Vice President's Office (VPO), the resident United Nations Food and Agriculture Organization (FAO) representative in Tanzania, an Environmental Officer at WWF Tanzania Country Office and a TMA official from headquarters in Dar-es-Salaam. Interviews at the local level were conducted in Kiswahili; those at the national level were in English and Kiswahili.

In addition to the interviews and discussion groups, we conducted observations on interactions among various actors involved in the PAR. For instance, at the national level we attended several conferences and meetings where the various actors were present. Our observations aimed at understanding participation and eliciting power relations during interactive processes among the actors. Throughout our research, we conducted an extensive document review to understand the motivations, processes and outcomes from interactive processes such as the PAR project.

Results and discussion

The RPA results have been analysed with a view to revealing the political factors that may hinder effective adoption of new and evidence-based policy recommendations for effective adaptation strategies to climate-change impacts in agriculture. We have investigated multi-stakeholder engagement throughout the policy process from policy design to implementation and the role of scientific research. Specifically, we wanted to know whether and how PAR researchers engaged with the various stakeholders across multiple levels of governance. We employ a nuanced articulation of power relations among actors in formal and informal policy spaces to argue that focusing on the politics of interaction can shed light on factors such as competing narratives, divergent interests and power amongst actors that may impede the application of sound policy strategies. By 'political factors' we refer to the power relations between actors, and the forces influencing those power dynamics. Actors often deploy power dynamics in attempting to shape the views and actions of others (see Gaventa 2006; Lukes 2005).

For the three levels – national, district and village – we present our findings and our interpretation of the various aspects of interactions between multiple actors across multiple governance levels in making and applying strategies for climate-change adaptation strategies. For each level we indicate who the main actors are, their interests, the spaces for interactions, and the narratives and counter-narratives they employ when interacting in the policy spaces identified. These components of the analysis are aimed at explaining the complex nature of actor relations, in order to shed light on what measures to take in navigating the policy landscape so as to achieve faster and effective use of research results.

Actors and policy spaces at the national level

We use national-level and local-level policy spaces to highlight the actors involved and the politics of interaction among them. We present and discuss the roles, interests and powers of the actors and how these affect interactions in such consultative spaces. National-level policy spaces include the Agriculture Sector Consultative Group, the Agriculture Sector Working Group of Development Partners and the multi-stakeholder National Policy Forum, as well as the project inception workshop. Local-level policy spaces include the field farm school and the Decision Making Forum (DMF).

The *Agriculture Sector Consultative Group* is convened by the Ministry of Agriculture, and brings together development partners, representatives of the government, the private sector and NGOs. This forum meets four times a year and is hosted by the Directorate of Policy and Planning of the Ministry of Agriculture, Food Security and Cooperatives. It is the most powerful forum for policy-making in agricultural development because it includes all the major players representing various interests and influence, and derives its legitimacy from being convened by the government. The second policy space is the *Agriculture Working Group of the Development Partners*, which meets monthly. 'Development partners' is a collective term for various multilateral and bilateral development and environmental agencies represented in Tanzania. They are coordinated by the FAO's country office and normally invite experts to give presentations on agriculture development issues in the country. This group draws its legitimacy from the multilateral and bilateral agreements signed between the Tanzanian government and other governments or organizations. The third policy space is the monthly *Policy Forum* breakfast debate organized by a national NGO, the Policy Forum. At these meetings, actors from various interest groups meet to deliberate on matters of concern and policy relevance. Policy Forum breakfast debates have gained recognition and appreciation as spaces for critical independent insights, unlike the first two policy spaces described above. They are highly regarded by government agencies, development partners, the private sector and civil society, so attendance and participation are usually very representative of the range of actors at the national level. This forum draws its legitimacy through documented representation by the various actors involved.

These three fora are highly influential in agricultural development policy at the national level. They provide opportunities for the major actors to meet and exchange ideas, and mutually influence their thinking on specific issues. In addition, at the time of project inception, the PAR organized a national workshop in Same District. This workshop was attended by a total of 37 participants from various parts of the country, representing different categories of stakeholders as regards climate change and variability. There were researchers from academic and research institutions, District Agricultural and Livestock Officers, extension officers from Same and Dodoma, and NGOs' representatives. Other participants included farmers from Same and Dodoma, representing the interests of farmers in semi-arid areas.

In addition to introducing the research project to potential stakeholders, the workshop was intended to involve them in identifying indigenous and recommended practices/strategies for soil, crop, water and livestock management; further, to identify the climate information needs of different stakeholders, and to involve stakeholders in setting criteria for the selection of villages for project implementation in Same District. Following up such a workshop through project progress feedback is crucial for continuous stakeholder engagement.

By using existing practical and bureaucratic and invited spaces, as well as creating a new space – the DMF – the PAR project was able to bring the main stakeholders together. Through the DMF and farm field school meetings, the engagement of local-level actors was made more continuous. The farm field school engagement brought together local actors – farmers, SAIPRO, input suppliers, agricultural extension officers and weather forecasters. The DMF, with 16 members drawn from local-level actors including district council officials, discussed weather forecasts by TMA and traditional weather forecasters as well as advice from agricultural extension experts, including the timing of farm preparations, planting, weeding, harvesting and the type of agricultural inputs to use. This interaction outcome has attractive benefits: for instance, suppliers can minimize the cost of doing business by stocking the 'right' agricultural inputs like seeds and industrial fertilizers at the right time, which in turn enables farmers to obtain these agricultural inputs in time.

Narratives and their contestation

Two categories of narratives emerged in our investigation: one related to climate change; the other to agricultural development and food security. On the climate change front, we found all actors held views in line with the narrative that 'Climate change is real and has huge impacts to vulnerable developing countries'. However, a few academicians interviewed in this study argued that inaction on the part of certain actors, particularly national governments and development partners, in making adaptation funds available indicates that such actors are little occupied with the urgency of dealing with climate change, despite their verbal rhetoric. We also found that climate debates in terms of whether what is being experienced is climate change or variability (see IPCC 2007 for definitions) is becoming evident. Some of those interviewed, particularly from the spheres of government and the academic world, wondered whether, at the household level, adaptation strategies could be anything different from the coping strategies already used by farmers in times of droughts and floods – i.e. that there is nothing new in the drive for adaptation to climate change. Others hold that such views are the result of limited awareness of climate change, with most Tanzanians being unfamiliar with the concepts of climate change and global warming (Hepworth 2010).

Although many interviewees from civil society, government and academic institutions accepted the reality of climate change and the need for adaptation to avoid its negative impacts, a few educated actors in government and academic institutions argued that climate change is a priority that has been imposed on the government by international conventions; and they question the urgency of dealing with it. In government circles, it is argued that the more basic pressing problems of food insecurity and abject poverty need immediate attention, and that the country lacks the capability for effective coping due to lack of the necessary resources. However, an interview with the VPO Division of Environment confirmed the government's interest and commitment to honour its international obligations under the Kyoto Protocol in order to maintain its good reputation and be able to benefit from the global funds expected to be made available through the Green Climate Fund (GCF) for mitigation and adaptation.

For farmers at the local level, the dominant narrative concerns climate variability and its impact on livelihoods. The District Agricultural Office has put considerable efforts into irrigation as a means for adapting to climate change/variability impacts. On the other hand, the District Meteorological Office works on weather forecasting, without much linkage to other district-level actors. The result is separate, uncoordinated and often ineffective weather-related advice to farmers. Moreover, putting more emphasis on irrigation and less on other adaptation measures is bound to produce more vulnerable communities in areas where there are no rivers, lakes or dams to provide water for irrigation. Mediating these uncoordinated efforts are NGOs like SAIPRO, which tries to address the problem holistically without adequate resources. Left in the middle are farmers who, without adequate support, resort to the traditional ways which they know well and can manage.

We then assessed the validity of the narrative that asserts 'agriculture as the backbone of the Tanzanian economy'. This shared narrative is important to the extent to which it influences prioritizing agriculture development issues, and demonstrates the divergent views among various actors. The narrative is intended to serve as a bonding ideology among actors in addressing a common objective. While most actors interviewed affirmed this narrative, reasoning that the majority of Tanzanians reside in the rural areas and engage in farming, we also found some actors who felt that the government narratives were just 'hot air'. There is a clear mismatch between the government ascribed discourse and its actual action. Several actors attribute this disparity to lack of sufficient resources (human, financial and technical) for translating policy statements into policy actions. Others, civil society actors in particular, disagree with the explanation of inadequate resources, arguing that the problem is poor prioritization by the government.

In light of changing climatic conditions, two narratives are dominant: planting of drought-resistant crops and early-maturing seeds; and the emphasis on irrigation farming to reduce reliance on rain-fed agriculture for food security. Both of these narratives are subscribed to by the government and farmers. The cultivation of drought-resistant crops has picked up, although farmers still plant their traditional staples despite their bad performance. Given the lack of reliable, effective weather information as well as of adequate agronomic advice, farmers have continued to suffer losses due to poor harvests. The climate change agenda has come as a blessing in disguise to the agriculture sector this time around. Considerable investments and resources are being committed to develop agriculture for economic growth and food security. The declining food security situation, which caused poverty to entrench itself in rural areas, has prompted the government and its sympathizers to act in favour of the sector. All interviewees acknowledged that climate change poses huge risks to this sector; measures taken seem to serve both improved food security and adapting the agriculture sector to the impacts of climate change.

Actor interests and power dynamics

Policy is driven by multiple interests. Various actors and organizations vie to get their own interests accommodated in policy. At the national level, the actors/organizations identified included those within the line ministries of agriculture and environment, development partners, academicians, NGOs, civil society and the private sector. We hold that the various actors in different ways have supported and enabled the research process, making possible the collaborative implementation of the PAR project. This culminated in a periodic information brochure presenting timely and relevant weather and agricultural advice information to stakeholders. PAR researchers together with SAIPRO were proactive in coming up with the research idea based on their long experience of agricultural development in Same District, hence gaining the upper hand in its initiation and implementation. The interests of officials of both the Ministry of Agriculture and the Division of the Environments are based on their policy objectives, so they would work towards achieving them. The director of national food security focuses on ensuring food security under the challenging changing climatic conditions. Similarly, the mandate of the VPO Division of the Environment is to facilitate policy proposals which support effective implementation of national climate-change policies and agreements. Government actors therefore occupy an advantageous position of influence when initiating a policy agenda. The interests of development partners vary. Some, like Norway and Sweden, are interested in supporting the management of Tanzania's natural resources, as they have done for over four decades; and in 2009 Norway signed a partnership agreement on climate and forests with the government of Tanzania. Other development actors, including the International Development Agency (IDA), the International Fund for Agriculture Development (IFAD), the Danish International Development Agency (DANIDA) and the Japan International Cooperation Agency (JICA), are long-standing supporters of agricultural sector development, and wish to consolidate the gains so far achieved by addressing the likely impacts of climate change on the sector.

At the local level, the Same District Commissioner gave the researchers the required support to conduct their studies. He deemed the project important because his district was increasingly suffering from chronic food shortages, and that it was his expectation that the research would succeed and translate into increased agricultural productivity and increased food security. We note, however, that the sustainability of such support is dependent on the individual qualities of the district commissioner as a leader as well as his continued presence in the position. Should this change, for instance if he were to be transferred, this support might cease, thus jeopardizing the process. During our meeting, he explained the measures he was taking to ensure sustainability – the creation of a system intended to contain all information about the project and plans. This, he hoped, would facilitate institutional memory and assist future office-holders in continuing with the implementation of project results.

Farmers, for their part, embraced the PAR project as a possible way out of their predicament of failing crops and abject poverty due to drought. As one farmer in Same stated,

> Changes in rainfall patterns are increasing in frequency, making it difficult for us to farm effectively. Last season I planted maize and the rains did not fall as expected, resulting into everything being destroyed. I could not replant when we were advised to do so because I lacked the inputs and money…

A villager from the group of traditional weather forecasters explained, 'The TMA forecasts are at zonal level. They don't take the local situation into consideration; so forecasts differ from place to place within the same zone, and traditional forecasts work well locally but not in zonal dimension.'

SAIPRO had worked with farmers in Same District for over a decade to combat food insecurity. It would like to see its long-term involvement and efforts in supporting the rural communities to achieve food security translated into success through climate-change adaptation. Suppliers of agricultural inputs are business-oriented actors who feel that project success would serve as an important planning tool in helping to minimize losses arising from stocking wrong agricultural inputs and at the wrong time. Late supply of inputs can mean that working capital is tied up in huge amounts of unsold farming inputs.

By matching narratives to the interests of these various actors, we can identify a convergence point where success can be achieved. Multiple interests do come with underlying power dynamics being played out among actors in the quest for getting their interests recognized and included in the research and policy process. Power relations are manifested in various forms, maintained through formal and informal rules of participation in policy spaces. The deliberative democracy approach legitimatizes democratic spaces formed by non-state actors.

Power relations between actors are not universal, in that there is no single most-powerful actor among the five categories of actors considered in this chapter: government agencies, development partners, civil society, private sector and local communities. Power relations – informal ones in particular – are mobile, depending on the point of engagement between the different actors and the issue at stake. For instance, a deliberation convened by the PAR researchers in collaboration with SAIPRO at the outset of the project automatically gave more power to the experts and the NGO as key actors, with the government and civil society on the opposite ends. Policy spaces facilitated by the academic groups tend to place more emphasis on the role of research for policy-making, giving less power to government agencies. Similarly, at Policy Forum breakfast debates, civil society actors commonly assume more powers and freedoms, with government agencies usually on the defensive side. Local communities, such as those involved in the farm field school at Bangalala as traditional weather forecasters, felt more empowered and capable of engaging with other actors through spaces organized within their locations and using less technical language. When asked about their opinion on their participation in the weather forecasting exercise they said that the project had given them a platform from which to show what they can do to help the community, and had enhanced their credibility and therefore respect among the community. By contrast, the strict rules in the development partners' group meetings and the government's agricultural sector consultative groups automatically restrict effective participation by other actors, especially local people and civil society, due to their design and special language, location and the fact that one must be invited.

These multiple and shifting power relations between actors are crucial for effective deliberation (Habermas 1989). They are a necessary condition for actors to freely and confidently demonstrate their capabilities and make their voices heard. Through these different spaces and power relations, particular groups may initiate action on the basis of lessons learnt in the process of implementing the research project, without having to wait for a top-down government policy process or campaign to encourage the adoption of new practices based on the research.

Making the case for continuous and multiple target stakeholder engagement

In this section we discuss the results of interactions between researchers and other stakeholders in the policy process, highlighting notable achievements as well as gaps. The interaction between PAR researchers and actors had, by the time of this study, resulted in several tangible outcomes at various levels. These include the establishment of a collaborative working relationship between the TMA, district agricultural extension officers, NGOs, traditional weather forecasters and input providers, in a way never seen before in Same and with considerable success. The nature of the collaboration that emerged when researchers, agricultural extension officers, weather forecasters (modern and traditional), input suppliers and members of the farming community came together was indeed unprecedented, as commented on by the farmers. The interaction offered a practical and effective means for collaboration, exchange and implementation of ideas, as well as facilitating coordination, enhanced trust among actors, a sense of recognition, respect and inclusion by actors. Here it should be mentioned that traditional weather forecasters had not been part of the initial research design: they were included through the engagement processes at the village level at an early stage of the research process. Another milestone was the establishment of a DMF by the Same District Council, facilitated by the PAR researchers. This collaboration has, as noted, resulted in an information brochure prepared by the DMF and issued at intervals, containing weather information forecasts and expert farming advice. Its distribution to farmers is facilitated by SAIPRO and agricultural extension officers. Because of the importance of weather information in planning of agricultural activities, the district TMA officer was co-opted into the highest district policy body – the full council – for the first time. These are encouraging achievements at the local level. The analysis provides insights into how PAR actors could not only seek to influence the policy process more effectively, but also be influenced in their research to make it more relevant to the intended stakeholders, at the national and local levels.

However, it should be noted that the success of this collaborative effort is heavily dependent on the robustness of the weather forecasts, made among other factors.[2] Another challenge in the policy process concerns its implementation. This hinges on the national- and district-level representative actors and/or institutions that attend meetings intended to bring actors together. Those who attend the meetings as representatives of their institutions may sometimes change from one meeting to the next, causing inconsistency and loss of continuity and institutional memory of the proceedings. This is even more detrimental to the intended objective of the interactive policy process, where there are no reporting-back mechanisms for representatives to their relevant organizations after the meetings.

Summary and recommendations

In this chapter we set out to investigate whether the politics of interactions during the policy process in terms of power relations and interests of relevant actors can help to narrow the gap between research and policy, and action for improved adaptation to climate change. We analysed whether and how PAR as an incremental research model can provide a departure from the 'business as usual' research processes. We deployed the three-lens approach to identify the actors involved in generating and applying knowledge for climate-change adaptation, their interests and the narratives employed in advancing their arguments, and the power relations among actors interacting through multiple policy spaces from the local to the national.

The answer to our research question proved to be in the affirmative: participation and interactions of relevant actors during the research process in terms of their interests and power relations can indeed contribute towards narrowing the gap, to facilitate better adaptation to climate change. The fact that there existed both shared narratives among actors as well as competing and contested narratives was a good starting point for multi-actor negotiation regarding climate-change adaptation in the agricultural sector. The existence of multiple competing and contested narratives and power relations between actors further served to test and strengthen the various interests and positions of different actors. Moreover, the use of existing and newly created multiple policy spaces, from the local to national level, has provided important avenues for individual and collaborative strategizing aimed at addressing adaptation to the impacts of climate change in Tanzania. The recognition and involvement of these actors from different levels in a collaborative participatory manner helped to make clear their interests, and contributed to making project outcomes more relevant to their interests and positions. Involving relevant stakeholders at the district/local government level through the farm field school and the DMF promoted ownership of the research process as well as results, and facilitated more rapid adoption of research recommendations.

One important prerequisite for the success of the RPA process is getting robust results from research. If the scientific information generated by the researchers and disseminated to users is incorrect or too vague, this may lead to considerable scepticism and loss of trust, with far-reaching consequences. This underscores the importance of getting the science right.

We argue that, while it is important to ultimately provide evidence for informed decision and policy-making at the national level, there is also a need to strategically engage actors from the national as well as the local levels of governance. This involvement should be participatory and should strive to adopt means that can enhance participation by local actors. In this way, the research process can achieve multiple policy contributions at the national and local levels while receiving feedback for improving the research process itself. In addition, research evidence is translated more rapidly into development practice when the relevant actors themselves apply the newly acquired knowledge. This RPA process has rejected the 'business as usual' practice where policy-oriented research is implemented by experts, with minimal participation of stakeholders, and results are disseminated to potential users *ex post facto*, denying the main stakeholders a chance to participate in making the research relevant to them by learning from it, influencing and owning it.

Our main recommendation to researchers on adaptation to climate change in particular, and development policy-oriented action research in general, is to design their research activity by identifying and continuously involving relevant actors at all levels, from the national to the local, in their differing categories and roles, such as policy-makers, civil servants, private sector and civil society. Technical research activity, coupled with a policy-process analysis involving actors' roles, their interests and power relations, will help to clarify the dynamics of interaction within the community and enable realistic and practical measures to be crafted, for effective policy implementation through faster translation of research results into development activities.

Acknowledgements

The authors would like to thank anonymous reviewers of this manuscript for providing constructive comments which helped improve the chapter. We also thank the CCAA project financed by the IDRC of Canada and coordinated by IDS, at the University of Sussex (UK), for support for the research upon which this chapter is based. We thank also Drs Oswald Mashindano and Natu Mwamba, who participated in the Tanza Kesho Consult (TKC) project team for the RPA research, and TKC staff members, for facilitating the research process.

Notes

1 Capacity to act, to exercise agency and to realize the potential of rights, citizenship or voice (Gaventa 2006)
2 Currently, only the weather forecasts by the meteorology experts are used and recognized as official weather information, although the traditional weather forecasts are also presented and discussed at the DMF, until more work on documenting the traditional knowledge on weather forecasting indicators is done. Interestingly, thus far, the forecasts have been close to the meteorology experts' forecasts.

References

Aaserud, M., Lewin, S., Innvaer, S., Paulsen, E.J., Dahlgren, A.T., Trommald, M., Duley, L., Zwarenstein, M. and Oxman, A.D. (2005). 'Translating research into policy and practice in developing countries: a case study of magnesium sulphate for pre-eclampsia'. *BMC Health Service Research* 5, 68.

Broad, K. and Agrawala, S. (2001). 'Integrating climate forecasts and societal decision making: challenges to an emergent boundary organization science'. *Technology & Human Values* 26(Autumn): 454–477.

Chinsinga, B., Mangani, R. and Mvula, P. (2011). 'The political economy of adaptation through crop diversification in Malawi'. *IDS Bulletin* 42(3), 110–117.

Eriksen, S. and Lind, J. (2009). 'Adaptation as a political process: adjusting to drought and conflict in Kenya's drylands'. *Environmental Management* 43(5), 817–835.

Fischer, G., Shah, M., Tubiello, F.N. and Van Velhuizen, H. (2005). 'Socio-economic and climate change impacts on agriculture: an integrated assessment, 1990–2080'. *Philosophical Transactions of the Royal Society B* 360, 2067–2083.

Gaventa, J. (2006). 'Finding the spaces for change: a power analysis'. *IDS Bulletin* 37(6), 23–33.

Habermas, Jürgen (1989). *The structural transformation of the public sphere: An inquiry into the category of bourgeois society.* Translated by Thomas Burger with the assistance of Frederick Lawrence. Cambridge, MA: The MIT Press.

Hanney, S.R., Gonzales-Block, M.A., Buxton, M.J. and Kogan, M. (2003). 'The utilization of health research in policy-making: concepts, examples and methods of assessment'. *Health Research Policy and Systems 2003,1:2.* BioMed Central. http://www.health-policy-systems.com/content/1/1/2 (accessed 15 November 2012).

Hennink, M. and Stephenson, R. (2005). 'Using research to inform health policy: barriers and strategies in developing countries'. *Journal of Health Communication* 10(2), 163–180.

Hepworth, N. D. (2010). *Climate change vulnerability and adaptation preparedness in Tanzania.* Nairobi: Heinrich Böll Foundation.

IDS (2006). *Understanding policy processes; a review of IDS research on the environment.* Knowledge, Technology and Society Team, Institute of Development Studies, University of Sussex.

IDS (2011). *Research to policy for adaptation: Linking African researchers with adaptation policy spaces.* Submitted by the Institute of Development Studies, Brighton, UK, with KIPPRA, Kenya, Chancellor College, Malawi, and TanzaKesho, Tanzania. Final Technical Report covering the period of March 2009–February 2011. Brighton: University of Sussex.

Ingram, K.T., Roncoli, C. and Kirshen, P. (2002). 'Opportunities and constraints for farmers of West Africa to use seasonal precipitation forecasts with Burkina Faso as a case study'. *Agricultural Systems* 74, 331–349.

IPCC (2007). 'Annex II: Glossary'. In Alphons P. M. Baede, Paul van der Linden, Aviel Verbruggen (eds). *Climate Change 2007: Full Report.* Cambridge: Cambridge University Press.

Keeley, J. and Scoones, I. (2003). *Understanding environmental policy processes: cases from Africa.* London: Earthscan/James and James.

Kulindwa, K. (2011). *Weather information for risk management, vulnerability reduction and agricultural productivity improvement in Tanzania.* Report prepared by TanzaKesho Consult Ltd (TKC), submitted to IDS Sussex.

Lukes, S. (2005). *Power: a radical view.* New York: Palgrave Macmillan.

Mendelsohn, R. (2000). 'Efficient adaptation to climate change'. *Climatic Change* 45, 583–600.

Naess, L.O., Polack, E. and Chisinga, B. (2011). 'Bridging research and policy processes for climate change adaptation'. *IDS Bulletin* 42(3), 97–103.

O'Brien, K.L. and Vogel, H.C. (eds) (2003). *Coping with climate variability: the use of seasonal climate forecasts in Southern Africa*. Aldershot: Ashgate.

Roncoli,C., Kirshen, P., Ingram, K. and Flitcroft, I. (2000). 'Opportunities and constraints to using seasonal precipitation forecasting to improve agricultural production systems and livelihood security in the Sahel-Sudan region: A case study of Burkina Faso, CFAR-Phase I' in *Proceedings of the International Forum on Climate Prediction, Agriculture, and Development*. Palisades, NY: International Research Institute for Climate Predictions

Roncoli, C., Kirshen, P., Ingram, K. and Jost, C. (2001). *Burkina Faso – Integrating indigenous and scientific rainfall forecasting*. Washington, DC: World Bank.

Stephenson, R. and Hennink, M. (2002). *Moving beyond research to influence policy: barriers and strategies for developing countries*. Opportunity and Choices Working Papers 2002/05, University of Southampton.

SUA (2009). *Managing risk, reducing vulnerability and enhancing agricultural productivity under a changing climate*. Progress Report, IDRC Grant Number: 104146001. Morogoro, Tanzania: Sokoine University of Agriculture.

UNEP (2011). *Livelihood security: climate change, migration and conflict in the Sahel*. Nairobi: United Nations Environment Programme (UNEP).

URT (United Republic of Tanzania) (2003). *Initial national communication under the United Nations Framework Convention on Climate Change (UNFCCC)*. Dar es salaam: Vice President's Office.

Vogel, C. and O'Brien, K. (2006). 'Who can eat information? Examining the effectiveness of seasonal climate forecasts and regional climate-risk management strategies'. *Climate Research* 33,111–122.

Walt, G. (1994). 'How far does research influence policy?' *European Journal of Public Health* 4, 233–235.

Ziervogel, G. and Zermoglio, F. (2009). 'Climate change scenarios and the development of adaptation strategies in Africa: challenges and opportunities'. *Climate Research* 40, 133–146.

14

LIMITED ROOM FOR MANOEUVRE

Indigenous peoples and climate-change adaptation strategies

Jakob Kronik and Jennifer Hays

Introduction

Indigenous peoples, estimated at about 380 million people in the world today, are identified primarily by their unique ways of life and connection to land – and also by their marginalized status in the states in which they live. Although their subsistence strategies are generally low-impact, recent research on the social dimensions of climate change has found that indigenous peoples remain among the most vulnerable to the effects of climate change; furthermore, they are often vulnerable in specific ways (Kronik and Verner 2010a; Mearns and Norton 2010; Nakashima et al. 2012). In addition to being highly dependent upon natural resources, as are other rural peoples, the very conditions necessary for the reproduction of their culture, social structures, and knowledge systems are also under severe pressure.

Since the beginning of this century, increasing attention has been paid to the importance of indigenous/local knowledge systems in the face of climate change – both for indigenous communities themselves and for human adaptation in general (Roncoli, Crane and Orlove 2009; Kronik 2010; Crate 2011; Pearce et al. 2011). Early work in this area has focused principally on the Arctic, an area particularly vulnerable to the already-measureable changes in temperature and sea level (see for example Cruikshank 2001; Krupnik and Jolly 2002; Nichols et al. 2004), and on observations of Andean ethnoclimatology (Orlove et al. 2000, 2002).

The research described in this chapter has found that, although local and indigenous knowledge plays an important role in adaptation strategies, this knowledge – and not least the institutions and practices necessary to maintain, develop, discard and disseminate it – are often overlooked or not fully understood in development strategies aimed at reducing risks. However, while the importance and sophistication of indigenous knowledge is well-documented, by itself it can rarely provide an effective approach to adaptation to climate change and variability today, because of the increasingly limited room for manoeuvre accorded to indigenous peoples.

Room for manoeuvre

In their exploration of the concept 'room for manoeuvre' Clay and Schaefer (1984) focus primarily on policy analysis and discourses, and how these, in conjunction with the narrowing of opportunities, can define and limit room for manoeuvre. In our use of the concept, we include people's ability to strategically exploit livelihood options, in particular for those peoples who rely heavily on natural resource use, such as small-scale rain-fed agriculture, pastoralism, and hunting and gathering. Climate change reduces general environmental opportunities in a direct way for such communities (Tol et al. 2000). There are clear parameters that constrain people's ability to react and adapt to changing conditions – limitations on water, arable land, or wild plant and animal resources, for example. As resource availability changes, people move to exploit other options; the more options open to them, the more 'room for manoeuvre' they have. Greater economic space and a capacity for diversification beyond and within natural-resource use, as well as political and legal space that allows for innovations and responses developed locally to evolve, increase the 'room' available for communities and individuals (see also Thomas and Twyman 2005).

Encompassed within this understanding of 'room for manoeuvre' are thus the notions both of constraints inherent in a given situation and the ability to move within – and potentially to contest – these constraints. *Room for manoeuvre*, understood as the opportunity to change plans or choose among different ways of doing something, entails several characteristics of *social resilience*, like the ability to adapt in the face of external social, political, or environmental stresses and disturbances (Luthar and Cicchetti 2000; Adger 2000) and the existing ecological and social preconditions for effective adaptive capacity that enable individuals or groups to respond to climate change (Olsson and Folke 2001; Brooks 2003; Berkhout et al. 2006). However, it is not only exogenous forces that limit societal adaptation – at least equally limiting can be the values, perceptions, processes and power structures within a society (Adger et al. 2009). To support more effective adaptation, a holistic approach is needed – one that takes into consideration the internal as well as external factors that drive and limit effective adaptation. In our understanding and use of it, the concept of *room for manoeuvre* better captures the decision-making processes that take place *within* local social-ecological systems, including cultural practices, institutions and knowledge systems, and relates these to opportunity structures and sources of pressure. At the individual, household, community and society levels, people, families and social groups need to adapt to actual and future consequences of climate change. Although climate change, and adaptation to it, tends to be described as sequential and pre-deterministic ('changes under way': O'Brien 2011), in fact, at each level, actors are influenced by particular goals (Berkhout et al. 2006), interests, worldviews, opportunity structures and other factors.

One way to respond to the questions posed by this volume is to ask: how can approaches to climate-change adaptation and mitigation serve to maximize people's 'room for manoeuvre' as individuals and as groups? Are current approaches to development doing this or are they – perhaps unintentionally – squeezing indigenous peoples into even tighter spaces? This chapter argues that the success of indigenous peoples' adaptation strategies depends not only upon the quality and appropriateness of cultural, technological and other practices, cultural institutions, and knowledge systems and their ability to interpret climate-change phenomena, but also upon the socio-economic, legal and political *room for manoeuvre* that they experience – and on their ability to challenge this space by exercising their rights.

To examine these dynamics, the studies described here looked at four overarching factors, as outlined in Table 14.2. The first is the *general impact of climate change upon indigenous peoples* – the specific ways in which climate change is altering earlier conditions in the regions in which the cases are situated. The second factor is the *vulnerability context*, which concerns how these changes relate to the particular livelihood strategies of indigenous groups, which often vary significantly from those of other sectors of the population. Following Adger (2006), we see vulnerability as a function of susceptibility to harm, sensitivity and lack of capacity to adapt. The third factor is the *livelihood and adaptation strategies of indigenous peoples* – including the nature of cultural practices and social structures that form a key component of maintaining access to resources.

In this chapter, we focus specifically on the fourth factor – how *current shifts in climate and environmental conditions are related to shifts in livelihood strategies, and cultural and social contexts* – and how all these are part of a broader global context in which multiple pressures influence people's room for manoeuvre in the face of drastic changes. We argue that 'development as usual', by focusing only on certain aspects of indigenous peoples' vulnerability, not only fails to address some of the most important limitations that they are confronting in the face of climate change (Adger et al. 2009), but in some cases serves to limit their room for manoeuvre even more. Further, a constructive approach to development must be based on a rights-based approach. We describe what this means in relation to indigenous peoples and climate change.

Assets and adaptation strategies in different vulnerability contexts

The research described in this chapter forms part of larger projects investigating indigenous peoples' adaptations to climate change (Kronik and Verner 2010a, 2010b; Kronik 2011; Kronik and Clément 2013). Here, the focus is on the interrelationships between various dimensions of adaptation to climate change as they relate to five particular case studies conducted from 2008 to 2011: three in Bolivia, Colombia and Nicaragua, 2008–2009 (Kronik and Verner 2010a, 2010b), and two among semi-nomadic Bedu of Syria and Tunisia (Kronik 2011; Kronik and Clément 2013), as outlined in Table 14.2. The original aim of the research was to understand if – and how – indigenous people perceive climate-change phenomena; how and why their access to livelihood assets have been affected over time; and what opportunities and obstacles they experience in the face of climatic and other changes. To capture the complexity of the impacts of climate change on poor and vulnerable indigenous communities, as well as their responses, communities were selected from larger eco-regions, in order to cover a wide range of climate-change phenomena, as well as social, cultural, economic and political contexts.

To facilitate systematic analysis of these complex variables in different contexts, the research described here has drawn on key elements of anthropological, social, institutional and environmental analysis, with a particular focus on capturing and understanding local vulnerability contexts, livelihood strategies and assets as well as opportunity structures. The conceptual framework and ensuing fieldwork strategy is inspired by the Sustainable Livelihoods Framework (SLF, from Department for International Development 2001), which seeks to provide a holistic and comprehensive picture of local livelihood options and how they change over time, as well as a picture of the complexity within a local situation. The Department for International Development's (DfID's) original SLF framework includes *human, social, natural, financial* and *physical* capitals, and provides a tool for assessing these interrelated influences on people's livelihood security. The SLF approach puts people (as opposed to resources) at the centre of the analysis; however, it lacks a comprehensive understanding of cultural assets, or *cultural capital* (as framed by Bourdieu 1973, 1986). In addition, the SLF was not developed to address climate-change issues, and the attention to human resources is often inadequate (Morse et al. 2009; de Haan 2012).

For the study described here, the SLF framework was used with modifications partially addressing some of these criticisms. *Cultural capital* was added, in order to fully consider this dimension of livelihood – which (as described below) is particularly important for indigenous peoples. Furthermore, institutional and environmental mapping and climate-change scenario exercises were developed and supplemented by open-ended inquiry and semi-structured interviews based on a series of concrete and ranked closed questions, with respondents selected through maximum variation sampling. The number, place, time and criteria of these questionnaires are presented in Table 14.1.

The data regarding key livelihood indicators collected among the Bedu in Syria and Tunisia are presented in Figures 14.1 and 14.2, graphed along with perceptions of drought intensity, shown as mean values for 2010 and 1990. As these figures show, the most important changes to the Bedu livelihood system can be explained in terms of decreasing access to social, cultural, financial and environmental assets.

TABLE 14.1   Overview of interviews

Bolivian Andes	38 with Aymara indigenous peoples from eight communities in the Titicaca Lake basin (3,810–4,200 metres above sea level) and Afro-Bolivian and Aymara (4,660–1,240 metres above sea level), April 2008.
Colombian Amazon	34 in 10 communities with indigenous peoples, distinguishing vicinity to urban centres in the Amazon, dependency on mature versus secondary forest, access to markets, public health and education, May 2008.
Nicaragua's Carib coast	41 with mestizo, Miskitu and Garífuna in three coastal and inland communities of the Atlantic Autonomous Regions of Nicaragua, March–April 2008.
Syrian steppe	63 in 15 communities with Bedu men and women in Palmyra ($N=32$), Raqqa ($N=28$) and Aleppo ($N=3$) regions of the Syrian Rangeland, the Badia, December 2010.
Tunisia arid, semi-arid	51 interviews in 20 communities and sites in the central and southern regions of Tunisia, February 2010 and November 2011.

This revised framework proved extremely useful for identifying and illuminating how different aspects of climate change and climatic variability affect people's assets, their livelihood strategies and livelihood outcomes, and ultimately their wellbeing. It also helps to identify entry points for increasing wellbeing, reducing vulnerability, improving food security, raising income or achieving more sustainable use of resources.

Case studies from Latin America, North Africa and the Middle East

Until recently, relatively little attention has been given to indigenous peoples' perceptions of, and reactions to climate change and variability in Latin America (notable exceptions include Orlove et al. 2000, 2002). The case studies referred to in this chapter illustrate the various types and levels of impacts from various climate-change phenomena and other contributing factors in specific eco-geographical regions, the variation in the strategies used to respond to these changes, and the constraints facing the people.

North Africa and the Middle East are particularly vulnerable to global warming, and Bedu populations in this region experience specific forms of vulnerability (the common Western term 'Bedouin' is actually a double plural; in the Arabic language they refer to themselves as *Bedu*). The Bedu continue to practise semi-nomadic pastoralism, though combined with the temporary migration of many family members (typically in the agricultural and construction sectors) in order to earn cash. Although they do not necessarily self-identify

TABLE 14.2 Climate change, impact, vulnerability context, livelihood and adaptation strategies and room for manoeuvre in the five case studies

Place	Bolivian Andes	Colombian Amazon	Nicaragua's Carib coast	Syrian steppe	Central and Southern Tunisia
People	Aymara	Uitane and Uitoto	Miskitu and Garífuna	Bedu	Bedu
Climate change[a] and general impact	Increasing mean temperatures, causing drought and glacier retreat; variations in seasonality marked by changes in patterns and intensity of rainfall, hailstorms, frosts.	Severe climatic changes occurring in the Amazon,[b] causing drought and irregularity of seasons, profoundly affecting tropical forests.	Increased intensity of extreme events, especially hurricanes, endangering entire ecosystems, and human lives. Gradual warming and acidification of the oceans threaten the viability of the mangroves and coral reefs.	Greatest warming in summer night-time temperatures, widespread warming of average and extreme minimum temperatures across the region, increased water scarcity.	Combined impact of increasing temperatures, reduced and variable precipitation and sea-level rise (increasing salt-water intrusion) are projected to increase water scarcity and frequency of droughts and flooding.
Vulnerability context: climate change impact on livelihood assets	Losses in production and profitability due to: increase in crop and livestock pests and diseases; reduced ability to produce small-scale crops due to shorter season and fewer viable locations; loss of wildlife. People express resignation to the situation and fatalism about the future of life as they know it.	Previously regular flow of rivers now out of sync with seasonal events that directly affect livelihoods; unprecedented changes in the timing of frosts, heavy rains and drought disrupt the agricultural cycle. Traditional knowledge and practices become obsolete under the influence of climate change; severe social, political and institutional impact.	Increased intensity of storms decreases access to natural resources (fisheries, forests, arable land), and destroys infrastructure and personal belongings. Greatly increased vulnerability of communities relying on mangroves and coral reefs.	Disturbances in seasonal rhythms affect the viability of crop and livestock production and the availability of food foraged from the wild. Longer dry seasons reduce the length of time that herds can graze the land. Loss of social and cultural assets that are vital to migration as a livelihood strategy and to community resilience.	Seasonal cycle of arboriculture species is affected by temperature peaks. Oases are particularly vulnerable to water scarcity and encroachment by urban areas and sand dunes. Feelings of shame and uncertainty make people unwilling to ask for loans as they would have done in the past.

Place	Bolivian Andes	Colombian Amazon	Nicaragua's Carib coast	Syrian steppe	Central and Southern Tunisia
People	Aymara	Uinane and Uitoto	Miskitu and Garífuna	Bedu	Bedu
Principal livelihood and adaptation strategies	Agriculture, including arable crop and livestock production. Crop production for own consumption and for sale at local markets. Livestock include sheep and cattle, llamas and alpacas. Cheese, wool, meat and livestock, are sold at the local markets. Experimentation is based on new knowledge in conjunction with the revival of older practices and customs (such as the use of canals in the lakeshore zone).	Indigenous peoples derive their livelihood mostly from forest and water resources, and depend heavily on fish and game for protein. Those close to urban centres depend on secondary forest horticulture, cash crops, commercial fishing, wage labour, tourism and sale of handicrafts. Greater access to markets, public health and education services can provide a buffer against many effects of climate change; those groups living more traditional lifestyles have less access to this.	Heavy direct and indirect reliance on natural resources for all populations. The Miskitu occupy all the productive zones in the area (fishing, agriculture and hunting) and are in a better position to adapt livelihood strategies in the event of hurricanes and storms. The Garífuna mostly inhabit the coastal and lagoon areas and are more vulnerable to climate change and other external influences.	Migratory pastoralism and herd management; intricate use of natural resources and livelihood strategies heavily dependent on cultural, human and social assets. Changes to their livelihood system are attributed to decreasing access to social, cultural, financial and environmental (grazing) assets. Diminishing size of sheep flocks, and the resultant lack of financial resources and collateral, have undermined social networks, community relationships and close kinship relations.	Pastoralism and agriculture, some using the traditional three-tier cultivation system of the oases. Vulnerability is intrinsically related to the diversity of income sources available to the family. Oases particularly vulnerable to degradation stemming from water scarcity and encroachment by urban areas and sand dunes, pressures that will be exacerbated by climate change.

continued …

Table 14.2 continued

Place	Bolivian Andes	Colombian Amazon	Nicaragua's Carib coast	Syrian steppe	Central and Southern Tunisia
People	Aymara	Uinane and Uitoto	Miskitu and Garífuna	Bedu	Bedu
Room for manoeuvre: possibilities and limitations	Strong indigenist and workers' unions translate into political, social and legal opportunities; however, barriers with the labour/indigenist government combine with pressure on resources from mineral and hydrocarbon extraction. Concessions negotiated with private and state-owned extractive industries are in areas coinciding with mega-biodiversity hotspots and indigenous territorial rights.[c] All these limit options for response in the face of environmental change.	Effects of climate change exacerbated by deforestation and forest fragmentation. In the western part of the Colombian Amazon, colonization, armed conflict, illegal crops and deforestation have had a great impact. Integration into mainstream culture can provide a buffer against the effects of climate change that groups pursuing more traditional lifestyles do not have; however, the latter have more control of forest resources. In the eastern part, indigenous peoples maintain greater territorial and cultural autonomy, but are more vulnerable to climate change variations.	After the hurricane flattened large tracts of forest, agricultural settlers had easy access to colonize indigenous territories, as a result limiting control over resources and ability to draw on certain adaptation strategies. Coastal communities are slowly inserting themselves into an incipient market economy (shrimp, lobster, timber, artisanal gold mining), giving them access to building materials and other goods that can make them better prepared to withstand climate change and variability events – but more vulnerable to market forces.	Traditional herding has become a business, contributing to a current lack of resilience to long-term droughts. Increased numbers of sheep necessitate investment in equipment and growth in the size of flocks results in increased pressure on grazing and water resources. Competition over edible vegetation leads to increased dependence on loans from feed traders. Reserves established by the government to protect fauna and flora decrease the natural grazing areas. The combined effect is a severe limitation of options.	Expansion of crops and arboriculture, overgrazing and detrimental use of machinery all play a role in land degradation. Respondents explained their lack of social capital in terms of shame and uncertainty about being able to repay debt. Social, financial and environmental livelihood assets are closely connected, and relevant to how people respond to changing conditions.

Notes
a Climate change scenarios and data from Christensen in Kronik and Verner (2010a), and Wilby 2010 and 2013.
b IPCC 2001 and 2007. Various phenomena including the El Niño Southern Oscillation, la Niña, winds from the Antarctic, and warming from the Caribbean.
c Humpreys-Bebbington 2012, p.140; Bebbington 2012, pp.14–15.

as indigenous people, the Bedu share many of the characteristics noted in the introduction. They have unique traditional management systems, well adapted to the harsh conditions of the desert, and which are affected in specific ways by climate change, as described in the following section.

In these studies, using the modified version of the SLF, it was found that, while indigenous peoples often have rich strategies for managing change, the foundations of their cultural practices and institutions are under severe pressure from a range of other sources, including cultural, social and political pressures; this is particularly well-illustrated by the data from the Bedu studies, as described in the following section. *Knowledge* also emerges as a key asset linking social, cultural and environmental assets, as described below. The presence of globalized development agents in every corner of the world exerts a combined pressure from the multiple stressors of global development. In some cases, climate change is not the most important stressor, but rather the trigger that makes apparent the limited space available to indigenous peoples for putting into practice their adaptation strategies. Strengthening local climate-change adaptation capacity is not only about improving technical adaptation skills, but also involves some fundamental changes, such as the application of their rights to land and resources, and access to consultation and free prior and informed consent; we return to this point later in the chapter.

How processes of change limit room for manoeuvre

In all areas studied, people were able to identify several interrelated ways in which environmental changes were affecting their livelihood options. For example, high-elevation Andean farmers described many processes of change that they have seen since the turn of this century: water scarcity caused by the melting of glaciers and alterations in the hydrological regime; increases in the intensity of rains and temperatures; hailstorms and frosts at unusual times of the year, and droughts. The changes put food security at risk and affect social stability, health and psychological wellbeing (see Table 14.2). Such findings in all areas confirm a fairly straightforward cause/effect relationship between changing climatic conditions and livelihood.

A particularly important finding of this research was that climate change is also having extreme effects on social structures – on the formal and informal institutions, networks, relations of trust, kinship and friendship that constitute the 'glue' of rural communities and have crucial implications for livelihoods. In indigenous communities, leadership structures, social norms and exchange networks are all connected in intricate resource-management systems, which in turn depend greatly upon cultural cohesion. To maintain their livelihood strategies, they depend heavily on cultural, human and social assets, including traditional knowledge systems and institutions that are now under increased stress – making them especially vulnerable to climate variability.[1] These knowledge systems are based on experiments with nature, juxtaposed with a stock of knowledge developed over time and passed on through generations. The ability to predict and interpret natural phenomena, including weather conditions, has been vital for survival and wellbeing and has also been instrumental in the development of local cultural practices, social structures, trust and authority.

The societal production of knowledge about nature's cycles has led to certain cultural practices. These practices, in turn, have resulted in the creation of *cultural capital* (see Bourdieu 1986), which includes the forms of knowledge described above, related skills and competences (including social competence), and the social generation of this knowledge – the practices and rituals through which it is reproduced. Structures are developed around these practices and rituals, with varying levels of formalization, including leadership and authority structures, education (or knowledge transmission) strategies and religious practices. These cultural institutions serve to maintain, develop and dispute information, allowing for continuity as well as flexibility to incorporate new information and adapt to the changing circumstances that are heavily affecting natural resource management, community health and coping abilities.

Advocating for an understanding of the concept of *room for manoeuvre* is a call for recognition of the need – and possibility – for creating the right kinds of spaces. It is also a call for an approach that can facilitate appropriate, innovative and creative adaptation, with principles of equity and social justice at its core (Thomas and Twyman 2005). Although the factors described interweave in varied ways, it is possible to identify some general patterns in how climate change and variability are impacting indigenous peoples around the globe. The sub-sections below describe the social and cultural impacts of climate change; the role of *knowledge* in adaptation to climate change; and how all these interact with other pressures experienced by indigenous peoples. We highlight some specific ways in which the cultural capital of indigenous peoples is connected to their resources, and how changes in these constrain the room for manoeuvre.

Social and cultural impacts of climate change

In Latin America, the elders and traditional leaders of the communities visited expressed virtually unanimous concern that the direct effects of climate change are not the only consequences – that social, political and institutional upheavals are also devastating. Traditionally seen as local experts, these formal or informal leaders lose credibility when climatic conditions become impossible to predict. Unprecedented changes in the timing of frost, heavy rain and drought are disrupting the agricultural cycle in ways that no one would ever have imagined. When such events recur, it undermines ritual practices, joint social memory and the ability of elders to maintain social order. Such social upheaval, in turn, leads to serious consequences for local governance of natural resources. When traditional authorities cannot guarantee abundance and prosperity, their status falls. People look elsewhere for solutions to their problems – by seeking other bodies of knowledge, and by migrating.

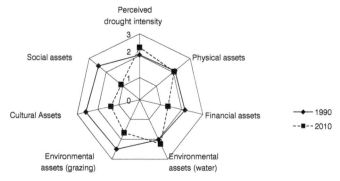

FIGURE 14.1 Bedu perceptions of drought intensity and assessments of key livelihood strategy indicators, Badia steppe region of Syria, 1990 and 2010 (source: fieldwork by Jakob Kronik, December 2010, 63 Bedu men and women in the Syrian Rangeland, the Badia)

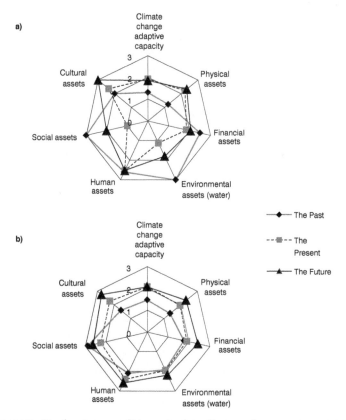

FIGURE 14.2 Production conditions under climate change pressure: perceived climate change adaptive capacity and livelihood assets, in semi-arid and arid Tunisia (a) areas with access to oasis management and (b) without access to oasis management (source: fieldwork by Jakob Kronik, November 2011, 51 men and women in the central and southern regions of Tunisia)

The relationship between cultural and social assets, livelihood and climate change was illustrated particularly clearly in the Bedu studies. In Syria, we found that the diminishing size of sheep flocks, and the resultant lack of financial resources and collateral, had undermined social networks, relationships to the communities and even close kinship relations. Local social security systems have been severely affected, including access to monetary and non-monetary loans from relatives and friends. While the Bedu interviewed all remained calm and controlled, and were always hospitable, their answers and rankings made clear the degree and significance of gradual social disintegration.

Respondents in Tunisia explained this lack of social capital in terms of shame and uncertainty. The most pronounced difference was found among respondents who had access to oases, as reflected in Figure 14.2a. They indicated that they would not ask friends for loans because they felt ashamed, because they would not be able to pay back the loan or because few people have anything to lend. Although other respondents indicated that they still had access to such loans from family and friends through their networks, the present is referred to with much uncertainty. It became evident that social, financial and environmental livelihood assets are closely connected, and relevant to how people respond to changing conditions (Kronik and Clément 2013).

The importance of knowledge in climate-change adaptation

Abundant research has shown that indigenous peoples are keen observers of natural rhythms, and that they have accumulated a large and sophisticated body of knowledge about annual seasonal cycles (Conklin 1954; Lévi-Strauss 1962; Nelson 1969; Johannes 1978; Chambers 1983; Descola 1994; Agrawal 1995; Rhoades and Nazarea 1999). More recent works have argued that recognizing this knowledge is vital for an understanding of climate change, and its impacts (Orlove et al. 2000; Krupnik and Jolly 2002; Robledo et al. 2004; Kronik 2010). The implications, however, are not always straightforward and vary greatly in different situations, according to multiple factors. In some places, this knowledge is becoming obsolete under the influence of climate change, and people's daily practices are increasingly failing to respond effectively to changes in precipitation patterns. The research described in this chapter found strong links between indigenous knowledge, adaptive strategies, leadership and social cohesion. Indigenous peoples emerge as those people *most aware of* and *most vulnerable to* climate-change phenomena and their effects (Kronik and Verner 2010a).

Pastoralism, forest horticulture and rain-fed agricultural livelihood systems all depend on predictable and well-established seasons. Indigenous peoples possess a strong awareness of complex ecological indexes of the timing of seasons. These natural rhythms serve to regulate, defend and maintain life by governing the interrelation of water, wind, heat, marine and terrestrial fauna, insects, wild fruits and human activities. Key informants in all regions visited report that the natural signs and indicators are now perceived as alarming. Seasons have become irregular; for example the once-regular flow and descent of Amazon rivers is now out of synchronicity with seasonal events (such as the ripening of wild fruits) that directly affect livelihoods (Kronik and Verner 2010a; see also Table 14.2).

While knowledge plays a critical role, it is also important to recognize that access to traditionally exploited natural resources does not always correlate with more effective adaptation, or more room for manoeuvre. For example, this research found that in the northern Amazon, the peoples most affected by climate change and variability are often those who have greater territorial autonomy, who derive their livelihood mostly from forest and water resources, and maintain an active and engaged ritual life. Such peoples place great value on the ecological diversity of mature forests. They depend heavily on fish and game for protein, maintaining health through their own means and knowledge, and their livelihoods rest on their abilities to interpret regular natural cycles and to act accordingly. Although they do have contact with mainstream society, participate moderately in the market economy, and have access to public health and education services, much of their livelihood depends on their traditional knowledge and management of natural resources. When these are threatened through climate change, the associated social and cultural breakdown is more destructive than it is for those who have greater access to other options. For example, communities in the Amazon and the Nicaraguan coastal indigenous communities are slowly inserting themselves into an incipient market economy with activities linked to national or international markets (artisanal gold mining, timber, shrimp, lobster), giving them access to building materials and other goods that can make them better prepared to withstand climate change and variability events. Having access to these alternatives when forest and agricultural options are compromised has allowed some 'room for manoeuvre'; without this, the chances of successful adaptation would be extremely limited and migration would increasingly become the sole option.

At the same time, this integration into markets can also have problematic aspects. It can increase dependency, and it influences people towards development models based on maximizing the extraction of resources – a model that, as we argue below, often increases people's vulnerability. In many cases, having secure rights and access to land would itself provide a buffer to this vulnerability (see section on adaptation, below). Thus the role of knowledge of the local environment as a cultural resource is crucial, but not always straightforward. It is very important not to oversimplify this. A limited focus on either the promotion of traditional knowledge *or* incorporation into local, national and global economies at the expense of the other will ultimately restrict options. 'Room for manoeuvre' emphasizes the need to recognize the advantages and disadvantages of various options, and to find solutions that maximize the 'space' in which people can respond to changing climatic – and political, economic and social – conditions.

Interrelated factors limiting room for manoeuvre

As noted, climate change is one of many factors affecting various assets; it leads to both direct and indirect changes in livelihood options, which are also combined with multiple other sources of pressure. In Nicaragua, for example, large tracts of formerly impenetrable forests that once prevented settlers and ranchers from accessing indigenous lands have been flattened by hurricanes; as a result, there has been encroachment into these lands (Kronik and Verner 2010a). Partially as a result of this encroachment, indigenous people interviewed in the two regions along the Caribbean coast said that 20 years after Hurricane Joan in 1988, they had yet to fully recover the abundance of forest resources (especially lumber and wildlife) that existed before the hurricane. In contrast, fish catches and agricultural yields regained their pre-hurricane levels within one to five years, making these livelihood options more resilient.

Changing economic models encouraged by the state and by international development agents have also had a profound influence. In Syria, while herding is a traditional occupation, it has also become a business. The effects of this transition contribute to the current lack of resilience to long-term droughts. Having greater numbers of sheep makes it both possible and necessary to invest in tractors and trucks to transport drinking water for the huge flocks, and expanding flocks put increased pressure on grazing and water resources. With competition over every straw of edible vegetation has come greater dependence on feed traders.

In Tunisia, natural rangeland degradation in the central and southern interior regions is mainly the result of decreasing and more-variable rainfall, coupled with the eradication of natural vegetation and subsequent erosion. According to Tunisian regional technical staff from the Gafsa, Médenine and Tataouine, the expansion of crops and arboriculture, overgrazing and detrimental use of machinery all play a role in land degradation. Traditionally, Tunisian agro-pastoralists would build fodder reserves during wet years to sustain their herds in dry years. Successive years of drought combined with increasing herd sizes and high-input agriculture result in a downward spiral of decreasing economic and social options as herders sell off herds at reduced prices to meet the increase in production costs.

Adaptation within limited room for manoeuvre – threats and opportunities

The over-exploitation of resources described above in the Bedu cases is not isolated, but part of the current development model based on maximizing the extraction of resources. Indigenous peoples' room for manoeuvre in adapting to climate change and in maintaining their livelihood options is severely limited by increasing pressure on resources, combined with a range of economic, political and social pressures, including wars and other political struggles, as well as the large-scale destruction of natural resources. Below we briefly describe the role of extractive industries. The types of situations we describe have been a primary focus of the global indigenous rights movement. Rights-based approaches have been fully outlined in international indigenous rights mechanisms, most clearly in the United Nations Declaration on the Rights of Indigenous Peoples (UNDRIP; United Nations 2007) and the International Labour Organization (ILO) Convention 169 on the international rights of indigenous and tribal peoples (ILO 1989). Particularly relevant is the principle of *free, prior and informed consent* (FPIC). Article 32 of UNDRIP states that FPIC must be obtained 'prior to the approval of any project affecting their land or territories and other resources, particularly in connection with the development, utilization or exploitation of mineral, water or other resources' (United Nations 2007). Below we briefly highlight some of the most relevant aspects of indigenous rights as they relate to the arguments in this chapter.

Extractive industries and development as usual

Extractive industries exert increasing pressure on indigenous peoples' livelihoods, access to assets and available options to react and adapt. Unprecedented growth in countries like China, India and Brazil, and the wish of governments to decrease dependence on energy sources from unstable regions (Asif and Muneer 2007) has increased the hunt for the resources required to fuel productive industries and for land for agro-industries to produce meat and biofuels for the growing middle classes (Dauvergne and Neville 2010). The search for and exploitation of oil, gases, coal, copper, rare earth minerals, timber, biofuel crops and pasture lands has increased the presence of powerful actors, and the attention of governments and international agencies in even the most remote areas of the world.

For governments and national actors, the extraction of these resources may be seen as a source necessary for funding social programmes (as in Andean and Amazonian countries), and bringing prosperity. However, as documented by numerous authors (see Bourgouin 2011:525; Bebbington 2012) extractive industries (especially mining, hydrocarbon and timber) have generally not lived up to the expectations of increased prosperity, poverty reduction and growth through long-term investments in socio-economic development. Quite the contrary: the direct impact on lands and territories, the tendency of extractive industries to bypass human rights concerns, and the impact on livelihoods (as through contamination of water and soil) have had serious negative impacts on peoples dependent on natural resources. In the Andean region, large parts of lands designated as protected areas and as indigenous territories have been identified as having the potential for mineral and hydrocarbon extraction, and concessions have been negotiated with private and state-owned extractive industries (Humpreys-Bebbington 2012). Several of these sub-soil resource-rich areas coincide with mega-biodiversity hotspots (Finley-Brook 2007;

UNDP 2010; Rieckmann et al. 2011) and major water drainage basins of the region. Some of these overlap with indigenous territorial rights (Bebbington 2012).

In some of these situations, as in the Bagua of Perú and in the case of El Territorio Indígena y Parque Nacional Isiboro-Secure (TIPNIS) of the Bolivian Andes, major conflicts between indigenous peoples and the government have divided indigenous groups. (In both cases, the governments have had to review their positions and respond to international criticisms.) Such situations increase the vulnerability of indigenous peoples, both because of the conflict and because they decrease land security. In the tropical forests of the Colombian Amazon, the profound effects of climate change are exacerbated by deforestation and forest fragmentation. Indigenous peoples find their livelihoods and options for responding to climate change and variability profoundly affected by extensive cattle ranching, agro-industrial palms and illegal coca plantations. This movement has been spurred by political violence, prompting people to leave violent areas, and by the appetite for land on which to grow industrial and/or illegal crops.

In principle, indigenous peoples have the right to fully participate in decisions affecting their livelihood. However, in practice, the extraction of natural and mineral resources, as well as the over-exploitation of grazing, water, land and other natural resources, is intimately linked to international and national political and commercial dynamics that are beyond the reach of the peoples described here. Decisions made at the highest levels of international policy and the political economy carry the potential to resolve long-term sustainable development issues for poverty-ridden regions; however, recent studies show that this is rarely the case. Instead, the presence of extractive industries seems to make local communities 'more polarized, more uncertain, more worried, and still poor' (Bebbington 2012:225; see also Bourgouin 2011). This is 'development as usual' at its worst.

Indigenous rights-based development

Indigenous peoples are not necessarily in principle opposed to extractive industries. There are many cases of their active engagement in mining or other extractive activities, or willingness to negotiate ways in which these can take place while still securing the long-term social, cultural and environmental conditions for sustained indigenous livelihoods. However, this is possible only when there is real consultation, capacity building and institutional strengthening of the parties involved – including local and national institutions and their civil servants – and with the full participation of indigenous peoples in decision-making processes. This is emphasized in the principles of indigenous rights, which also embody a deep recognition of communal rights to land and resources. An approach that adheres to these internationally agreed-upon principles, and addresses the structural causes of poverty and vulnerability, would allow the possibility of alternative strategies for development, rather than focusing primarily on incorporation into mainstream economies. It would also emphasize the rights of peoples to choose the most appropriate strategies for themselves. Some communities may opt for entry into the mainstream economy, as indicated in Table 14.2 and discussed above. Where people have secure rights and access to land, they can often more effectively negotiate their participation in wider economies, and they are far less vulnerable as a result.

Discussion

As pointed out in the introduction and other chapters of this book, predominant development patterns do not appear to be mitigating climate change or reducing vulnerability but in fact leading in the opposite direction. There are several ways in which this happens. One overarching pattern is the tendency to address climate change as an isolated factor – rather than as one of many factors and linked to holistic subsistence strategies and social structures. Another is the tendency for development initiatives to focus on development models that are ultimately a part of the problem. This chapter has highlighted some of the specific ways that both of these play out for indigenous peoples.

Changing circumstances change long-established ways in which people relate to one another – as individuals, communities and cultures. Social changes like crumbling leadership and authority structures, and increasing unwillingness to ask for help from neighbours, can have as much impact on people's livelihood possibilities as the environmental impacts. However, such social changes are often difficult to foresee and are not taken into consideration in predictive models about the impact of climate change. Turner et al. (2008) argue that losses that are indirect and cumulative are more likely to be invisible in environmental decision-making. Such losses typically include cultural and lifestyle losses, loss of identity, self-determination and influence, and changes which for those experiencing it represent 'loss of order in the world' (ibid. p.4). Similarly, Adger et al. (2009) argue that specific losses of physical places involve the loss of attendant cultural and social significance that is often invisible to the prevailing calculus. This is supported by our data as well.

Furthermore, the goals and by-products of international and national 'development' often have severe impacts on indigenous peoples' ability to adapt to climate change. These can be both direct (such as the reduction or contamination of natural resources on which they rely, through mining or other extractive industries), and indirect (such as the pressure placed upon indigenous communities when their neighbours exploit their land and resources in order to respond to market demands). All these pressures serve to limit indigenous peoples' room for manoeuvre as they struggle to respond to new constraints in the face of changing climatic conditions.

People's room for manoeuvre can be improved through various concrete measures, such as providing access to information about the global and national dimensions of climate change and culturally sensitive institutional support from international development agencies, government offices and surrounding society. However, strengthening indigenous peoples' local adaptive capacity requires more than good practices and meteorological information. Numerous cases have shown that, without secure rights to land and resources, and the capacity to fulfil livelihood aspirations in the territories they inhabit, this assistance will rarely suffice. A conscious approach to climate-change adaptation and mitigation must include an understanding of how knowledge systems have developed under different circumstances, and with different drivers and processes.

In some cases, indigenous peoples have the relevant knowledge and socio-cultural structures to respond to climate-change phenomena, but have been restricted by other limiting factors – largely imposed through extractive industries and government policies. In the Colombian Amazon case, the exercise of rights and autonomy, and the practice of cultural livelihood strategies, have proven to be no guarantee for successful adaptation. Likewise, in the case of Syrian Bedu herders and Tunisian oasis managers, official development policies and failure to regulate the market have resulted in increased pressure on environmental resources, and has restricted local livelihood options and increased vulnerability. Some indigenous peoples are compelled to change their livelihood so dramatically that they lose vital conditions for the development and reproduction of their culture. Indigenous knowledge, institutions and practices may be rendered superfluous, lost or temporarily forgotten – thereby reducing the adaptive potential for these communities, and perhaps for humanity in general.

A strengthening of current international efforts to protect indigenous peoples' rights to land and natural resources is crucial. This includes models of collective ownership, consultation and participation based on rights, and regulatory frameworks such as ILO Convention 169. It will involve strengthening the inclusion of representatives from indigenous peoples' organizations in national and local climate-change adaptation initiatives. Participatory processes need to be implemented at the design stage and followed through to the final project evaluation. Adaptation measures should focus equally on processes and outcomes, applying participatory strategies to build resilience, including the strengthening of strategies and increased support to help indigenous communities adapt to climate change and variability, acknowledging the diversity of their livelihood strategies and the role and efficiency of their cultural institutions. This support must be rooted in, or at a minimum must respect, the traditional knowledge of indigenous peoples and the co-development of technology and technical advice on agricultural practices that are culturally, environmentally and economically appropriate.

This chapter has argued that indigenous peoples' ability to adapt to local environmental changes resulting from global climate change is constrained both by a changing set of parameters (rainfall, temperature, water and soil quality, game availability) and also by pressures on social, political and economic dimensions which limit their room for manoeuvre in adapting to changes. We have argued from a poverty alleviation perspective, and from a rights-based perspective. The concept of 'room for manoeuvre' can also be applied on a larger scale. Although the effects of climate change may be the most severe for indigenous peoples and others with land-based livelihood strategies living in highly vulnerable ecosystems, they will ultimately affect all of humanity. As we struggle to adapt our responses to the changes that are already happening and to prepare for those that are predicted, it would be wise to recognize the value of the myriad of human adaptive strategies – knowledge, skills, means of transmission, economies, social structures – that have been honed in local environments over centuries. Failure to allow for these strategies to develop is tantamount to limiting our own room for manoeuvre when adapting to changing conditions on the planet that we all share. The world needs approaches to climate change and to 'development' that are viewed, not as unidirectional aid, but as a collaborative exercise focused on improving the wellbeing of all peoples, and recognizing the value of the diversity of human knowledge, culture and adaptive strategies in a rapidly-changing world.

Note

1 The IPCC's Fourth Assessment Report (IPCC 2007) points out that there are 'sharp differences across regions and those in the weakest economic position are often the most vulnerable to climate change and are frequently the most susceptible to climate-related damages, especially when they face multiple stresses. There is increasing evidence of greater vulnerability of specific groups.'

References

Adger, W. N. (2000). 'Social and ecological resilience: are they related?' *Progress in Human Geography*, 24 (3), 347–364.

Adger, W. N. (2006). 'Vulnerability', *Global Environmental Change*, 16, 268–281.

Adger, N. W., Dessai, S., Goulden, M., Hulme, M., Lorenzoni, I., Nelson, D.R., Naess, L.O., Wolf, J. and Wreford, A. (2009). 'Are there social limits to adaptation to climate change?', *Climatic Change*, 93, 335–354.

Agrawal, A. (1995). 'Dismantling the divide between indigenous and scientific knowledge', *Development and Change*, 26 (3), 413–439.

Asif, M. and Muneer, T. (2007). 'Energy supply, its demand and security issues for developed and emerging economies', *Renewable and Sustainable Energy Reviews*, 11 (7), 1388–1413.

Bebbington, A. (ed.) (2012). *Social Conflict, Economic Development and Extractive Industry*. New York: Routledge.

Berkhout, F., Hertin, J. and Gann, D.M. (2006). 'Learning to adapt: organisational adaptation to climate change impacts'. *Climate Change* 78:135–156.

Bourdieu, P. (1973). 'Cultural reproduction and social reproduction', in R. Brown (ed.) *Knowledge, Education and Cultural Change*. London: Willmer Brothers Ltd.

Bourdieu, P. (1986). 'The forms of capital', in J. G. Richardson (ed.) *Handbook of Theory and Research for the Sociology of Education*, 241–258. New York: Greenwood Press.

Bourgouin, F. (2011). 'The politics of large-scale mining in Africa: domestic policy, donors, and global economic processes', *Journal of the Southern African Institute of Mining and Metallurgy*, 111, 525–529.

Brooks, N. (2003). 'Vulnerability, risk and adaptation: a conceptual framework', Tyndall Centre Working Paper 38. Tyndall Centre for Climate Change Research, University of East Anglia, Norwich.

Chambers, R. (1983). *Rural Development: Putting the Last First*. London, New York: Longmans Scientific and Technical Publishers.

Clay, E. and Schaefer, B. (1984). *Room for Manoeuvre: An Exploration of Public Policy in Agriculture and Rural Development*. London: Heinemann.

Conklin, H. C. (1954). *The Relation of Hanunoo Culture to the Plant World*. New Haven, CT: Yale University Press.

Crate, S. A. (2011). 'Climate and culture: anthropology in the era of contemporary climate change', *Annual Review of Anthropology*, 40, 75–94.

Cruikshank, J. (2001). 'Glaciers and climate change: perspectives from oral tradition', *Arctic*, 54 (4), 377–393.

Dauvergne, P. and Neville, K. J. (2010). 'Forests, food, and fuel in the tropics: the uneven social and ecological consequences of the emerging political economy of biofuels', *Journal of Peasant Studies*, 37 (4), 631–660.

De Haan, L. J. (2012). 'The livelihood approach: a critical exploration', *Erdkunde*, 6(4), 345–357.

Department for International Development (DfID) (2001). *Sustainable Livelihoods Guidance Sheet*, http://www.nssd.net/pdf/sectiont.pdf.

Descola, P. (1994). *In the society of nature: A native ecology in Amazonia*. Cambridge: Cambridge University Press.

Finley-Brook, M. (2007). 'Green neoliberal space: the Mesoamerican biological corridor', *Journal of Latin American Geography*, 6 (1), 101–124.

Humpreys-Bebbington, D. (2012). 'State–indigenous tensions over hydrocarbon expansion in the Bolivian Chaco', in A. Bebbington (ed.) *Social Conflict, Economic Development and Extractive Industry*, 134–152. New York: Routledge.

International Labour Organization (1989). *Convention Concerning Indigenous and Tribal Peoples in Independent Countries* (ILO No. 169), http://www.ilo.org/ilolex/cgi-lex/convde.pl?C169

IPCC (2001). Third Assessment Report 'Climate Change 2001', http://www.grida.no/publications/other/ipcc_tar/?src=/climate/ipcc_tar/.

IPCC (2007). Summary for Policymakers. Climate Change 2007: The Physical Science Basis. Contribution of Working Group I to the Fourth Assessment Report of the Intergovernmental Panel on Climate Change, in S.D. Solomon et al. (eds) *Contribution of Working Group I to the Fourth Assessment Report of the Intergovernmental Panel on Climate Change*. Cambridge: Cambridge University Press, http://www.ipcc.ch/publications_and_data/ar4/syr/en/spms5.html

Johannes, R. E. (1978). 'Traditional marine conservation methods in Oceania', *Annual Review of Ecology and Systematics*, 9, 349–364.

Kronik, J. (2010). *Living Knowledge – The Making of Knowledge about Biodiversity among Indigenous Peoples in the Colombian Amazon*, PhD dissertation. Saarbrücken: Lambert Academic Publishing.

Kronik, J. (2011). 'The Bedu of the Syrian Rangeland', in D. Verner (ed.) *Syria Rural Development in a Changing Climate. Increasing Resilience of Income, Well-Being, and Vulnerable Communities*, 98–118 (unpublished due to the ongoing conflict).

Kronik, J. and Clément, V. (2013). 'Socioeconomic effects of climate change in Central and Southern Tunisia', In D. Verner (ed.) *Adaptation to a changing climate in the Arab countries: a case for adaptation governance and leadership in building climate resilience*, 79–120. New York: World Bank.

Kronik, J. and Verner, D. (2010a). *Indigenous Peoples and Climate Change in Latin America and the Caribbean*. Washington, DC: World Bank.

Kronik, J. and Verner, D. (2010b). 'The role of indigenous knowledge in crafting adaptation and mitigation strategies to climate change in Latin America', in R. Mearns and A. Norton (eds) *Social Dimensions of Climate Change: Equity and Vulnerability in a Warming World*, 145–172. Washington, DC: World Bank.

Krupnik, I. and Jolly, D. (eds) (2002). *The Earth is Faster Now: Indigenous Observations of Arctic Environmental Change*. Fairbanks, AL: Arctic Research Consortium of the United States (ARCUS).

Lévi-Strauss, Claude (1962). *La pensée sauvage*. Paris: Plon.

Luthar, S. S. and Cicchetti, D. (2000). 'The construct of resilience: implications for interventions and social policies', *Development and Psychopathology*, 12 (4), 857–885.

Mearns, R. and Norton, A. (eds) (2010). *Social Dimensions of Climate Change: Equity and Vulnerability in a Warming World*. New Frontiers of Social Policy. Washington, DC: World Bank.

Ministère de l'Environnement et du Développement Durable (DGEQV)/FEM/PNUD (2008). *Etude de la vulnérabilité environnementale et socio-économique du littoral tunisien face à une élévation accélérée des niveaux de la mer dues aux changements climatiques et identification d'une stratégie d'adaptation*. Tunis: Ministère de l'Environnement et du Développement Durable.

Morse, S., McNamara, N. and Acholo, M. (2009). *Sustainable Livelihood Approach: A Critical Analysis of Theory and Practice*. Geographical Paper No. 189, University of Reading.

Nakashima, D. J., Galloway McLean, K., Thulstrup, H. D., Ramos Castillo, A. and Rubis, J. T. (2012). *Weathering Uncertainty: Traditional Knowledge for Climate Change Assessment and Adaptation*. Paris: UNESCO/ Darwin: UNU.

Nelson, R.K. (1969). *Hunters of the Northern Ice*. Chicago, IL: University of Chicago Press.

Nichols, T., Berkes, F., Jolly, D., Snow, N.B. and the Community of Sachs Harbour. (2004). 'Climate change and sea ice: local observations from the Canadian western Arctic', *Arctic*, 57: 68–79.

O'Brien, K. (2011). 'Global environmental change II: from adaptation to deliberate transformation', *Progress in Human Geography*, 1–10. http://phg.sagepub.com/content/early/2011/11/10/0309132511425767.

Olsson, P. and Folke, C. (2001). 'Local ecological knowledge and institutional dynamics for ecosystem management: a study of Lake Racken Watershed, Sweden', *Ecosystems*, 4 (2), 85–104.

Orlove, B., Chiang, J. C. H. and Cane, M. (2000). 'Forecasting Andean rainfall and crop yield from the influence of El Nino on Pleiades visibility', *Nature*, 403, 69–71.

Orlove, B., Chiang, J. C. H. and Cane, M. (2002). 'Ethnoclimatology in the Andes', *American Scientist*, 90, 428–435.

Pearce, T., Ford, J. D., Duerden, F., Smit, B., Andrachuk, M., Berrange-Ford, L. and Smith, T. (2011). 'Advancing adaptation planning for climate change in the Inuvialuit Settlement Region (ISR): a review and critique', *Regional Environmental Change*, 11, 1–17.

Rhoades, R. F. and Nazarea, V. D. (1999). 'Local management of biodiversity in traditional agroecosystems', in W. W. Collins and C. O. Qualset (eds) *Biodiversity in Agroecosystems*, 215–236. Boca Raton, FL: CRC Press.

Rieckmann, M., Adomßent, M., Härdtle, W. and Aguirre, P. (2011). 'Sustainable development and conservation of biodiversity hotspots in Latin America: the case of Ecuador', *Biodiversity Hotspots 2011*, 435–452. Springer Link.

Robledo, C., Fischler, M. and Patiño, A. (2004). 'Increasing the resilience of hillside communities in Bolivia: has vulnerability to climate change been reduced as a result of previous sustainable development cooperation?' *Mountain Research and Development*, 24 (1), 14–18.

Roncoli, C., Crane, T. and Orlove, B. (2009). 'Fielding climate change in cultural anthropology', in S. A. Crate and M. Nuttall (eds) *Anthropology Climate Change From Encounters to Actions*, 87–115. Walnut Creek, CA: Coast Press.

Thomas, D.S.G. and Twyman, C. (2005). 'Equity and justice in climate change adaptation amongst natural-resource-dependent societies', *Global Environmental Change*, 15, 115–124.

Tol, R. S. J., Fankhauser, S., Richels, R. G. and Smith, J. B. (2000). *How Much Damage Will Climate Change Do? Recent Estimate, Research Unit Stability and Global Change*, Centre for Marine and Climate Research, Hamburg University, Hamburg.

Turner, N. J., Gregory, R., Brooks, C., Failing, L. and Satterfield, T. (2008). 'From invisibility to transparency: identifying the implications', *Ecology and Society*, 13 (2), 7, http://www.ecologyandsociety.org/vol13/iss2/art7/.

UNDP (2010). *Biodiversity and Ecosystems: Why these are important for Sustained Growth and Equity in Latin America and the Caribbean Colombia: Status Report*. New York: UNDP.

United Nations (2007). *United Nations Declaration on the Rights of Indigenous Peoples* (UNDRIP). UN General Assembly Resolution 61/295, http://www.un.org/esa/socdev/unpfii/en/drip.html.

Wilby, R. L. (2010). *Climate Change Projections and Downscaling for Jordan, Lebanon and Syria*, Draft Synthesis Report, World Bank background paper. New York: World Bank.

Wilby, R. L. (2013). 'A synthesis of climate change scenarios and impacts', in D. Verner (ed.) *Tunisia in a Changing Climate: Assessment and Actions for Increased Resilience and Development*, New York: Sustainable Development Department, Middle East and North Africa Region of the World Bank.

15

CLIMATE CHANGE AND DEVELOPMENT

Adaptation through transformation

Karen O'Brien, Siri Eriksen, Tor Håkon Inderberg and Linda Sygna

The climate is changing, and there is growing recognition that the social dimensions of vulnerability and adaptation must be brought to the forefront of development policies and practices. Until now, adaptation has most often been approached in an instrumental way, by promoting technical interventions and capacity-building programmes aimed at helping people to minimize the risks associated with specific climate impacts, such as higher temperatures, more frequent droughts, larger storm surges or greater flooding. Adaptation is being absorbed into prevailing approaches to development and 'mainstreamed' into every domain and sector, from health, education and governance, to agriculture, water resources, infrastructure and many others. In fact, the unprecedented risks associated with climate change – in the near term but especially in the long term – indicate that transformation of development itself may be required if we are to deal with climate change impacts, adaptation and vulnerability, along with other social and ecological challenges.

The lessons from this book show that integrating adaptation into 'development as usual' often ignores the real factors that drive vulnerability – like the interests, power relations and structural factors that systemically perpetuate uneven development, environmental degradation, resource depletion and growing global emissions of greenhouse gases. The cases presented in this book show that adaptation is a question of much more than a set of projects or interventions to reduce specific impacts of climate change: adaptation includes the dynamics of living with change while also transforming the processes that have contributed to vulnerability in the first place. Adaptation is a social process that involves empowering individuals, households, communities, institutions and states, not only to react and respond to the impacts of change, but also to challenge the drivers of risk and promote alternative pathways to development.

This broader view of adaptation does not mean that technical measures are unnecessary or unimportant. Drought-resistant seeds, flood barriers, early warning systems, water harvesting, malaria control, drip irrigation and other such responses will remain critical to the lives and livelihoods of millions. Nonetheless, such measures are not sufficient for dealing with vulnerability in a world where development processes themselves often contribute to inequities and reduce response options, all the while moving the world along a trajectory towards dangerous climate change. The current high-risk situation means that it is time to consider how adaptation, mitigation and development can, together, contribute to shared outcomes that are equitable, ethical and sustainable.

In this concluding chapter, we consider what it means to transform paradigms and practices so as to enhance social equity, resilience and environmental integrity in the face of climate change. Synthesizing some key findings about adaptation from the chapters, we present a framework or 'roadmap' that can be used to navigate what Pelling (2011) refers to as 'adaptation as transformation'. We begin by discussing why transformative responses to adaptation and development are necessary. Focusing on three interacting spheres of transformation, we describe entry points for adaptations that reduce vulnerability and contribute to outcomes for global sustainability, of which social equity, resilience and environmental integrity can be considered key components. Finally, we offer some recommendations relevant to those working in bilateral and multilateral aid organizations, in governments and in research, all of whom can potentially play key roles in promoting the transformation of paradigms and practices in support of global sustainability.

Transformative responses

Sustainable development is a challenging social goal in a world where planetary boundaries are being crossed, and where thresholds and tipping points threaten the stability of important Earth system processes (Lenton et al. 2008; Rockström et al. 2009). A new language of the Anthropocene is being developed to describe an era where human development pathways have had, and will continue to have, considerable influence on the conditions under which humanity may or may not thrive (Steffen, Rockström and Costanza 2011). Science has increasingly shown that the future climate will depend on the types of development pathways that are pursued (IPCC 2013, 2014a, 2014b). Within this context, climate-resilient pathways are defined as sustainable development trajectories that combine adaptation and mitigation to reduce climate change and its impacts (Denton et al. 2014). These are seen as iterative and evolving processes for managing change within complex systems. Importantly, they draw attention to the need for transformative responses, rather than merely continuation of 'business as usual' (ibid.). Thus, adaptation becomes part of a larger process that includes transforming development paradigms and practices alike to achieve global sustainability.

Adaptation may take various forms, from vulnerability and exposure reduction on the ground through development planning and practices, to transformations within the practical, political and personal spheres of change (IPCC 2014b, see SPM Box 1). Transformative responses apply to all the actions, decisions, approaches or behaviours that contribute to systemic changes. They often involve questioning the assumptions underlying incremental, business-as-usual approaches and dominant paradigms (O'Brien 2012). However, the concept also introduces some confusion, as transformation may be approached in various ways: for example, there are two different but related facets of transformation currently discussed in the literature on adaptation to climate change.

On the one hand, there is a growing recognition that some impacts of climate change will call for transformational adaptations that will alter the nature, composition and/or location of activities or systems (Brooks et al. 2011; Kates, Travis and Wilbanks 2012; Denton et al. 2014). As described by Kates et al. (2012), transformational adaptations may involve actions or interventions on a larger scale, with greater intensity and over longer time-periods than previously experienced. Examples here may include large-scale resettlement of coastal communities, or a dramatic expansion of permaculture and agro-ecology to feed a growing population sustainably in a changing climate. They may also involve adaptations that are new or unprecedented in a given region or system, such as new types of risk-sharing arrangements. Finally, they may involve adaptations that transform places or lead to a shift in the location of activities. Transformational adaptations are already evident in response to climate variability and change (Marshall et al. 2012). It is expected that they will be increasingly necessary in some locations and for marginalized or vulnerable groups. They may include, for example, a shift to pastoralism or agropastoral production systems in areas that become too dry for agriculture (Brooks et al. 2011), particularly if climate change mitigation efforts are unsuccessful (Denton et al. 2014). Importantly, this type of transformation is a proactive or reactive response to the impacts of climate change, which are more or less taken as a given.

On the other hand, however, a transformational approach to adaptation can also focus on reducing risk and vulnerability in the first place (Pelling 2011). This type of adaptation involves altering the very systems and structures, economic and social relations, and beliefs and behaviour that contribute to both climate change and vulnerability (O'Brien 2012; Denton et al. 2014). Rather than directly responding to the impacts of climate change, such transformations seek to alter the risks to global development and human security posed by climate change. As Pelling (2011: 86) puts it, transformation is concerned with the wider and less visible roots of vulnerability: 'These lie in social, cultural, economic and political spheres, often overlapping and interacting. They are difficult to grasp, yet felt nonetheless. They may be so omnipresent that they become naturalized; assumed to be part of the way the world is.' Such transformations are not politically neutral: they inevitably challenge or promote some interests and agendas over others (Smith and Stirling 2010). All the same, transformations of development pathways towards more equitable and sustainable low-carbon societies stand out as among the most important adaptations to climate change, not least because this approach can reduce the need for transformational adaptations to the *impacts* of climate change.

Attempts are underway to identify criteria and metrics for assessing transformation, and there is a frantic search for good examples of transformational adaptation. It is important to recognize that, like adaptation, transformation is more often a process than an event, and often takes place amidst uncertainty – as when old ways of doing things no longer yield the desired results but new ways of being and doing are not yet clear or firmly established. That said, conditions can be created to support transformations that are both equitable and sustainable, and these are often linked to learning, leadership, empowerment and collaboration within and across groups, sectors, organizations or institutions (O'Brien 2012; Denton et al. 2014). Recognizing that the concept of transformation can be difficult to operationalize, below we explore what adaptation can look like through the lens of transformation.

Adaptation through a transformation lens

The case studies in this book offer valuable insights for reducing vulnerability through adaptation. Many of them emphasize the importance of taking the local context and key features of local adaptive capacity as a starting point in designing interventions, recognizing that these contexts are situated in larger structures and societal processes that drive vulnerability. While this may seem an obvious point, adaptation planning has often been criticized for being delinked from local needs and vulnerability contexts, and for approaching community adaptation in a very simplistic manner (Pelling 2011; Vincent, Næss and Goulden 2013; Schipper et al. 2014; Nightingale this volume). There have been calls for more integrated and holistic approaches to adaptation (O'Brien and Hochachka 2010; Schipper et al. 2014); the challenge now lies in putting such approaches into practice.

A broader and more holistic approach to adaptation involves viewing the vulnerability context from different spatial and temporal perspectives, but also through different lenses of abstraction. Below, we refer to three interacting 'spheres' of transformation to show how adaptation processes may be transformed to support climate-resilient pathways for sustainable development. These spheres – the practical, political and personal (see Figure 15.1.) – can be considered as distinct yet related arenas or entry points for realizing change (Sharma 2007; O'Brien and Sygna 2013; Denton et al. 2014). Underlying this conceptualization is the recognition that the technical and behavioural changes essential to successful adaptation are almost always facilitated or constrained by larger systems and structures, which are in turn influenced by diverse and often competing worldviews and paradigms (O'Brien and Sygna 2013). We now turn to each of the three spheres, and how the findings of the chapters in this book relate to them.

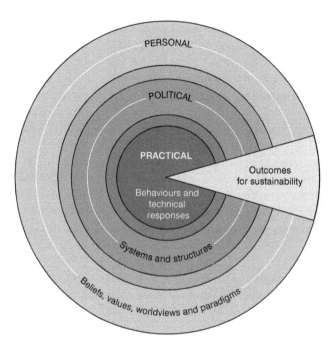

FIGURE 15.1   The three spheres of transformation (source: based on O'Brien and Sygna 2013)

Adaptation through transformation in the practical sphere

Adaptation strategies and measures tend to focus on the practical sphere, where outcomes and benefits can be most easily measured and monitored. Adaptation in the practical spheres includes a wide array of technical responses, ranging from hard structural measures, such as infrastructure and technological projects, to soft policy measures such as climate services and behavioural changes. Trærup and Christiansen (this volume) distinguish three types of technologies for adaptation: hardware, software and orgware. Their research acknowledges the importance of hardware (e.g. capital-intensive technologies), but also of software such as improved soil, water and crop management, ecosystem restoration, improved extension services. Moreover, orgware relating to the ownership and institutional arrangements, such as the creation of water-user associations and adaptive co-management schemes, is recognized as important to adaptation processes.

We have seen how adaptation in the practical sphere has been an important goal of many development interventions. This is exemplified by efforts in the Lake Victoria Basin to optimize timing for planting crops through the use of climate information accessed by mobile phones, develop drought- and flood-resistant seed varieties, or improve carbon storage in soils (Gabrielsson Chapter 5). It can be seen in the Afar State Adaptation Plan of Action's emphasis on de-stocking herds, restricting free-range grazing, and introducing mixed farming and irrigation systems (Eriksen and Marin Chapter 10). Further, it can be seen in efforts to provide information about climate change and culturally sensitive institutional support to indigenous groups (Kronik and Hays Chapter 14).

Nonetheless, practical adaptations alone are insufficient to reduce vulnerability in the short and long term: indeed, in some cases they actually increase vulnerability, such as in the case of Afar pastoralists (Eriksen and Marin Chapter 10). Wamsler and Brink (Chapter 4) have shown how institutional assistance can reinforce existing inequalities and create barriers to adaptation: for instance, projects that depend on materials and technologies that cannot be locally maintained, or that deprive people of their livelihoods, or offer a false sense of security. Ochieng et al. (this volume) point out that the heavy promotion of environmental conservation measures often overlooks the significance of other activities, such as charcoal production, as important adaptive measures and livelihoods.

The success or failure of these responses in relation to the goal of achieving climate-resilient pathways for sustainable development often depends on the larger political, economic and cultural systems and structures in which these solutions are embedded. As Nightingale (this volume, p. 226) argues, 'when absolute quantities and qualities of resources and services are assumed to determine the ability of people to adapt, it masks how those with greater social and political power can harness negative changes in resources for their own benefit'. Although many adaptation efforts claim to take the local context *into account*, taking the vulnerability context as a *starting point* for development actions demands a deeper understanding of how various structural processes and relations, such as gender and power relations, political processes and inequities, act to generate vulnerability.

Adaptation through transformation in the political sphere

The success or failure of actions in the practical sphere – including their feasibility and scalability – is influenced by systems and structures that constitute the political sphere of transformation. It is here that decisions, rules, regulations, agreements, incentives and priorities are discussed, negotiated, decided or imposed, and where some interests and agendas are prioritized over others. It is in the political sphere that problems and solutions are identified and defined, and conflicts of interest may emerge; it is also here that collective action and social movements can make a difference by directly challenging the systems and structures that contribute to vulnerability.

Many of the chapters in this volume support the need for greater attention to adaptation within the political sphere. For example, Nightingale's research (see Chapter 12) in Nepal shows that access to and control over assets and resources are primarily constrained by political and economic factors, not biophysical or environmental ones. The findings of Nagoda and Eriksen (this volume) support this, as they show that food and seed distribution to vulnerable households and villages in Nepal does not reduce vulnerability in the long term, but actually reinforces inequities and vulnerability, particularly when poor or low-caste groups are barred from risk-spreading strategies or pushed to lower-yield lands. Vedeld and colleagues (Chapter 7) emphasize that adaptation is a process, rather than an outcome. Central here is the capacity of cities and urban communities *to act* and deliberately change or adjust urban development plans. Participation is as much about having influence and taking ownership (both top-down and bottom-up processes) as it is about creating channels for exchange of adaptation knowledge.

Contributions in this volume also show how shifting the focus of adaptation to the political sphere is a way of facilitating inclusion and distributional justice. Gabrielsson (Chapter 5) draws attention to the need for increasing the political voice of women to enable them to influence future development, which means narrowing the gender gap in local political leadership. Limited room to manoeuvre in the political sphere undermines individual and collective agency and access to the practical adaptations that can directly reduce vulnerability, whether through loans, farming education, or access to and use of drought-resistant seeds. Similarly, Kronik and Hays (Chapter 14) call for moving beyond improving technical adaptation skills, to include application of indigenous rights to land and resources, and to consultation and free and informed consent. This is particularly important in the case of extractive industries, which have put increasing pressure on livelihoods, access to assets and available options for adaptation. Securing rights to land and resources is critical to building adaptive capacity among indigenous peoples.

Adaptation through transformation in the personal sphere

It is important to recognize that actions in the political sphere are influenced by the subjective views and perceptions associated with the personal sphere of transformation. The personal sphere represents individual and collective assumptions, beliefs, values, worldviews and paradigms. These are often used to define the goals or objectives of systems, who can and should benefit, and in some cases even the role of individual and collective agency in making changes within the political and practical spheres. Although many assume that systems and structures are fixed or given, the personal sphere draws attention to the social and cultural constructions of rules, norms and behaviours that influence social-ecological systems.

Several authors in this volume show that beliefs and assumptions play an important role in how systems and actors are viewed. The beliefs that adaptation practitioners bring to the project can influence the types of responses and outcomes achieved. Challenging the assumption that the poor are passive victims and instead recognizing them as highly adaptive implies that their social innovation can play an important role in adaptation (Wilk et al. this volume).

Wamsler and Brink (this volume, pp. 75–6) emphasize the importance of challenging such assumptions:

> The way that marginal at-risk settlements are viewed influences the types of solutions proposed for them. City authorities and aid organizations may choose to focus on how appalling conditions are, and therefore look for ways of clearing or replacing such 'eyesores'. Alternatively, they can recognize and tap into the wealth of knowledge, experience and capacities that people living in such areas possess and, within that perspective, their need for more disaster-resilient housing, water and sanitation. This second view opens the way to a different path: one that can lead to sustainable transformation, not least by changing the power relations that dictate the management of risk.

Gabrielsson (Chapter 5) emphasizes the role of values, norms and traditions in defining the space for responding to climate change in the political sphere. Livelihood diversification plays an increasingly important role in communities in the Lake Victoria Basin, but gender-differentiated rights and responsibilities often limit the opportunities for women. She argues that empowerment has the potential to challenge the very norms and structures that contribute to vulnerability.

Moving forward: transforming paradigms and practices

The three spheres of transformation are relational and interacting, and indicate multiple entry points for adapting to climate change in ways that can contribute to climate-resilient development pathways. However, most development interventions to date have focused on the practical sphere, with responses often directly linked to current variability or observed and projected changes in climate conditions and associated impacts. This is not surprising, as the success of adaptations in the practical sphere can be readily measured and assessed according to a range of benchmarks and indicators, such as reduced flood losses, increased crop yields, lower morbidity and mortality during heat waves, or through lower air pollution levels, improved water access and quality, reduced carbon dioxide (CO_2) emissions or increased access to renewable energy.

However, overemphasis on adaptation interventions in the practical sphere is unlikely to address the underlying drivers of vulnerability to climate change that reside in the political and personal spheres of transformation. It precludes seeing adaptation as an opportunity for social reform or as a reason to question the values that drive social injustice and inequalities in development and an unsustainable relationship with the environment (Pelling 2011). Most adaptation projects have preserved existing structures and relationships, instead of challenging them and contributing to transformative change (Ireland and McKinnon 2013).

Development practitioners can play a key role in shaping the adaptation process – as mediators facilitating dialogue between the various actors involved in adaptation decisions including local communities, businesses and national authorities, and through their on-the-ground actions and identifying of entry points and specific tools for development work. The entry points for reducing vulnerability to climate change are not always obvious. Often, important leverage points for transformation in the political and personal spheres are overlooked in adaptation strategies and plans. In discussing systems change, Meadows (1999) has pointed out that most attention goes towards low-impact interventions, some of which counterintuitively exacerbate the problem at hand. In contrast, very little attention goes to the higher leverage points of increasing information flows, redefining the goals of the system, or transforming the paradigm from which the systems arise. In the following, we present six recommendations for adaptation interventions that address adaptation through all three spheres of transformation, again with reference to the findings in the chapters of this volume.

Recommendation 1: prioritize building contextual knowledge among development actors

This recommendation is perhaps the simplest and most obvious to emerge from the chapters in this volume, but is also one of the most challenging, for it has several implications for how development actors operate. First, prioritizing contextual knowledge requires that the policy-makers and practitioners involved in adaptation efforts are 'close to' the local context: they must get to know and understand the local context well. This means understanding not just the day-to-day context of project work in the practical sphere, but also the systems and power relations in the political sphere, as well as the beliefs, values and worldviews in the personal sphere. This takes time and often builds on personal experience. Administering adaptation efforts through staff who are frequently rotated to new settings, or operating remotely through a set of standard procedures or project criteria, will not be adequate. The people themselves, and the way they relate to the local community and to other development actors, are what matter here. Community-based adaptation has much to offer in terms of methods and approaches (Schipper et al. 2014). Second, and related to this, taking the local context as a starting point demands that development actors themselves reflect on their own position in political and social relations, including what they themselves see as 'good' adaptation and 'good' development. This may mean questioning individual and shared assumptions, and being open to new types of knowledge and new ways of thinking about adaptation and development. This means, in particular, that development and climate finance institutions need to strengthen their own social science capacity and knowledge of methods and tools. Without this, contextual knowledge is unlikely to contribute to the transformative changes needed to reduce vulnerability and promote global sustainability.

Recommendation 2: create spaces for engagement and negotiation between diverse interests and actors

As pointed out in several contributions to this volume, transformation in the political sphere will require development actors to shift their mode from focusing on implementation of practical actions to placing primary attention to adaptation as a process. This directs attention to negotiations and the creation of spaces for the emergence of cross-scale relationships and shared power in communities with diverse formal and informal governance relationships. As Ensor et al. (this volume) point out, the focus of adaptive capacity needs to be structural, rather than technical, hence local politics must be taken seriously. Drawing on their case study from Mozambique, they underscore the need for flexible, adaptive governance systems that can foster adaptive capacity, showing how power sharing, knowledge and information, and experimentation and testing can contribute to greater resilience.

Engagement means much more than consulting and informing local communities in development efforts: it requires creating arenas for negotiation and promoting power-sharing relationships through collaborative actions, for example in adaptation experiments or tests of alternative livelihood or infrastructural approaches. Development actors can serve as mediators between government and community interests. For example, Wamsler and Brink (Chapter 4) note that government and development actors can support urban dwellers in negotiating their needs and rights through shared learning dialogues. It also means addressing the politics of interactions that are important in the production and application of scientific knowledge, including the role of power relations and interests in planning for adaptation. Using a three-lens framework to examine actors, narratives and interests, Kulindwa and Mshale (Chapter 13) describe how social transformations may be promoted by conjoining research and policy processes. This underscores the significance of multi-stakeholder engagement through forums that enable actors to meet and exchange ideas. Several of the chapters point out that these systemic changes may require a shift in individual and collective mindsets, including among development actors, as a means of increasing the ability of social actors to influence the long-term resilience of their social-ecological systems through changes in the social and political context. Here, transformations in the personal and the political spheres are closely related.

Recommendation 3: empower the most vulnerable into planning and decision-making processes

Although creating space for dialogue between diverse interests is important, it is seldom sufficient for empowering the most vulnerable. While most adaptation projects strive to include vulnerable groups, the processes of selecting who is to participate are often highly politicized. As pointed out in the chapters by

Gabrielsson (Chapter 5) and Eriksen and Marin (Chapter 10), empowering vulnerable groups in adaptation processes means giving priority to the vulnerable in planning and decision-making processes, for example marginalized women over men, or pastoral groups over irrigation farmers. The voices of the vulnerable must be accorded political influence – not only in adaptation planning but also in development strategies, which includes choosing development futures (Eriksen and Marin this volume).

The negotiating table is usually tilted against the most vulnerable through norms, customs, rules and social/political relations that determine who is included and whose interests are heard, and that often make the vulnerable invisible. Empowering those who suffer structural injustices in planning and decision-making processes is not only a way of strengthening their adaptive capacity; it can also tackle the structural causes of vulnerability, for instance by challenging the norms and structures that create vulnerability in the first place (Gabrielsson; Nagoda and Eriksen, this volume). As Kronik and Hays (Chapter 14) point out, empowerment is a deeper process than mere participation or inclusion of indigenous knowledge: it is about the basic ability to exercise rights.

Development models and approaches such as agricultural investments shape the vulnerability context, as West (Chapter 8) points out. Kronik and Hays (Chapter 14) show that development initiatives have tended to be based on the very developmental models that are part of the problem, such as economic growth led by extractive industries that undermine the human rights, resource access, livelihoods and adaptation options of indigenous groups. Instead of mainstreaming adaptation into development plans, development plans themselves may need adjusting based on the needs and strategies of the vulnerable – an essential point. It is clear that development actors usually have to work within existing structures and institutions – sometimes the very same social and political structures that disempower vulnerable groups. Addressing social hierarchies and power structures may be considered outside the mandate of most development actors. However, as Nagoda and Eriksen (Chapter 11) point out, these actors can nonetheless identify how their interventions and processes exacerbate or alter such structures and strive to create situations and 'safe spaces' where the most vulnerable have a voice and conflicts can be aired.

Recommendation 4: extend the time frame for activities

The findings presented in this volume point to a growing need to accord greater weight to long-term perspectives and wider and multiple goals when planning and prioritizing adaptation. The chapters show that vulnerability-reducing interventions can be time-consuming and resource-intensive, which necessitates a wide and long-term focus that is participatory and process-oriented. As such, the time frames of development activities need to be significantly altered. This recommendation is in line with observations by Brooks et al. (2011), who note that since many aspects of climate change and adaptation unfold over long time frames, longer-sighted approaches are needed for planning, implementation and assessment of activities.

Extending the time frame also concerns the way sustainability is understood and approached. Adaptation processes can play an important role as a vehicle for transformation of development pathways to include enhanced equity, as well as in avoiding carbon and vulnerability lock-in and path-dependencies. A long-term commitment to the process by development actors is required if such long-term changes are to be realized. It may also call for new project goals that focus on a wider scope of impacts, both in terms of types and time-horizons. This will require some important changes in funding structures, as three- to five-year project cycles (currently the norm) are usually too short to accomplish long-term social goals. In summary, development agencies and funders will need to consider longer time perspectives in their support.

Recommendation 5: include more social and process-oriented indicators in monitoring and evaluation

The importance of building contextual knowledge makes it inappropriate and inadequate to administer projects through a standard set of criteria. As pointed out by Brooks et al. (2011: 14), '… there is no easily definable single metric for adaptation … due to the fact that the functions and goals of adaptation will be different in different contexts'. Also, there are no universally and neutral measures of success: 'the question of success is not simply to be decided on scientific, rational, objective, or procedural grounds, but is in important ways normative, historically contingent, and context specific' (Moser and Boykoff 2014: 2).

Monitoring and evaluation systems, if expanded to include more social and process-oriented indicators and analyses, can provide a starting point for improved focus on social structures and sustainability. Yet there is a need to go beyond present tools, or to combine several types of tools, to capture interactions across scales, including national level structures and processes, qualitative and social aspects of the vulnerability context, and longer-term impacts of actions on social change and development pathways. Although cost–benefit analyses address the efficiency of a project in terms of the ratio of benefits to costs, they tend to have a narrow focus on climate as an isolated factor affecting a particular parameter such as water supply and demand (Nkomo and Gomez 2006). These do not capture the wider vulnerability context, nor other important aspects of success of a project, including feasibility, efficacy/effectiveness, acceptability/legitimacy, equity and sustainability (Brooks et al. 2011). Such approaches need to be complemented with other types of evaluation methods, such as social return on investment (SROI), to evaluate the impacts on stakeholders, identify ways to improve performance and enhance the performance of investments.

It may be necessary to develop more qualitative and participatory tools that contribute to creating arenas for raising and negotiating conflicting interests and perceptions, as well as new or expanded approaches to measure value and performance in an adaptation context. The latter might include building on multi-criteria analysis (MCA), which permits balancing among multiple, potentially competing objectives, including social, environmental, technical and economic objectives, or on flexible and forward-looking decision-making (FFDM) (see Jones et al. 2014). Several frameworks have emerged to guide the selection of adaptation projects, and the monitoring and evaluating of their outcomes, including the Pilot Programme for Climate Resilience results framework (Climate Investment Funds 2012). There are also a growing number of frameworks that focus on local vulnerability, risk management, adaptation strategies and livelihoods, such as the International Federation of Red Cross and Red Crescent Societies 'Vulnerability and Capacity Assessment' (VCA) and the International Institute for Sustainable Development (IISD)-driven 'Community based Risk Screening Tool – Adaptation and Livelihoods' (CRiSTAL).

While such frameworks often capture vulnerability at the local level and provide insight into the national institutional context, they seldom examine the political and social relations and processes involved in adaptation and the contribution of adaptation actions to transforming development pathways. Importantly, since adaptation as a social process is driven by changes in all sectors, not just by formal adaptation interventions, all development sectors need to systematically include analysis of underlying social structures and the vulnerability context of each project or investment. This means identifying the most vulnerable groups and individuals, the social and political relations that create such vulnerability, how practical actions may affect the intersectionality of relations of gender, caste, ethnicity and livelihood groups, as well as the contribution of the intervention to transformations in the practical, political and personal spheres, and to climate-resilient development pathways more generally. The chapters in this volume provide several examples of how this can be done.

Recommendation 6: challenge assumptions and introduce learning and reflexivity into adaptation processes

Perhaps the most important, yet also most difficult, entry point for transformative change is to challenge the beliefs, assumptions, worldviews and paradigms that influence adaptation processes and practices. As noted in several contributions to this volume, adaptation is a process that involves learning and reflection. For example, Nightingale points out that formal adaptation policy processes should include regular revision mechanisms in order to take account of the dynamic character of vulnerability. Further, Wilk et al. (this volume, p. 173), argue that recognizing spinoffs from development that can support adaptive capacity 'requires ongoing, conscious open-minded appraisal of new technological and socio-economic phenomena, and weighing of their advantages, disadvantages and potential uses'.

What does it mean for development actors themselves to engage in processes to build reflexivity about their own values and positionality relative to the structures, relations and development pathways that drive vulnerability? It may mean creating internal processes and discussion spaces to highlight different perceptions and interests, or to draw attention to the very lack of awareness and understanding of the vulnerability context within organizations. It may also require a reorientation of the way that development actors, including bilateral and multilateral agencies, non-governmental organizations (NGOs) and governments, carry out their work. By definition, these actors usually work in the practical sphere. However, their actions can and often do drive changes (deliberately or unintentionally) in the political sphere. An increased awareness of the relationships among changes in the practical, political and personal spheres is essential to transformations towards more sustainable development pathways.

Transformations in the personal sphere can serve as a catalyst for new approaches to adaptation in the political and practical spheres, but they are nonetheless challenging. Tearfund, a UK relief and development agency, reflects on the difficulties and challenges of their own internal transformation process:

> Embarking on this transformative journey through a process of co-creation generated more ownership of the process amongst staff, but it also proved time-consuming and exhausting and created uncertainty that needed to be managed. While some members of staff were very committed to the cause from the beginning, others were unsure and needed more time to engage with the issues. Continuously questioning the status quo and engaging in system thinking is a complex and uncomfortable challenge that bears the temptation to fall back into old patterns of thinking and working.
>
> (Tearfund 2014)

Conclusions: a new role for development

The complexity and urgency of climate change means that rather than sidestepping difficult issues, it is time to face them head on. Adaptation involves more than simply accommodating the impacts of climate change: it is also about confronting the societal context in which these changes are occurring. This means moving beyond impacts-oriented adaptation to tackle the underlying sources of vulnerability that are often determined by social, economic and political relations. Critically, it involves challenging the processes and conditions that are creating vulnerability and risk – including economic development models that undermine the cultural and material basis for community well-being and perpetuate reliance on fossil-fuel energy sources (Pelling 2011; Redclift 2012). It also necessitates challenging the ways of 'doing development'.

The chapters in this book offer insights on the types of social science analyses needed to better understand the relationship between adaptation and development. They also provide a range of frameworks and analytical tools that can be used to assess adaptation options. These include frameworks for analysing people's efforts to reduce and adapt to urban risk (Wamsler and Brink Chapter 4), or for placing attention on multi-level, multi-sectoral analysis of the barriers and potential for risk management inherent in the governance and political context (Vedeld et al., Nightingale this volume). Such frameworks recognize policy-process analyses of actors' roles and power relations as a necessary part of more participatory adaptation approaches. Eriksen and Marin (this volume) outline principles of sustainable adaptation, showing that a focus on vulnerability contexts, political and social relations and empowerment in adaptation efforts can potentially transform development pathways. The frameworks and tools employed in adaptation practices will vary across contexts; what is most important, however, is reflection about the assumptions and understandings of vulnerability upon which each tool builds, and which facets of vulnerability each tool and approach address and, more importantly, do *not* address.

Climate change may mean adapting to higher seas, more water/less water, stronger winds, more intense heat, ecological changes and so on. Yet the implications of these changes are not simply that society has to 'adapt' better. This, as Paulo Freire (1970) emphasized, translates into practice as taking the world as a given, without questioning the very systems and structures that drive climate change, vulnerability, inequality and poverty (O'Brien, St. Clair and Kristoffersen 2010; Pelling 2011). As a phenomenon, climate change calls for questioning our collective assumptions about the continuity of energy-intensive economic growth, about availability and access to adequate water and food resources, about the permanence of coastlines, the security of livelihoods, the predictability of 'extreme' climate events, and many other aspects of ecology and society that have been taken for granted or considered 'manageable' within the dominant development paradigm. What these changes should be telling us is that it is time to rethink current development pathways, and to make stronger links between current actions and future outcomes.

The need to move towards climate resilient pathways raises many important questions: What processes contribute to climate resilient pathways in different contexts, and how can such processes be catalysed and supported? Given that there is no clear blueprint for actions, what are the key aspects of adaptation and transformation processes that can be monitored and evaluated? How can adaptation trigger ethical change in development pathways, especially in relation to existing power asymmetries, and social inequities? These questions are likely to be answered through a combination of research and practice, which draws attention to the importance of reflexivity and learning. It is clear, however, that climate change and its impacts present considerable risks to development, and adapting to these risks without addressing the drivers of vulnerability represents a missed opportunity to pursue transformations to sustainability. Adaptation through transformation has the potential to become an inclusive, engaging and empowering process that contributes to alternative and sustainable development pathways.

References

Brooks, N., S. Anderson, J. Ayers, I. Burton and I. Tellam. 2011. *Tracking Adaptation and Measuring Development*. London: IIED.

Climate Investment Funds. 2012. *Revised PPCR Results Framework*. Washington, DC: Climate Investment Funds.

Denton, F., T. Wilbanks, A.C. Abeysinghe, I. Burton, Q. Gao, M.C. Lemos, T. Masui, et al. 2014. 'Chapter 20 IPCC: climate-resilient pathways: adaptation, mitigation, and sustainable development'. In *Climate Change 2014: Impacts, Adaptation, and Vulnerability. Contribution of Working Group III to the Fifth Assessment Report of the Intergovernmental Panel on Climate Change*. Cambridge: Cambridge University Press.

Freire, Paulo. 1970. *The Pedagogy of the Oppressed*. New York: Continuum.

IPCC. 2013. 'Summary for policymakers'. In *Climate Change 2013: The Physical Science Basis. Contribution of Working Group I to the Fifth Assessment Report of the Intergovernmental Panel on Climate Change*, edited by T.F. Stocker, D. Qin, G.-K. Plattner, M. Tignor, S.K. Allen, J. Boschung, A. Nauels, Y. Xia, V. Bex and P.M. Midgley. Cambridge: Cambridge University Press.

IPCC. 2014a. 'Summary for policymakers'. In *Climate Change 2014, Mitigation of Climate Change. Contribution of Working Group II to the Fifth Assessment Report of the Intergovernmental Panel on Climate Change*. Cambridge: Cambridge University Press.

IPCC. 2014b. 'Summary for policymakers'. In *Climate Change 2014: Impacts, Adaptation, and Vulnerability. Contribution of Working Group III to the Fifth Assessment Report of the Intergovernmental Panel on Climate Change*. Cambridge: Cambridge University Press.

Ireland, P. and K. McKinnon. 2013. 'Strategic localism for an uncertain world: a postdevelopment approach to climate change adaptation'. *Geoforum* 47(4): 158–166.

Jones, L., E. Ludi, E. Carabine, N. Grist, A. Amsalu, L.Artur, C. Bachofen, P. Beautement, C. Broenner, M. Bunce, J. Mendler de Suarez, W. Muhumuza, P. Suarez and D. Zacarias. 2014. *Planning for an Uncertain Future: Promoting Adaptation to Climate Change through Flexible and Forward-Looking Decision Making. Executive Summary*. London: Overseas Development Institute.

Kates, R.W., W.R. Travis and T.J. Wilbanks. 2012. 'Transformational adaptation when incremental adaptations to climate xhange are insufficient'. *PNAS* 109(19): 7156–7161.

Lenton, T.M., H. Held, E. Kriegler, J.W. Hall, W. Lucht, S. Rahmstorf and H.J. Schellnhuber. 2008. 'Inaugural article: tipping elements in the earth's climate system'. *Proceedings of the National Academy of Sciences* no. 6:1786. doi:10.1073/pnas.0705414105.

Marshall, N.A., S.E. Park, W.N. Adger, K. Brown and M.S. Howden. 2012. 'Transformational capacity and the influence of place and identity'. *Environmental Research Letters* 7. http://iopscience.iop.org/1748-9326/7/3/034022

Meadows, D. 1999. *Leverage Points: Places to Intervene in a System. Sustainability Institute Papers*. Hartland, VT: Sustainability Institute.

Moser, S. and M. Boykoff. 2014. 'Climate change and adaptation success: the scope of the challenge'. In *Successful Adaptation to Climate Change: Linking Science and Policy in a Rapidly Changing World*, edited by S. Moser and M. Boykoff, 1–33. London: Routledge.

Nkomo, J.C. and B. Gomez. 2006. *Estimating and Comparing Costs and Benefits of Adaptation Projects: Case Studies in South Africa and the Gambia*. A final report submitted to Assessments of Impacts and Adaptation to Climate Change (AIACC). Washington DC: The International START Secretariat.

O'Brien, K.L. 2012. 'Global environmental change (2): from adaptation to deliberate transformation'. *Progress in Human Geography* 36(5): 667–676.

O'Brien, K. and G. Hochachka. 2010. 'Integral adaptation to climate change'. *Journal of Integral Theory and Practice* 5(1): 89–102.

O'Brien, K., and L. Sygna. 2013. 'Responding to climate change: the three spheres of transformation'. Paper given at 'Transformation in a Changing Climate' Conference, 19–21 June, Oslo, Norway.

O'Brien, K., A. Lera St. Clair and B. Kristoffersen. 2010. 'The framing of climate change: why it matters'. In *Climate Change, Ethics and Human Security*, edited by Karen O'Brien, Asunción Lera St. Clair and Berit Kristoffersen. Cambridge: Cambridge University Press.

Pelling, M. 2011. *Adaptation to Climate Change. From Resilience to Transformation*. London: Routledge.

Redclift, M. 2012. 'Living with a new crisis: climate change and transitions out of carbon dependency'. In *Climate Change and the Crisis of Capitalism: A Chance to Reclaim Self, Society and Nature*, edited by M. Pelling, D. Manuel-Navarrete and M. Redclift. New York: Routledge.

Rockström, J., W. Steffen, K. Noone, Å. Persson, F.S. Chapin, E.F. Lambin, T.M. Lenton, M. Scheffer, C. Folke, H.J. Schellnhuber, B. Nykvist, C.A. de Wit, T. Hughes, S. van der Leeuw, H. Rodhe, S. Sörlin, P.K. Snyder, R. Costanza, U. Svedin, M. Falkenmark, L. Karlberg, R.W. Corell, V.J. Fabry, J. Hansen, B. Walker, D. Liverman, K. Richardson, P. Crutzen and J.A. Foley. 2009. 'A safe operating space for humanity'. *Nature* 461(7263): 472–475.

Schipper, E. L. F., J. Ayers, H. Reid, S. Huq and A. Rahman. (eds.) 2014. *Community-Based Adaptation to Climate Change*. London: Routledge.

Sharma, M. 2007. 'Personal to planetary transformation'. *Kosmos Journal*, Fall/Winter, 31–35.

Smith, A. and A. Stirling. 2010. 'The politics of social-ecological resilience and sustainable socio-technical transitions'. *Ecology and Society* 15(1): 11.

Steffen, W., J. Rockström and R. Costanza. 2011. 'How defining planetary boundaries can transform our approach to growth'. *Solutions* 2(3): 59–65.

Tearfund. 2014. *Blog on Theory and Practice. Project Doughnut – How Tearfund's Advocacy Department Has Started a Journey from Single Issue Lobbying Towards Systemic Change*, 29 January 2014. (Accessed 25 May 2014.) Available from http://www.smart-csos.org/blog-on-theory-and-practice/106-project-doughnut-how-tearfund-s-advocacy-department-has-started-a-journey-from-singe-issue-lobbying-towards-systemic-change.

Vincent, K., L.O. Næss and M. Goulden. 2013. 'National level policies versus local level realities – can the two be reconciled to promote sustainable adaptation?' In *Changing Environment for Human Security: Transformative Approaches to Research, Policy and Action*, edited by L. Sygna, K.L. O'Brien and J. Wolf. London: Earthscan.

INDEX

Information in a table is indicated in **bold** and information in a figure is shown in *italic*.

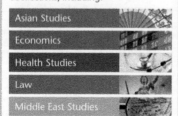